THE AFRICAN SYNOD

THE AFRICAN SYNOD

Documents, Reflections, Perspectives

Compiled and edited by the
Africa Faith & Justice Network
under the direction of Maura Browne, SND

ORBIS BOOKS

Maryknoll, New York 10545

The Catholic Foreign Mission Society of America (Maryknoll) recruits and trains people for overseas missionary service. Through Orbis Books, Maryknoll aims to foster the international dialogue that is essential to mission. The books published, however, reflect the opinions of their authors and are not meant to represent the official position of the society.

ORBIS/ISBN 1-57075-038-6

Contents

Foreword

Sister Maria Rita Matiku, IHS

Musoma, where the Immaculate Heart Sisters' Center is located, is a typical rural town of nearly one million people on the shores of Lake Victoria in northeastern Tanzania.[1] Like many rural towns in Africa, it has no television and newspapers seldom reach us. Yet, I would wager that every one of Musoma's 300,000 Catholics knows about the African Synod and has discussed the major themes at parish meetings.

I do not know if the Catholic community in the rest of the continent is so well informed, but I can say with certainty that the Synod will impact every one of Africa's 102 million Catholics.[2] Whether one was satisfied or disappointed by the Synod, it was a pivotal moment in the history of the Church in Africa. What took place before and after the Synod in grassroots communities and local parishes across the African continent may be even more significant than the actual gathering of Bishops in Rome from April 10 to May 8, 1994.

I was privileged to be one of twenty-four women auditors in attendance, representing the Conference of Major Superiors in Tanzania. I did not know what to expect when I arrived in Rome. Some theologians, observers, and bishops were critical that the gathering was not being held on African soil and others were concerned that Rome would exert too much control.

The fact that women and lay people could not be full participants was another drawback as was the time limit of eight minutes for each bishop's intervention. In spite of these very real limitations, there is much to celebrate and share. Participants debated openly and freely about critical issues affecting ordinary people's lives—issues like marriage, AIDS, corruption, female circumcision, polygamy, poverty, foreign debt, healing, traditional religion, and ethnic conflict. No topic was either too profane or too sacred to bear scrutiny.

A continent rich in oral tradition, dance, song, and music, Africa lent its unique gifts to the liturgies that graced each day. The presence of the Holy Father throughout the first weeks of deliberations (until he fell and broke his hip), reassured participants of his interest in the gathering and did not appear to inhibit the free exchange of ideas. The very strong focus on justice and peace indicated a growing awareness of the Church's role in society while the focus on inculturation revealed the need for radical changes in how the Christian message is proclaimed and lived.

The Church in Africa will never be the same if the 67 propositions put forward by the Synod fathers are implemented. Endorsed by Pope John Paul II in his Post-Synodal Apostolic Exhortation, these propositions offer a concrete blueprint for revitalizing and Africanizing the Church.

This includes proposals to promote dialogue with African traditional religions, permit the veneration of ancestors, champion the rights of women and include them in ministry and decision-making, develop a theology of the Church as Family, and to create commissions on marriage that include married couples. In the public sphere, the bishops called for an end to arms sales to Africa, forgiveness of the foreign debt, the destruction of torture chambers, protection of the environment, and an end to corruption and dictatorship.

In spite of the importance of this historic event, there is a danger that the wealth of debate and discussion will be lost or forgotten. For that reason alone, this volume on the Synod is welcome indeed. While it does not contain every intervention by individual bishops, it preserves the most cogent points that were raised as well as debate that took place before and after the historic event.

The first section contains the history leading up to the Synod, including some of the outstanding preparatory documents from around the continent, as well as expressions of disappointment and fear that the process would be controlled by the Vatican.

The second section presents the highlights of the Synod itself, focussing on concrete propositions for action put forth by participants as well as some of the most quoted interventions. In section three, several outstanding Church leaders and theologians, including Jean-Marc Éla of Cameroon and Bénézet Bujo of Zaire, share their hopes for a truly African Church. Section four looks toward the future, examining implications for local churches, women, justice and peace, and the mass media.

The volume concludes with the Apostolic Exhortation delivered personally by Pope John Paul II when he visited East, West and Southern Africa in September 1995. Representing the conclusions of the official Church, the message captures the major hopes and concerns expressed by the Synod fathers.

In editing the book, attention was given to retaining the style and wording of individual authors. Thus, non-inclusive language has been retained in many cases, revealing the bias of male contributors to the volume. Another limitation is the lack of women's voices. This too is an accurate reflection of the current position of women in the African Church as well as in society. While this is rapidly changing, women are still grossly underrepresented in decision-making and leadership positions in local churches throughout the continent.

Thanks to Orbis Books and the Africa Faith and Justice Network, this historic moment in the Church's life in Africa will be preserved. My hope is that these documents will continue to be debated by the Christian community in Musoma and in villages, towns, and cities throughout the African continent as well as in our sister churches all over the world. Although many problems exist, the Church in Africa has demonstrated that it has a message of life and hope for the global community.

Notes

[1]The Immaculate Heart Sisters of Africa are a diocesan community founded by Maryknoll Father J. Gerard Grondin in 1955 and trained by the Maryknoll Sisters. The community presently numbers more than one hundred members who work in the dioceses of Musoma and Shinyanga as well as with Rwandan refugees in Rulenge Diocese. Sister Rita Matiku is the current mother general.

[2]John Baur, *2000 Years of Christianity in Africa: An African History 62-1992* (Nairobi: Paulines Publications Africa, 1994), p. 524.

Part I

Preparatory Work

The Birth and Development of a Local Church

Difficulties and Signs of Hope

Elochukwu E. Uzukwu

The church in Africa was born old.[1] The midwives awaited the birth and the child itself really had no choice in the matter. Thus, from the time of the first evangelization by western missionaries until and even after Vatican II, structures such as churches; primary, secondary and catechetical schools; seminaries; convents; and hospitals sprouted. Foremost in the mind of the evangelizers was the establishment of a church and, naturally, they turned to western European church structures and often transplanted them intact in Africa, with remarkable effects. A glance at the statistics compiled by Barrett shows a steady growth of Christians (including Roman Catholics), especially between 1900 and 1970.[2]

The missionaries' successors, chosen and appointed by the missionaries, continued their strategy and shepherded the flock. However, having been schooled in prudential compliance to authority and tradition, they lacked initiative. The desire expressed by the late Cardinal Malula in 1959 for a truly African church in an independent Africa was more an exception than the rule. Church leaders who operated in a feudalistic institution were much concerned with power and authority. It seems that this inherited pre-Vatican II feudal image of the church constitutes even today the greatest obstacle to the emergence of dynamic local churches in Africa.

The Second Vatican Council broke through this authority-conscious model of church and projected an image of the church as the people of God. Each member is called to holiness and to participate fully in the life of the church; ministry is exer-

Elochukwu E. Uzukwu, a Nigerian Spiritan priest, is on the faculty at the Spiritan International School of Theology, Attakwu, Enugu, Nigeria. An earlier version of this essay appeared in *Concilium* 1992/1. Revised and reprinted with permission.

cised for the good of the body of Christ. This new vision of church encouraged local churches in Africa to respond to local needs. In Zaire, for example, the church had to respond to the local context in its theology, its liturgy, and the form of its leadership. Yet, the very structure of authority within the church made the birth of local churches extremely difficult, as has been shown by attempts in East Africa to develop small Christian communities (SCCs).

The church in East Africa, functioning under the umbrella of the Association of Member Episcopal Conferences of Eastern Africa (AMECEA), resolved to evolve a more active and responsive church—one that would be self-ministering, self-propagating, and self-supporting. To ensure the dynamic witness of the church at the grass-roots level, AMECEA decided as early as 1976 to establish SCCs. Ten years later, an evaluation of the SCCs noted some achievements. However, it was felt that the project had not attained its overall purpose. It had not been implemented in many dioceses, and where it did operate, its "major problem" was linked to clerical resistance and control:

> Some dioceses have done little to encourage SCCs in practical terms. . . . SCCs are clerical-centered with little and at times no initiative at all from the laity. . . . Some priests fear that if such communities are not properly managed other sects may spring up. There has been over-supervision of the SCCs due to fears of the dangers of the emergence of "splinter groups" and "schisms." . . . Thus SCC leaders are not allowed to take full responsibility. . . . Other people do not like changes. They want to continue things as they always did. . . . When the laity are responsible the clergy tend to be very strict. Good recommendations from the Christian communities are not welcome.[3]

While this new style of being church through the small Christian community results from the breath of the Spirit, its implementation rests in the hands of those who exercise authority in the church. The SCCs appear to threaten the command structure of the church and those in power are not ready for change. While AMECEA sees initiative and responsibility as fundamental to the emergence of a dynamic local church, the clergy insist on initiating and supervising in order to ensure right doctrine and right practice. One can only agree that preserving right doctrine and practice (Titus 1:11, 2:1) is a value to be maintained in the church and that care must be taken to control those whose ears itch for novelties (2 Tim. 4:3). But African clergy appear to have exaggerated their fear of novelties in the SCC experiment and to be unduly burdened by their legacy of European Christianity, which they are unwilling to cast off. The pyramid of ecclesiastical administration ensures that the bishops are the extension of the pope, the priests are the extension of the bishops, and the laity are the extension of the priests.

While the church's mission of service (Mark 10:45) equips it to introduce change into society at the grass roots, because of its outmoded command structure, the church risks becoming but a spectator in the present drama of life in Africa—a drama that may determine the future of the continent and the role of the black race in the global village. By maintaining its ideology of authority in all areas, including the vital area of formation, the church persists in shielding candidates for the priest-hood and religious life from the very real concerns of life in Africa. For the foresee-able future, ministers in the church may be in Africa but not live as Africans.

Today the major concern in Africa is *hunger*. But the issue in the church is *power*. Among the qualities required to function as a good priest or religious, obe-dience takes priority. In a continent where 50 percent of the people live in absolute poverty and an estimated 400 million are living in extreme poverty in 1995, candi-dates for the priesthood and religious life are assured of food and the other material necessities of life by foreign agencies and by local contributions of the laity. Re-moved in this way from ordinary concerns, they are rendered incapable of appreci-ating in a practical way the lot of the majority of Africans; the root causes of pov-erty escape them at the most practical level. However, because they are fed they are dependent. Instead of abandoning the dependency syndrome by directing attention to the needs of Africa, they are often diverted by the hands that feed them to a preoccupation with the concerns of the church of Rome—its laws, its rituals, its doctrines—which are imposed on the mass of believers, whether or not they are tangentially related to contextual problems.

It seems to me that the Association of Member Episcopal Conferences of East-ern Africa (AMECEA) has instinctively put its finger on the solution to the prob-lem of the local churches in Africa—grass-roots mobilization—in its decision to undertake the "systematic formation of small Christian communities" as the "key pastoral priority in Eastern Africa."[4] However, the church in Africa needs to go one step further by reforming its leadership structures. In traditional Africa before the period of colonial dictatorship, two political systems were prevalent: the first con-centrated authority in the hands of one man (the king, who was assisted by a coun-cil), and the second dispersed authority in the community (with leadership in the hands of heads of families, kindreds, and associations). Under these two systems, despite abuses, leadership was preferred to kingship.[5]

Leadership was also the controlling idea of ministry in the various churches of the New Testament established by the apostles. No matter how centralized a New Testament church might have been,[6] feudalistic structures were unheard of. The church in Africa should allow itself and its patterns of ministry to be influenced both by Africa's traditional political systems and by the New Testament experi-ence. Today the need for the church in Africa to demonstrate leadership has be-come even more urgent. In a continent where authority is expressed in terms of the arrogant exercise of power, the church in Africa is called upon to present an alter-native pattern of building community. It must break with the feudalism of the past in order to allow grass-roots communities, such as the small Christian communi-ties, to assume their responsibilities in the tradition of the New Testament churches.

Signs of Hope

In many parts of Africa, national episcopal conferences have already celebrated their centenary of evangelization. Maturation, though difficult, is in progress. The courageous decision by AMECEA to establish SCCs has enabled some communities to experience reflecting on the word of God and applying it directly to their social context. AMECEA countries have also established, to some extent, local patterns in catechetics and liturgy. The primary emphasis given to inculturation by the Zairian episcopal conference has affected the development of consecrated life, pastoral leadership, liturgy, and theology. Inculturation in this region goes beyond the *Roman Missal for the Dioceses of Zaire*. Similar experiences that give local characteristics to the church include, among many others, the Cameroonian mass, the rite of Christian initiation in Burkina Faso, and the Christian marriage rite in Chad. Today, Africa's five Catholic faculties of theology (Kinshasa, Enugu, Port Hartcourt, Nairobi, and Abidjan are expected to make the African local experience the starting point of their theological reflection.

In addition, the church has helped African nations cope with the trauma of post-colonial independence. National and regional episcopal conferences have taken positions against military dictatorships, ethnic and religious intolerance, poverty and oppression. The Symposium of Episcopal Conferences of Africa and Madagascar (SECAM) has worked to promote evangelization as integral human promotion and has criticized infringements of human rights. All these are signs of hope of an evolving local church that will help demarcate the African church insofar as the church leadership courageously embraces the freedom of the children of God. True catholicity requires both diversity and unity.

Other signs of hope lie in an area not immediately under the control of the church hierarchy. Generally throughout Africa today the search for security and for integral well-being has assumed unprecedented dimensions. Christians of all denominations, Muslims, and practitioners of traditional religion rub shoulders at any center that promotes healing, whether it be sponsored by Christian churches, Muslim organizations, or adherents of African traditional religion. The problems that drive them to such centers are mixed: sicknesses of all descriptions, infertility, fear of witchcraft and sorcery, lack of progress in business enterprises, fear of armed robbers and secret societies, and so on. The benefits of modernization, such as western technology, education and medicine, and the insistent teaching of Christianity are unable to arrest this cry for help.

However, patterns of response to this hunger for integral well-being are developing into an authoritative tradition of experience. While this movement may be interpreted as folk religion, evidence[7] seems to indicate that it is rather a preference for a framework to interpret reality that is African in origin rather than received from western Christians. This framework, based on the authority of the ancestral experience, locates human beings firmly in the cosmos and insists that their integral well-being is the ultimate reality and meaning. To realize this, the physical and spiritual dimensions of life in the cosmos (all of which are actualized in human beings) must function harmoniously.[8] The vehicle of this ancestral experience is traditional African religion. A religion of structure, it introduces harmony and rhythm into everyday life. Its worldview integrates the social, economic, political, personal, and cosmic dimensions of life.

The African encounter with Christianity and modernity has failed to satisfy the yearning of Africans for integral well-being. The West, informed by the Enlightenment and Cartesianism, moves toward isolation and separation. The West affirms the autonomy and independence of each human discipline, and secularization limits religious practice (Christianity) to a particular area of human life.

African Christians thus experience a predictable conflict. Their problem is not only how to convert a religion of salvation (Christianity) into a religion of structure, but also how to make the benefits of modernity function in their holistic vision of the universe. A popular African Christian belief is that faith in Christ brings healing. In other words, the guarantor of security, the God-Christ who ensures harmony in the cosmos, must heal bodies as well as spirit. The decision by many African Christians to search for integration in their world is a way of insisting that life in the cosmos should move toward relationship and harmony instead of toward separation or isolation. In this manner the authority of the ancestral experience maintains its vigor in a changing world.

Many committed Christians believe that it is not necessary to return to their ancestral religion to live an integral life. For them, this core of the ancestral experience is a universal vision of humankind that is expressed in any religious tradition, including Christianity. Faith in Christ is complemented by the ancestral experience, not diminished. It is at this crucial point—where Christians decide to trust their experience, and forward-looking pastors are compelled to respond to the reality of the Christian life in Africa—that I see a central sign of hope for Christianity in Africa.

It is important to insist that ordinary lay Catholics in Africa take the initiative in resolving their life-problems. Pastors who learn from the laity's experiences are privileged to reexamine the meaning of salvation in Christ for the masses of African believers. One Nigerian priest, for example, has developed a liturgy for healing, rituals for peace among feuding villages, contract rituals among business associates, and purification rituals following suicides. Many other priests throughout Nigeria, Cameroon, and other countries devote themselves to devising relevant Christian responses to ordinary life situations in their regions.

On the whole, the experience of alienation by practicing Catholics in Africa is a reality that the church cannot simply wish away. Although courageous and charismatic pastors propose local solutions, there is a remarkable lack of coordination of these responses. Each pastor becomes an expert, and abuses are not wanting. A reformed and renewed church leadership must be clearly in tune with the problems of its region, and it must direct its attention to this African hunger for integral well-being. A true commitment to inculturation that promotes the integral well-being of humankind in each context should become its guiding principle. Theological reflection to this end should reinterpret the entire Christian experience and propose ways for its practice in contemporary African society. In this way, the full force of the message of Christ will be consonant with Africa's hunger for integral well-being.

Notes

1. O. Bimwenyi-Kweshi, "Religions Africaines, un 'lieu' de la Théologie Chrétienne

africaine," *Religions Africaines et Christianisme*. Colloque International de Kinshasa, 9-14 January 1978, Vol. II (Kinshasa 1979), p. 168.

2. David B. Barrett, ed., *World Christian Encyclopedia* (Nairobi, 1982), p. 782.

3. Joseph G. Healey, "Four Africans Evaluate SCCs in E. Africa," *African Ecclesial Review* (29.5, 1987), pp. 266-77.

4. AMECEA Bishops, "Guidelines for the Catholic Church in Eastern Africa in the 1980s," *African Ecclesial Review* (16.1, 2, 1974), pp. 9-10.

5. M. Fortes and E. E. Evans-Pritchard, *African Political Systems* (London, 1940).

6. Raymond E. Brown, *The Churches the Apostles Left Behind* (New York, 1984).

7. "Healing and Exorcism—The Nigerian Experience." Acts of the First Missiology Symposium of the Spiritan International School of Theology, Enugu, 18-20 May 1989 (ready for publication); E. Milingo, *The World in Between* (Maryknoll, NY: Orbis Books, 1986); M. P. Hegba, *Sorcellerie et Prière de Délivrance* (Paris: Inades Édition, 1982).

8. E. M. Zeusse, *Ritual Cosmos: The Sanctification of Life in African Religions* (Athens, Ohio, 1979), pp. 3f.

2

The Life of the Church

Frederick Chiromba

The documents of Vatican II provide a good place to begin to explore the theme of the renewal that can come about through inculturation. *Lumen Gentium* proposed the new model of the church as the people of God, a communion of believers in the Lord Jesus Christ. This is a model that suggests brotherhood and sisterhood, solidarity, and the equality of all people as children of God, called to the same supernatural destiny by and in Christ, the only mediator between God and humanity. As a consequence of this model, we realize that everywhere in the world there is a growing sense of brotherhood and sisterhood and solidarity among peoples. Gestures of mutual help continue to multiply. Of late we have also come to realize that we are jointly responsible for our environment. What happens to the environment in a remote corner of the globe can have repercussions everywhere. The foul air you breathe out, I breathe in!

The church of Vatican II, understood as the people of God, is a church present in the world. The church is neither separated nor far away from the world. She is in the world, in the heart of the peoples, in order to be the "salt of the earth and the light of the world" (Mt. 5:13-14). The church of Vatican II is engaged in the world, which she seeks to save from within rather than by avoiding it. There are many different ways to be present in the world and to understand the presence of the church in the world. As Jesus said, "You are in the world, but not of the world," (Jn. 17).

The church exercises a sanctifying presence in the world. Its mission belongs to all the baptized. The whole people of God is sent to the world to evangelize the world and to be witnesses to Christ. All Christians are responsible for the church's mission by virtue of the common priesthood of the faithful, which, however, not only differs in degree but in essence from the ministerial or hierarchical priesthood. Nevertheless, both are ordered one to another and each in its own proper way shares

---

Frederick Chiromba, a priest of the diocese of Mutare in Zimbabwe, is Dean of Studies at Chishawasha Seminary.

9

in the one priesthood of Christ (*LG*, 10). While the mission is one, the missionaries are different. This atmosphere requires a true sense of co-responsibility, dialogue, and sharing in teamwork rather than working in splendid isolation. It is with this background of the church that we now examine the role of inculturation.

Inculturation

By now inculturation has become a familiar term, even though it was still missing from the 1991 *Oxford English Dictionary*. Briefly, as used within the church, inculturation refers to the insertion of the Christian faith in a people's cultures. Pope John Paul II has used the term several times to express the need to help people welcome Jesus Christ in their own culture. Inculturation is about feeling at home in one's faith and the culture of our time. In the New Jerusalem, everyone will feel at home, and that process has to begin now through inculturation, which can challenge the bad and lift up the good in each culture. As church, we must organize ourselves in such a way that newcomers feel at home and that we find ourselves at home with them. We have to be faithful to ourselves and to them.

Inculturation, often seen as a slow process, is based on the incarnation of Jesus. So many people were attracted by Jesus. It was not his money that attracted his contemporaries, because he had none. It was not his background, which was very simple. His appearance was probably very ordinary. It was not his academic learning which attracted them; he simply did not have it. He was not a politician. Neither was it his miracles that people sought; in fact, at critical moments Jesus failed to hold a crowd. But still people flocked to Jesus because of the ease with which they could be themselves in his company. They discovered their deepest selves in the words of Jesus: Nicodemus, Zachaeus, Levi, the Roman officer, the adulterous woman, the Samaritan woman, Martha, Mary, the Twelve, and so many others. All of us can feel at home with Jesus because he responds to our deepest consciousness. His approach—first, by becoming man and, second, his attitude toward us—assures us of the fullness of life. He makes us feel at home because that is what love does, it takes away all fear. It allows us to be ourselves, bringing together our splendor and giftedness. Thus, we can realize the vision of St. Irenaeus who remarked, "The glory of God is man fully alive!"

So far, the way the church has often been viewed in Africa can best be compared to staying in a hotel room. A person can go to a hotel, smartly dressed, with the necessary cash and time to spare. Once there, one often experiences great difficulty in feeling at home in the hotel room. The lay-out, the decorations, the furniture, everything, in fact, is imposed on you by the management. Whether a person is young or old, all get the same kind of room. Feeling at home cannot come from the management; it can only come from the grassroots, your background and the person or people you are. To make others and ourselves feel at home or inculturated in the church, the Second Vatican Council proposed to us the model of the church as the people of God in communion. The people of God in their small communities in all their variety are the core and substance of the church. The Good News finds its roots in such communities and nowhere else. The model of the church as the people of God has confidence in the capacity of the Christian communities themselves to discern the Spirit and to realize the Gospel at the grassroots level.

The Setbacks for Africa

Irish stew is a nourishing dish. It is composed of various vegetables and meat that are cooked together but nevertheless maintain their identity in gravy. The Irish would most likely be disappointed if they could not tell the potatoes from the carrots in the finished product. Such is the disappointment of the African who is absorbed into a church that forces him or her to lose his or her identity. Different people react in different ways, by leaving the church altogether, by forming independent churches, by practicing their Christianity on Sunday and adhering to their cultural heritage for the rest of the week, and so on. For a long time Christianity has been equated with Western culture in such a way that by embracing one, one had to embrace the other. Most often Africans have had to discard their culture and identity at the door when entering their church, which they also have erroneously understood to be the white man's religion. Generations of Africans have come and gone with this institutionalized misconception of Christianity.

According to Professor John Mary Waliggo of Uganda, three factors have tended to undermine the emergence of an African Christianity and church: a) the black color of Africans, b) Africa's different way of life, and c) Africa's different religious belief and practices. Waliggo's observations can help us to situate the African person. In the field of inculturation, the first thing to know is the situation in which a person is located. It requires, as a minimum, knowledge of the history of a community or country, its failures and successes, its sufferings and joys. Nothing is trivial (V. Shirima, *A Light on Our Path*, p. 74).

The Black Color of Africans

Most people of the North coming to Africa encountered black people for the first time. Black became the distinguishing mark of an African and the most determinative factor in the relationship between Europeans and Africans. In these contacts it was taken for granted that the white color was normative and ordinary and thus black became the abnormal and extraordinary.

By the time people of the North actually met black people, both the word black and the concept of blackness had already been included in the languages of the North and taken on negative connotations. Even before the sixteenth century, the *Oxford Dictionary* described black in these words: "deeply stained with dirt, soiled, dirty, foul, having dark or deadly purposes, malignant, pertaining to or involving death, deadly baneful, disastrous, sinister . . . iniquitous, atrocious, horrible, wicked, indicating disgrace, censure, liability to punishment." Black was an emotionally partisan color, the handmaid and symbol of debasement and evil, a sign of danger and repulsion.

White was the very opposite of black. "White and black connoted purity and filthiness, virginity and sin, virtue and baseness, beauty and ugliness, beneficence and evil, God and the evil." It is in this perspective that words such as blackmail, black death, black magic, or black market acquire their meaning; many Africans continue to use these expressions, often to the amusement or initial embarrassment of people of the North.

Among the thousands of myths surrounding black Africans originating in the North are cultural laziness, highly imitative but never creative, intellectually retarded or inferior, always in search of a master, incapable of self-control especially sexually, unable to plan, incorrigible lying, possessing infectious diseases and the initial source of AIDS, and so on.

However much some Africans have tried to do so, they cannot alter their skin color without some very detrimental consequences. Black Africans who have lived in the North for centuries retain the same skin color as that of their ancestors who lived in Africa. All of us—Africans and non-Africans—need to strip away our prejudices. I quite understand why an African cleric rejects the use of black vestments for mourning. It is equally understandable when an African minister of baptism rejects putting a white cloth over the head of a beautiful black baby. To do so would create a contrasting insult, similar to that which St. Jerome confronted in translating the biblical text "black but beautiful." In the tradition of color, black and beautiful simply do not go together.

Black is very important in our inculturation process in Africa. It is the *black* God, the *black* Jesus, the *black* church that Africans can fully identify with. The black Madonna and the black St. Peter in St. Peter's Basilica make a lot of sense to Africans. Black can be beautiful equally with all other colors. None is superior. Christianity and the church must enter all colors and be decorated and accepted in all colors. Inculturation must form a new theology with the power to eliminate racism and to accept all peoples as they are. Missionaries who work in Africa are still challenged to treat their African counterparts as totally equal in all ways; missionary institutes that have begun to recruit Africans must ensure that those new members are fully accepted and treated as equals and are able to bring with them their Africanness, their blackness, and their identity.

The African Way of Life and Culture

Many non-Africans find it hard to believe that African cultures can add to the very understanding of Christianity and the church. Most models we use at present—both theological and ecclesiological—are still too eurocentric. We have yet to unveil the beauty of the church, the bride of Christ, in all its colors and cultures. For all intents and purposes, the center of gravity of the Christian church seems to be shifting quite drastically and quickly from Europe to the so-called Third World. It is this "third church" that may in the near future find itself with the task of re-evangelizing the first and second churches.

Inculturation in Zimbabwe

Deriving inspiration from the second Vatican Council, the late Cardinal Malula of Kinshasa/Zaire, always insisted on a theology of the local church. He saw the priest as the facilitator of this theology, creating, founding, and uniting Christian communities in order to form a well-inculturated local church.

The local church in Zimbabwe can boast of having covered some distance in inculturation since Vatican II, mainly in the area of liturgy. Apart from church music and dancing, there is also a popular burial rite and the less popular anniversary rite (*kurova guva*). The Zimbabwean church must realize that it has only begun the journey of inculturation. Despite the popularity of the burial rite, it is clear that the rite does not totally incorporate local traditions. Sometimes a funeral is delayed for hours while traditional rites are performed. We need to go beyond the rite itself to develop a theology of death and of the dead in a local context. Until the time when Christianity learns to theologically penetrate our African world view, we will be left with two separate theologies. For the African Christian, in time of crisis, both have to be satisfied, one in a Christian way, but the other one traditionally.

Only local theologians can help the church to arrive at a synthesis of the two. If we are serious about inculturation we cannot help but ask ourselves: How many local theologians do we have, people who have specifically studied theology after their seminary or university training, who are committed to this task? This is where we must begin.

3

An Analysis of the Church in Africa

New People Media Centre

The final aim of any legitimate missionary endeavor is to establish a truly local church in the shortest period possible. This is the powerful lesson we learn from the Acts of the Apostles, the letters of the Apostles, and the early church tradition. The fulfillment of a mission endeavor occurs when a foreign missionary, surrounded by a well-trained local clergy and a committed evangelizing laity, is able to resign all pastoral work into their hands and to move on to the regions beyond.

Despite the three major waves of missionary evangelization in Africa—the evangelization of the early centuries, the missionary movement at the end of the fifteenth century, and the nineteenth-century missionary activities—the African "missions" have not yet been able to become truly local churches. The essential conditions for a mission endeavor to become a truly local church include the following:

1. There should be sufficient local personnel to consolidate the faith, minister to the Christian communities, and spread the good news throughout the region. These should include local bishops, priests, religious, catechists, lay leaders, and a sizable number of committed and well-trained laymen and laywomen who live in stable and evangelizing families.

2. The entire Christian faith expressed in daily life, in doctrine, in worship, in catechesis, and in spirituality should be fully incarnated in and enriched by the local mentality, language, culture, and aspirations of the people. This involves not only the meaningful translation of the Bible, but also the achievement of a specific integral identity of the local church that is open to the universality of the Catholic church. The church must be seen and understood as being indigenous and local, and not as foreign, or a colonial imposition or importation.

3. A local church should manifest the maturity and vocation of being missionary to other parts of the country, the continent, and the world not yet evangelized. It is

This essay first appeared in *Cast Away Fear* (Nairobi: New People Media Centre, 1994). Revised and reprinted with permission.

in doing so that it manifests a sense of confidence, its integral and equal partnership in the universal church, and its constant need to be both local and universal at the same time.

4. A local church becomes truly local when it has made a clear and gradual achievement of self-reliance in the means that both maintain and consolidate as well as promote all aspects of its integral evangelization. It is only then that the local church becomes a giving church to needy local churches elsewhere, although it remains open to receive in times of emergency and for specific tasks, but not for its normal organization and evangelization.

5. A church becomes truly local when it has successfully developed and matured its own theology or theologies which manifest its attempt to understand and express its living faith. This will be a unique contribution to the world church and will serve as the sure basis for its growth in its specific identity, and in the ever challenging reality of being universal and open for enrichment from other cultures and contexts.

6. A church becomes truly local when it has been able to develop indigenous forms of religious life, priestly formation, and family spirituality that are inspired by its unique character, culture, history, actual context, and vision for the future. It is through these indigenous forms that the local spirituality develops and imbues the entire church, thus making possible the emergence of various ministries necessary to sustain society and the people of God within the local church and beyond.

7. A church becomes truly local when it develops a model of communion of all the people of God working together for the promotion of the kingdom of God. In such a model of being church, the hierarchical, clerical, and institutional aspects of church are organized and seen as truly serving the community, empowering the laity to take up their role in all aspects of the church—from decision-making to implementation. This kind of church is able to tap the talents of each member and section of the community; it is sensitive to and respectful of the human dignity and equality of all the people; it evangelizes itself on the basis of social justice. Such a church can survive future problems and be assured of permanency because it is firmly based on the community as a whole rather than a few individuals, as in the clerical model of church.

8. A church becomes truly local when it has discovered how to live and witness its faith creatively, peacefully, and respectfully amid other Christian traditions and other religions. Such a discovery leads to the emergence of genuine ecumenism and religious dialogue, bringing with it the characteristics of cooperation, mutual respect, and a serious search for common human and religious values that can transform society.

9. A church becomes truly local when it identifies with the genuine aspirations of the society where it exists and, above all, with the anxieties, suffering, and problems of the poor, the marginalized, the oppressed, the voiceless, the vulnerable, the old, and the sick. It is such an identity that defines the church's ministry of liberation and transformation and makes ministry not only an integral part of society, but its very leaven. Such an identity clarifies the relationship with the state and makes the church's prophetic mission always relevant to the changing contexts of the people

and society as a whole. Even where it is a very small minority, the church should never be accused of being, or be regarded as, foreign or irrelevant.

The Concrete Reality

Using these nine criteria, what we see in the Catholic church in Africa clearly indicates that the various churches that have celebrated five, two, or one hundred years of evangelization have not yet become truly local churches. The last hundred years have witnessed great accomplishments by both the work of missionaries and the work of "local" churches. Nearly five hundred dioceses have been erected in Africa, and the majority are presided over by local bishops. The number of priests and religious women and men has increased each year. Similarly, dedicated lay leadership has emerged in several African "local" churches, especially since Vatican Council II. Each African country is blessed with hundreds, if not thousands, of committed lay ministers who take care of local communities.

Despite some serious criticisms, the quality of Catholic life in Africa is relatively high. Family life has its basic problems, but it has produced many women and men committed to each other, to the church and society, and to holiness. The churches and chapels, schools, hospitals, orphanages, and development projects throughout the continent continue to bear the eloquent signs of love and commitment of missionaries, their successors, and the laity of each generation. Without those basic infrastructures of liberation, African independence could hardly have been conceived, let alone achieved.

Numerous men and women, both local and missionary, have sacrificed their lives for the good of the church and society in Africa. Generous benefactors abroad and within Africa itself have sustained the services rendered by the church and above all supported the structures of evangelization. The African church is, therefore, not only a hope for the universal church, but once it becomes fully local, it has the potential to be an inspiration to others.

These successes should not lead to complacency or to overlooking the serious mistakes of the past methods of evangelizing Africa. If we judge Catholicism by the nine principles previously listed, it would seem that there is no church in Africa that can be called truly local. The presence of a local bishop in a diocese does not automatically make a church local. Despite a gradual increase in the number of local priests, many Christians in several countries and dioceses in Africa feed more on the good news proclaimed by catechists than on the eucharist celebrated by priests. Instead of the African church organizing the sending of its missionary sons and daughters to other continents, this process has been largely "taken over" by international missionary societies that recruit candidates on their own without the necessary and enriching relationship that should exist between the sending and the receiving local churches. After more than one hundred years of evangelization, the Bible has been fully translated into only a handful of local languages. Despite initial attempts at inculturation since Vatican II, the church in Africa still appears foreign and sometimes also colonial to the local people. Every African diocese still depends heavily on financial assistance from Rome and elsewhere to carry out its essential services of formation, catechesis, and evangelization.

African theologians are still in their infancy stage and not fully supported or promoted to create the specific identity of the African church. The forms of religious life, priestly formation, and family spirituality are borrowed from elsewhere and as such cannot fully inspire the local community. The hierarchical, clerical, and institutional model of church still dominates and for many Christian Africans, this model of church minimizes the active role of the laity and the African sense of community and participation of all believers.

Ecumenism and religious dialogue receive little emphasis, while religious conflicts and fundamentalism appear to be on the increase. In several countries, especially where Christianity is the minority faith, there is a sense of isolation and failure to identify with the genuine aspirations of society. All over the continent the church does not seem to have made a clear option for the poor and the oppressed, nor has it dedicated itself to their total liberation and welfare. The prophetic mission is often compromised and the church fails to be truly leaven for the transformation of the entire society.

Why Has This Happened?

First, the defective ecclesiology and missionary methods of the nineteenth century resulted in African "missions" that continue to be at great risk of never becoming fully local churches. The failure to understand what a truly local church is and to plan for its implementation has often resulted in identifying missionary work with conversion, preaching, and baptizing rather than with the primary goal of establishing a self-supporting, self-ministering and self-propagating eucharistic community.

Second, some Christian missionaries, due to the situation of their times, tended to come to Africa with more faith and enthusiasm than a clear vision or well-planned program of work. They could not propose a schedule for their systematic withdrawal within a reasonable time to enable the local "mission" to become a truly local church. Their African successors have tended to follow similar methods, without putting a clear priority on the establishment of a truly local church.

In addition, the vulnerability of African cultures and people to outside cultures and foreign agents weakened Africa's resistance to that which was not advantageous. The African trait of not wanting to annoy or shock the friendly foreigner prevented the clear articulation to outsiders of what Africans really wanted. This silence has been detrimental and it explains the lack of constructive challenges to the church on the part of Africans. The fear of being misunderstood by missionaries or by the authorities of the universal church has made the African church either a silent church or a "yes-church," a church that is praised for its great obedience and conformity but never for its courageous innovation and creativity, its identity or its relevance.

No mission can ever achieve full maturity or a specific identity unless it is fully trusted and given the necessary freedom to think, plan, and implement what it critically judges to be proper, genuine, just, and relevant. The African church has not yet attained this full trust and freedom, despite a prophetic call from several church documents and gestures to that effect. The African Catholic church tends to continue thinking, evangelizing, and behaving in a way inconsistent with its own character and identity; it gives the impression that it is a church with no authority of its own.

Whereas a prophetic and courageous transition from Judeo-Christianity to Gentile-Christianity was made in the first century, a similar transition from eurocentric Christianity to world Christianity has not yet been clearly and prophetically achieved in the twentieth century. As a result, the universal church is still missing the great enrichment and beauty it could gain from various identities of the local churches.

Concrete Proposals for the Synod

1. Every missionary and church endeavor in Africa should be based on a fundamental vision, principles, and pastoral methods that clearly and consciously aim at establishing fully local churches in Africa, churches with all the characteristics of being self-supporting, self-ministering, and self-propagating in the shortest time possible.

2. As a living community of the Catholic church, the churches of Africa must become the actors—the subjects—and take responsibility for the planning and implementation of what they judge good, just, and relevant for themselves and their members in a true spirit of autonomy, seeking their identities as local churches.

3. The Catholic church in Africa retains its respect and dignity as equal in all matters to other local churches. It sees itself as mature and growing in that maturity. The church in Africa fully trusts that it can make a critical analysis of itself and of Christian preaching and come out with innovations and solutions that are orthodox.

4. The Synod should encourage the Catholic church in Africa in very clear terms to develop its own identity and to utilize fully its freedom to enrich its growth and contribute to the beauty, growth, and vision of the universal church.

5. In carrying out its missionary vocation within the continent of Africa and to other areas and other peoples, the African church wishes to establish living links between itself and the world around it. This vocation should be carried out with the full knowledge of the local church and in dialogue with the missionary societies and bishops' conferences. This is a crucial issue for mutual challenge and enrichment.

6. The Synod should establish the priority of meaningful translations of the Bible into all the local languages of Africa in order to ensure that African Christianity is scripture-centered. The Synod should design a realistic program and clearly define the necessary means to achieve this project in cooperation with other Christian denominations.

7. Africa is very much in need of its own liturgical rites that can enable it to celebrate in truth its faith and to build truly African Christian communities through worship. The challenge of the African church is to exploit fully Africa's cultural heritage, its symbols and symbolism, its history and actual context, and its theological thinking and reflection. Such African rites will serve as one of the pillars of

truly local churches, especially in the celebrations of the vital sacramental moments of life. Such rites will assist in eliminating dualism and at the same time give the legitimate opportunity to the African church to enrich the universal church and all the communities that belong to it.

8. In this same way, the African Catholic church ought to develop its own particular applications, emerging from within, of the universal canon law in order to deal adequately and effectively with the full way of being church: church leadership, sacramental life, and the entire organization and administration of the local churches in Africa. The present code already encourages this. Guided by the general principles of the new code, an African canon law would go a long way toward establishing the unique identity of the African church and empowering it with that specific autonomy necessary to be true to itself, to the mission of the universal church, and to its own people and context.

9. The Synod should encourage the development of authentic African theologies that could provide a way to understand faith and the principles on which the African Christian identity is based and appreciated within the one universal church of Christ. It is the duty of such theologies to keep the African church always thinking and reflecting, alive and dynamic, and above all always able and willing to accept challenges and criticisms from all corners. Through the twin processes of liberation and inculturation, African theologies can provide a sure basis for the coherent development of the African church.

10. The African church should be encouraged to develop indigenous forms of religious life, priestly formation, and family spirituality so that it may courageously undertake new ministries of justice, peace and reconciliation, development education, service to refugees and displaced persons, protection of children and other vulnerable categories of society, ecumenism and religious dialogue, all of which are crucial to contemporary society.

11. The African church is challenged to be more a communion of believers at the service of society and to accentuate less the institutional model of being church. It is this community model of church that can fully involve laymen and laywomen, religious men and women, youth, and intellectuals in the mission of Christ. Such a model can work to eliminate injustice and inequality in the church while at the same time utilizing fully the African sense of community for the integral evangelization of the continent.

12. Any African local church that judges that it has achieved the necessary level of self-reliance should be encouraged to ask that it be removed from the care of the Congregation for the Evangelization of Peoples and be placed under the Congregation of Bishops. This should be the visible sign that a particular church has become a truly local church.

The Historical Background of the African Synod

Engelbert Mveng

Preparatory discussions for the African Synod began as early as 1984 when the Ecumenical Association of African Theologians (EAAT) organized its first consultation on the theme of an African council of bishops. The project for an African council received an encouraging response from African intellectuals and then from African theologians, a large part of the African episcopate, and even from the Holy Father. This resulted in positive expectations, enthusiasm, and optimism on the part of African theologians. The Symposium of Episcopal Conferences of Africa and Madagascar (SECAM) set up a theological committee (COMITHEOL) to provide materials for reflection on the possible preparation of this event. The Catholic members of EAAT then organized two consultations at Yaoundé in Cameroon and Kinshasa in Zaire.

Certainly the theologians underestimated the potential difficulties and obstacles that could bar the way to an African council of bishops. So, after reviewing these early consultations, I shall discuss these obstacles and show how and why, while the talk was originally of an African council, what finally took place instead was an African synod. A significant development in the growth of the church in Africa, this synod can also mark a decisive step toward an African council of bishops.

The Yaoundé Consultation (April 11-12, 1984)

A Short History

Organized by EAAT, and under the presidency of Monsignor Tshibangu, auxiliary bishop of Kinshasa, fifteen Catholic theologians from Zaire, Cameroon, Nige-

Engelbert Mveng, a Jesuit theologian, poet, and artist, was director of the Department of History at the University of Yaoundé, Cameroon. An earlier version of this essay, translated by John Bowden, appeared in *Concilium* 1992/1. Revised and reprinted with permission.

ria, Ghana, Benin, and the Ivory Coast took part in this consultation. It began with a brief report on the origin and development of the idea of an African Council, noting the following significant steps in the development of African theology:

1. In 1956 *Des prêtres noirs s'interrogent* (Paris: Présence Africaine), the first distinctive statement by African theologians, was published in French.

2. In 1962-63 three significant events occurred: (a) a motion passed by Catholic African students at their seventh congress, held in Fribourg (April 1962) called for an African episcopal assembly to be held; (b) the Society for African Culture (SAC), speaking through two lay persons (Alioune Diop and Georges Ngango) expressed its desire to Pope Paul VI for African participation in the Second Vatican Council and made suggestions about the future of the church in Africa; and (c) in 1963 *Personnalité africaine et catholicisme* (Paris: Présence Africaine) was published under the aegis of SAC, expressing aspirations for an authentically African Christianity.

3. Vatican II clarified the notion of particular churches and defined the process of their growth to maturity. At Lyons, in December 1982, Cardinal Gantin stated that an African Council had already been spoken of in the corridors of Vatican II.

4. October 1974 saw an official declaration by the African bishops present at the Synod of Bishops in Rome on (a) promoting evangelization as shared responsibility, and (b) replacing the theology of adaptation with the theology of incarnation.

5. In September 1977 a colloquy held at Abidjan under the aegis of SAC on the theme of "Black Civilization and the Catholic Church" passed a resolution calling for an African Council (reported in the bulletin *Pour un Concile Africain*, Paris, 1978).

6. In 1981 three African theologians (Abbé Bimwenyi, secretary general of the Episcopal Conference of Zaire; and Fathers Meinrad Hebga and Nicholas Ossama) visited Europe under the aegis of the SAC and gave a series of lectures in Paris, Lyons, Brussels, and Louvain to explain the proposal for an African Council.

7. The Symposium of Episcopal Conferences of Africa and Madagascar (SECAM) examined the project, and charged its secretary-general with creating a task force to undertake an in-depth analysis and express its views on the proposal for an African Council.

8. EAAT, founded at Accra in December 1977, identified itself with the wish for an African Council and included this among its major study projects in 1980.

9. In May 1980 the episcopate of Zaire expressed the desire for an African Council to John Paul II on his visit to Kinshasa.

10. In April 1983 Cardinal Malula, in the name of the episcopate of Zaire, repeated to the pope the same desire for an African Council, "which would allow our churches to take stock of the present situation of Christianity and to establish in consultation an adequate basis for the integral evangelization of our continent in the future."

11. On April 23, 1983 in Rome, replying to a second group of bishops from Zaire, Pope John Paul II expressed his agreement in principle with the project for an African Council. He added: "Besides, I have already spoken of the vital need for consultation between all the bishops of Zaire; moreover, I think that to respond to a

desire which you have expressed about the whole African church, a consultation is also necessary at this level in one form or another, to examine the religious problems facing the whole of the continent, obviously in liaison with the universal church and the Holy See. But that would leave intact the responsibility of each bishop in his diocese."

12. In October 1983, under the presidency of Cardinal Zoungrana of SECAM, the African bishops present at the Synod of Bishops in Rome examined the project for an African Council and opted for the formula of an African Council in place of an African Synod.

13. In November 1983 a COMITHEOL document was sent to all the episcopal conferences of Africa and Madagascar on the project for an African Council. This document stated: "EAAT was one of the bodies, along with SECAM, which seized on the idea and the desire for an African Council expressed by the Abidjan Colloquy in 1977."

14. In April 1984 at the EAAT consultation, Catholic members of EAAT studied the project for an African Council in order to submit a report on their reflections to the president of SECAM. The secretary-general of SECAM and the president and secretary-general of COMITHEOL had indicated their intention of attending the meeting in Yaoundé but were unable to because of the political situation in Cameroon. As a result COMITHEOL was represented by Monsignor Peter Sarpong, the president of EAAT and a member of COMITHEOL.

This historical sketch clearly demonstrates that the project for an African Council was from its beginnings a fully ecclesial project and that it was of utmost interest to the Catholic theologian members of EAAT.

Definition and Nature of the African Council

In conformity with Canon 439.1, this would be a particular regional council, at the level of Africa. The canon speaks directly of a particular plenary council bringing together the particular churches of an episcopal conference. In this case the council would be sought at the continental level, and it would bring together all the particular churches that are part of SECAM.

A plenary council, that is, one which is held for all the particular churches belonging to the same conference of bishops, is to be celebrated as often as it seems necessary or advantageous to the conference of bishops, with the approval of the Apostolic See (Canon 439.1).

In accordance with Canon 439.1 the African Council would be convened at the level of SECAM by its president, but the prior approval of the Holy See would be required. With reference to Canons 439 through 446, taking account of the necessary characteristics of a particular council at a regional level, the Council would bring together all the bishops, who would be joined by representatives of all the people of God in Africa, meaning priests, religious and duly chosen laity, and foreign missionaries working in Africa (other than bishops who would participate in their own right), who would be invited to the degree that they might have positive contributions to make.

In a special category, SECAM could invite a delegation or representation from the Holy See, but this delegation would have no voting rights. As observers, SECAM could also invite the categories that were represented at Vatican II, namely ecumenical representatives from Africa and even from outside the continent or from other episcopal conferences.

The basic proposal was to take stock of the current state of Christianity in Africa, to create conditions for the development of the Christian religion so that it could establish deep roots, and to make a general survey of the current religious situation in Africa. It also proposed to explore and examine future directions for Christianity in the following sectors: theology and the doctrinal situation, liturgy, spirituality, overall pastoral orientations and options, and the activity of the church in African society.

Several suggestions and clarifications were put forward by the consultation.

1. A preamble should be produced on the historical and theological foundations of the African Council.

2. Since this was a Catholic project, the Catholic members of EAAT were involved, and they indicated they would be ready to make their specific contributions to the preparation and holding of the African Council. At that time they were working under the aegis of the highest authorities in SECAM and in communion with them.

3. Those taking part in the Yaoundé consultation recommended (a) establishing immediately three preparatory technical committees for the three major language groups—Anglophone, Francophone, and Luso-Hispanophone; (b) setting up a central technical coordinating committee; and (c) designating a technical committee to take charge of the needed material infrastructure and finance, to be responsible for estimating the cost of the preparations and holding the sessions, and to examine sources of finance inside and outside Africa.

4. The members of the Yaoundé consultation sought to establish a list of specific problems needing discussion by the central commission, after consultation with all the people of God in Africa. They identified the need to stimulate work and research at every level within the church: parishes, Christian communities, major seminaries, faculties of theology, research centres, associations, and so forth. Each of these commissions was to include specialized subcommissions on the general situation of Africa, pastoral questions, doctrinal questions, the responsibility and mission of the church in contemporary African society, law, and church discipline.

5. Members of the consultation recognized that to ensure the full success of the Council it would be necessary to conscientize and mobilize the whole of the African episcopate. Those taking part in the consultation resolved to send a letter to Cardinal Zoungrana, president of SECAM, and Monsignor Sarpong, president and secretary-general of EAAT, and I was instructed to take this letter to the president of SECAM.

6. The consultation recommended that the whole church in Africa should devote itself to prayer for the full success of the African Council.

The Kinshasa Consultation (February 23, 1986)

The second consultation for the project of an African Council, held at Kinshasa, Zaire, was attended by fifteen African theologians from Zaire, Cameroon, Rwanda, Burundi, Nigeria, and Ghana. Under the presidency of Monsignor Tshibangu, auxiliary bishop of Kinshasa and founding member of EAAT, the agenda included a determination of the state of the project for an African Council since the Yaoundé consultation. It also specified that the consultation should assess the present situation and determine a procedure to be followed.

As secretary general of EAAT, I presented a brief report on current preparations for the Council that summed up the work of the two theological commissions—COMITHEOL and the Catholic group of EAAT. I reported on a number of documents and reports prepared during 1983 and 1984 by both groups that surveyed the range of historical, pastoral, and theological questions relating to the possibility of an African Council. We also began to discuss the possible organization and preparation of such an event. It seemed that the more theoretical phase of the project of an African council was drawing to a close and a new stage—a move toward action—was being envisaged.

The Move toward Action

The step necessary to move forward was a form of ecclesial consultation to provide information for Africa's Christian people, to sensitize and mobilize them. The fact that Pope John Paul II referred to an African Council on his trip to Africa in 1985 demonstrated that he was aware of the planning work completed by the time and that, moreover, he appeared to sympathize with it. This was great encouragement for African Catholics.

In keeping with this need for consultation, two surveys were undertaken of the views of the African episcopate: the first questionnaire was sent to the African episcopal conferences by SECAM, and the second was sent to each African bishop by the Sacred Congregation for the Evangelization of the Peoples. The results of these surveys were not made public.

The August 1985 visit of Pope John Paul II to Africa marked an important stage in the development of the project of an African Council. Speaking to African intellectuals in Yaoundé on August 13, the pope referred to the African church authorities with specific mention of the episcopal conferences, SECAM, and the Council.

At that time, information had not yet been provided to the Catholic people of Africa, nor had they been sensitized or mobilized. It was agreed that SECAM should immediately produce a monthly information bulletin to provide a link with all the episcopal conferences and the Holy See. This bulletin would take stock of the real significance of the African Council, its objectives, and the stages in its preparation. A second step would be to disseminate the same information widely at the level of episcopal conferences, dioceses, and right down to parish level. The reactions and suggestions of pastors, theologians, and the faithful would then be communicated monthly to the SECAM secretariat. Consultation participants further proposed that EAAT organize sensitizing missions, with Abbé Mushete Ngindu and myself in charge of French-speaking Africa, and Father Elochukwu E. Uzukwu, Professor Brookman-Amissah, and Father Mutiso Mbinda in charge of English-speaking areas.

At the parish level, it was suggested that bishops call for campaigns of prayer so that the Spirit of the Lord might be the inspirer and promoter of this African Council.

At the theological level, the organizing committee also suggested that SECAM create a group of theological experts to be responsible for organizing reflection seminars for the regional episcopal conferences. Kinshasa consultation participants stressed that it would be helpful for the theologians to avoid offending the African episcopate by giving the impression of preempting or forcing its decisions. Their prime concern should be the interests of the churches of Africa in communion with the universal church. It was noted that to that date only eleven out of the thirty-five episcopal conferences that received the SECAM survey had responded. It was noted that the standing committee of SECAM, planning to meet on February 24, 1986, would certainly address this question, and that even if a majority of these responses turned out to be negative, the work of the theologians was significant in that it would continue to make the churches of Africa sensitive to the problems of the people of God in Africa.

Participants at the Kinshasa consultation also discussed what purpose the Council would serve and what would happen after the Council, considering that the Catholic church in Africa had not yet "digested" Vatican II. It was generally agreed that the African Council would be a starting point, not a destination as had been the case in China and the United States in the previous century. The Council would be seen as a sharing of experiences between African churches and not the concern of a single church, such as that of Zaire, and it would in fact be the extension and implementation in Africa of Vatican II.

Finally, given the extraordinary upsurge in conversions in Africa, the African "boom," it was necessary for the church in Africa to take stock, to develop strategies for its second evangelization (most of the churches were celebrating their centenaries), and to give itself the means to control and guide the rapidly increasing numbers of the faithful. Several African dioceses either had organized or were in the process of organizing synods. In fact, given the absence of information and awareness among the African churches, there was an ongoing need to organize regular information at episcopal conferences and colloquies (as, for example, on the subject of *Ad Gentes* and its application). Such regional meetings would both sensitize and inform. Thus, it would become obvious, for example, that the idea of the Council, born at Abidjan in 1977, was not a Zairian affair, as had been rumored, nor was it even exclusively French-speaking, since English-speaking bishops and theologians had been working on it from the beginning.

In discussing the aims of an African Council, the participants reflected on the role of the laity in such an assembly. While the very existence of SECAM could justify the calling of a Council, the primary partners calling for a Council were the people of God and their daily problems and the very progress of history on the African continent. If such discussion did not take place, the churches of Africa could face the Africa of the year 2000 in disarray. As a result the participants suggested specific measures to inform and sensitize the people of God, including, as mentioned above, the creation of a SECAM information bulletin and the organization of special missions.

At that time, the consultations had not yet touched directly on a proposed date for the Council. The plenary assembly of SECAM at Kinshasa in July 1984 put a good deal of emphasis on the need to devote time for an in-depth preparation. Considering the experience of other plenary councils (such as those of the United States and China in the nineteenth century, and Indochina in 1934), the year 1990, approximately five years later, would be a reasonable date. The immediate preparation of those previous plenary councils did not take more than a year at most, and communications were less developed.

The earlier plenary councils lasted around two weeks, although the churches represented were less dispersed than those of the whole of the African continent. It was suggested that on the one hand the Council could last one month and on the other hand that it could confer a conciliar status on SECAM, which would allow it to prolong the work of the Council in its later sessions.

The actual convening of the Council might occur as follows: First, SECAM, through its president, would submit the entire Council dossier to the Holy See, seeking its approval. Second, after approval of the Holy Father, the standing committee of SECAM would be approached to prepare the convocation. Third, the president of SECAM would proceed to convene the Council.

The consultation participants suggested that two brochures be produced, one in French and the other in English, containing the texts of all the documents on the project for an African Council developed by COMITHEOL and EAAT. These brochures would be distributed among African bishops, major seminaries, faculties of theology, and key Christian groups.

The Yaoundé consultation developed quite a complete plan for the Council, including a projected budget, while recognizing the need for a special consultation for detailed planning. Participants saw an immediate need to compile a list of the entire African episcopate from the *Annuario Pontificio* and a list of expert theologians by disciplines and by African language zones.

The consultation also considered where the Council could be held. Suggestions included Kinshasa, Abidjan, Yaoundé, Nairobi, Harare, and Ibadan, among others. It was estimated that at least 700 people would be invited, including theologians and representatives (400), guests (50), theologians and representatives of the people of God (200), technicians and others (50). In all, there should be provision for 1,000 guests that would include lodging, food, local transport, a secretariat, simultaneous translation, post, and telecommunication.

Allowing for inflation, a budget of approximately 1.5 billion CFA was projected. It was estimated that a good deal of this money would come from Africa: from African Christian heads of state if the approaches were made at the highest level; by special collections from the faithful; and from Christian movements (such as

Christian women's groups). It would also be possible to count on the Holy See and the generosity of traditional Christian organizations throughout the world.

From the African Council to the African Synod

The documents and consultations cited above repeatedly attempted to survey the major problems and to find answers to questions that appeared to pose obstacles to the African Council. However, while problems were indeed identified and other pertinent questions were asked, it is not true that answers were found commensurate with all the questions.

Problems Posed by Canon Law

The first and perhaps most serious problem lay in the African reading of the new *Code of Canon Law* (1983). That reading seemed to be unaware of the imprecisions of—not to say the gaps in—the new code. For example, the debate on episcopal conferences and their attributions was far from having been resolved satisfactorily. The doctrine and practice of *particular councils*, which were so developed in the early churches and which underwent a real renewal in the nineteenth century, seemed to have been telescoped in this last code. The *plenary councils*, which played such a key role in the mission countries in the nineteenth century (the Baltimore councils) and the beginning of the twentieth (the plenary councils of China, Japan, and Indochina, for example), having been reduced to the one level of episcopal conferences, no longer seemed to match the whole range of particular national, regional, and provincial councils held throughout the centuries in the churches of both East and West. The *ecumenical council* itself appeared in the new code only as one of the prerogatives of the Sovereign Pontiff, who has the power to convene it, to preside over it, and to promulgate its acts.

When the theologians of COMITHEOL and my colleagues of EAAT invoked Canons 439-446 of the new *Code of Canon Law*, or when they referred to Canon 439.1 to define an African Council, they were putting the cart before the horse, so to speak. They had not yet shown in any way how the definition of an episcopal conference given by the Code could apply to SECAM, the Symposium of Episcopal Conferences of Africa and Madagascar. Even those unlettered in canon law, like myself, could see that SECAM did not correspond to any of the ecclesial structures envisaged in the *Code of Canon Law*. A symposium, in the primary meaning of the word, is a friendly meeting over drinks. Such a gathering has neither statutes nor jurisdiction nor power. (Those who have some acquaintance with SECAM are aware of these gaps.)

Even more amazing was the negative reaction of the great majority of the members of SECAM in Kinshasa in 1984 and later in Lagos when the question was raised of giving SECAM statutes, which could have made it an association of episcopal conferences, as happened in Latin America. Indeed, it was these statutes that made possible the now historical assemblies of Medellín and Puebla. It is difficult to see how SECAM, without legal existence, statutes, or power, could have convened a plenary council on a continental level.

Lack of Consensus in Africa

This legal void was not the result of ignorance or negligence on the part of the members of SECAM. It stemmed directly from the lack of consensus that divided them. Not only was there no agreement on the significance, function, role or scope of SECAM itself, there was also division over the opportunities, the content, the program, and the powers of an African Council. The emotional character of some of the debates emphasized the differences of opinion between English-speakers and French-speakers, conservatives and progressives, and supporters and opponents of inculturation. High emotion quickly produced scapegoats: first, among the African theologians, who were christened "problem theologians"; second, in the Zaire episcopate, which had been accused of continental hegemonism; and finally in the person of a man who, in the opinion of some of us, was an authentic father of the African church, Cardinal Malula, Archbishop of Kinshasa.

Without doubt, the COMITHEOL and EAAT documents took into account the support of African bishops—not to mention the pope—for an African Council. Unfortunately, this support was insufficient in itself to put an end to the differences or to fill the legal void. The primary need was incontestably for the African episcopate to free SECAM from its aporia by conferring a canonical existence on it, thus providing the conditions for convening a Council. At the very moment when there was the most talk of an African Council, we were forced to note that there was not yet an authority in Africa capable of convening such a Council. And it was not up to the pope to do this; canon law made no provision for it.

Pros and Cons of Synod or Council

The announcement of an African Synod or, better, a Synod of Bishops on the Evangelization of Africa, could only provoke contradictory reactions. For some it was a final authoritarian stop to the project for an African Council, which was presented in some quarters as a short cut toward an African schism. The most pessimistic proclaimed a real return to fetishism. Some missionaries seized the opportunity to defend their work in Africa against an African church promoted in haste, hardly having emerged from paganism, and always ready to lapse back into it. Others, less pessimistic (and these included the African theologians), saw the calling of an African Synod as the quite logical gesture of a pope who, tired of waiting for the African episcopate to take responsibility, took it upon himself to do what the law allowed him to do—convene a Synod of Bishops and designate the evangelization of Africa as its central theme.

Of course, some of the African episcopate applauded, believing that the pope had purely and simply taken sides with the opponents of an African Council. That was a gross error! Besides, the problems connected with an African Synod belong within the general perspective of the application of Vatican II, which was the very reason for the creation of the Synod of Bishops. The preceding Synod of Bishops of Europe could not but have reassured even the most timid and the most hesitant. That having been said, however, the perspective of an African Council was different. Not only could the proposed Synod *not* bar the route to the Council, the Synod might seem a necessary and salutary step toward the preparation of an African Council, given the questions and aporias that I enumerated here.

Although the Synod of Bishops of Europe did reassure some people, the proposed African Synod was a quite different matter. There is a great contrast between Europe and Africa. Europe is increasingly unified in political, economic, cultural, and religious terms, and in Europe the Catholic church, present everywhere, plays a dynamic and unifying role. On the other hand, Africa experiences vast political, economic, cultural, and social disintegration. In Africa, the Catholic church, overwhelmed by an uncontrollable flood of conversions, struggles to cope with people with their backs to the wall—impoverished, starving, without a future, without guides, and with no reason for hope.

At the same time, the African church is being overwhelmed by the bureaucracy of baptisms to computerize, registers to fill, collections, intentions at mass, and the need to beg alms from overseas benefactors night and day. Such a church is increasingly absent from the places and institutions in which all of Africa desperately tries to gather together to strategize for its own survival; the Catholic church does not attend meetings of the Organization for Africa Unity, the Lagos plan, the UNO Economic Commission for Africa, or the All Africa Conference of Churches. So our church, despite its massive numbers, seems to be exiling itself on the dramatic periphery, leaving the center to the sinful structures that risk stifling it.

In my opinion—and in the opinion of others—the only possible solution in such circumstances seemed to be a Synod of Bishops on Africa. The hesitations that surrounded its convocation, the silence that reigned for more than a year after its first announcement, the whispers surrounding its preparation, all produced an atmosphere of mistrust, a real malaise. This was compounded by a useless clumsiness in certain Vatican circles that betrayed practices totally alien to the gospel that were reminiscent of our former oppressors. Media coverage was astonishing, as were rumors of "black lists" emanating from Rome that circulated in Africa, suggesting an order to African bishops to remove the famous "problem theologians," the very theologians who attempted to make an African contribution to theological research at the end of this twentieth century.

The Nature of the Synod of Bishops

The first Synod of Bishops on Africa should begin by identifying priorities and choosing a limited number of themes to pursue in depth. In early discussions, little weight was attached to questions such as the missionary effort and the specific contribution of Africa to the evangelization of the world of the twenty-first century. Inculturation was treated with the same haste, not to mention levity. Problems relating to strictly African forms of the consecrated life, to the contextualization of the spiritual life, to the sacralization or the profanation of poverty in Africa, to a legalistic and oppressive ecclesiology in which canon law ignores and stifles the gospel, the transition in Africa from a dependent church to a sharing church—all these problems were skated over or forgotten in the official preparatory questionnaire. This led us to ask: What is the ultimate object pursued through the synod? Is it the growth of the church in Africa? Or will the synod stifle it?

A Synod of Bishops for Africa has a place in the providential process of the growth of the church on our continent. It must be prepared for with all the seriousness that such an event merits for it is a visitation of God in the biblical sense of the word. This visitation is at the same time a questioning and a call to conversion, but not only of infidels. It is above all the conversion of the people of God who are in Africa. The synod can help us discover the gap between the call that the Lord addresses to us and the meanness of our responses. It can reveal to us the reality of an African church that is a free gift from God and that is already there before us, often without us or despite us. It can help us to discover, to accept, to assume, and to promote this gift of God. The synod can help us discover the African bride of Christ, which is the church on our continent with all its beauty and its ugliness, with the stigmata of five centuries of oppression and martyrdom, and of the anthropological annihilation of Africans on all the continents. It can help us to meet the gaze of our mother the church in Africa, which sounds out our hearts and asks us gravely: "How long will I have to wait for the day when you achieve in me what is lacking in the Catholic dimension of the body of Christ? Where will you finally make yourself the truly African Catholic church?"

A synod can also help us to recognize the church in Africa, living and present today, with its people of God rich in their immense poverty, with its Christian families, its clergy, its cardinals, its bishops, its priests, its religious, men and women, its thinkers, its theologians, its Christian artists, and its spiritual masters. For it is through all these people now that the church of Jesus Christ will build itself up on our continent. We do not need useless questions to take us half a century backwards, sterile questions about an African theology, an African liturgy, or African Christian art. They already exist; they are part of the African church.

That is why the preparation of this synod caused problems. Would this synod sweep the table clean, would it be like the first harvest? Why were the people of God in Africa ignorant of the whole preparation of this synod? For whom, and why, was it being prepared? Why were authentic African theologians being systematically removed? Why were the spiritual masters of our continent being ignored? Why was the impression being given that this was a matter for Vatican officials, both in Rome and scattered throughout Africa among the ranks of the clergy and in the official institutions? So many embarrassing questions.

These questions show that the synod, both a divine visitation and call to conversion, was viewed as a decisive step to allow the church in Africa to discover itself and to become aware of the many challenges that the future poses. By the grace of God this synod could be an opportunity for the church of Africa to discover its conciliar dimension and once again to lay the foundations of a true communion of the churches of Africa to build the kingdom of God on our continent in solidarity and charity.

The synod could offer the African episcopate the occasion for conveying a legal structure and a moral persona on SECAM, just like that of CELAM in Latin America. Such an assembly could then give itself conciliar structures with periodical sessions. If the church of Africa today is not equipped for convening a council, we think, we desire, and we pray that the Synod of Bishops for Africa will constitute a real prolegomena to an authentic African Council.

A Critical Review of the *Lineamenta*

Justin S. Ukpong

Following the announcement by Pope John Paul II on January 6, 1989, to convene a Special Assembly for Africa of the Synod of Bishops, the *Lineamenta* (outline) for preparing for this synod was promulgated at the general assembly of the Symposium of Episcopal Conferences of Africa and Madagascar (SECAM) in Lome in July 1990. The theme of the synod, "The Church in Africa and Her Evangelizing Mission Towards the Year 2000: 'You shall be my witnesses' (Acts 1:8)," was presented in the *Lineamenta* in two major sections. Following a brief history of the evangelizing of Africa, the first part dealt with the meaning and necessity of evangelization. The second part identified and analyzed five different tasks of evangelization in Africa, namely: proclamation of the good news of salvation, inculturation, dialogue, justice and peace, and the means of social communications. The *Lineamenta* concluded with a questionnaire on each of the above five tasks of evangelization.

I propose to appraise the *Lineamenta* from the perspective of the African church experience and raise issues for further discussion. I shall seek to bring out the philosophical, theological, and methodological assumptions that frame each section. Thus, my focus is not only on what the *Lineamenta* says but also—and most importantly—on the assumptions that lie behind what it says, and its methodological presuppositions.

Background

The primary discussion in the *Lineamenta*, the five tasks of evangelization, is prefaced by a brief history of the evangelization of Africa and a clarification of the

Justin S. Ukpong, a Nigerian Spiritan priest, is deputy rector of the Catholic Institute of West Africa in Port Harcourt, Nigeria, where he teaches New Testament and African theology. An earlier version of this essay was published in *Concilium* 1992/1. Revised and reprinted with permission.

concept of evangelization. Clearly the concept of history as *magistra vitae* (teacher of life) underlies the historical presentation. History is a retelling of the past in order to learn lessons for the present, the basis of the idea that history repeats itself. Also, it becomes clearly evident that history is the story of the victors. The *Lineamenta* also conveys a deep impression of the defeat of Christianity and the triumph of Islam.

Given the fact that the synod's theme is the *future* evangelization mission of the African church, this approach does not seem very helpful. The history of the evangelization of Africa ought to have been presented in such a way as to provide the proper vision, inspiration, and commitment needed for the African church to create a new history in the third millennium. For history is not necessarily a presentation of dead facts but rather a matter of interpretation of facts; the purpose of the interpretation determines the selection and organization of facts and their interpretation. Moreover, history is created by human beings participating in events; it does not happen by itself. Thus, history repeats itself when knowledge of past events has not been utilized to create new situations.

The church in North Africa flourished and then dwindled away. While early attempts to evangelize West Africa did not meet with lasting success, today the church in sub-Saharan Africa flourishes. First, instead of interpreting the North African story as a defeat of Christianity, we should interpret it from a forward-looking perspective that involves looking beyond the obvious to the less apparent to seek historical meaning. We should not interpret this history as the story of the victors but as the story of the victims seen as possible real heroes. This is indeed the paradigm of the historical meaning of the passion-resurrection event whereby Jesus, the "victim" of death in human eyes, was in fact the victor-hero. What should be highlighted is the struggle of North African Christians to maintain the faith. This struggle led to the survival of the Coptic and Ethiopic churches, which have managed to weather the storm of Muslim aggression until the present time.

Second, we should see a connection between the North African story and today's sub-Saharan stories. We should look on the church in North Africa as having accomplished a mission, and we should see its "demise" as a symbol of the seed of Christianity sown in African soil that still sprouts and flourishes today in sub-Saharan Africa. In this way, African Christians south of the Sahara can claim in a historical sense their own Christian heritage. In this way, too, the realities of the present church in Africa will be viewed seriously as the raw material of a new history.

With regard to the concept and necessity of evangelization, in Africa today the question is less a matter of clarifying these concepts than of identifying the type of evangelization needed. Africa needs evangelization that is integral and dialogical. It should be *integral* in the sense that the gospel message should permeate all aspects of the people's lives—religious, economic, political, cultural, social, and so on. This implies a theology of evangelization that holds in creative tension the material and spiritual aspects of the people's lives and views them as complementary. *Dialogical*, as opposed to monological, means that evangelization should be concerned not only with giving the Christian message to a people but also with how the people's context shapes the interpretation of Christianity and its message.

Task 1: Proclamation of the Good News of Salvation

Against a backdrop of competing proclamations of the gospel by various religious sects in Africa, an authentic proclamation of the gospel today is rightly emphasized as the most essential task of evangelization. However, in my opinion, certain elements that are vital to such proclamation are neglected in the *Lineamenta*. First is the fact that Jesus Christ himself is the good news of salvation and was also the first proclaimer of the good news. This calls for the centrality of Jesus and of the Bible in the proclamation and in the lives of Christians. We must constantly ask what Jesus' attitude was toward certain issues, persons, or situations. Unless the centrality of Jesus is recognized both in what is preached and in the life-style of the preacher, we run the risk of not preaching "the truth of the gospel" (Gal. 2:14).

Authentic proclamation of the gospel also demands that its recipients be seen as an important factor in the proclamation process. Recipients are not mere passive objects but active participants in the proclamation process; they should not be treated as a *tabula rasa*. The proclaimer must take into account not only the recipients' background but also their contribution to the hermeneutical process of appropriating the message of salvation. Today African Christianity has entered a new phase of its life. Africa is no longer to be considered as the *object* but rather as the *subject* of evangelization. This says more than that Africans have become agents of evangelization. It says that Africa is no longer to be seen as a land out there to be conquered by a gospel message read through the lenses of another culture. Africa is first and foremost a land that is also heir to the patrimony that is the gospel message, which it must appropriate with its own resources. The African church must search for its authentic Christian self-definition and its authentic interpretation and expression of Christianity. In turn the African church must set free the Christian message for appropriation and interpretation by African Christians. Authentic proclamation also implies addressing contemporary issues. Hence, the African church must identify the pressing religious, economic, social, and political issues facing Africa today as challenges calling for the prophetic voice of the church.

Finally, the African Synod must face the question of how to tap the human and material resources in Africa and organize them toward indigenous growth in evangelization. How many new insights have the local churches in Africa brought to the task of evangelization in recent years? With the large numbers of trained local clergy, the church must address, for example, the need for new catechisms, for organizing parish structures to respond to current needs, for restructuring the ministry, the liturgy, and rituals. While much has been done in Zaire in this respect, other regions need to go beyond simply introducing traditional music into the liturgy.

Task 2: Inculturation

The presentation on inculturation rightly links inculturation with the biblical mandate to evangelize all peoples and traces the genesis of this practice to apostolic and ecclesiastical traditions. However, the *Lineamenta*'s analysis does not sufficiently follow through on this basic insight and its hermeneutical implications.

First, the text interprets inculturation only in terms of the gospel influencing cultures; there is no indication that it also involves bringing new dimensions to the understanding of the gospel. Thus, in the encounter between gospel and culture (the process of inculturation), culture is supposed to be "transformed" to accept Christianity (no. 47), and criteria are established to determine which cultural values may be assumed into Christian practice (nos. 50, 51). Nothing is said about a possible reinterpretation of the gospel message in the light of a new cultural experience. Although the text actually mentions instances of such reinterpretation in the New Testament (no. 47), it does not utilize the insight hermeneutically.

Because of their hermeneutical importance in this context, two different examples in the New Testament deserve mention. The first is the admission of Gentile Cornelius into the church without circumcision (an important case of inculturation). This entailed not only conversion on Cornelius' part but also a reinterpretation of the Christian faith on the part of Peter and the other apostles for whom this had hitherto been unthinkable. The second example worth noting is that in the New Testament we find not only a Jewish but also a Hellenistic interpretation of the one Jesus. Scholars have pointed to some christological titles in the New Testament that appear to come from a Palestinian background (such as the reference to Jesus in Acts 3:13-26 as "servant" and "prophet" like Moses), and others that appear to emerge from a Gentile Hellenistic background (such as the title *soter*, savior).[1] Above all, regarding New Testament foundations for inculturation, it is important to mention the example of Jesus' use of Jewish culture to present the Good News, and the letter to the Galatians wherein Paul argues that Gentiles need not adopt a Jewish cultural identity in order to be Christians.

The relation between faith and culture is expressed in the text in terms of faith taking "from culture those elements which are suitable to illustrate her mysteries, while culture seeks to appropriate to herself the truths revealed, at times through a tiring effort" (no. 50). In view of an earlier reference to inculturation as a "synthesis between culture and faith" (no. 48), I would suggest that the relation between faith and culture would be better seen in terms of faith influencing and challenging culture from within, and in culture influencing the interpretation and expression of faith.

The two approaches have different practical consequences. If inculturation is understood with the former approach, it is enough to interpret the Christian faith from a foreign perspective and then select from African culture (for the purpose of inculturation) only those elements that fit that perspective. Using the latter approach, the totality of African culture is exposed to the Christian faith, which in the process causes the dead wood in the culture to fall apart, while authentic cultural insights help to shape the interpretation and expression of faith. Thus, faith influences culture at the same time as culture influences the interpretation of faith; culture does not just struggle to appropriate divine truths, but rather it opens itself to be totally influenced by faith. This does not occur in the abstract (as opposed to the impression given in the former approach), but in concrete human communities and in individuals.

A second question I would like to ask is if evangelization is really "inconceivable without inculturation" (no. 47). Would it not be more correct to say that evangelization is inconceivable without *some measure* of inculturation? Or, better yet, to say that effective evangelization demands inculturation? If evangelization were inconceivable without inculturation and if inculturation were denied as "the encounter of the Good News with all people of the earth through the *instrumentality* of their culture" (no. 47, emphasis mine), we would not be debating questions of inculturation in sub-Saharan Africa today after nearly a century of continuous evangelization. Indeed, the gospel was announced to Africa through the framework of European culture, while only those elements of African culture that fitted into that framework were incorporated in the process. African culture as such was not really considered or utilized as an *instrument* of evangelization. Attempts were even made to have it replaced by European culture, which was considered better and more "Christian."

Since inculturation is perhaps the most significant issue on which the African church has made progress, it would have been helpful for the *Lineamenta* to present a broad outline of the issues as a means of raising consciousness about future expectations. So far, the practice of inculturation in Africa has remained mostly at the level of peripheral liturgical adaptation. The Synod Fathers should move beyond this.

Inculturation has serious implications for both the African church and the universal church. The church's life and beliefs are no longer to be thought of in monolithic terms, but in terms of a diversity of cultures. This implies the affirmation, in practical terms, of the differing cultural identities of peoples within the universal church and of the need to empower these peoples to interpret and express their own Christianity. It implies, too, the movement of churches that were formerly at the periphery to the center of the life and activity of the church universal. The universality of the church should now be expressed in terms of a communion of churches and a sharing of power in collegiality rather than in terms of uniformity and conformity to one pattern.

Fully implemented, inculturation involves both challenge and risk—a challenge to the local churches to define their authentic self-image, and the risk of the boat of the church's universality (as this has been hitherto understood) being rocked in the process. Karl Rahner's theological analysis that our epoch (with its transition from European to world church) is parallel to the transition from Jewish to Gentile Christianity is very helpful here.[2]

Task 3: Dialogue

The *Lineamenta* acknowledges dialogue as a means for the church to fulfil its mandate to preach the gospel to all creation. It also analyzes the circumstances of dialogue at different levels and seeks to point to the challenges of dialogue in Africa at each level. Unfortunately, nowhere does the text proffer a definition of dialogue. And when we ask, "Dialogue for what?" no amount of teasing of the text yields a substantive answer. This makes it difficult to form a clear image of the reality or the perspective under discussion.

I propose adopting a working definition of dialogue to guide our discussion. Based on Pope John Paul II's definition of interreligious dialogue,[3] I understand dialogue as *an approach in relating with other people that assumes the freedom and legitimacy of these people to be themselves and that promotes understanding and respect for them, including their faith situation.* The purpose of dialogue is to learn and be enriched by knowledge of the other and not to force change on the other or confront the other with advantage.

Omitted from the text is one significant factor that has given rise to the practice of dialogue today—the church's de-emphasis of a triumphalist self-image. This understanding is informed by an ecclesiology that sees the church as always in need of reform and self-evangelization. Vatican II speaks of the Catholic church sharing in the blame of Christian disunity (*Unitatis Redintegratio*, 3). Dialogue is possible only when the *other* is regarded as a partner and not as an addressee.

In my opinion, the statement that "without dialogue the Church cannot proclaim the Good News" (no. 55) seems inaccurate. If in practice this were so, then dialogue would not be a modern issue. The good news has been proclaimed in Africa for over a century and yet we are only now discussing dialogue. It would be more accurate to say that evangelization by its very nature calls for dialogue, and that any approach to evangelization that is not dialogical is inadequate. Another serious reservation for me is the lack of discussion of intra-ecclesial dialogue. This is dialogue within the church itself—among the hierarchy, clergy and religious, and between these groups and the laity.

Similarly, the analysis of dialogue with African traditional religion appears to miss a central point that distinguishes this dialogue from dialogue with other non-Christian religions. African traditional religion is an integral part of the African world view, and it is basically what informs the day-to-day existence of average African Christians. Today the average African Christian is severely torn between the African and the Christian world views. The primary purpose of dialogue in this case is to integrate the two world views so as to give the African Christian an integrated religious personality. In this context, dialogue takes place first and foremost in the minds of individual Christians; it is basically non-verbal and absolutely fundamental. The issue is to help Christians (and not just neophytes and catechumens) engage in this dialogue. At one level, this involves formal study and analysis of African traditional religion; at another level, it involves interaction with its practitioners.

Another criticism I offer is that the text is based on the institutional model of dialogue rather than the people-of-God model. The institutional model conceives of dialogue primarily—though not exclusively—in terms of relations between institutions, while the people-of-God model conceives of dialogue primarily in terms of the interactions between people belonging to these institutions. Assuming an institutional model poses problems when analyzing dialogue with African traditional religion (no. 69), as African traditional religion does not apply this model. Also, the text consistently speaks of the "church" being in dialogue, and there is no doubt that the institutional church is meant. Furthermore, the "concentric circle" approach to identifying dialogue partners, whereby the Coptic and Ethiopic Orthodox churches are seen as the closest neighbors, is meaningful only in the institutional framework.

On the other hand, in the people-of-God framework the focus is on individual Catholics as participants in dialogue. While some African Catholics have practitioners of traditional religion or Muslims or Protestants as their closest neighbors, they may never have seen or known of the existence of Coptic or Ethiopic Christians. In this framework, therefore, it is not possible to speak of one group, particularly the Coptic and Ethiopic Christians, as the closest neighbors.

While the institutional model is suitable for analyzing dialogue at the level of the universal church, which is the context of Pope Paul VI's *Ecclesiam Suam*, it is a very poor candidate at the level of the local church, which is the focus of the *Lineamenta*. By its very nature the institutional model implies that dialogue is verbal, formal, and structured, while at the level of the local church dialogue is more often than not informal, unstructured, and non-verbal. This explains why, even though different forms of dialogue are identified early on and in spite of the fact that dialogue is acknowledged to go beyond structures, the analysis itself does not consider these insights.

About 80 percent of African Catholics live in rural communities where relationships are close, and one may find people belonging to three or four different dialogue groups (namely, practitioners of African traditional religion, Protestants, Muslims, and Catholics) in one community. Some forms of dialogue involve the interaction of people from all these groups together at the same time, such as when finding common solutions to the community's problems. This is the most rudimentary and functional form of inter-religious dialogue in Africa, but the *Lineamenta's* analysis gives it no consideration.

In the light of the fact that dialogue has not made much progress in Africa despite Africa's society being religiously pluralistic, the *Lineamenta* presentation of this very important aspect of the Church's mission should have sharply focused on giving inspiration and a sense of direction and commitment on this matter. Discussions on dialogue today should analyze the modality, grounds, and goals of dialogue and, in the case of non-Christian religions, evaluate them theologically. A major task of the Synod should be to interpret the meaning of these religions in the light of God's universal saving activity in history. The pluralistic nature of African society should allow us to make a meaningful and original contribution in this area.

Task 4: Justice and Peace

The focus of the *Lineamenta* presentation on justice and peace is that action toward justice and peace is constitutive of evangelization and that this is part of the mission of the church in Africa. The presentation shows concern for theological soundness as evidenced in the biblical analysis and exposition of the church's teachings, and for stock-taking of where Africa is in the practice of justice and peace.

Because justice and peace are burning issues in Africa today, the text, in spite of its limited scope, provokes much reflection. First of all, with regard to the theological foundations, even though it is acknowledged that concern for human needs was bound up with Jesus' mission, there is a need to state clearly and with emphasis that Jesus' practice of evangelization constitutes the paradigm for the church's evangelization activity today. The church's mission today is a participation in and a continuation of Jesus' proclamation of the kingdom. Thus, the kingdom of God must be seen to be no less the theme of the church's proclamation than it was of Jesus'. This leads to a central question in the biblical analysis, "What sort of kingdom did Jesus preach?" and to the hermeneutical question, "To what extent is the African church faithful to this?"

This central question is not adequately broached in the biblical analysis of the *Lineamenta*. The biblical texts cited to show Jesus' concern for the human condition of people should have led to a presentation of the total image of Jesus the evangelizer, as this is the unifying meaning of Jesus' actions in respect of the poor. We search in vain for such an image, yet this understanding is crucial to complete the analysis and to properly develop the hermeneutic that follows.

Contrary to some contemporary conceptions (or misconceptions), the kingdom that Jesus preached does not refer to something purely spiritual that has nothing to do with material things. The Jews did not separate the spiritual from the material. The kingdom that Jesus preached signified the transformation of the totality of our world in its material and spiritual aspects, which includes individual conversion, human well-being (spiritual and temporal), and the restructuring of social relations, the political order, the economic order, and so on. There must be no confusion between Jesus' statement "my kingdom is not of this world" (John 18:36), and the "kingdom of God" preached by Jesus. While Jesus preached the transformation of our world as an indication of God's reign over the world, he did not in any way set himself up as an earthly king. This is the mission that Jesus inaugurated and that he commanded the church—and each Christian—to undertake. It is within this program that individual actions of Jesus have meaning.

In answering the hermeneutical question "To what extent is the church in Africa faithful to Christ in pursuing this program?" the text outlines the church's present contribution and admits, in what seems to be an understatement, the continued presence of some worrying economic, social, and political situations. There *are* crucial urgent problems of justice and peace in Africa today that the church must address.

If the gospel has the efficacy to transform human society, as the text admits, and if these issues are still plaguing Africa in spite of the church's presence there for more than a century, it would seem that what is needed is for the church not so much to redouble its efforts as to review the totality of its approach to evangelization. The appropriate question to ask, therefore, should be: "How do we make the good news a force to change the human lot in Africa, a force to empower Africa's poor to respond to their situation as a challenge rather than see it as a fate to which they have to submit and about which they can do nothing?"

This is the crucial question that ought to occupy the Synod fathers in respect to justice and peace in Africa. To answer this question effectively calls, first of all, for what may be termed, for want of a better term, a *prophetic ecclesiology*. In other words, in its self-understanding the church is committed to active involvement in the lives of the oppressed and the poor, and to promoting and participating in the struggle for a just society as a central aspect of its mission. Second, a *prophetic ecclesiology* calls for a concerted program of action at the grassroots level, which, nurtured by the word of God, will turn powerless citizens into agents of change who take their future into their hands. Third, it calls for a deepening commitment to Christ in his identification with the poor and oppressed.

Task 5: The Means of Social Communications

The text points to the need for particular churches to use the available means of social communications, both traditional and modern, and to train church personnel in communications as part of their evangelization effort. The proliferation of references to radio, cinema, television, and video is, in my opinion, wrongly attributed to large-scale illiteracy (no. 88). The fact is that the illiterate do not own this technology. A second somewhat confusing point for me is that the text advocates examining "the more widely used African languages . . . to see if they can be put to use in the proclamation of the gospel message" (no. 91). This seems strange as African languages are already being used throughout Africa to proclaim the gospel message.

While there is a stress on the responsibility of receivers of communication to be selective (no. 92), no corresponding stress is laid on the need for communicators themselves to be selective in what they put forth for public consumption. Their duty to be selective should be equally stressed.

Communication itself is a fundamental human right. Communication is a basic structure of society, and it certainly is at the heart of evangelization. The church should not fail to make a meaningful contribution to the discussion. This raises certain concerns about the text under review. First of all, the text focuses on the communication of the gospel alone, not on communication in general as it affects the communication of the gospel. Second, the text is mainly interested in the instrumental aspects of communication and not in the reality of communication. Thus, it does not probe the meaning, nature, and modalities of communication.

The church's mission of proclaiming the good news demands that the process of this proclamation should also be good. The church's duty must start with a critique of the communication process itself. Questions of interest to the Synod fathers should have included:

— How can the church influence the theories, policies, and practice of communication in favor of the poor and the voiceless, both generally and within the church?

— To what extent is modern mass communications concerned with human promotion?

— How can communication be placed at the service of peace, justice, and development?

— What does the church say about the monopolization and manipulation of communication?

It is very evident that the underlying model of communication operative in the text is the vertical one-way model whereby messages produced by a few (regarded as depositories of knowledge), and addressed to all, flow from the top downwards. This is faulty communication. Today communication is being seen more as a process of exchange and sharing. When so democratized, communication fulfills its proper function in society of enhancing social existence. Communication tools, which are to be used to transmit the "Christian vision . . . to the African people" (no. 89), should also be used to enable the African people to express and share their own perceptions of the Christian message among themselves and with others.

If the extent of the text indicates its rating on the scale of its importance to evangelization, communication deserves more attention than it received in the *Lineamenta*, given its importance as the most fundamental process of evangelization. To date, in fact, the participation of African churches in the new world communications order has been minimal. The Synod could have been seen as an appropriate occasion for launching the African church into the new orbit of world communications.

Final Comments

My reading of the *Lineamenta* left me with an impression of a heavy agenda for the African Synod, and a gnawing question, "Is the Synod not going to have too much on its plate?" Clearly, just one of the topics in the *Lineamenta* could have sufficed as subject matter for the Synod. All the same, the Synod must be looked upon as the *kairos* of the African church—a moment to take stock of the past and to utilize that knowledge to create a new future for the church in Africa.

However, the Synod will not fulfill that promise unless it is seen as an occasion for African Christians to give voice to their daily struggle to clarify for themselves what it means to be church; unless that voice is given a hearing; and unless there is a critical awareness of this within the African church itself. It must be noted that Christianity will never take root in the hearts of Africans unless there is a struggle by African Christians themselves to understand the Christian faith and unless that struggle is encouraged.

The Synod is Africa's *kairos* in another sense as well. It is the time to come face to face with the issue of the irruption of the African church—its sudden entry with a great impact onto the world church scene. This calls for a paradigm shift in the perception of what it means to be church. It also poses a challenge to search for a new way of being church, and to articulate the need for not just a Synod but for an African Council to address the enormous and complex realities of the African church situation. Indeed, there is also a need for such councils in other regions of the world to clarify issues that have emerged since Vatican II. Such councils would eventually prepare for a general council, to wit, Vatican III, to be held sometime in the third millennium to gather up the loose ends of the post-Vatican II era.

Notes

1. An overview of this may be found in Leopold Sabourin's *Christology: Basic Texts in Focus* (New York: Alba, 1984).

2. See Karl Rahner, *Theological Investigations: Basic Theological Interpretation of the Second Vatican Council* (Vol. XX) (New York: Crossroad, 1981), pp. 77-89.

3. See the "Address of the Pope at the Conclusion of the Plenary Assembly of the Secretariat," in *The Attitudes of the Church Towards the Followers of Other Religions: Reflections and Orientations on Dialogue and Mission* (Vatican City: Secretariatus Pro Non Christianis, 1984), p. 4.

Some Proposals for the African Synod

African Synod Communication Working Group (Nairobi)

The Synod itself, not only the discussion of the initial working paper (*Lineamenta*), should be seen as a participatory process in the spirit of the African way of palaver (talking together) toward a consensus. Synodal work should favor participation and the dialogue should not end with the promulgation of the final working paper (*Instrumentum Laboris*). Bishops and delegates should be given ample opportunity to express their ideas. Enough time should be allowed during the Synod for the bishops and delegates to report back to their home dioceses and to discuss the issues in the grassroot communities. This will help initiate a truly participatory process in the African church.

Two major sessions of the Synod can be foreseen, the first in June 1993 and the closing session in late 1994. In between, more regional or specialized sessions could be held on topics such as dialogue with Islam or inculturation.

The venue should be in Africa. If there is to be more than one session, the venue could change so that synodal sessions would be held in different geographical and cultural areas, such as an opening session in Kinshasa, intermediate sessions in Addis Ababa or Luanda, and a closing session in Nairobi.

The Synod should be characteristically African. Delegates should be provided with proper facilities to do good work, but at the same time stress should be placed on simplicity and sharing. For instance, local Catholics, in the spirit of African hospitality, could be mobilized to provide accommodations and transport for the delegates. In other words, in all aspects and to the degree possible, an African expression should be given to the Synod. This is a challenge.

The number of delegates should be such as to substantially and truly represent all African Catholics. Delegates (women and men, adults and youth) from grassroot communities, movements, and associations should be present, as well as delegates of diocesan priests and religious (women and men). Representatives of other churches and religions should also be welcome in the spirit of African solidarity. This wide representation is essential at such a crucial moment for the Catholic Church in Africa. Moreover, the delegates will assist in bringing the conclusions of the Synod back to the grassroots. The process will not infringe on the freedom of the bishops to take their final decisions.

These proposals aim at enhancing the African expression of a Synod that should be truly African and truly Catholic.

Our Bishops Want Family on Synod Agenda

Inter-regional Meeting of the Bishops of South Africa (IMBISA)

The following is a shortened version of the response by the Zimbabwean Bishops to the *Lineamenta* (provisional agenda) of the Synod of Bishops' Special Assembly for Africa. It was drafted based on responses to the *Lineamenta* from all parts of the church in Zimbabwe and was submitted to the Synod secretariat in Rome to be used for the preparation of the agenda proper.

On the Proclamation of the Good News of Salvation

While the Catholic population in Zimbabwe keeps growing in absolute terms, it is shrinking in relative terms. The Catholic church, though present as a strong community with an impact on national life beyond its numbers, is nevertheless a minority in Zimbabwe. Therefore, there is a need for a more united and unified Catholic community. A unified pastoral policy that also promotes creativity and freedom would help.

The Catholic church in Zimbabwe has undertaken a serious consultation of its members on the matter of the African Synod. The best and lasting result of the consultation was raising the consciousness of Catholics who were asked about their feelings toward the church today.

On Inculturation

The country is experiencing rapid change as three differing systems of beliefs and values intermingle: the local African culture, international Western-type culture, and Christianity. Christianity tries to influence and mold the first two systems of belief, but culture is quite fluid today both in Zimbabwe and in Africa as a whole.

In speaking to the Catholic laity in Harare, Zimbabwe, on September 11, 1988, Pope John Paul II rightly said:

> African traditional culture is centered on the family. Africa cannot flourish unless its families survive present social upheavals. The African family must find new strength, reaffirm the positive values contained in tradition, and assimilate a more personal dimension of understanding, commitment and love.

The bishops of Africa cannot talk about inculturation without talking about the family, since "African traditional culture is centered on the family." This topic must be included in the agenda.

Very high percentages of Catholics live in unions that canonically speaking are invalid. Many have never had their marriages blessed in church, and others may finally do so after many years of marriage. As a result, a very large number of adult Catholics are barred from the sacraments. The result is a *eucharistic famine* in Zimbabwe and elsewhere in Africa. The African Synod may need to look at the canonical norms for marriage so that Catholic couples may have their as yet invalid unions solemnized (convalidated) more easily.

But we believe that there is a more profound reason for Catholics not marrying formally in church. Many lack a proper understanding of Christian marriage. Very often the man is most reluctant to commit himself for life to one woman, even though she may have borne him a number of children. This is understandable if he is not a Christian and is asked to marry in church only because of his Catholic wife. Catholics refusing to consent to a Catholic marriage indicates something more serious: though baptized and taking part in church life, such Catholics reject their faith when it makes a concrete and practical demand on them. This shows that we have not fully evangelized even those who are considered and consider themselves full members of the church.

Recognizing that culture is dynamic, we would like to say that we feel that African family culture is in mortal danger. The migrant labor system, social and geographical mobility, unemployment, housing shortages, the corrosive influence of the Western neo-pagan culture, and many other factors are destroying the traditional family and its many positive values. It is only through "assimilating a more personal dimension of understanding, commitment, and love" (Pope John Paul II in Harare, September 1988) that the African family culture can be saved.

This "more personal dimension of understanding, commitment, and love" must be fostered through a thorough catechesis in preparation for marriage, starting with youth, and it must be celebrated, for all to see, within the community. It would be foreign to our culture to deny this new inner and personal reality its corresponding outward and social expression.

It is precisely this new element of the gospel that will preserve the old values of our African family culture. It is precisely this new element, meaning this personal commitment for life to the one beloved, expressed in the liturgical celebration, that is needed to save the heart of the African culture of old, namely, the family. If the family is ailing and undernourished in the sacramental grace of the church, then the whole church becomes ill and cannot perform its evangelizing mission properly.

In the context of inculturation we must also consider the priestly ministry. Apart from marriage, the question of ministry is the other Achilles' heel of the Catholic church in Africa. The number of ordained priests and their age level is totally inadequate to the number of Catholics in Africa. This is a second cause of the genuine eucharistic famine in a suffering Africa.

Some of our pastoral priests ask the African Synod to look at celibacy and to consider the ordination of *viri probati* (mature married men who have proven their commitment to the church through long service). We as bishops are aware of the church's determination, reaffirmed at the Synod of Bishops in 1990, to uphold the immense value of a celibate priesthood. The total commitment to service of the celibate priest makes him indispensable for the great task of evangelization.

But just as evangelization goes together with inculturation, since only a gospel rooted in the African soil can be convincing, so also celibacy must be related to the most basic values of African culture and become a sign that is intelligible in terms of those values. Here the teaching of the universal church will have to be complemented by the teaching of the African Synod.

Our traditional Zimbabwean culture is quite familiar with the need for certain people who have key roles in religious rituals to be either persons no longer sexually active or persons who abstain from sexual relations at least for limited periods, for example, as long as the rain-making ceremonial lasts. We may mention also the virgins (*mbonga*) serving at the shrine of the Mwari cult in the Matopos near Bulawayo.

Fecundity, having offspring, is of the highest importance in our culture, not only in economic terms but also in spiritual and religious terms. This desire to give life, to cherish and foster it and even make great sacrifices for it, is a very great value. Fecundity of a physical nature must go together with fecundity of a personal and spiritual nature. There is a spiritual fatherhood that helps create the family of the children of God without which even our natural families could not flourish.

The Synod will have to discuss an African understanding of celibacy and the lifestyle of priests that goes with it, starting with the formation of our future priests in the seminaries.

Dialogue with African Traditional Religion and with New Religious Movements

The Synod must concern itself with sickness and death. Emotional reactions toward sickness and death drive Catholics back to the old ancestral worship system or to new syncretistic or fundamentalist sects if the Catholic church is perceived as having no power, no "Spirit." We have an urgent need to help African Catholics deal better with healing and suffering in human life.

This also indicates a failure in our basic catechesis of the faith; after baptism there is no further instruction for the faith to grow and mature. There is an urgent need to respect, encourage, and empower all baptized Catholics so that they play their part in the mission of the church. Formation of the laity is the great task.

Justice and Peace

The people of Africa are disappointed with political and social models of society (such as the one-party state) that have only resulted in corruption, poverty, and civil strife. When the bishops and shepherds of the church assemble for the African Synod, Africa expects from them words of moral and spiritual guidance based on the universally valid social teaching of the church.

Women are the backbone of the church in Africa. Women recognize that Christ in his Church, symbolized by Mary his mother, gives them their full human dignity, and they accept this good news with joy, precisely because society at large in many ways fails to accord them proper respect. As a result, the Church must promote the full human dignity of women. As co-workers of Christ and essential agents of evangelization, they seek their proper place in the ministry and leadership of the church. Like the laity as a whole, women need to be given better formation and be offered greater responsibility within the Christian community.

Women's role in society is changing fast. Catholic women themselves will have to select what is good and valuable in traditional culture and make it part of a new culture. Guided by a Christian sense of service and following the model of Mary, they will carry out their tasks as wives and mothers, givers and protectors of life, both in the workplace and in public life.

At present, social development is much more supported than the work of evangelization. A more balanced view of the mission of the church is needed.

Means of Social Communication

The channels of communication between the church in Africa and Europe are often better developed than those within the church of Africa herself. The African Synod should find ways and means for us Africans to talk to one another and exchange our own insights and experiences.

For this reason also the African Synod must take place on the African continent. The interest of the whole people of God will be greater if the Synod is truly an African event. The communion model of the church in the *Lineamenta* could be a way to involve clergy, religious, laity, and other churches.

8

Statement

Catholic Theological Association of Nigeria (CATHAN)

The Catholic Theological Association of Nigeria sponsored a workshop on the *Instrumentum Laboris*, the final working paper of the Special Assembly for Africa of the Synod of Bishops called "The Church in Africa and Her Evangelizing Mission Towards The Year 2000—'You Shall Be My Witnesses' (Acts 1:8)."

When His Holiness, Pope John Paul II, announced in January 1989 the convoking of a Special Assembly for Africa of the Synod of Bishops, the Catholic Theological Association of Nigeria (CATHAN) joined other African Christians in greeting the announcement with enthusiasm and hope. When the *Lineamenta* for the Synod of Bishops in Rome was distributed, CATHAN again joined other African Christians in an in-depth study of the document. To that end, a special CATHAN workshop was held at the St. Thomas Aquinas Major Seminary in Makurdi, Nigeria, in July 1991. The outcome of that workshop was duly made available to the Catholic Conference of Nigerian Church and to Rome. The General Secretariat of the Synod of Bishops has since gone further to produce a "Working Paper" (*Instrumentum Laboris*) for the Synod based on responses to the *Lineamenta* received from the particular churches of Africa.

CATHAN again deemed it worthwhile to carry out an in-depth study of this latter document in view of the Synod itself, which the Holy Father has now scheduled for Rome, beginning from the Second Sunday of Easter, 1994. Once again, the forum was a workshop, this time at the Spiritan International School of Theology, Attakwu, Enugu, from July 5-8, 1993. For three days, some fifty-five members of the Association pondered the content of the *Instrumentum Laboris*, looking at the main theme of the Synod with its five sub-themes, namely, evangelization, inculturation, dialogue, justice and peace, and the means of social communication.

The workshop concluded with a report, the text of which is here produced. CATHAN wishes humbly to make this document available yet again to the Nigerian hierarchy and others whom divine providence will assign the task of representing Nigeria at the Special Assembly for Africa of the Synod of Bishops in Rome next year. It is our ardent hope and prayer that it will contribute in some small measure toward an effective participation of the Nigerian church in that historic event of the universal church.

Evangelization

The church's mission to evangelize derives from the Lord's mandate: "Go, therefore, make disciples of all the nations . . ." (Mt. 28:19). Through the ages the church has responded to this command of the Lord to evangelize using various methods according to different situations and times. Africa remains grateful to God for his word which she has received through the missionaries and acknowledges her responsibility to carry on the Lord's mandate. The CATHAN workshop reviewed the theme of evangelization as presented in the *Instrumentum Laboris* and, having studied the issues raised in the document and the actual practice of evangelization in Africa, notes the following:

1. That the faith has been planted and has taken root in Africa;

2. That God has blessed the young churches in Africa in terms of numbers, indigenous vocations, and leadership;

3. That missionary work in Africa has also brought Western education, medical and social services, and contributed generally to enhancing the quality of life of many Africans;

4. However, we note that missionary work in the past did not pay adequate attention to the important role of African culture in evangelization. Consequently, the language, concepts, and world-view in which the Christian message was presented were alien, and this made its impact on the people and its reception by the people less effective than it could have been. For example, symbols used in the liturgy, catechesis and prayer did not always communicate the message of the gospel to the people;

5. The work of evangelization has been too controlled by the church's hierarchy, and this made it difficult to adequately respond to the genuine concerns of the people.

Recommendations

1. For evangelization to be effective, the Gospel message should permeate every aspect of the people's life: social, economic, political and cultural. Furthermore, the people's context should shape the mode of presentation of the Gospel to them.

2. Africans should be recognized as subjects of evangelization and not merely as objects.

3. The practice of evangelization should be democratized; namely, by allowing initiative and creativity at all levels among the agents of evangelization, and thereby respecting the principles of subsidiarity and co-responsibility.

4. The African sense of community and communal life invites us to develop the

concepts of fellowship, brotherhood, and sisterhood as the goal of evangelization.

5. The workshop suggests that the Synod of Bishops for Africa in Rome should not be the end of the discussions on evangelization in Africa; rather, it should be seen as a forum for initiating a discussion that should be ongoing.

6. The workshop regrets that the Synod is not being held in Africa.

7. We join other African Christians in expressing the hope that the Synod will be a springboard to an African Council to be held on African soil. In addition, we recommend that such a Council take place before the year 2000.

Inculturation

The miracle of Pentecost is very illustrative of the goal of inculturation: "We hear them preaching in our own languages about the marvels of God" (Acts 2:11). In this light, we see inculturation as a dialectical process, involving an interpenetration of the Gospel message and a culture that leads to the appropriation of the Gospel message by the people of that culture. What is inculturated is not Christianity as received and expressed in another culture, but rather the Gospel message itself: the Christ event—Jesus' life, death, and resurrection as interpreted by a living faith community. The workshop has reviewed the progress of inculturation in Africa and makes the following observations:

1. The church in Africa rejects the theology of adaptation, which is no more than "nativizing" the Roman church. Rather, the African church opts for a theology of inculturation and incarnation.

2. We affirm that the African world view has many positive elements, which, under the light of the Gospel, can form the basis for an authentic African Christian life.

3. We therefore reject the earlier negative attitude toward the African world view.

4. Christianity can be enriched by some basic principles of the African world view: (a) a keen awareness of the presence of the sacred in all aspects of life; (b) the attitude of life enhancement, that is, that religion should be concerned with integral human well-being; and (c) emphasis on communality in Christian living.

5. It is to be noted that the gains of inculturation in Africa listed in the *Instrumentum Laboris* are limited to external forms of worship, to the neglect of emergent African rites, such as the Zairean Mass, the Nzon-Melem Mass in Cameroon, the Moore Initiation in Burkina Faso, and the Rite of Naming Ceremony among the Yoruba of Nigeria. These could well serve as inspiration to the other churches of Africa and elsewhere.

Recommendations

1. We recommend that the Synod call the attention of the local ordinaries and the territorial ecclesiastical authorities to the powers granted them in *Sacrosanctum Concilium* (22 and 40) to initiate experiments and recommend for approval laudable liturgical inculturation.

2. As a practical expression of the concept of the church as the people of God, sharing in the common priesthood of Christ, we recommend that lay ministries be created in each Christian community, reflecting the traditional role, structures, and present needs of the community.

3. In African societies women play a vital role in the social and ritual aspects of the life of the community. We recommend that ministries be so diversified as to make room for the indispensable role of women as members of Christ's body.

4. We recommend the creation and promotion of small Christian communities as an effective means of evangelization at the grassroots level.

5. In view of the fact that inculturation requires a great deal of research, experimentation, and resource personnel, it should be adequately funded.

6. We recommend that groups of African local churches aspire to seek ways and means of developing indigenous African rites.

Dialogue

"The truth I have now come to realize is that God does not have favorites, but that anybody of any nationality who fears God and does what is right is acceptable to him" (Acts 10:34,35). This experience of Peter provides us a biblical and theological basis for dialogue.

1. *Instrumentum Laboris* observes that dialogue is expressed in four ways, namely, through a dialogue of life, a dialogue of deed, through specialists, and religious experiences. However, we note that *Instrumentum Laboris* did not elaborate sufficiently on these.

2. The workshop welcomes the affirmation in *Instrumentum Laboris* of the need for dialogue within the church and between particular churches.

3. There is a need to form the Catholic faithful adequately in their own faith in order to equip them to engage in effective dialogue with members of other Christian churches and those of other faiths.

Justice and Peace

Action for justice and peace is a constitutive dimension of the ministry of Jesus (Lk. 4:16-19). Jesus declared that he came to set the oppressed free and to proclaim the Lord's year of favor. This entails sharing our common heritage, namely, the bounties of God and nature on the basis of mutual acceptance of one another as co-heirs in Christ. In this sense, justice and peace imply mutual respect, acceptance, fellowship and inclusion.

Observations

1. It is evident that the Christian conception of justice and peace has done a great deal to liberate humanity and to enhance the awareness of human rights (for example, the right to life of twins who are protected today as opposed to the earlier practice of killing them).

2. The present awareness of the injustice that has been meted out to women and to the less privileged of the society can be attributed to the impact of Christian teaching on justice and peace.

3. Justice and peace should be the focus of evangelization, rather than being seen as a mere "link," as is proposed in the *Instrumentum Laboris* (112). Human promotion is not just an incidental aspect of evangelization.

Recommendations

1. It is necessary to set up justice and peace commissions in parishes and dioceses, whose job will be to animate and create the required awareness in matters of human rights and human promotion.

2. Tribunals should be set up for settling intra-church disputes and for the arbitration of cases.

3. There should be proper education of Christians on the role of some Christian organizations in the promotion of justice and peace, such as the Young Christian Workers (YCW), Young Christian Students (YCS), Holy Childhood, Caritas, and so on.

4. Dioceses should train personnel through whom the impact of the justice and peace commissions might be felt. Such training should involve the lay faithful.

5. The church should take the lead in defending and promoting human rights within her own ranks.

6. The justice and peace commission should take a cue from civil rights groups whose aim is to defend and fight for the rights of the marginalized in society. This body should serve as a pressure group concerned with dismantling oppressive systems in church and society. It should not limit itself solely to fund-raising and development projects.

7. The monarchical structure of the church needs to be deemphasized in favor of participation, subsidiarity, and collegiality.

8. The over-dependence of the African church on the West should give way to interdependence and mutual sharing of riches, both spiritual and temporal.

Means of Social Communication

The biblical-theological basis for communication is well expressed in Jesus' injunction to his disciples to proclaim openly on house tops what they heard from him in hidden places (Lk. 12:3). God spoke to his people in the Old Testament in language and imagery familiar to them. Christ also used parables and stories to communicate the message of salvation. Through the ages the church has made use of the language available to her in communicating the Gospel message.

Recommendations

1. The traditional means of communication, such as town criers, the talking drum, bells, and cannon shots should be employed, alongside the modern means of

communication, like the print and electronic media, for a more effective communication of the Good News.

2. While the ideal would be for the church to own radio and television stations, in countries where this is not possible, the church should endeavor to sponsor regular religious programs on state-owned media.

3. The Bible should be made available in our languages and at affordable prices to facilitate communication of the Good News. Other theological, devotional, catechetical, and religious literature should be similarly disseminated. For this purpose, provision should be made in the budgets of local churches and special grants sought to finance this vital apostolate.

4. It is an advantage for the church to own print media for the promotion of evangelization. We recommend the pooling of resources at the provincial and national levels toward the establishment of a virile national newspaper.

5. The weekly bulletin in parishes can also serve as an effective means of communication, especially when themes of the Gospel message are expounded for easy assimilation by the congregation.

6. Mass rallies, crusades, open-air services, and Catholic outreach are all to be encouraged as possible ways of communicating the Good News.

7. It is necessary to establish a data bank for effective storing of information to facilitate evangelization in Africa.

8. Priests are urged to make effective use of their Sunday homilies. The principles of African rhetoric, which involves a two-way traffic in communication, dialogue, and audience participation can be effectively utilized in evangelization.

9. Talented members of the church who are versed in various areas of the church's life should be invited and encouraged to give exhortations and reflections at liturgical celebrations, even if they are not ordained ministers.

10. Funds should be made available for research into and collection of data in African legends, proverbs, riddles, and folktales to help more effective proclamation of the Word.

11. Seminaries should include social communication in their academic programs.

12. The use of African music, songs, dances, and drama should be fostered as means of communication since Africans are well known to love and appreciate music and dance.

Appendix: African Christology

Jesus' question to his disciples, "Who do you say I am?" (Mk. 8:29), is a challenge to every Christian and Christian community to continuously deepen their faith in Christ. Peter's confession of the Christ invites African Christians to a profession of their faith in Christ drawn from their experience and in their own categories.

We note with regret the absence of an African Christology in *Instrumentum Laboris*, for Christ is the subject of evangelization, inculturation, dialogue, and communication. With St. Paul, what we preach is Christ, and Christ crucified (1 Cor. 1:23). The phenomenon now gaining support among our people of professing Christ as one's "Lord and Personal Savior" shows the people's willingness to submit themselves to Christ as the organizing force of their lives.

Recommendations

The African Christian's knowledge of Christ is not limited to what we find in dogmatic theological formulations. Therefore, we recommend that:

1. Christ be presented to the Africans in concepts that are familiar to them, such as Jesus the Healer, Jesus the Ancestor, Jesus the Master of Initiation, Jesus the King, Jesus the Medicine Man (*Dibia, Onisegun, Nganga*), Jesus the Giver of Destinies (*chi, ori*), Jesus the Great (*Orisa,* the great Spirit Mediator), Jesus the Conqueror, Jesus the Fearless One (*Onwuatuegwu*), and the like.

2. There is thus a need to affirm the people's understanding of Christ within their own cultural context for a more effective and enduring evangelization.

9

Lay People Must Be Empowered

Theological Institutes for the African Synod

After meeting at Kinshasa in June 1991, the Catholic Institute of Yaoundé (Cameroon), the Catholic Institute of West Africa (Port Harcourt, Nigeria) and the Catholic Faculty of Kinshasa (Zaire) published a declaration on the African Synod. First, the representative of these three well-known African Catholic institutes expressed their approval and joy for the convocation of the Synod, seeing it as a privileged moment of grace that must be utilized to provoke all the people of God in Africa to commit themselves to evangelization and inculturation. They also stressed the importance that such a Synod could have for the growth of the universal church. They also felt they should state some reservations and put forward some propositions and recommendations. The following excerpts are from their document.

Reservations

The *Lineamenta* is an important document that invites people to freely submit opinions for the Synod, but this process has not yet sufficiently involved all people. If the Gospel is to be truly part of the African scene, the people have to be given the chance to take full responsibility for the inculturation of the Gospel message in their own lives, so much so that they feel the urgency of passing it on to their fellow Africans. In this sense, the activity of the Christians in the early church is an example for all of us. In acting thus, they will face the challenge of the African Muslims in all that concerns Islam and its rapid expansion in the continent.

Without this personal acceptance of and lifelong engagement to the Gospel message, the church in Africa today could experience a fate similar to—or even worse—than that experienced in North Africa during the Islamic invasion. While the church in Africa seems to be developing in terms of the creation of new dioceses, ordinations to the priesthood, and religious professions, alarming signs of a continuous exodus of our Catholics to join the African indepedent churches, the new religious sects, Islam, and traditional religions abound. We interpret this as a clear indication that the laity do not feel at home in the Catholic church and that the Catholic church has not yet succeeded in meeting the various aspirations of the African people.

During the Synod the church in Africa will meditate on her nature and mission and on the authenticity of her witness to Christ. It is only by this process that the African church will become conformed to the vision of the church as the people of God, according to the documents of the Second Vatican Council. Without being exhaustive, we wish to enumerate a certain number of fundamental areas of the church's life that require urgent attention.

1. The voice of the laity must be heard.

2. Liturgy, as the re-actualization of the sacred, should be based on the sacred Scriptures and on the patrimony of the church. Traditional African values, enriched by African symbols, music, and dance, should be introduced.

3. The church as the people of God should be structured in such a way that it becomes evident that authority is a charism of service and that the lay ministries— of both men and women—may receive their important and integral place.

4. The Synod should study all the African problems from an African perspective, such as matters concerning the structures of the church, its discipline, marriage, the position of women in the church and in society, and African traditional values. The Synod should aim at the emergence of an African rite and a code for the African church.

5. The Church should take very seriously the vision of the African people and its multi-dimensional impact on the life and environment of her Christians: an inculturated and vital spirituality, the relation between the Catholic faith and politics, the problems of social justice, religion and economics, dialogue and human rights, and Christians active in the church as well as in society.

Recommendations

Given the recognized importance of the Synod as a *kairos* for the church of this continent and the urgent necessity of involving the people in the process, we recommend:

1. The forthcoming African Synod should be seen as a first step toward an African Council. This Council, on a continental level, could stimulate spiritual renewal and church growth.

2. Any such Council would have to be thoroughly prepared for, during a period of some years, according to the methodology drawn up for the Seventh Plenary Assembly of SECAM at Kinshasa in 1984. It should imply the involvement of the individual by the intermediary of the family, the small Christian communities, the out-station, the parish, and then the diocese, on the provincial and national levels to culminate in a national event.

3. The forthcoming Synod has to determine the way in which an African Council is to be prepared.

4. Bishops, priests, religious, and laity (men and women) should be invited to

participate actively in the present Synod. Theologians, representatives of Catholic institutes, sociologists, anthropologists, and other experts in important and varied areas should be included in the membership of the Synod. By their advice the experts will contribute to the solution of certain religious and human problems that Africa is facing: for example, poverty, hunger, disease, ignorance, the threat of Islam, selfish and exploiting governments, the process of establishing democracy, and above all the relevance of the Catholic church in Africa today.

5. The Synod should also invite as observers the representatives of other Christian confessions and the other great religions of the world.

With firm faith and confidence in God who leads his African people, this Synod will give birth to a New Pentecost in communion with and for the enrichment of the universal church. This will result, in Africa and elsewhere, in a more efficacious and effective proclamation of the Gospel. This will not be effected without a serious and integral involvement of the laity to bring about the Africa Pope Paul VI of happy memory called the "*Nova Patriu Christi*"—the "New Homeland of Christ."

10

Seven Mission Subjects

Oyo Diocese, Nigeria

When studying the *Lineamenta* in preparation for the forthcoming Synod for Africa, we appreciate that many subjects are proposed for the agenda of the Synod, but strongly feel that several other subjects clamor for treatment as well. We list seven of them.

1. *Inculturation*. Nowhere does the *Lineamenta* seem to be aware that the matter of inculturation has importance for the whole of the Catholic church. As the brief historical survey shows, a non-inculturated church cannot survive and in fact does not survive among the young of our days. The Synod should be aware that "inculturation is urgent and necessary *hic et nunc* for the whole church."

2. *Structures of the church*. It is not enough to argue that inculturation is urgent and necessary and to sketch how it can be done, if there are no structures within which it can happen. Pluriformity has no future within centralized structures. The Synod must clearly urge for decentralization for the sake of the survival of a truly African Catholic church.

3. We wish that the Synod would address the question of the *permanent diaconate*. Is it not strange that the African church has so few permanent deacons? The reason for their absence might reveal how African bishops and priests feel about this and other ministries.

4. The *Lineamenta* fails to address the real problem of finance. A church that is financially dependent on foreign sources should find ways to preserve its independence even while admitting its poverty. The Synod should be very clear on this so that overseas partners may know how to avoid help that becomes patronizing colonialism.

5. *Religious neo-colonialism*. Africa is inundated with messages of Euro-American origin, ranging from the wonderful power of Coca-Cola to the presidential political system and the indispensable need for a home computer. Euro-American evangelism imports religious ideas, often with great financial backing, bringing

sects and religious movements in great number. Catholic evangelism is only a part of this phenomenon. On this subject also the Synod should be very clear to avoid help that is appreciated but that risks becoming alienating colonialism.

6. *Dialogue with government*. Experience shows that the Catholic church in Africa has a checkered record in matters of dialogue with governments. At times she has identified too much with a government and at other times she has wielded more power than a young independent government; often she has been accused of not supporting the legitimate programs of new or independent governments. The Synod should address this problem. There is an African way of dialogue, and Roman documents on the relation between church and government may well need to be inculturated.

7. *Justice and peace* and *development* are part of evangelization, as the *Lineamenta* rightly points out. The relation between the two takes on particular traits in Africa. The average African Christian is hardly aware of this. The Synod should clarify this relation and find terms easily understood in Africa to express this relationship. One matter that claims for a clear African statement is population control.

11

An Open Letter to the Holy Father

An African Synod without Africa?

New People Editorial Staff (Nairobi)

Holy Father,

The editorial staff of the New People Media Center would like to make known to you our reaction to your announcement that the African Synod—forgive us, if in spite of all evidence we continue to use this name for an event that your collaborators in Rome call the "Special Assembly for Africa of the Synod of Bishops"—will be held in Rome in April 1994. Here are our thoughts after carefully reading the *Instrumentum Laboris*, or Working Paper, which supposedly is the result of the reflection of African Catholics.

The Venue and the Preparation

While you were in Kampala, a member of our staff was in the hall where the bishops were waiting for you and he heard the murmur of disappointment when, a few minutes before your entrance, they were told that the Synod would be held in Rome. Those who planned for this anticipated announcement did not want you to hear the expression of the bishops' disappointment. Yet minutes after the conclusion of the session, most bishops were able to put up a smile and show enthusiastic support for Rome as the venue of the Synod. Only a few could blurt out, "It's terrible, but don't quote me." In all of them the smile was hiding a deep wound.

In deciding where to hold the Synod, two major aspects were involved. First, the logistics aspects. From this point of view one could discuss at length if it would be better to hold it in Rome or, let's say, Lagos: the possibility of accommodation, communications, and so on would be considered. Second, the symbolic aspect. Holding the Synod in Africa or Rome would send a clear message. The choice of Rome would stress the link with the Pope, while the choice of Africa would have stressed the recognition that Africa is truly "the new homeland of Christ," as Pope Paul VI called it. It would emphasize the potentiality of African Catholicism and the nearness of the church to the poor and suffering people who are the real stronghold of the Catholic faith in Africa. We believe that there would be no logistic impossibility in holding the Synod on African soil. The choice of Africa would have been of enormous significance for all of us living on this continent, more important than affirming our union with the Pope, which is already very clear and is not an issue. Both answers to the two aspects, the logistic and the symbolic, are however debatable and they do not touch the essence of our faith.

Passive Obedience

Due to the African tradition of respect for the elders and superiors combined with the authoritarian attitude of the Roman curia, a good number of African bishops have developed an attitude of passive obedience. The slightest divergence from any thought, opinion, or suggestion coming from Rome is perceived as heretical. Unanimity has become a must and is too often a straitjacket. A unanimous and enthusiastic attitude must be put forward to Rome, even to the extent of sacrificing the truth.

An example is what you were told about the preparation for the African Synod. Since you asked, when announcing the Synod in 1989, "all members of the people of God who live in Africa to prepare actively for the Assembly," the General Secretariat for the African Synod, for instance, wrote in its letter following your announcement of the date for holding the Synod, that "It can be affirmed without exaggeration that the whole Church in Africa became involved in the synodal process." This is not only an exaggeration, it is a lie.

In the very words of the newsletter of the Ethiopian Catholic Secretariat dated August 1992, "There has been very little discussion or writing on the Synod, and to the best of our knowledge almost nothing at grassroots level." And Ethiopia is a country which, because of its long Christian tradition, is supposed to give a highly qualified contribution to the synodal discussions.

A *New People* correspondent went to a university campus in Kenya to interview the students. Out of twenty-seven students who defined themselves "practicing Catholics, or active in a Catholic movement or association," only three had ever heard of the African Synod, and these did not have any idea of what it was.

On the other hand, the atmosphere of secrecy surrounding the preparation for the Synod did not favor the participation of the people. The international bureaucrats making up the Roman curia have only themselves to blame if the participation has been poor. We know by experience how difficult it is to get real news on the Synod preparation. We remember that when the *Lineamenta* was distributed some bishops thought it was a secret document and hid it in the deepest corners of their desk drawers. While we write, we know we belong to the privileged few who had a chance of seeing the Working Paper. Many bishops we know have not yet received their copy. No wonder that for the majority of African Catholics the African Synod is still a mysterious code word.

Holy Father, do not allow your collaborators to misinform you. The members of the local church in Africa who are aware of the African Synod are not happy with the decision to hold the Synod in Rome, and the participation of the people of God in its preparation has been minimal. To speak of what happened so far as a "genuine African event" adds insult to injury.

The Working Paper

A thorough examination and reflection on the *Instrumentum Laboris* or Working Paper has further dampened our spirit. Reading the *Instrumentum Laboris* one can hardly guess that we are dealing with a Synod on Africa. A first glance at it shows that there are 171 quotes. All of them come from the general documents of the church, with Your Holiness being by far the most quoted. There is not a single quote from your numerous African apostolic trips; all your quotes are general documents, such as encyclicals and exhortations addressed to the whole church. The documents of Vatican Council II come in second place, followed by Paul VI, (almost exclusively *Evangelii Nuntiandi*), with just one quote from his trip to Uganda in 1969. Not even mentioned is *Africae Terrarum*, the first document of this kind dealing explicitly and uniquely with the African situation. After Paul VI there are documents of Roman congregations, pontifical councils, and commissions. At the bottom of the line, the Symposium of Episcopal Conferences in African and Madagascar (SECAM) is quoted five times.

It is as if there were no local "magisterium," no local teaching church! Yet in Africa we have about five hundred bishops organized at continental and regional levels. Haven't these bishops and episcopal conferences written anything worth quoting on inculturation, dialogue, or justice and peace? Haven't they contributed to the present African scene with statements and pastoral letters on all sorts of moral problems? Why have their contributions been dismissed so lightly? Why not give value to the pastoral approach emerging from these documents?

There were more references to African situations in the *Lineamenta* than in *Instrumentum Laboris*. The historical introduction of the *Lineamenta*, which could have helped to contextualize the document, has disappeared. In its place there is an introduction whose main purpose seems to be to pre-empt all possible objections to the practicalities of the Synod, to lower expectations, to cut the Synod down to size.

It is true that now and then it is written that "the responses to the *Lineamenta* call the attention to . . ." and a list of problems follows. But even by weaving together all the references to the "African situation" present in *Instrumentum Laboris*, it is not possible to have a real picture of the vitality, the achievement, the difficulties, the temptations, or the failures of the African Christian communities. Yet we still hope that at the Synod a more concrete and vibrant image of African Catholicism may emerge. Otherwise what will come out will be irrelevant to the great majority of Africans.

Vitality of Local Churches

What we find more frustrating and even offensive for all of us members of local churches is the fact that the vitality of the Christian communities through the signs of holiness, martyrdom, and endurance in time of persecution is hardly perceptible.

The local churches of Africa do not emerge from *Instrumentum Laboris*; they are reduced to a list of arid problems. Where are the people? The hopes, dreams, joys, struggles, anguish of the African people are not present. Where is Jesus? We hope that the Synod, by a miracle of the Holy Spirit, will make the dry bones of this text come alive, and put in front of us Jesus walking, questioning, calling us to conversion in the context of our villages and towns, forests and deserts, schools and drinking places. There is a thirst for truth and dignity and beauty in the hearts of our brothers and sisters that only Jesus can satisfy.

It would be nonsensical for us to flatter you, Holy Father. But we must stress that we find in your attitudes and in the speeches you give when you visit African countries a deep and compassionate knowledge of our life and problems. We do not find this knowledge in the text of *Instrumentum Laboris*, yet the Preface and the Introduction go to great length to convince us that it is the fruit of a truly African process of participation.

Does the Spirit Speak to the Churches?

In the introduction of Bishop Schotte, the General Secretary of the Synod, it is written that "the percentage of responses, (is) so far the highest ever recorded for a Synod." One wonders where the richness of these responses has disappeared.

It is true that according to the methodology prescribed in the Preface to the *Lineamenta*, the voice of the grassroots had to undergo a rather severe trimming: responses from the church communities and groups within a diocese were sent to the local bishop who made use of such information in drafting his response. The bishop's response was then forwarded to the episcopal conference of which he is a member. Finally, the submissions from the episcopal conferences arrived at the General Secretariat.

Since the bulk of the reflections and contributions do not seem to have entered into *Instrumentum Laboris*, one is prompted to conclude that the Synod is going to be more an occasion to familiarize the bishops of Africa with the documents of the church rather than a real discernment on the concrete life of the Christian communities living in the African continent. Our expectations were greatly different. We would have liked a humble and bold listening to what "the Spirit tells the local churches" in Africa, according to the language of the book of Revelation.

This impression is reinforced by the fact that in the paragraphs of *Instrumentum Laboris*, whole title is "toward the future," one finds expressions of this kind: "observing the rules for fruitful ecumenism, according to the directives and practice of the church" and "seeking to implement at local level the ecumenical programs of the universal church . . . the Pontifical Council for Promoting Christian Unity has prepared a document to guide such ecumenism on the local level."

The methodology followed in the document also shows this type of approach. The methodology of seeing, judging, and acting does not enjoy the preference of those who prepared the document. They prefer to go back to the methodology of the texts of systematic theology of pre-Vatican II, starting from the thesis whose validity is "proven" through Bible texts and documents of the church, going down to the applications to daily life.

Which Model of Evangelization?

Another aspect of the mentality underlying *Instrumentum Laboris* deserves some attention. It appears as if Africa should only learn from the universal magisterium of the church, while the universal church cannot learn from Africa and the variety of Christian experiences present here. We have learned from Vatican Council II, especially *Gaudium et Spes*, from the missionary theology of the last half-century, and from our own personal experience and missionary ministry that the church "gives to the world, and receives from it."

What has the universal church actually learned and continues to learn from Africa? What does the Spirit say from Africa to the local churches of other continents? What does the Spirit say to the central government of the church, especially regarding the present style of leadership?

In *Instrumentum Laboris* we read: "Inculturation is, therefore, an ongoing process, never a finished product" (65) and "today inculturation appears to be an urgent task for the church in Africa" (67). Our question is: Is there any room left for experimentation, for a reflection that is not a mere repetition of what is stated in official documents? Where is the freedom for the missionaries of today, the kind of freedom available to the missionaries who evangelized Europe?

Inculturation without profound reflection is impossible. Why then is there so much fear of African theologians? Why do new rules make them responsible only to the secretary of the Synod rather than to the Synod fathers? Will their voices be heard at all in Rome during the Synod? At Vatican II the bishops were entitled to have a personal theologian. Was that experience so harmful as not to be repeated at the level of a Synod on Africa? In the Preface to the *Lineamenta* the faculties of theology were mentioned in the list of those invited to contribute to the Synod. In fact, their participation was discouraged and their proposals have had no impact on *Instrumentum Laboris*. The "Higher Theological Institutes" are mentioned a couple of times (27, 107) and it is said that they "should be further developed" and "should continue to do research in this area (the African Traditional Religion) and make proposals to the bishops." What about the proposals they have already made? How long are they supposed to continue to make proposals which are systematically ignored?

We are convinced that true inculturation will come from the small Christian communities and the heroic effort of many Catholics to live their faith in their places of work and leisure as well as in their chapels. The aseptic libraries of theological institutes are only one instrument of reflection over this rich Christian life growing in Africa. The first inculturation is holiness and martyrdom shining through the life of Catholics: the one and the other are present in Africa. We do not find them anywhere in *Instrumentum Laboris*. We do hope that the Synod may correct this lacuna!

Is "reformulation" (111) enough? Is the inexhaustible mystery of God in Christ already totally unveiled? For Africa will there only be reformulations? Has the mystery of the Father, the Son, and the Holy Spirit been probed so deeply that all that is left now for new human groups who enter the church is to only "reformulate"? As for the liturgy, are we just to "translate"? In the Synod on Evangelization, in 1974, the missionary theology of adaptation was abandoned in favor of the richer idea of inculturation. Is this idea now to be resurrected?

Facing the Challenges of the Moment

Holy Father, in spite of all the prophets of doom, we are convinced that Africa is living a very positive moment, a *kairos*, a moment for critically evaluating the present situation and the past decades.

The challenges facing us in the political, economic and cultural fields are signs of the times for the Church to read. At the same time there are challenges which we could call internal to the life of the Church. With great disappointment we see the *Instrumentum Laboris* does not seem to face them squarely.

A non-Catholic friend with whom we have shared our reflections on the *Instrumentum Laboris* asked us:

Where in this document are the great unfolding process of democratization, the dramas of civil wars and refugees, the anguish of the AIDS victims, the questioning gaze of the malnourished children, the enormous positive energy of our youth, the awakening giant that is the African woman? Where is Africa?

As for the internal challenges of the Church, for instance, while the *Instrumentum Laboris* speaks about the formation of priests—in such general terms that the text could be valid for Brazil, France and Vietnam as well as for African countries—the problem of the African priest in the Catholic Church is not even posed in its real terms.

Neither is there any serious and exhaustive reflection on the situation of the African family. In particular, the problems raised by Christian marriage in the context of Africa are not posed. There are a few lines here and there, and these are sprinkled with "shoulds" and "oughts." Have we not learned that this is hardly a way to solve problems?

These are only examples. The disheartening impression is that where there is a problem to be tackled, the authors of the *Instrumentum Laboris* turn and look away.

Holy Father, we were enslaved and colonized by Lisbon and London and Paris. We are now brutalized by Washington and the faceless bureaucratic world powers residing in New York and Geneva. In spite of all this, the promise of total liberation brought by Christ is taking roots in our hearts. Will this promise now wither and dry under the stern indifferent gaze of a Church behaving like a stepmother rather than a mother?

If the Church will not be with us as an understanding and loving mother, to whom will we turn? To the African independent churches? To the new American sects from the Bible belt? To Islam? Many of our sisters and brothers have already done so; many more will follow them, if they find in these religious expressions a more merciful God, a community more rooted in our traditions, a better response to our spiritual and material needs.

We are afraid we see even in our most courageous bishops some signs that they are also ready to concede defeat. We are afraid they might give up the battle for a truly African Catholicism. Some think: "The bureaucrats in Rome wanted the Synod, let them have it, and let them follow it. We will simply ignore it." Then, truly, the vital unity with the Pope and the circulation of grace in the body of Christ will suffer, and it will be a bitter victory for those who have opposed the emergence of an African Catholicism.

Holy Father, the message of the Synod must be a message of hope. In the words of Vatican Council II, "The future of humanity lies in the hands of those who are strong enough to provide coming generations with reasons for living and hoping" (*GS*, 13). At the conclusion of the reflections we have shared with you, we are left only with questions. Does this African Church have a future? Will she be able to stand up and deserve one? Will she provide the generations to come with reason for hope?

The courageous and simple faith of many of our African brothers and sisters gives us the audacity to answer YES. The timidity and fear for any risk of the Church bureaucrats based in Europe as well as in Africa makes us less sure.

United with you we pray that the Holy Spirit will take the African Synod by storm, and lead all of us down paths we cannot imagine.

Part II

The Synod

12

Admission of Guilt

Northern Theologians

We, Christian men and women from Europe, gathered in Initiative Kindugu, salute the entire church of Africa on the occasion of your Synod 1994. With you, we desire this Synod to become a milestone on your journey toward being a truly African church. As Europeans, we have reason to turn to you. In grief and pain we acknowledge the countless wrongs inflicted on African people. We are ready to identify ourselves with the sins of our ancestors. We have begun to examine the ways in which we ourselves up to this day have taken part in the oppression of and contempt for your dignity and self-determination, politically, economically, eco-logically, culturally, and even ecclesiologically. We confess having both individu-ally and communally contributed in various ways to existing social structures as well as to ecclesial paternalism. We regret not always having played our part to undo such injustice. It seems impossible to assess the extent of such sin or even to redress it. We dare ask for forgiveness of yourselves and of your ancestors only before God and His son Jesus Christ who reconciled us to Himself and to one another through His own suffering and death.

We are resolved never to let the memory of our wrongdoings fade but to strive for conversion with courage and self-denial. God alone can bring about the heal-ing. With you we beseech Him for it.

May God instill in you the conviction and determination to realize the call Pope Paul VI expressed in Uganda in 1969, namely, to root deeply the Christian faith in African soil. We are becoming increasingly aware of the reaching demands this call makes on all of us. Christians everywhere in the world are in need of the revelation God desires to make through the African church. We need and we want to learn from you because we are convinced that God's Spirit has entrusted you with new and wonderful gifts.

Signed by many religious, clerics and lay people, including Pedro Casaldáliga, Erwin Krautler, Bernhard Häring, Notker Wolf, Peter Hunermann, Wolfgang Hoffmann, Giuseppe Alberigo, Norbert Greinacher, Walbert Buhlmann, Hans Küng.

13

Message of the Synod

Synod Documents

Dear Brothers and Sisters in Christ,

Christ is risen, Alleluia!

1. Like Mary Magdalene on the morning of the resurrection, like the disciples at Emmaus with burning hearts and enlightened minds, the Special Synod for Africa, Madagascar, and the Islands, proclaims: *Christ, our Hope, is risen. He has met us, has walked along with us.* He has explained the Scriptures to us. Here is what the Bishops of Africa, together with all the participants in this holy Synod, "united with Him alive for ever and ever and I hold the keys of death and of the abode of the dead" (Rev. 1:18).

2. Right from its first session on Monday, 11 April 1994, the Special Assembly for Africa of the Synod of Bishops received from Christ himself its profound significance, namely, the Synod of Resurrection, the Synod of Hope. And as St. John at Patmos, during particularly difficult times, received prophecies of hope for the People of God, we also announce a message of hope. At this very time when so much fratricidal hate inspired by political interest is tearing our peoples apart, when the burden of the international debt and currency devaluation is crushing them, we, the Bishops of Africa, together with all the participants in this holy Synod, united with the Holy Father and with all our Brothers in the Episcopate who elected us, we want to say a word of hope and encouragement to you, the Family of God in Africa; to you, the Family of God all over the world: *Christ our Hope is alive; we shall live!*

3. At this hour of special heavenly goodwill for the land of Africa which Paul VI "on the morrow of the Council prophetically called 'the new fatherland of Christ,'" our whole being cries out with joy and thanksgiving to the living God for the great gift of the Synod: to the Father, whose *family* we are, to the Son, from whom derives our *brotherhood* which overcomes fratricidal hate, to the Spirit of love, who molds us into images of the Blessed Trinity.

4. To the Supreme Pontiff, His Holiness Pope John Paul II, who took the initiative in calling this Synod, and who was present during all the general assemblies

until the time of his accident, following attentively with love and encouragement, how shall we not say that we know he loves Africa with a deep fatherly and constructive love? Our heart knows this and is grateful.

5. Greetings to you, People of God in Africa, Madagascar, and the Islands! You prepared this Synod actively and with enlightened zeal through your responses to the questionnaire contained in the Outline document (*Lineamenta*) and through your reflections on the Working Document (*Instrumentum Laboris*). Besides, you have supported it with your prayers to ensure its success. And a success it was. Indeed, the image we have of you now is one that more effectively touches and motivates us for the work of evangelization in our continent.

6. Right from the opening celebration on Sunday, 10 April, presided over by the Holy Father with 35 cardinals, one patriarch, 39 archbishops, 146 bishops and 90 priests, this universality was experienced in a liturgy reflecting the inculturation going on in the African continent. Africa brought to this historic assembly the most deeply felt expression of the efforts at inculturation in which the whole people participates with a joy that is faith in life itself. St. Peter's Basilica reechoed with the sound of tam-tams and xylophones, of castanets and gongs, which for us mark the rhythm of the struggle between life and death. That this should happen on this Second Sunday of Easter when Christ triumphed over death gave the occasion a particularly rich significance. As Pope John Paul II would remind us in his homily: Africa is a land loved by God.

7. The Synod just concluded has been for us the occasion to experience brotherhood, collegiality, and ecclesial communion as in a family. All the bishops experienced the universality of the church, which is not uniformity but rather communion in diversity compatible with the gospel. They were all aware that "as members of the body of bishops which succeeds the college of apostles, they are consecrated not for one diocese alone, but for the salvation of the whole world" (*Ad Gentes*, 38).

8. *Evangelization.* The first two weeks enabled us to listen to the churches of Africa through the interventions of the Synod fathers around the central theme, "The Church in Africa and Her Evangelizing Mission toward the Year 2000: 'You will be my witnesses' (Acts 1:8)," under five subheadings, Proclamation, Inculturation, Dialogue, Justice and Peace, and Means of Social Communication.

9. *Evangelization as Proclamation.Evangelization is the proclamation of the Good News of salvation realized in Jesus Christ and offered to all.* This first proclamation ought to be centered on Christ, the same yesterday and today, the enduring and ever new manifestation of God's goodness toward us. In Him the Spirit is given us to accomplish our sanctification and to transform the world. Unchanging in its content which is Christ, this evangelization will be "new in its ardor, new in its method, and new in its mode of expression" (John Paul II). Therefore it is not a theory but a life, a meeting of love which radically changes our life, today as at the beginning of the church.

The Spirit which gives the power to bear witness to Christ, dead and resurrected, sets the apostle on his missionary journey. It is the same Spirit which prepares all humanity for this meeting with Christ, in order to establish the Church, assembled by his Word and nourished by the Sacraments.

Therefore this first proclamation ought to bring about this overwhelming and exhilarating experience of Jesus Christ, who calls each one to follow him in an adventure of faith.

This experience is characterized by an irresistible desire to share it. It must be communicated to the many in our continent and the whole world who have not heard the Good News. The faith contains in itself a missionary urgency. The certitude of having discovered in Jesus the "pearl of great price" of the Kingdom of God brings about a transformation, which in turn implies newness of life. It demands a detachment, it uproots and launches one on mission both within one's country and outside to the ends of the earth. This initial Christian experience is sealed by the sacraments of Christian initiation. Within the established church catechesis continues this experience in a more systematic way, through pastoral activity, organizing the liturgical and sacramental life, as well as the missionary task—all forms of evangelization. To evangelize is to bring about life in Christ, the unique Redeemer of mankind. The Church in Africa, at this turning point of her history, should more than ever center herself on Christ and submit herself to the guidance of His Spirit which works in each individual and in the Church already constituted as the work of Christ. This Spirit impels toward proclamation to all peoples.

This focusing on the foundational experience of the Church is the first reason for calling this Synod.

10. *Homage to the Missionaries.* The effort made by missionaries, men and women, who worked for generations on end on the African continent, deserves our praise and gratitude. They worked very hard, endured much pain, discomfort, hunger, thirst, illness, the certainty of a very short life span and death itself, in order to give us what is most dear to them: Jesus Christ.

They paid a very high price to make us the children of God. Their faith and commitment, the dynamism and ardor of their zeal have made it possible for us to exist today as Church-Family for the praise and glory of God. Very early then we rejoined in their witness by great numbers of sons and daughters of the land of Africa as catechists, interpreters, and collaborators of all kinds.

11. May their example animate not only our young men and women whom institutes are today recruiting in large numbers for the evangelization of peoples, but equally the local churches they founded. When these churches will see new institutes emerging from their bosom, institutes which demonstrate their solicitude for the whole Church, their demonstration to carry the Gospel to the yet unevangelized parts of the world, then the work of the missionary institutes would have achieved its true purpose. Their work continues as cooperation among the churches (cf. *Redemptoris Missio*, 39, 85).

12. In the cordial dialogue and collaboration with the mission institutes, working on the African continent and in communion with the See of Peter, the churches in Africa which take the initiative to found institutes of consecrated life and for the missions unmistakably show that a new stage in the evangelization of Africa has now begun. In the past only the missionary institutes from the northern hemisphere were evangelizing Africa. At the end of a century, the statistics speak eloquently:

95 million Catholics. But this represents only 14 percent of the total population of Africa. From this it follows that the primary proclamation is still both urgent and necessary, especially since other spiritual and religious currents are gaining ground. The new stage that has started demands from our churches creativity and historic initiative. These initiatives well thought out and discerned in prayer cannot fail to receive the encouragement of this holy Synod. All our local churches should burn with missionary ardor.

13. Such was and still is the proclamation that the apostles and their successors passed on throughout the last twenty centuries. At each new epoch, with the Greeks and with the Latins, with the Anglo-Saxons and the Germanic peoples, the proclamation of the Word always brought about a profound transformation of individuals and of peoples, a transformation that is a new creation. It was fidelity to the biblical structure of revelation. Evangelization appeared clearly to all under its double aspect as Proclamation of the Word of Salvation and Inculturation. From this emanates a double demand of witness for each particular church and each baptized person, namely to welcome the Good News down to the roots of our cultures and to carry it to all peoples, even to the ends of the earth. An evangelization limited only to the dimension of proclamation would be disfigured, for it is in a dialogue of love of which the inculturation of the message is the necessary second moment.

14. *Evangelization: Inculturation and Holiness*. This dialogue of love with God the Holy One carries with it an unavoidable demand which all feel deeply, and which many enunciated with insistence and theological depth: holiness. When the Word takes on our nature, he purifies it of sin and he bestows on it his most fundamental and most beautiful attribute, namely holiness. When he takes up his due place in a culture, he awakens all the energies of the first creation which it expresses, investing them with the power of his redemption.

15. But the culture which gave its identity to our people is in a serious crisis. On the eve of the twenty-first century when our identity is being crushed in a mortar of a merciless chain of events, the fundamental need is for prophets to arise and speak in the name of the God of hope for the creation of a new identity. Africa has need of holy prophets.

16. *To be witnesses*. Like the incarnation, inculturation reaches its summit in the paschal mystery in which Christ gives testimony to the truth even with his blood; on the cross he recapitulates all that is true and holy in cultures to use them in manifesting the Blessed Trinity. He is the First Witness.

17. The baptized person who receives from the risen Christ the mandate to bring evangelization to its term and who responds to it becomes in his turn a witness. He evangelizes the cultural roots of his person and of his community and takes up the socio-economic and political challenges in order to be able to express the message in his own words and in a new dynamic of life which transforms the culture and the society.

18. *The domains of inculturation*. The field of inculturation is vast; the Synod which has so strongly insisted on its spiritual dimension by the place it accords to witnessing demands that none of its dimensions, theological, liturgical, catechetical, pastoral, juridical, political, anthropological, and communal be lost sight of. It is

the entire Christian life that needs to be inculturated. A special attention should be paid to liturgical and sacramental inculturation, because it directly concerns all the people who are already participating in it. Among other basic conditions that will enable it to touch the lives of the people, there is the translation of the Bible into every African language. We also need to promote the personal and communal reading of the Bible within the African context and in the spirit of tradition.

19. Many concrete practical domains for inculturation, which seeks to encompass the whole of life, were discussed: health, illness, and healing according to traditional methods; marriage; widowhood; and still other areas.

20. The Church-Family has its origin in the Blessed Trinity at the depths of which the Holy Spirit is the bond of communion. It knows that the intrinsic value of a community is the quality of relation which makes it possible. The Synod launches a strong appeal for dialogue within the Church and among religions.

21. *An appeal for dialogue with traditional religion.* Particular attention should be paid to our customs and traditions in so far as they constitute our cultural heritage. They belong to oral cultures and their survival depends essentially on the dialogue of generations to assure their transmission. Corporate personalities, wise thinkers who are its guarantors, will be the principal interlocutors in this phase of profound change in our cultures. A dialogue with the guarantors of our cultural values and of our traditional religion (ATR) structured around the cultural heritage is strongly recommended in our local churches.

22. *Dialogue with our Christian brethren.* We call for the intensification of dialogue and ecumenical collaboration with our brethren of the two great African churches of Egypt and Ethiopia and with our Anglican and Protestant brethren. We wish together to bear witness to Christ and to proclaim the gospel in all the languages of Africa. The presence at this Synod of our brothers of the churches and ecclesial communities of Africa has been deeply appreciated by all and we are grateful to them for addressing the Assembly and for their participation in its work.

23. *Dialogue with Muslims.* We assure our Muslim brethren, who freely lay claim to faith in Abraham (cf. *Nostra Aetate*, 3), that we wish to collaborate with them, everywhere on the continent, in working for the peace and justice which gives glory to God. The living God, Creator of heaven and earth and the Lord of History is the Father of the one great human family to which we all belong as members. He wants us to bear witness to him through our respect for the faith, religious values, and traditions of each person. He wants us to join hands in working for human progress and development at all levels, to work for the common good, while at the same time assuring reciprocal respect for the religious liberty of individual persons and that of communities (*Redemptoris Missio*, 39). God does not want to be an idol in whose name one person would kill other people. On the contrary, God wills that in justice and peace we join together in the service of life. As servants of his Life in the hearts of men and in human communities, we are bound to give to one another the best there is in our faith in God, our common Father.

24. To the local churches, the Church-as-Family churches of Africa, the People of God in assembly throughout the world, it is primarily to you that we *proclaim*

Jesus Christ (cf. 1 Cor. 1:23) and it is from you that we wish to have re-echoed that He was put to death but is alive, that He gave his life for the world and that He gave it in abundance. The Synod has highlighted that *You are the Family of God.* It is for the Church-as-Family that the Father has taken the initiative in the creation of Adam. It is the Church-as-Family which Christ, the New Adam and Heir to the nations, founded by the gift of his body and blood. It is the Church-as-Family which manifests to the world the Spirit which the Son sent from the Father so that there should be communion among all. Jesus Christ, the only-begotten and beloved Son, has come to save every people and every individual human being. He has come to meet each person in the cultural path inherited from the ancestors. He travels with each person to throw light on his traditions and customs and to reveal to him that these are a prefiguration, distant but certain, of Him, the *New Adam, the Elder of the Multitude of Brothers which we are.*

25. Envy, jealousy, and the deceit of the devil have driven the human Family to racism, to ethnic exclusivism, and to hidden violence of all forms. They have led to war, to the division of the human race into first, second, third, and fourth worlds, to placing more value on wealth than on the life of a brother, to the provocation of interminable conflicts and wars for the purpose of gaining and maintaining power and for self-enrichment through the death of a brother. But Christ has come to restore the world to unity, a single human Family in the image of the trinitarian Family. We are the Family of God: this is the Good News! The same blood flows in our veins, and it is the blood of Jesus Christ. The same Spirit gives us life, and it is the Holy Spirit, the infinite fruitfulness of divine love. But for such a church to exist, we must have priests who live their priesthood as a vocation to spiritual paternity, Christian families that are authentic, domestic churches, and ecclesial communities that are truly living. For that reason the Synod spent a long time considering the qualities needed by these pastoral agents and their formation. It makes a first appeal to the diocesan priests, their primary collaborators in evangelization.

26. *To diocesan priests.* Your priestly ordination has made you representatives of Christ, the Pastor and Spouse of the Church. The Synod which has dwelt on the mystery of the Church, gives thanks to God for the great gift which you represent. It expresses thanks to you for having accepted with generosity to dedicate your lives to the Church-as-Family. The Synod therefore invites you to keep in mind the grace which you have received and to allow to be dynamic within you. You are called to reproduce in yourselves together with Christ the perfect sonship of the Father, whose all-powerful and creative love is faithful, patient, merciful, and the gracious source of plenty. You are called in the Son to respond to every work of the Father in the particular situation of your parish community in which there should be no distinction of persons. In fact the parish is the concrete place where you serve the universal mission, in which some of you already take part as priests of *Fidei Donum.* Mindful of the communion of the priestly fraternity, you will support and care for your brothers in the priesthood, realizing that you too are cared for and often supported. You will lead a life of profound pastoral charity, filled with care for all.

Fidelity to celibacy which is inseparable from chastity has, as you know from experience, its source in an intense love of Christ. Be faithful to the life of prayer and spiritual combat which maintain and deepen this love. This is the condition of your credibility as you dedicate yourselves to pastoral work in the Church. Do not be found wanting in the matter of God's wonderful plan to make us his family. Africa, which loves family life, reveres the father figure. Do not disappoint her. The Church counts on you to exercise faithfully this spiritual fatherhood without sparing yourselves.

27. *The Christian family.* The vitality of the Church-as-Family, which the Synod wishes to highlight, can only be effective insofar as all our Christian families become authentic domestic churches. It is there in effect that you, fathers, mothers, and children, live, in the image of the Holy Family, the richness of the love which is in the heart of God. It is there that you learn to share and to increase in the love of God and of men. The extended African family is the sacred place where all the riches of our tradition converge. It is therefore the task of you Christian families to bring to the heart of this extended family a witness which transforms from the inside our vision of the world, beginning from the spirit of the Beatitudes, without forgetting the various tasks that are yours in society.

28. *The Church-as-Family and small Christian communities.* The Church, the Family of God, implies the creation of small communities at the human level, living or basic ecclesial communities. In such communities, which are cells of the Church-as-Family, one is formed to live concretely and authentically the experience of fraternity. In them the spirit of disinterested service, solidarity, and a common goal reigns. Each is moved to construct the Family of God, a family entirely open to the world from which absolutely nobody is excluded. It is such communities that will provide the best means to fight against ethnocentricism within the Church itself and, more widely, within our nations. These individual Churches-as-Family have the task of working to transform society.

29. *Save the family.* This International Year of the Family is also the one in which the ecclesial consciousness of Africa, begun after Vatican II, has, in the heart of this holy Synod, borne the good fruit of the Church as the Family of God (cf. *Lumen Gentium*, 6).

30. During this Synod, we became aware of certain orientations of the preparatory document for the Cairo Conference. These create a situation in which there is a deliberate intention to impose, with strong financial backing, on the nations of the world as a whole the liberalization of abortion, the promotion of a life style without moral reference, and the destruction of the family as it was willed by God. We all condemn this individualistic and permissive culture which liberalized abortion and makes the death of the child simply a matter for the decision of the mother. We condemn the enslavement of man to money, the new god, through which pressure is put on the poor nations to force them to choose options in Cairo which are contrary to life and morality.

We appeal to all men of good will to take action with a view to putting a stop to this anti-life plan and we appeal to all believers to join with us in uninterrupted prayer that this plan may not see the light of day. The Church, which has been and continues to be dedicated to work towards human promotion and the development of peoples, is contributing together with the United Nations to the success of the International Year of the Family. The Synod, in union with the Holy Father, and with the universal Church, makes an appeal to the fifty-three African nations and to all the signatory nations of the Universal Declaration of Human Rights who will be present at the forthcoming World Conference on Population and Development in Cairo: "Do not allow the African family to be ridiculed on its own soil"; "do not allow the International Year of the Family to become the year of the destruction of the family."

31. *The Church-as-Family at the service of society (Justice and Peace).*

The Synod occupied itself extensively with the grave cultural, socio-economic and political problems of the continent during these critical and crucial years, full of uncertainty and chaos, of convulsion and upheaval. The Synod wishes to reiterate to all the sons and daughters of Africa that in the midst of all these torments our hope of liberation lies in the Redeemer of Mankind who gave his Spirit in order that we might resolutely assume our responsibilities.

32. The Savior has bestowed on us those two great gifts of the Kingdom of God which He is in person: Justice and Peace. The Synod demands greater justice between North and South. There should be an end to presenting us in a ridiculous and insignificant light on the world scene, after having brought about and maintained a structural inequality and while upholding unjust terms of trade! The unjust price system brings in its wake an accumulation of the external debt which humiliates our nations and gives them a regrettable sense of inferiority and indigence. In the name of our people we reject this sense of culpability which is imposed on us. But at the same time we appeal to all our African brothers who have embezzled public funds that they are bound in justice to redress the wrong done to our peoples.

33. By the same token we do not wish to deny our responsibilities as pastors. We have not always done what we could in order to form the laity for life in society, to a Christian vision of politics and economics. A protracted absence of the lay faithful from this field has led them to believe that the faith has nothing to do with politics. This Synod encourages all Christians who are so gifted to become engaged in the political field, and we invite all without exception to educate themselves for democracy. The sanctification of the temporal order is a characteristic proper to the secular vocation of the laity (cf. *Lumen Gentium*, 31). There is a need for prophets for our times, and the whole Church should become prophetic.

34. If we desire peace, we should all work for justice, we should foster the rule of law. In many cases, people have turned to the Church that she might accompany them as they set out on the journey of the democratic process. Consequently, democracy should become one of the principal routes along which the Church travels together with the people. Hence education toward the common good as well as toward a respect for pluralism will be one of the pastoral tasks which are a priority for our times. The lay Christian, engaged in the democratic struggle according to the spirit of the gospel, is the sign of a Church which participates in the promotion of the rule of law everywhere in Africa.

35. *An appeal to political leaders.* The "fullness of love" (Eph. 3:15-19), which is holiness, should also be sought in politics, which Pius XI defined as "the highest

form of charity." The Synod prays that there will rise up in Africa saintly politicians and saintly heads of state. They will be men who love their people to the end, and who wish to serve rather than be served. It is their duty to work for the restoration of dignity to our countries and to promote brotherhood. Thus they will hold in check the lust for hegemony, both internal and external, which sows the seeds of division and hate which give rise to wars. We thank our brothers in the military for the service that they assume in the name of our countries. We remind them however that they will have to answer before God for every act of violence against the lives of innocent people.

36. We salute with joy the democratic process which has begun in many countries of our continent. We hope that this process will be consolidated and we take particular pleasure in sharing the joy that is in the hearts of the people of South Africa, after so many decades of suffering and lack of mutual understanding. We share in the yearning of so many other people who still yearn after the establishment of the rule of law in their countries. We pray that all obstacles and resistance to the establishment of the rule of law may be promptly removed, thanks to the concerted action of all the protagonists and to their sense of the common good. May brotherly dialogue rather than the use of arms resolve all tensions! The Synod denounces and emphatically condemns the lust for power and all forms of self-seeking as well as the idolatry of ethnicity which leads to fratricidal wars. These are the things which bring on Africa the shame of being the continent where the greatest number of refugees and displaced persons are found.

37. *Support for refugees, displaced persons and war-torn populations.* The continent is burning and bleeding in many places. The cries of the people of Rwanda, Sudan, Angola, Liberia, Sierra Leone, Somalia, and parts of Central Africa rend our hearts. United with the dozens of millions of refugees and displaced persons, we ask the United Nations to intervene in order to re-establish peace. So many of our brothers and sisters from numerous countries of the continent live in exile because of dictatorship and all kinds of violence and are thus prevented from using their talents in the service of their own people for justice, tranquillity, and peace. To all, the Synod expresses its union in heart and prayer and invites them to put their hope in Christ, who has assumed and continues to assume all their sufferings for a new heaven and a new earth. Let them remember that "hope never fails" and let them offer their suffering as an ardent prayer to obtain peace for Africa.

38. *The poor, the sick and the victims of AIDS.* To all of you, brothers and sisters, tried in your dignity by misery, sickness, and all sorts of suffering, moral or physical, especially by AIDS which is claiming so many lives in our continent, we express our compassion and we pray for you to the Father of mercy and consolation. May He deign to make his presence felt to widows and orphans.

39. *Social workers and development agents.* We wish to thank in a special way all the men and women, especially the religious, engaged in the service of the suffering members of the African family. They manifest the face of Christ in His continual love toward the sick and the handicapped. We also express our gratitude to all Christians and to all men of good will who are working in the fields of assistance and health-care with Caritas and other development organizations.

What they have accomplished in enabling many families to improve their lot gives us reason for hope.

40. *Our Christian brothers and sisters in the Northern hemisphere.* With all our apostolic conviction, we turn to our Christian brothers and sisters and to all people of good will in the Northern hemisphere. We request them to intervene with those in responsible political and economic positions in their respective countries as well as those in international organizations. It is imperative that there be a stop to arms sales to groups locked in conflict in Africa.

41. It is a matter of urgency to find a just solution to the problem of the debt which crushes the greater part of the peoples of the continent and which renders futile every effort at economic recovery. Together with the Holy Father and the Pontifical Council for Justice and Peace, we ask for at least a substantial, if not a total, remission of the debt. We also simultaneously call for the formation of a more just international economic order, in order that our nations may eventually be able to take their place as worthy partners. Our continent also suffers from continual degradation arising from the terms of trade, from the use of Africa as a dumping ground by the over-industrialized societies, from the imposition on our societies of socio-economic measures from abroad which lead to life styles that are contrary to the dignity of the African as indeed of all men and women. We ask our brothers and sisters of other continents to see to it that due respect is given to Africa and Africans, as well as those of them who have immigrated to the Northern hemisphere. Only thus shall we succeed in building up the world family which the Creator invites us to form together on this earth, which he has given us to administer for the common good of humanity.

42. We are grateful to our brother bishops of the Special Assembly for Europe of the Synod of Bishops for having recently launched an appeal to the same effect:

The cries of the suffering Christ come to us today with particular force from the South of the planet, a place where peoples in extreme poverty call from us a solidarity which is bold and efficacious against the hunger, the innumerable obstacles, and injustices which afflict them. It is demanded of us that we respond to these appeals with concrete options. These include the abolition of the arms trade, the opening of our markets, a more equitable settlement of the international debt, as well as anything else which, in those regions, may promote the development of the culture and the economy together with the growth of democracy. Moreover, Europe herself would well benefit from the spiritual riches of other countries and cultures (Final Declaration of the Synod of the Bishops of Europe, n. 11).

43. *Examination of conscience of the churches of Africa.* The churches in Africa are also aware that, insofar as their own internal affairs are concerned, justice is not always respected with regard to those men and women who are at their service. If the Church should give witness to justice, she recognizes that whoever dares to speak to others about justice should also strive to be just, in their eyes. It is necessary therefore to examine with care the procedures, the

possessions, and the life style of the Church.

44. In other respects the Synod has made a serious examination of the question of the financial self-reliance of our churches. Each of the Catholic faithful should make his own examination of conscience. Our dignity demands that we do everything to bring about our financial self-reliance. The first step in this direction is transparent management and a simple life style which is in keeping with the poverty, indeed the misery of our people. In no way should this search for financial self-reliance be confused with a closing in on ourselves. On the contrary we seize this occasion to thank the Pontifical Mission Aid Societies, our sister churches, the religious institutes, and other non-governmental organizations (NGO) which have helped us up to the present, and we invite them to continue to do so as an expression of their communion with us. We would cease being the genuine church of Christ if we closed in on ourselves. The Church-as-Family is one of free and generous circulation of both goods and personnel.

45. *The means of social communication.* The Synod paid great attention to the mass media. Two important and complementary aspects surfaced: the mass media as a new and emerging cultural universe and as a series of means serving communication.

46. First of all, they constitute a new culture that has its own language and its own specific values and counter-values. For this reason, like any culture, the mass media needs to be evangelized. The Synod requests that all the agents of evangelization become familiar with the media and that those who work full time therein be sustained by their pastors who will be mindful of their necessary spiritual nourishment.

47. If this world of communications "is the first Areopagus of the modern age," apostles must be formed to witness therein and to speak with competence of the Word of truth and of life who is the Communicator par excellence. The Church owes it to itself to foster creativity in this area: as long as we remain only consumers in this domain we run the risk of changing our culture without wishing to and without even knowing that we are doing so.

48. The media are also, as their name indicates, means, traditional and modern, in the hands of communicators. That is why the Synod recommends that the churches do everything for formation in the use of these means for proclamation. They should initiate the faithful and especially the young to have a critical judgement of what the media produces. It is recommended that the local churches exploit judiciously the hours that are available to them on regional and national stations.

49. *Formation.* The program of formation desired by the present Synod is one which is aimed at leading candidates resolutely along the road to sanctity. It envisages the formation of people who are truly human, well inserted in their milieu and who bear witness therein to the Kingdom which is to come. This is done by means of evangelization and inculturation, of dialogue and involvement in justice and peace, as well as by means of a presence in the new culture constituted by the world of the mass media.

50. It is necessary that the program in houses of formation, especially in seminaries and novitiates, reflect the concern manifested by this Synod to see inculturation

and the social teaching of the Church taken very seriously.

51. *Formators in seminaries and novitiates.* There is truly reason to thank God for the vocations increasing everywhere in Africa, priestly vocations as well as vocations to the consecrated life. We should respond to this grace with a real sense of responsibility, being concerned with the quality of our vocations discernment process, setting up criteria for admission and formation. We must make available to seminaries priests capable of carrying out effectively the formation program. We urgently ask the Episcopal Conferences and our brother bishops who might have such formators available to put them generously at the service of this essential work.

52. To you, dear brothers and friends, who have the direct responsibility for the formation of future priests, the Synod expresses very deep gratitude. Your bishops know that you are constantly at work so that the People of God will never lack servants who are truly men of God, knowing how to be, in all simplicity, "all things to all men" (1 Cor. 9:22). Your mission is a very great one for the Church on the African continent. On the quality of your life and on your fidelity to your commitments depend the credibility of what you are teaching the seminarians and the success of the formation that you are giving them. If your intellectual competence is not put at the service of a holy life, you will be increasing in the Church the number of priest functionaries who will not give to the world the only reality that the world expects from them: God. You will be watchful about this. Do not forget the words of Paul VI, repeated by John Paul II: "People today put more trust in witnesses than in teachers, in experience than in teaching, and in life and action than in theories" (*Redemptoris Missio,* 42 and cf. *Evangelii Nuntiandi,* 41).

53. *Schools, cultural and research centers, institutes and universities.* In a world that is constantly and rapidly evolving, they are the privileged centers where our societies must adapt to the international context, remaining open to the future, thanks to the education and formation of the youth and thanks also to research. The great task, a difficult but exalting one, that the Synod entrusts to them is that of defining with rigor, and transmitting effectively, our cultures in all that they have that is viable and transmissible, being careful always to find the possible meeting points with other cultures. What should characterize them in the times in which we live is the establishment of a system of collaboration with the resource persons in our own lands, the wise bearers and guarantors of our traditions.

54. If our countries expect such centers to become places in which the mastery of science and technology fosters further development, they likewise expect them to become, at the same time, privileged places for the remolding of our traditional cultures confronted by modern rationality.

55. The Church in Africa on its part hopes that they will work for the sanctification of man's intelligence and that with her they will develop the rational criteria for a lasting inculturation.

56. *African theologians.* Your mission is a great and noble one in the service of inculturation which is the important work site for the development of African theology. You have already begun to propose an African reading of the mystery of Christ. The concepts of Church-as-Family, Church-as-Brotherhood, are the fruits

of your work in contact with the Christian experience of the People of God in Africa. The Synod knows that without the conscientious and devoted exercise of your function something essential would be lacking. The Synod expresses its gratitude and its encouragement to you to continue working with your distinctive role certainly, but in communion with your pastors so that the doctrinal riches which will flow from this Assembly may be deepened for the benefit of our particular churches and the universal Church.

57. *The lay faithful.* The Church-as-Family is orientated toward the building of society which she seeks to inspire by the spirit of the Beatitudes. The task of the faithful lay person, who through Baptism and Confirmation participates in the three great functions of Christ, priest, prophet and king, is to be the salt of the earth and light of the world, especially in those places where only a lay person is able to render the Church present. A certain idea of the Church produced a type of lay person who was too passive. The Church-as-Family is a church of communion. All pastors are invited to develop a pastoral program, in which the laity rediscover their proper place and importance. As for you, dear sons and daughters, concentrate resolutely on the grace of your Baptism and Confirmation and utilize every initiative which the Holy Spirit will give you, so that our Church may rise to the challenge of her mission.

58. *Religious: priests, brothers and sisters.* You have made a total gift of yourselves to reveal to Africa and to the world the beauty and grandeur of the life of the Church and its purpose. Religious life, contemplative or active, has a value in itself to manifest the holiness of the Church. You will succeed in inculturating religious life in Africa only by assuming, as it were, by representation and anticipation, the profound values that make up the life of our cultures and express the end pursued by our peoples. In this way you will give cultural hospitality to Christ, chaste, poor and obedient, who has come not to destroy but to fulfil. Your fidelity to your religious consecration and your communion with the local Church are for everyone signs of the Kingdom.

59. *Catechists.* Yours is the duty to assure the daily organization of village communities and urban neighborhoods, in order to make of them living fraternal groups, vital cells of the great ecclesial family. You are the primary collaborators of the priests in their ministry of evangelization. The Synod which has had the joy of participating in the beatification of one from among you, Isidore Bakanja, hopes that you may receive and transmit a formation truly centered on Christ, making you and all who through you enter the Church authentic witnesses of the faith.

60. *Seminarians and candidates for the consecrated life.* The theme of the Synod "You will be my witnesses . . . toward the Year 2000" concerns you very specially. The Church counts on you to make your own and live in depth the riches of this Synod. Enter generously into the ideal which is proposed to you. Be convinced that spiritual formation is the key to the whole of your formation.

61. An intense prayer life and a generous spiritual combat will enable you to properly discern your vocation and to grow as witnesses who know in whom they "have put their trust" (2 Tim. 1:12). Evangelization and inculturation, whose internal link is witness, should be the beacons that enlighten the coming century which

will be yours. Seminary discipline should become self-discipline and the expression of your maturity. Strive after the simple life style of laborers for the gospel in solidarity with all the poor of our continent; by your manual labor share in the concern of the local church to support itself.

62. *Young people*. The Synod was deeply conscious of the youth of Africa and of the local churches. It recognizes in Christ the primary source of this youth. The Synod also finds in your youth a source of dynamism and of renewal. Your great numerical strength is a sign of divine blessing on this Africa which loves life and freely communicates it to the future generations. Your desire for participation expresses a sense of responsibility which is for us a reason to give thanks.

63. The tasks of evangelization, inculturation, justice, peace and the means of social communication which received particular attention from the Synod cannot be achieved without your generous commitment. But how can this be done without dialogue with you? The call to live dialogue was also one of the fundamental preoccupations of the Synod. We desire to intensify it with you. You represent more than half of the population of the continent. You are a blessing for our peoples. The Synod desires that in every country a solution be found for your impatience to take part in the life of the nation and of the Church. For its part and as of now, the Synod asks you to take in hand the development of your countries, to love the culture of your people, and to work for its revitalization through fidelity to your cultural heritage, through a scientific and technical spirit, and above all, through the Christian faith.

64. The Synod of Hope is not unaware that you, young people with diplomas but without work, are faced with a difficult situation. It prays for you and asks your churches and the leaders of your countries to invent new models of development able to integrate the enormous potential that you represent, a potential impossible to utilize in the current materialistic and economy oriented model of society. It sympathizes with all the young Africans scattered all over the countries of the Northern hemisphere for the purpose of studies and who, because of unemployment, cannot return to put their competence at the service of their country.

65. *Women*. We render homage to you our mothers, our sisters! This Synod of Hope reflected on the alienations that weigh upon you. They come from a traditional vision of man and of the world and in this manner they manifest clearly one of the major forms of the structure of sin engulfing our African societies. They also come from the unjust structures of the present world.

66. The Synod requests that woman be given quality formation to prepare her for her responsibilities as wife and mother, but also to open for her all the social careers from which traditional and modern society tend to exclude her without reason. The Synod asks that woman be given once again that place which corresponds to the real importance conferred upon her by the responsibilities she already exercises.

67. Convinced that "to educate a woman is to educate a people," your bishops and all those who participated in this holy Synod are determined to take every measure to see your dignity fully respected. During this Synod, the Holy Father

beatified two mothers of families, Elisabetta Canori Mora and Gianna Beretta Molla. We join in this homage that the Holy Father addressed to you on that occasion:

> We desire to render homage to all courageous mothers who consecrate themselves without reserve to their families, who suffer in giving birth to their children and who are ready after that to endure every fatigue and to face every sacrifice in order to transmit to their children the best that is in them. . . . How extraordinary at times is their sharing in the solicitude of the Good Shepherd! (Homily of the Holy Father for the Beatification of Isidore Bakanja, Elisabetta Canori Mora and Gianna Beretta Molla, 25 April 1994).

68. We greet with deference all consecrated women of Africa and Madagascar and of the whole world. We encourage them to persevere in their holy vocation and to assume joyfully the grace of spiritual motherhood that Christ offers to them in the Church. We are convinced that the quality of our Church-as-Family also depends on the quality of our women-folk, be they married or members of institutes of the consecrated life.

69. As participants in the bringing about of full human development, you will be a source of hope for our continent in this hour of crisis, if you know how to imitate Mary, the new Eve, the Mother of Christ, the Redeemer of mankind.

70. *Thanksgiving.* In thanksgiving for the faith that we have received, and inspired by great joy, we turn toward the year 2000 which is approaching. We are filled with hope and determination to share the good news of salvation in Jesus Christ with every man and woman. That is our prayer and we invite the whole Family of God to pray with us and with Mary, the figure of the Church, for a new Pentecost.

71. O Mary, Mother of God, Mother of the Church, thanks to you, at the dawn of the Annunciation, the whole human race with its cultures rejoiced in knowing itself capable of the Gospel. On this eve of a new Pentecost for the Church of Africa, Madagascar, and the Islands, together with the people entrusted to us, in communion with the Holy Father, we unite ourselves to You, so that the outpouring of the Holy Spirit may make our cultures places of communion in diversity, and may make of us the Church-Family of the Father, the Brotherhood of the Son, the image of the Trinity, anticipating the Reign of God and working with all for a Society that has God as its Builder, a society of Justice and of Peace. Amen!

14

Propositions

Synod Documents

The Synod wishes that these Propositions, which the Fathers regard as of great importance, be presented to the Supreme Pontiff, in addition to the documents used in the course of its work, namely, the *Lineamenta*, the *Instrumentum Laboris*, the *Report of the General Secretary*, the *Relatio ante disceptationem*, the *Relatio post disceptationem*, the *Reports of the Circuli Minores* and their discussions.

Proposition 1

The Synod Fathers therefore request the Holy Father to publish at an opportune time a document on "The Church in Africa and Her Evangelizing Mission toward the Year 2000, 'You shall be my Witnesses' (Acts 1:8)."

Context of Proclamation in Africa

Proposition 2

Rejoicing at the many blessings brought to Africa during so many centuries of evangelization, thanking God for the many graces received, we also share deep concern and call for a new and urgent thrust in the evangelization of African men and women, wounded in their dignity by the scourges of the colonial past, oppressed by wars, disturbed by so many sects, manipulated by local and foreign means of social communication, and victims of ideologies alien to their own cultures.

The Synod wishes, therefore, that the post-synodal Apostolic Exhortation should refer to the actual situation of Africa so as to help determine pastoral and missionary priorities and address the message of salvation to the men and women of the continent.

Proposition 3

The Synod recalls that to evangelize is to proclaim by word and witness of life the Good News of Jesus Christ, crucified, died and risen, the Way, the Truth and the Life. Witness of life has a strong persuasive force in proclaiming the Gospel, especially in places where explicit proclamation of Jesus Christ is not possible.

Evangelization touches society and human beings in every aspect of their existence. It is therefore expressed in manifold activities, and in a particular manner in those activities which our Synod has chosen as fields of action: proclamation, inculturation, dialogue, justice and peace, and the means of social communication.

Proposition 4

The new evangelization should be centered on a transforming encounter with the person of the living Christ. In evangelization the role of the Holy Spirit must be stressed for a continuing Pentecost, where Mary, as in the first Pentecost, will have her place.

The African believes in God the creator from his traditional life and religion and thus is also open to the full and definitive revelation of God in Jesus Christ, Emmanuel, the Word made flesh. Jesus the Good News, is God, who saves the African, who loves the African, who gives the African rain and life and children and health and prosperity, and saves him from oppression and slavery.

For these reasons and in the light of the mandate from Christ, the Good News must be announced to all peoples of the continent, to the members of African Traditional Religion, to those who seek submission to God in Islam, to those who have lost the sense of God. Together with new evangelization, efforts must be continued in encouraging first evangelization.

Proposition 5

Sanctity, the living expression of our configuration to Christ, should be presented as the purpose of evangelization. Entrance into the Kingdom of God demands a change of mentality and behavior and witness of life in word and deed, a life nourished by the reception of the sacraments, particularly the Eucharist, in the Church, the sacrament of salvation.

The Bible in Evangelization

Proposition 6

The revealed Word of God in Sacred Scripture is owed special reverence and has a primary role in awakening faith. In the first place it has been entrusted to the Church. Therefore as far as the Bible, the written word, is concerned, it is not the individual but the Church that has determined its books and oversees its authentic interpretation.

In continuing the mission of the Church in Africa and to better proclaim the Living God and the Person of Jesus Christ, we recommend as part of Christian formation that efforts be intensified to allow proper access to the Word of God in the Scriptures (*Dei Verbum*, 22) through:

a) Bible translations into local languages (in collaboration with other Christian churches where possible);

b) putting the Bible into the hands of all the faithful and from their earliest years;

c) in-depth biblical formation of the clergy, religious, and catechists as well as the laity in general;

d) provision of all or parts of the Bible with study-guides for use in prayer, family and community study, etc. for the faithful;

e) well-prepared celebrations of the Word, Bible exhibits, etc.

f) Reactivation of the biblical center for Africa and Madagascar (SECAM) and the creation of similar structures at all levels for the promotion and coordination of the biblical apostolate.

Proposition 7

Since the revelation of Jesus as Christ is given us in the Bible which has been entrusted to the Church and is interpreted by her, it should be the point of reference for evangelizer and evangelized. This does not make superfluous catechisms based on the Bible, rethought according to each culture and produced in conformity with the Catechism of the Catholic Church.

The Church as the Family of God

Proposition 8

The mystery of the love of the Triune God is the origin, model and purpose of the Church (*LG*, 4; *AG*, 2; *GS*, 40), a mystery which finds suitable expression for Africa in the image of the Church-as-Family. For this image emphasizes care for the other, solidarity, warmth of relations, acceptance, dialogue and trust. It shows also how authority is exercised as service in love.

Baptism initiates one into this family of God and calls for a conversion which overcomes all particularisms and excessive ethno-centrism, thus allowing the faithful to live with these differences in reconciliation and in true communion as brothers and sisters.

To this end, personnel and resources should be shared between particular churches; seminarians should be formed so as to be open to service beyond the bounds of their own diocese; the most suitable candidates for episcopacy chosen irrespective of ethnic background; and bishops are invited to discuss the problem of tribalism openly and in a spirit of brotherly love.

It is earnestly desired that theologians in Africa elaborate the theology of the Church-as-Family with all the riches contained in this concept, showing its complementarity with other images of the Church (such as People of God). Meanwhile we encourage the development of an African ecclesiology based on the Church-as-Family.

Proposition 9

The Church-as-Family cannot reach its full potential unless it is broken up into communities which are small enough to permit close human relations. For this reason the small Christian communities (SCCs) have already been recommended by the African Bishops at the 1974 Synod. The holy Synod recommends that such communities be created and given life in urban and rural pastoral care. There is no need to elaborate on their value as instruments of transformation and healing. In fact they are places for:

—evangelizing of the communities themselves;

—bringing the Good News to others;

—praying and listening to the word of God;

—promoting the responsibility of the members themselves;

—learning to live as Church, treating the real problems of life in the light of the Gospel.

The Fathers of the Synod insist that these SCCs should be permeated by the universal love of Christ who breaks down the barriers and natural alliances of clan, tribe, or other interest groups. It is in such communities that Jesus Christ is known, loved and served in a personal and communal way.

Missionary Vocation of the Church

Proposition 10

The Church is by its nature missionary. Faith grows through sharing it with others. As the Church in Africa grows, we recognize our indebtedness for the gift of faith and our duty to share it with others. Seeing that the majority of people living on the African continent have not yet heard the Good News of salvation, the Synod recommends:

a) that missionary vocations be encouraged;

b) that in each country and diocese cells be established of the four Pontifical Mission Societies;

c) that where possible priests, brothers, sisters, and lay missionaries be encouraged to serve as *fidei donum* in needy countries of Africa or in other parts of the world;

d) that prayer, sacrifice, and alms for the mission work of the Church be encouraged and actively supported.

Agents of Evangelization

Proposition 11

The primary agent of evangelization is the Holy Spirit who gives life to the entire Church (*DV*, 4).

By virtue of baptism and confirmation, each and every Christian (clergy, religious, and laity) is called upon to evangelize according to his or her possibilities. Each person must know God and also make him known; love God and also make him loved; serve God and also bring others to serve him.

The complexity of the actual situation does not allow improvised action; formation is necessary for all.

Laity

Proposition 12

The laity are becoming increasingly conscious of their vocation and role in the Church. They wish to carry out the mission entrusted to all the baptized, namely, to proclaim Jesus Christ. To help achieve this, the Synod exhorts and proposes that schools or centers of biblical and pastoral formation be established in parishes, dioceses, countries, and regions of Africa. Special attention should be given to formation of the leaders of SCCs.

As witness to the faith in daily life is an act of evangelization of first importance, the Fathers ask that Christian decision-makers receive a suitable formation in the social teaching of the Church so that they may witness to the faith in their milieu.

Catechists

Proposition 13

The role of the catechist has been and remains a determinant force in the implantation and expansion of the Church in Africa. The Synod recommends that catechists not only receive a sound initial preparation (for example, through a two-year course) but that they continue to receive doctrinal formation as well as moral and spiritual support. Regular meetings should be organized for catechists so that they can discuss together how best to prepare their classes and devise plans for pastoral action, and so on. Bishops should give special attention to catechists and to their conditions of life and work. The parish priest should also carefully respect the special place of the catechist in the community.

Voluntary catechists also should receive adequate formation and encouragement.

Family

Proposition 14

a) The Christian family is the first cell of the small Christian community. It has its model and spiritual source in the Holy Family of Nazareth and has been rightly called the "domestic Church." As such, it has the vocation to be an agent of evangelization. It must also be conscious of the three-fold mission of Christ: priestly, prophetic, and royal.

The Christian family is a privileged place for evangelical witness because of its quality of life, the love between the members, and its hospitality. It ought to be a place of human and spiritual growth for parents, children, the youth, and the aged. For this, it is necessary to promote movements of the Apostolate of the Family.

b) Diocesan organisms for natural family planning in Africa and Madagascar are facing great financial difficulties, thus finding it impossible to employ permanent staff, to budget for the future and to make long term plans for their work.

Agencies for population control, on the other hand, have huge sums at their disposal. Besides, the methods of natural family planning are scientifically effective and trustworthy, have no dangers or side effects and are acceptable to the consciences of millions of Catholics.

The Synod addresses a formal request to organisms which dispose of funds for fertility control to give to agencies for family planning in Africa and the Third World access to these funds with the usual norms for financial control but with no conditions which may oblige persons to act against their conscience.

Proposition 15

Youth are both the subjects and objects of evangelization. For this reason it is necessary that the care of youth be explicitly developed within the overall pastoral plan of dioceses and parishes.

The Synod is attentive to the grave problems which face African youth today:
—illiteracy;
—idleness and hunger;
—drugs;
—recruitment into armies and armed partisan groups.

Special attention should be given to youth in inculturation because of the cultural uprooting caused by insertion into the modern and urban civilization.

The Synod asks the dioceses of Africa and Madagascar to establish suitable pastoral programs for youth in which they will be enabled to discover quite early the importance of generosity in the gift of self—the only way in which the human-person can develop. Such programs should have as objectives both human and professional formation.

Proposition 16

a) In the Church understood as the Family of God, religious life has the particular function not only to indicate to all the call to holiness (*LC*, 4347) but also to witness to fraternal life in community. Therefore all who live the consecrated life are called to respond to their vocation in a spirit of communion and collaboration with the bishops, clergy, and laity.

Since Africa has been, from the first centuries of Christianity, the cradle of monastic and cenobitic life, the bishops of Africa and Madagascar, conscious of the importance of contemplative life in evangelization, shall have it at heart to foster and support vocations to the contemplative life in their dioceses.

b) For all religious, it is important to ensure that:
—vocations are properly discerned remembering that quality is more important than quantity;
—a minimum education requirement for aspirants be fixed at national level;
—solid human, spiritual, doctrinal, apostolic, and missionary formation programs be provided;
—ongoing formation is also essential;
—those who are capable should be given the opportunity to follow higher studies or professional training;
—theological, scriptural, and pastoral ministry courses should be organized for religious brothers and sisters in the seminaries;

—adequate provision be made for care in old age;

—ongoing spiritual support be given to all religious communities.

c) The Synod requests that the vocation to brotherhood, with its own specific charism and service in the Church and in society be understood—and more highly valued. A solid spiritual, intellectual, and professional formation is indispensable.

d) The Synod requests that in founding new religious institutes in Africa greater prudence and better discernment be made, taking into account the criteria indicated in *Ad Gentes* 18 and *Perfectae Caritatis* 19. Once these institutes have been founded they must be helped to acquire juridic personality and to enjoy autonomy in finance and their own apostolic projects.

e) Religious institutes that do not have houses in Africa are not allowed to come seeking new vocations without prior dialogue with the local ordinary.

f) All religious communities should be noted for their missionary zeal and their availability to exercise their particular ministry where major needs of mission are evident either within or outside their country.

Permanent Deacons

Proposition 17

The permanent deacon, as an ordained minister and therefore as an agent of evangelization, should be duly acknowledged, fostered, and encouraged.

Future Priests

Proposition 18

The Synod Fathers affirm that today more than ever there is need to form our future priests to the true cultural values of their country, to a sense of honesty, responsibility, and integrity. They shall be formed in such a manner that they will have the qualities of the representatives of Christ, of true servants and animators of the Christian community under them, solidly spiritual, available, dedicated to evangelization, capable of administering the goods of the Church with efficiency and transparency and to live a simple life as befitting their milieu.

Seminarians should acquire affective maturity and should be both clear in their minds and deeply convinced that for the priest celibacy is inseparable from chastity. They should receive adequate formation on the place and the meaning of consecration to Christ in the priesthood.

Each episcopal conference, while maintaining the principal lines of the formation of priests as required by the universal Church, must study the special needs and context of their countries.

The criteria for the admission of candidates should be established, and the process of screening candidates should be done, with great care and in consultation with the families and the small Christian communities.

The Fathers noted that with the increase of vocations there is urgent need to improve programs of formation so that candidates will be led to a life of faith, a life of deep prayer and good example. Thus future priests will become witnesses of the Good News and effective apostles of evangelization.

Proposition 19

Formators/educators in major seminaries should be outstanding not only for their intellectual abilities but also and especially for their human, pastoral, moral, and spiritual qualities.

In view of the fact that many of our seminaries do not have qualified educators, the Synod requests the setting up of centers for the training of spiritual directors.

Proposition 20

The Synod deeply acknowledges the apostolic work of priests, diocesan and members of institutes, which they accomplish in Africa and Madagascar. It is aware that the new evangelization of our peoples demands of them faithfulness to their vocation in full communion with their bishop and in the total gift of themselves to their mission.

Given the necessity of continuing formation in all disciplines, the Synod Fathers ask that the ongoing formation program recommended in *Pastores dabo vobis* be effectively put in place and that the accompaniment of young priests be considered as vital.

After ordination, priests should be placed for a suitable time under the guidance of an experienced and good pastor. The Synod recommends that especially in the early years after ordination priests be invited to live in a community of priests. This would help them develop the spirit of cooperation in the exercise of their ministry.

Bishops

Proposition 21

In order to allow bishops to have an *aggiornamento* which will render them more capable of accomplishing their role as those most responsible for evangelization, it would be opportune for Episcopal Conferences to provide them with renewal or updating courses.

Proposition 22

In the spirit of Church-as-Family those responsible for local churches and for institutes of consecrated life and societies of apostolic life shall promote dialogue through the creation of mixed groups for consultation as a witness of fraternity and a sign of unity in the service of the common mission.

Mutuae relationes (1978) has presented the mystery of the Church as one body in which, "all are members of one another" (Rom 12:5; 1 Cor 12:13), all are invited to become a "visible sacrament" destined to give witness to and announce the Gospel. Conscious of the progress made since the publication of this document but also taking account of the new lights and possibilities offered by the concept of Church as family, the Synod Fathers call for a revision of *Mutuae relationes* and a better definition of the place of religious life in the local Church.

The Synod further proposes that both at diocesan and conference levels, besides the presbyteral council, structures be set up for ongoing dialogue between bishops and the diocesan clergy on the one hand and between bishops and the various religious institutes on the other. There should furthermore be joint planning in the different areas of activity.

Proposition 23

The laity are more and more engaged in the mission of the Church in Africa and Madagascar. Almost everywhere this participation and initiative have reached a high level. This result is in large measure due to the dynamism of the movements of Catholic Action, apostolic associations and movements, and new spiritual movements.

The Synod Fathers request that this thrust should be pursued and developed among all the laity, adults, youth and children (cf. *Relatio ante disceptationem*, 11).

Proclamation and Schools

Proposition 24

Catholic schools are at one and the same time places of evangelization, integral education, inculturation, and initiation to the dialogue of life among young people of different religions and social backgrounds. The Synod Fathers recommend to the Churches in Africa to foster the Catholic school, especially professional and technical schools, as a contribution to the program "education for all." Special attention will be given to educators.

The Church will give equal attention also to the Christian education of pupils in non-Catholic schools. For universities there will be a program of religious formation which corresponds to the level of studies.

Proclamation and Higher Institutes in Africa

Proposition 25

The Catholic universities and higher institutes of Africa have a prominent role to play in the proclamation of the salvific Word of God. They are a sign of the growth of the Church as they help to internalize theological truths and praxes. They serve the Church by:

a) providing trained personnel;

b) studying important theological and social questions for the benefit of the Church;

c) developing an African theology;

d) promoting the work of inculturation especially in liturgical celebration;

e) publishing books and publicizing Catholic truth;

f) undertaking appropriate assignments given by the bishops;

g) contributing to a scientific study of cultures.

We strongly recommend that bishops provide qualified staff, send suitable students, and give full moral and financial support.

Proposition 26

In this time of generalized social upheaval on the continent, Catholic cultural centers offer to the Church the possibility of presence and action in the field of cultural change. They constitute in effect public fora which allow the Church to make widely known, in creative dialogue, the Christian convictions on man, woman, family, work, economy, society, politics, international life, the environment—convictions which are the soul of all authentic human and Christian culture. They are also places where one can learn to listen to ideas, sometimes contradictory, but always exchanged in an atmosphere of respect and tolerance. The Christian faith has insights to propose to African society.

Material Means of Evangelization

Proposition 27

"From the start the Christian community should be so organized that it is able to provide for its own needs as far as possible" (*AG*, 15). Apart from the human resources evangelization requires material and financial means; such means are far from being adequately available in our dioceses in Africa. It is therefore urgent, indeed a priority, that the particular churches of Africa examine the ways and means of providing their own needs and assuring their self-reliance.

Therefore the Synod urgently calls on episcopal conferences, dioceses and all Christian communities in our churches, each according to what concerns it, to do what they can so that this self-sufficiency becomes effective.

Besides, the Synod calls on our sister churches all over the world, to be more generous to the pontifical mission aid societies and through their own aid organizations, to provide assistance to poorer dioceses and to invest in projects that will generate resources with a view to arriving at a progressive self-reliance in our churches.

Theological Basis of Inculturation

Proposition 28

Jesus Christ the Son of God made man, crucified and risen in glory, is the center and model of every aspect of the Christian life. The incarnation of the Son of God is the principle and model of inculturation. In the light of the mystery of the incarnation, inculturation, as a project of communion in diversity, is thus rooted in the mystery of the Trinity. Christ is "at home" in our cultures.

Furthermore, the Gospel itself becomes the principle that purifies, guides, animates and elevates the culture, transforming it in such a way that there is a new creation. There is need for every culture to be transformed by Gospel values in the light of the paschal mystery.

Proposition 29

Inculturation in its process as well as its aim is a priority and urgent matter in the life of the churches of Africa in view of a firm rooting of the Gospel in the Christian communities and in the Church-as-Family. The Synod Fathers commit the churches in Africa to this far reaching and long term task. They recommend the prudence and discernment necessary for such a delicate enterprise. However, local churches should be given trust and freedom to accomplish this great task.

Proposition 30

Inculturation is a demand of evangelization. It is the fruit of listening, welcoming, or reflecting on and assimilating the Good News of Jesus Christ, the Son of God (Mk. 1:1). Inculturation is the work of the Holy Spirit who leads the Church into the whole truth (Jn. 16:13) and grants it to her to express in all cultures the wonderful deeds of God. That is why inculturation must be carried out within the Church.

The Synod recommends that inculturation brings together in trusting collaboration the small Christian communities and the researchers under the responsibility of bishops and episcopal conferences.

Criteria of Inculturation

Proposition 31

Considering the rapid changes in the cultural, social, economic, and political domains, our local churches must be involved in the process of inculturation in an ongoing manner. The Synod emphasizes that the project of inculturation will respect the two following criteria:

    a) compatibility with the Christian message, and

    b) communion with the universal church.

In the process of inculturation noble elements of the culture can be utilized. Those elements contrary to Christian values must be dropped. In such cases suitable substitutes must be found in order not to create a vacuum. In all cases care should be taken to avoid syncretism.

Areas of Inculturation

Proposition 32

Inculturation is a movement toward full evangelization. It seeks to dispose people to receive Jesus Christ in an integral manner. It touches them on the personal, cultural, economic, and political levels so that they can live a holy life in total union with God the Father, under the action of the Holy Spirit.

The Synod recommends to the bishops and to the episcopal conferences to take note that inculturation includes the whole life of the church and the whole process of evangelization. It includes theology, liturgy, church structures, and life. All this underlines the need for research in the field of African cultures in all their complexity.

The Synod thanks God for the abundant fruits which the efforts of inculturation have already brought forth in the life of our churches. The Synod Fathers invite pastors to exploit to the maximum the numerous possibilities which present church regulations provide in this matter.

Inculturation and Formation of Agents

Proposition 33

Inculturation is one of the greatest challenges of evangelization for the churches of Africa and Madagascar as we move toward the third millennium. It is the expression of the Christian experience of the community (clergy, religious, laity, the theologians, artists, and so on) tapping the talents of each one. Therefore, the Synod asks for:

a) the establishment of commissions, structures and centers for the training of personnel at the episcopal conference and diocesan levels;

b) that the faculties and other institutes and centers already existing in Africa and Madagascar become each in its cultural area institutions that promote interdisciplinary research and reflection, experimentation, and documentation (*AG* 22);

c) that higher institutes and major seminaries in liaison with the Congregation for Catholic Education design programs of priestly formation in this direction so as to form personnel capable of promoting an authentic inculturation.

Areas of Application

Proposition 34

Inculturation of the liturgy, provided it does not change the essential elements, should be carried out so that our people can better understand and live our liturgical celebrations. It is therefore recommended that those parts of the liturgical celebration which can be changed in order to enhance an intelligent, conscious, and meaningful participation in it should be inculturated according to agreed norms. The different cultures should open themselves progressively to the values of the Gospel. Liturgical rites in their turn should be carriers not only of artistic beauty but also of the Christian message.

Proposition 35

We strongly affirm the Church's teaching on the unity and indissolubility of marriage as of divine origin. We also note with satisfaction that most African cultures ideally uphold the same essential properties of marriage.

However, there is the problem of so many Catholics who are being excluded from the sacraments because they have contracted marriage in a form not recognized by the Church.

In affirming monogamy as the Christian teaching and therefore rejecting polygamy, the Synod strongly urges that those involved in polygamous unions be treated with respect, justice and compassion. All concerned must be evangelized and helped to come closer to Christ.

Therefore, the Synod recommends that episcopal conferences create commissions on marriage in Africa which will include married couples. Their aims will be to study all the questions concerning marriage from the point of view of theology, sacramentals, liturgy, and canon law with special reference to cultural questions.

Proposition 36

In many African communities, the ancestors occupy a place of honor. They are part of the community together with the living. In many cultures, there are clear ideas of who merits to be called an ancestor. Were many of these not seeking God with a sincere heart? The ancestors are venerated, a practice, which in no way implies worshipping them.

We therefore recommend that ancestor veneration, taking due precaution not to diminish true worship of God or to play down the role of the saints, should be permitted with ceremonies devised, authorized, and proposed by competent authorities in the church.

The Spirit World

Proposition 37

The African belief is that good spirits bring fortune while bad spirits cause harm. This is where the problem of witchcraft comes in.

For our societies it constitutes a constant danger to peace and harmony among our people. It even compromises some efforts of integral development undertaken by our Christian communities. The Synod hopes that a multi-disciplinary research team be urgently put together in order to look into and clarify this problem which is complex, obscure, and widespread.

In order to minister to the faithful, we need to preach the power of Christ over every evil spirit. That is why there is need for holy men and women, who by the sacraments and sacramentals and by prayers of deliverance can help the afflicted. One should not neglect the modern means afforded by clinical psychology and para-psychology.

Dialogue

Proposition 38

Evangelization continues the dialogue of God with humanity and reaches its apex in the person of Jesus Christ. The attitude of dialogue is the way of being for the Christian within the community and with other believers and men and women of good will.

Dialogue in the Church

Proposition 39

Aware of belonging to a Church-Family, Christians are earnestly invited to practice first of all this dialogue between themselves at all levels:

—between particular churches and the Apostolic See;

—between particular churches on the continent itself and those of other continents;

—and, in the particular church, between the bishop, the presbyterate, consecrated persons, pastoral agents, and the faithful;

—among various rites within the Church.

The spirit of dialogue allows for a respect for the competence of each level of authority and leadership, and guarantees the application of the principle of subsidiarity. It is therefore recommended that the Symposium of Episcopal Conferences of Africa and Madagascar (SECAM), the regional associations of bishops' conferences, and national episcopal conferences and dioceses, have structures and means which guarantee an exercise of this dialogue.

Ecumenical Dialogue

Proposition 40

Linked to Jesus Christ by their witness in Africa, Catholics are invited to develop an ecumenical dialogue with all their baptized brothers and sisters of other Christian denominations, so that the unity for which Christ prayed might be realized and so that their service to the peoples of the continent may make the Gospel more credible in the eyes of those who are seeking for God. In a common concern for truth and charity, but with patience and prudence, it would be convenient to assure that there are ecumenical translations of the Bible, to work out together a Christian theology of development and open a common accord for a more just and brotherly society where the rights of persons would be respected.

In order that ecumenism be promoted and abuses in this field prevented, it is necessary that all agents of evangelization, especially priests, be given a solid ecumenical formation. In addition, and in accordance with the directions given by the Holy See, every episcopal conference should have a commission for ecumenism, while at the diocesan level there should be at least a special office entrusted with this pastoral task.

Dialogue with Muslims

Proposition 41

This effort of dialogue ought to embrace equally all Muslims of good will. Christians should not forget that there are many Muslims attempting to imitate the faith of Abraham and to live the demands of the Decalogue.

Catholics are in addition invited to practice with them a dialogue of life in the family, at work, at school, and in the public life, of a kind which will bring about the realization of a just society where a veritable pluralism guarantees all freedoms, and especially religious freedom. This encompasses the freedom of persons and of communities to profess publicly their faith, as well as the freedom to change one's religion, to meet in common worship and to erect structures for such purposes, and to exercise educational and charitable work.

To facilitate such an undertaking on the part of Christians at the local, regional or national level, it is desirable that commissions and institutes be created to form and to be informed on positive interreligious dialogue with reciprocal respect for the spiritual values of each of them.

It is essential that we be vigilant in the face of dangers which come from certain forms of militant Islamic fundamentalism. We must become more vocal in exposing their unfair policies and practices, as well as their lack of reciprocity regarding freedom of religion.

African Traditional Religion

Proposition 42

It is evident that the dialogue with African Traditional Religion must continue because African Traditional Religion still has an influence on the African and often directs the way of life of even the best of Catholics. There are positive values in African Traditional Religion which could stand the Church in good stead. The central doctrine of African Traditional Religion is the belief in a Supreme Being Who is Creator, Giver of Everything, Just Judge, Eternal, and so forth. Adherents of African Traditional Religion are worthy of respect. They are believers in God and in spiritual values. Such beliefs and values will lead many to be open to the fullness of revelation in Jesus Christ, through the proclamation of the gospel.

National episcopal conferences should give African Traditional Religion more attention. Derogatory language, such as "heathenism" and "fetishism" must be avoided when describing African Traditional Religion. There is also need for courses in ATR in seminaries and houses of formation, while research must be intensified in order to discover those elements which are compatible with the Gospel.

Proposition 43

Finally, it is necessary that this spirit of dialogue equally inspire the relations of African Christians with local political powers and international institutions, whether political, economic, or cultural, in such a manner that a North-South dialogue as well as South-South dialogue may be established and developed to assure better the necessary solidarity based upon mutual respect

Appeal to Prayer

Proposition 44

The Synod asks for prayers all over the world for peace in every country or region where there are tensions and violence caused by religious intolerance so that the people there will find peace and concord.

The Situation of Injustice in Africa
and the Church's Prophetic Role

Proposition 45

Integral development implies respect for human dignity and this cannot be realized unless in justice and peace.

a) For some years now Africa is the theater of fratricidal wars which are decimating populations and destroying their natural riches. These wars are caused, among other reasons, by tribalism, nepotism, racism, religious intolerance, and the thirst for power reinforced by totalitarian regimes which trample with impunity the rights and dignity of the person. Populations crushed and reduced to silence submit as innocent victims and resign themselves to all these situations of injustice.

b) Even today there are many countries where chambers of torture exist and these are specially equipped to inflict terrible sufferings upon people.

The Synod asks all the heads of state and of government to destroy these establishments wherever they exist and to demand of their subordinates to treat every citizen as a human being with due respect to the Charter of the Rights of Man and of Peoples.

c) The Church shall continue to play its prophetic role and be the voice of the voiceless.

The Synod condemns all these situations and calls upon the consciences of heads of state and those in charge in the public domain to guarantee ever more the liberation and development of their peoples.

d) The Church defends the rights of all, especially the marginalized. She condemns clearly all those foreign manipulations and interests that connive with corrupt local leaders to pillage our national resources.

Among the most marginalized in Africa, the Synod draws the attention of governments and partners in development projects to the workers and the rural populations constrained to flee the villages to cram into the towns.

e) The Synod asks for the suspension of international isolation through embargoes which bring suffering to populations. Conflicts are to be resolved by dialogue. To succeed in such a mission, there is need for personal conversion and a deep sense of prayer.

Structures

Proposition 46

Aware that gross violations of human dignity and rights are being perpetrated in many countries of Africa, in particular, the right to life from the moment of conception and the right to essential freedoms, the Synod asks episcopal conferences to establish justice and peace commissions at various levels, including that of the parish. These will awaken the Christian communities to their evangelical responsibilities in the defense of human rights.

Formation

Proposition 47

Formation of clergy, religious, and laity imparted in the area of their apostolate should lay emphasis on the social teaching of the Church. Each according to his state of life should be specially trained to know his rights and duties, the sense of the common good and its service, honest management of public goods, and the proper manner of participating in political life in order to intervene in a credible manner against social injustices.

Women

Proposition 48

The Synod appreciates the indispensable contribution which African women make to family, church, and society. In many African societies and sometimes even the Church, there are customs, and practices which deprive women of their rights and the respect due to them. The Synod deplores this. It is imperative that women be included in appropriate levels of decision making in the Church and that the Church establish ministries for women and intensify efforts toward their formation. Each episcopal conference must champion the rights of women especially with regard to widowhood, brideprice, pregnancy, delivery, single mothers, justice in marriage, adequate remuneration for their work, and give them spiritual assistance. The role and place of women in Church and society should be further studied by special commissions to be established by the episcopal conferences. These commissions should cooperate with government agencies where possible.

Arms and Debts

Proposition 49

a) The Synod Fathers as pastors and citizens exhort the heads of state and their governments in Africa not to crush their peoples with internal and external debts. Associating themselves with efforts already being made, the Fathers ask the International Monetary Fund and the World Bank and all other foreign creditors to alleviate the crushing debts of African Nations. And it also urges the episcopal conferences of the industrialized countries to present this issue consistently to their governments and to organizations concerned.

b) The sale of arms is a scandal since it sows the seed of death. This Synod appeals to all countries that sell arms to Africa to stop doing so. It also implores African governments to move away from huge military expenditure and put the emphasis on the education, health and well-being of their people.

c) The Synod recommends that episcopal conferences intensify their efforts at dialogue with their governments. They should continue issuing public statements on matters affecting the lives of the people and act together. There is also a value in networking with other groups both within and outside their own countries. The

Synod Fathers urge conflicting parties to renounce the recourse to arms and to solve their problems through dialogue.

d) Episcopal conferences throughout the world should educate the faithful on Catholic social teaching about the crushing external debts and the scandalous sale of arms to African governments. Thus also can be developed supportive public opinion.

Health Problems of Africa

Proposition 50

These can be summarized under the following headings:
—malnutrition;
—lack of hygiene;
—disease and high mortality rate.

The Synod proposes the following:

a) the promotion of the pastoral care of health as a task to do with man's integral salvation;

b) the setting up of specific formation in theology, bioethics, and health care attached to this specialized apostolate;

c) support of lay Catholic associations for the defense and protection of life;

d) organization of the health education and medical services at all levels.

The Synod appeals to international organizations and those concerned with political and commercial matters linked with demographic problems to let themselves be led by principles of good ethics.

AIDS

Proposition 51

The Synod is deeply concerned about the spread of AIDS and the dramatic misery it is bringing to so many families in Africa. This spread is due in part to conditions of poverty and misery which exist in the continent. For this reason, the bishops pray for men of science all over the world that their laudable efforts in scientific research may attain the wished-for objective as soon as possible. Besides, the bishops exhort all, especially the families and health staff, to offer those sick of AIDS the care and the affection they expect. The companionship, joy, happiness and peace which Christian marriage and fidelity provides, and the safeguard which chastity gives must be continuously presented to the faithful, particularly the young.

Financial Assistance

Proposition 52

While encouraging the churches in Africa to be more self-sacrificing in the effort to become self-sufficient, it is demanded that the older churches continue to support them in the spirit of solidarity.

The Church in Africa gives thanks for the humanitarian help that Africa receives from international organizations. However, she feels the duty of reminding them that the projects of development should meet the real needs of each country or region and when offering help no unilateral conditions should be imposed. We also note that financial help is more easily given for social works than for evangelization. We ask for collaboration between Catholic organizations and the particular church, so that the latter can receive priority assistance in her task of evangelization.

Refugees and Displaced Persons

Proposition 53

The phenomenon of refugees and displaced persons in Africa has reached tragic dimensions: tens of million of men, women and children are forced away from their homes and their lands. The Synod asks the local churches:

a) to offer material assistance, in collaboration with the international agencies and with the aid of Catholic organizations, to refugees and displaced persons during their exodus in the camps and in the process of repatriation.

b) to give priority to the pastoral care of refugees and displaced persons assigning to this ministry priests and religious of their own language and culture, and announcing the Gospel's message to those among them who are not Christians.

c) to work effectively to eliminate those situations of violence and injustice which are at the root of forced migrations;

d) to include specific programs in the formation of clergy and pastoral workers on the problems of human mobility in Africa.

Given the magnitude and plight of refugees and displaced persons in our countries this Synod cries with anguish to the Organization of African Unity and all governments having diplomatic relations with those African countries from whence the refugees come or the displaced persons live, to remedy without delay the causes which are surely a disgrace to their image and to Africa.

The numerous African refugees, displaced persons and students, who live outside the continent of Africa especially in Europe and North America must also be assured adequate pastoral care, in cooperation with the churches of their countries of origin. Those among them who have attained working experiences and academic degrees useful and necessary to the development of their native countries should be encouraged to return to their homelands.

Poverty

Proposition 54

Given the underdevelopment and poverty under which Africa is suffering, while acknowledging the efforts already under way in view of development, the Synod calls on industrialized countries to promote real growth on the continent by paying fair and stable prices for its raw materials. It further calls on African governments to adopt appropriate economic policies in order to increase growth, productivity, and job creation. It urges them to develop regional cooperation.

The Synod deplores corruption in public life and the banking of embezzled funds in foreign countries. We ask people of integrity in our own countries and abroad to investigate ways of having these monies returned to what are already poor nations.

Environment

Proposition 55

The present ecological conditions and the damage caused by deforestation and industrial pollution are matters of grave concern. The Synod urges that controls be put in place to prevent the dumping of toxic waste and the pollution of Africa's waterways and coasts. In sermons, articles, and catechesis as well as in programs in schools, care of the environment and the integrity of creation must be inculcated. At local level, parishes should organize programs of education and practical action, such as the planting of trees.

Democracy

Proposition 56

It is necessary and urgent to establish the rule of law in our countries to safeguard the rights and obligations of the citizens. The Church, therefore, should intensify her education of consciences so as to help our people to put in place political systems that would respect human dignity and the fundamental freedoms of citizens.

Means of Social Communications

Proposition 57

In faithfulness to Christ who is the Communicator par excellence the Church is aware of her duty of fostering social communications *ad intra et ad extra.*

a) The Church should promote communications from within through a better diffusion of information among her members.

b) The Church ought to use the full range of traditional and modern techniques of social communications so as to fulfill efficaciously her evangelizing mission.

c) Episcopal conferences and dioceses should develop pastoral plans of communications as part of their total pastoral planning.

She ought to give particular attention to traditional forms of the media which are less costly and more accessible.

Proposition 58

The media, whether private or public, should constitute a service for the people. Therefore, the churches in Africa are called to do all that is possible so that this objective might be safeguarded and that access to them might be guaranteed to every person without exception.

Proposition 59

The presence of Christian communicators also in Church, private, and state media is indispensable for evangelization. Therefore, they should be given all necessary encouragement.

a) Technical and professional formation need to be based on a sound human and religious formation;

b) Catholic universities are centers for reflection, research and the promotion of culture. The Synod recommends the creating of a chair for social communications. At the same time programs of formation on the diocesan and national levels should be established.

Proposition 60

The spoken word is a unique aspect of African culture. Therefore the Synod recommends:

—the setting up of local radio stations;

—better collaboration between the Vatican radio and local radio stations;

—the setting up of a radio station for the entire continent so that the voice of the Gospel might be heard throughout the continent in both urban and rural settings;

—that efforts be made to secure a satellite channel for the Church in Africa and Madagascar.

Proposition 61

The Synod requests of the episcopal conferences, families, educational groups, and heads of Christian communities to seek to safeguard the dignity of women and to pay particular attention to pornography and violence in films that now invade the media, which, instead of communicating moral values, carry contrary messages of degradation to the point of corrupting the conscience of our people, especially the young.

The Synod greatly deplores the very negative portrayal of the African in the media as a humiliating insult and calls for its immediate cessation. We also ask African governments, on their part, to grant due freedom to the media.

Proposition 62

In order to assist our Christian communities to have access to useful audiovisual and reading materials, the Synod requests the opening of diocesan and parochial libraries and audiovisual centers. It makes an appeal to sister churches of the world to facilitate this in the spirit of solidarity for the co-production of interesting and useful works.

Proposition 63

The Synod has noted the need for a more dynamic and better coordinated use of the means of social communications. It therefore recommends the creation of diocesan and national commissions for communications and the revitalization of the Pan-African Episcopal Committee of Social Communications (CEPACS).

Proposition 64

This Synod, conscious that it can do nothing without divine favor, assistance, and support (cf. Jn. 15:5), urges that the spirit of prayer, individual and communitarian, be fostered:

—The Lord Jesus, whom the Father has sent, will be in a special manner in our midst and active through us;

—The Holy Spirit, whom Jesus has given to his Church, will lead us to the goal here proclaimed.

May Our Lady, the Mother of Africa, be with our churches!

15

Some Interventions

On Justice and Peace

Cardinal Bernard Yago, Archbishop of Abidjan (Ivory Coast)

The promotion of people, their integral blossoming, the respect for their dignity and rights, and the establishment of justice and peace are basic parts of evangelization. They are the signs by which we may recognize that the Kingdom of God has arrived. Numerous pontifical documents bring this up.

Faithful to this teaching, the missionaries, from the beginning, supported human promotion through schools, dispensaries, and actions for development on their part. The bishops and the episcopal conferences, sometimes, take courageous stands to denounce injustices and to remind people of the social doctrine of the Church. But one must admit that if the actions on behalf of human promotion are developed in an organized way, those regarding justice and peace are less thorough. This comes back to our culture which makes people too dependent on collectivity and customs and also on the political situation of our countries where dictatorship of the sole party has imposed silence upon all of us until these last years.

Fortunately, things are changing with the advent of multiparty systems and the birth of movements such as the League for the Rights of Man and the ACAT (Christian Association for the Abolition of Torture). The intellectuals have found the freedom of speech again. The Church, in which our people have great trust, must accomplish a great deal in our countries in the domain of justice and peace by:

a) Teaching social ethics from childhood and at all ages while clearly and forcefully insisting that the Good News announced must be proved by actions that are not only charitable, but also in the search for social justice and the fight for the respect of human beings.

b) The establishment of "justice and peace" commissions in the dioceses with well-formed and supported lay people, because the transformation of the social

---

These Interventions first appeared as press releases.

structures is the task of the lay people, among whom are women, an unending treasure of generosity and piety.

The present Synod should send a pressing plea to our Christian elite to get involved in the political and economic, as well as professional organizations and in the diverse associations working for human promotion to breathe into them the evangelic spirit.

Telesphore George Mpundu, Bishop of Mbala-Mpika (Zambia)

The commitment on the part of the Church to promote justice and peace as integral to evangelization in Africa is not a commitment to a project or to a program, but to a way of life. It is a commitment of love that follows upon a conversion to the Gospel of Jesus Christ. Perhaps for too long we Christians have looked upon our mission of evangelizing as a spread of religion rather than a call to conversion. As a consequence, an overly spiritualistic Catholicism has been emphasized, with the issues of justice and peace seen as non-essential to our faith.

Yet we have the clear teaching of the Church that "action on behalf of justice and participation in the transformation of the world . . . (is) constitutive to the preaching of the Gospel" (1971 Synod of Bishops, *Justice in the World*). Truly, without active involvement in justice and peace, we have no evangelization, we have no Christian community.

But do we really believe this and show our belief in the priorities of our ministry of evangelization in Africa today? On this continent we share the Good News of Jesus amidst much that is bad news in terms of human suffering: wars and tribal conflicts, refugees and displaced persons, famines and diseases, hunger and illiteracy, economic failures and political chaos, structures of oppression and violations of human rights.

Our evangelical message must have a transforming impact on these situations of bad news or it simply is not credible Good News for our people!

The justice and peace way of life embraces a spiritual compassion with the suffering, a social solidarity to empower the poor and oppressed, a political effort to change unjust structures and a cultural commitment to non-violence. Such a way of life must be taught beginning with basic catechesis for children and must be central to the Christian formation of adults. It must enter into our celebration of the Eucharist and the Sacraments. It must characterize the attitudes and behavior of our own church institutions.

We know that the commitment to justice and peace as integral to evangelization requires not only word, but also witness. The clear and courageous witness of church officials and church institutions is essential in the promotion of justice. The wages we pay to church workers, our honest accountability in the use of money, our respect for the rights of women, our openness to dialogue and consultation, our priority option for the poor, and so forth, are a few of the justice issues upon which we will be judged and on which our credibility will be assessed.

As chair of the Zambia Episcopal Conference, I can tell you that the Zambian church's clear teaching on justice and peace issues has in the past few years played a major and recognized role in our country during the political transformation to democracy and the economic struggle for development. Yet there still are many Christians, including priests, religious, and lay leaders, who do not accept that the promotion of justice and peace is essential to the task of evangelization. They seem to feel that it is only a hobby or a side-line for those who are not fully engaged in what they would consider to be true pastoral work.

Speaking on behalf of the Zambia Episcopal Conference I, therefore, urge that this African Synod makes very clear in our final statement a re-emphasis on the central place which the promotion of justice and peace must have in our evangelization efforts. At this moment in the history of our continent, we can only echo the words of Paul, "Woe to me if I do not preach the Gospel" (1 Cor. 9:16), a Gospel which includes as a constitutive dimension the commitment to "action on behalf of justice and participation in the transformation of the world."

Medardo Joseph Mozombwe, Bishop of Chipata (Zambia)

Every day Christians throughout the world pray the Lord's Prayer. In some translations, we express some of our deepest human needs by the words: "Forgive us our debts."

This petition has a special profound meaning for Africans, and particularly for us who live in the AMECEA countries, in whose name I make this intervention.

The external debt owed by our African countries south of the Sahara is truly staggering, amounting today to a total of US$185 billion, over 110 percent of our combined gross national product (GNP). The burden of repaying even a modest share of only the interest due on that debt is stifling the fragile economies of our countries, endangering our new democracies and imposing immense hardship on the poor who make up the majority of our people. Without significant relief coming very soon to the problem of managing our debts, we face very little future prospect of effectively improving the lives of our sisters and brothers.

The decade of the 1980s has been described for Africa as a lost decade. Economic indicators such as per capita GNP growth and social indicators such as health and education levels declined over the course of the decade and have not yet begun to improve. Directly related to this decline has been the rapid fall of African countries into the debt trap as these figures dramatically demonstrate: 1980 US$56 billion; 1985 US$98 billion; 1990 US$172 billion; today, an estimated US$185 billion.

The structural adjustment programs proposed (and imposed) by the International Monetary Fund and the World Bank have meant curtailment of government spending on social programs such as health and education, retrenchment in the employed work forces, rapid increases in the price of basic necessities such as mealie-meal, and devaluation of the national currencies.

Our Synod theme of integral evangelization demands that we consider this justice issue of the debt of our African countries. The living out of the Good News that is the coming of the Kingdom of justice and peace is being blocked and undermined by economic injustices that disregard the basic conditions for human dignity and integral human development. Jesus' mission of proclaiming the Good News to the poor is our mission as Church and therefore we must necessarily address the conditions within which the poor are greatly suffering.

The debt problem is not simply an economic issue. It is fundamentally an ethical issue because it is radically a human problem, affecting the well-being of families, the survival of the poor, the bonds of community, and the security of the future. That is why it is an issue that this African Synod cannot ignore. We must speak out clearly and forcefully.

What do we want at this moment? The United Nations reports that the high debt repayment burden, which now consumes about one-third of the continent's total export earnings, "constitutes a large leakage of resources otherwise available for financing growth and development" (Report of Secretary-General Boutros Boutros-Ghali, 2 December 1993). The 1986 statement of the Pontifical Commission for Justice and Peace, "An Ethical Approach to the International Debt Question," emphasizes that "Debt servicing cannot be allowed to strangle a country's economy; no government can morally demand of its people privations incompatible with human dignity."

Paul Bakyenga, Bishop of Mbarara (Uganda)

There are several main areas which the Church should emphasize.

First, there should be an emphasis on the practice and promotion of justice and witnessing to poverty. I refer to the appeal of the Synod of November 1971 on "Justice in the World." Ordained ministers should not only preach justice but also practice it and give witness to a life of poverty and simple living. Africa is crying out for political justice, which future priests should be aware of. A question is raised as to whether the provision of Canon 287 could be applied more in Africa, so that priests could be more active in using legitimate political means to influence society.

Second, there is a need for more involvement and sharing of lay people in the priest's ministry. Would catechists be allowed to administer anointing of the sick, especially as they are nearest to the sick people? Could they also witness at marriages (Can. 1112)?

Third, leadership should be first proven in the local community. The training of priests in the local community and the evaluation of candidates by the local community where they work should be taken seriously. A number of priests are not good leaders and yet they are put at the head of communities and they feel ill at ease. To remedy this, candidates for priesthood should be approved first by the community, before being ordained.

The local community should have an active role in deciding on who should or should not stay in active ministry. The local community, with guidelines of the episcopal conferences, should be allowed to decide on who is or is no longer fit to remain in active ministry, without having to refer to Rome; Rome could then be informed of the decisions of the local churches.

Benedict Dotu Sekey, Bishop of Gbarnga (Liberia)

I speak on behalf of the Liberian bishops, on my own behalf and on behalf of the many Liberians for whom the last four and one-half years have been a nightmare of untold proportions. It is a small attempt to add my voice to what my brother Arch-bishop Francis mentioned a few days ago on the whole notion of justice and peace as found in *Instrumentum Laboris* (IV, 111).

Some of us in this Assembly come from countries torn apart or decimated by tribal and civil wars, from countries where the fruits of efforts made over many decades of evangelization to establish this very Kingdom have collapsed over-night. In their place have emerged institutionalized lies and complete disregard for the sanctity of human life, desecration and massacre, injustice, hatred, and war. In such a situation it is those who are innocent who become easy prey and victims. In such a situation the Church quite often is not spared; its personnel and institutions become targets.

The question often asked in a crisis situation is: What are church leaders doing about the situation? A fair question indeed. When church leaders speak up, they are threatened with public flogging. Again, when they speak up they are told by the mass media to confine themselves to the pulpit and not to get involved in politics, as if one loses the right of citizenship by the mere fact of becoming a church leader. Very often when they speak they are ignored and when things come to a climax people ask: "What are church leaders saying?" Maybe the question should be re-phrased to read: "What are those who are following the church leaders saying?"

The Church is the Body of Christ so when one member of the Body suffers, the rest of the Body suffers too. When the Church in one part of Africa suffers, the rest of the Church in Africa and the universal Church suffers. This is why we feel strongly and appeal to this venerable Synod that wherever there are conflicts in parts of Africa and the Church in those areas is rendered voiceless, the rest of the African Church should speak out with a strong voice of solidarity, communion, support, and solace on behalf of those local churches that are suffering. The voice of the African Church through its national and regional episcopal conferences, together with that of the Holy Father, will be a deterrent to those who take the lives of our people for granted.

In conclusion, the Liberian church is very grateful to the Holy Father for his untiring efforts on behalf of Liberia. We also thank those brother bishops and oth-ers who through their prayers and support eased, even if temporarily, the pain of our people.

16

Forgive Us Our Debts

*Open Letter to Our Brother Bishops
in Europe and North America*

The Bishops of Africa

Dear Brothers in Christ,

Africa is home to hundreds of millions of the poorest people on earth. They are shackled with a burden of unpayable debt, which is both a symptom and a cause of their poverty. It is a symptom because they would not have borrowed if they were not poor; it is a cause because the crushing burden of debt repayments makes them poorer still.

The bishops of Africa taking part in the African Synod pledge ourselves to uncompromising solidarity with the poor and make their cry known: Forgive us our debts. We address our appeal to the bishops and faithful of our sister churches in Europe and America, and in particular to justice and peace commissions and groups. Your churches have supported us faithfully and generously in terms of personnel and finance and we are conscious of an unpayable debt of gratitude. We know that we can continue to depend on your generous support as we appeal to you on behalf of the debts that cripple our people's lives and blight their hope for the future. This debt has become unpayable because of a combination of factors. Some of these factors are internal to Africa and can only be remedied by changes within Africa. Other factors are external to Africa and African governments have no control over them. It is now over a decade since former President Nyerere of Tanzania asked a poignant question: "Must we starve our children to pay our debts?" The Pontifical Commission for Justice and Peace offered a very eloquent answer to this question in its 1986 statement entitled *An Ethical Approach to the International Debt Question.* This document calls for sharing the consequences of the debt crisis between debtors and creditors. It says: "The burden should not fall disproportionately on poor countries . . . it is morally wrong to deprive a nation of the means to meet the basic needs of its people in order to repay debt." Another document of the same commission states, "The needs of the poor take precedence over the wants of the rich."

The right of the Church to intervene in political and economic affairs is limited in any part of the Church. Yet the social teaching of the Church is part of her mandate to go and teach all nations. These are times when justice compels us to speak publicly on these matters. If we remain silent and inactive, whether in Africa or the countries of the North, we may appear as cowards or accomplices rather than as champions of justice. We have the right and duty to enlighten the consciences of the decision-makers. The question of African debt offers an opportunity for the bishops of Africa to work in partnership with their fellow bishops in Europe and America to seek a just and speedy way of resolving it.

For our part in Africa, we pledge ourselves to address the internal factors that contribute to the debt crisis. The Church in Africa has always been a fearless champion of human rights and democracy; we reaffirm our resolve to continue to use non-violent ways to overcome corruption, oppression, and economic mismanagement among our government officials, military, and ruling elite. We ask our sister churches in Europe and America to help to bring about a swift and just resolution of our problem of unpayable debts. This is inextricably linked with unjust conditions of world trade where the price of our commodities has collapsed to an all-time low. It is also related to the urgent need for reform of the structural adjustment programs which cause great suffering among the poor.

We are confident that our appeal will be heeded and provide an opportunity for the Church to make its own the joys and hopes, the sorrows and anguish of suffering people in Africa.

We the undersigned:

Bishop Dennis H. de Jong, Ndola, Zambia
Archbishop Michael K. Francis, Monrovia, Liberia
Archbishop Joseph Henry Ganda, Freetown & Bo, Sierra Leone
Archbishop Lawrence Henry, Cape Town, South Africa
Archbishop Polycarp Pengo, Dar es Salaam, Tanzania
Archbishop Gabriel Zubeir Wako, Khartoum, Sudan
Archbishop Laurent Monsengwo Pasinya, Kisangani, Zaire
Archbishop Charles Vandame, N'Djaména, Chad
Archbishop André-Fernand Anguilé, Libreville, Gabon
Archbishop Emmanuel Wamala, Kampala, Uganda
Archbishop Jean-Marie Cissé, Sikasso, Mali
Archbishop Isidore de Souza, Cotonu, Benin
Archbishop Adam Kozlowiecki, Potenza Picena, Zambia
Bishop Amadeus Mzarikie, Moshi, Tanzania
Bishop Boniface Setlalkgosi, Gaborone, Botswana
Bishop Tarsizio Gabriel Ziyaje, Lilongwe, Malawi
Bishop Gregory Eebolawola Kpiebaya, Wa, Ghana
Bishop Bernard Ratsimamotoana, Morondava, Madagascar

Bishop Paulino do Livramento Evora, Praja, Cape Verde
Bishop Julien K. Mawule Kouto, Atakpamé, Togo
Bishop Théodore-Adrien Sarr, Kaolack, Senegal
Bishop Jean-Baptiste Somé Diébougou, Burkina Faso
Bishop Joseph Edra Ukpo, Ogoja, Nigeria
Bishop Telesphore George Mpundu, Mbala-Mpika, Zambia
Bishop Alberto Setele, Inhambane, Mozambique
Bishop Paul L. Kalanda, Fort-Portal, Uganda
Bishop John O'Riordan, Kenema, Sierra Leone & Gambia
Bishop Bernard Bududira, Bururi, Burundi
Bishop Evaristus Thatho Bitsoane, Qachas'Nek, Lesotho
Bishop Louis Ncamiso Ndeovu, Manzizi, Swaziland
Bishop Francis Xavier Mugadzi, Gweru, Zimbabwe
Bishop Philippe Kourouma, N'Zérékoré, Guinea
Bishop Edouard Mathos, Guifi, Central Africa Republic
Bishop Cornelius Fontem Esua, Kumbo, Cameroon
Bishop Medardo Joseph Mazombwe, Chipata, Zambia
Bishop Antoine Marie Maanicus, Bangassou, Congo
Bishop Francisco João Silota, Chimoio, Mozambique

Rome, April 1994

Part III

Reflections on the African Church and the Synod

17

The Church in Africa Today

Sacrament of Justice, Peace, and Unity

Michael Kpakala Francis

Introduction

In the readings for the feast of the Baptism of our Lord, the Church applies the words of the prophet Isaiah to Jesus Christ:

> Here is my servant whom I shall uphold . . . upon whom I have put my spirit; he shall bring forth justice to the nations . . . a bruised reed he shall not break, and a smoldering wick he shall not quench, until he establishes justice on the earth. I, the Lord, have called you for the victory of justice . . . (Is. 42:1, 3, 4, 6).

The responsorial psalm re-echoes with the response: "The Lord will bless his people with peace." And in the Acts of the Apostles we are admonished by St. Peter:

> I begin to see how true it is that God shows no partiality. Rather, the man of any nation who fears God and acts uprightly is acceptable to him. This is the message he has sent to the sons of Israel, the Good News of peace proclaimed through Jesus Christ who is Lord of all (Acts 10:34-36).

Thus, the mission that Jesus was embarking on included, as an essential element, the attainment of peace and justice for all mankind. As it was the mission of Christ, it continues to be the mission of his Mystical Body, the Church, the People of God.

Justice, peace, and unity are words that sound so strange to us on the continent

---

Michael Kpakala Francis is the archbishop of Monrovia, Liberia. This essay was first published in *Africa: The Kairos of a Synod* (Rome: SEDOS, 1994). Revised and reprinted with permission.

of Africa. The violation of the fundamental rights of the peoples of Africa is a daily occurrence. For nearly thirty-five years the peoples of Africa have suffered so much; our leaders have shown their real and true colors—they do not care about our people but only themselves. The Church in many countries has been the lone voice of sanity. The Church must stand up to the political, social, and moral evils that beset Africa today. The Synod must address itself to the problem of justice, peace, and unity in Africa.

The Liberian Experience

On 14 April 1980, Master Sergeant Doe led a coup d'état against the Tolbert regime. The coup was universally popular, especially among the tribal people. It even had some support among the Americo-Liberians, although it had all the appearance of the natives coming into power and the relegation of the settlers to the background.

The euphoric acceptance of Doe's People's Redemption Council (PRC) did not last long. The excessive, murderous, and atrocious acts perpetrated against the Americo-Liberians disenchanted many people in Liberia and abroad. As the months wore on, the new regime proved to be worse and more detestable than the one it had overthrown. Since the members of the PRC were illiterate, the only concept of government it had was the one it had lived under—a corrupt oligarchy. Corruption was a *modus vivendi*; nepotism, a political virtue; and self-service the ultimate goal. Tribalism caused Doe to rid himself not only of Americo-Liberians but also of native people other than his own ethnic group—the Krahn.

Non-Krahn people were perceived as actual enemies or potential rivals. Personal loyalty to Doe was confused with (if not identified with) patriotism and loyalty to Liberia. Opposition to and criticism of Doe was treason and sedition. Coercion, suppression, and repression flourished during the Doe era. Inevitably and inexorably Doe's government became a Krahn hegemony, much more intensely corrupt, much more repressive and murderous than any preceding government had ever been. In place of the old dichotomy of settler versus native, a new one came on the scene—the Krahn versus everyone else.

The whole conflict has only infinitely intensified the tensions and rivalries among the Liberian peoples. Hatred, deep-rooted animosity, desire for revenge are its legacy. Reconciliation is and will be a difficult task. A whole generation has been deformed. Instead of being nurtured in the highly disciplined cultures of their ethnic groups, inculcating obedience and reverence, our youth have been trained and practiced in arrogance, disregard, and disrespect for persons and human life. They have been exposed to wielding power and authority by the gun, to acquiring wealth by use of the gun. They have been indoctrinated not to hesitate to use the gun to kill. Schooled to be remorseless, they have become caricatures of human beings. Many are severely traumatized by the horrors they have witnessed and the horrors they have perpetrated. They are now young adults, asocial and antisocial people with no academic learning, no vocational skills, and who are utterly incapable of fitting gainfully into society. They are the potentially criminal components of post-war Liberia.

The Local Church and the Civil War

The Church has suffered very much by the deaths of many of her personnel, by the destruction of her institutions, and the displacement of her flocks. We, the pastors, have suffered physically and mentally at seeing brothers and sisters fighting each other. But what is most painful is the destruction of a whole generation of young boys and girls by warlords.

The Church, in spite of all the suffering she has undergone and is still undergoing, has tried to speak out against injustice and the violation of the rights of our people, to create an atmosphere for some normalcy in the country, and to rebuild our institutions and render pastoral, educational and medical care to our flocks and others. Though peace has not been achieved as yet, the process is irreversible.

In many ways the Liberian experience is a microcosm of what has happened throughout sub-Saharan Africa. In Liberia the overthrow of the Americo-Liberian hegemony unleashed hidden and unsuspected forces. We lived in a dream world with unrealistic, idyllic images of ourselves as kindly, peace-loving, and brotherly Africans. In somewhat the same way other countries emerged from the overlordship of their colonial masters only to become embroiled in more complex, more deep-rooted, and less soluble problems and hostilities that characterized their conflicts with the colonial powers.

The African Experience

The African Way of Life

It is true that a basic and common insight among us Africans in regard to man is that he exists and is what and who he is by reason of birth, and birth from a definite pair of parents, therefore deriving from and belonging to a nuclear family and an extended family. Of all our surrounding environment, the most outstanding and intriguing object for us is the human person. And the immediate, fundamental, overpowering observation about man is that in order to be, he is born. A very close link exists here between existing and being born, between being real and being alive, between life and reality. So we easily pass into animism.

Coming back to man, the social aspect in his regard predominates over the individualistic aspect. A man exists as a person, naturally and necessarily enmeshed in a web of relationships. His very existence, his reality is bound up in those relationships. These relationships provide the most prolific, the most profound, the most intense sources of motivation for living and for action. The Kantian categorical imperative finds no resonances in our African psyche. Cold, legalistic enumerations of abstractly conceived duties pale in comparison with the stimulation to performing or omitting actions, to accounting acts good or bad, which stems from the commitments inherent in relationships. So it is that morality, humaneness, tender and compassionate feelings are largely co-terminal with relationships.

Beyond the perimeters of these relationships, the sense of obligation toward another is scarcely perceived. The existence of rights or claims inherent in another upon oneself are not strongly experienced, nor acknowledged apart from relationships. There exists in our culture the very lofty concepts of human dignity and of the respect and obligations due to the human person. A man is perceived as good in proportion to his loyalty to these relationships and to his meticulous fidelity in acquitting himself of all the ensuing requirements.

The relationships extend beyond the nuclear family; they include the extended family, the quarter, the clan, and the tribe. But beyond that they dim and fade out completely. So there are limits to the relationship. The lofty ideals of humane and just conduct have a certain intra-group limitation. Furthermore, in the past the subsistent economies, the labor-intensive processes of agriculture, the cohesive lifestyles of mutual interdependence within the ethnic societies served to enhance customs of brotherliness experienced and confined within definite demographic boundaries. They inhibited the opportunities for greed, wealth, power, and prestige. Individual and group competition and rivalries were held to a minimum. It would not be an exaggeration to say that a stifling conservatism marked these ethnic societies in every way and from every point of view. But a chain is only as strong as its weakest link. When all the links held firm and strong a deceptive peace prevailed; when anyone gave way even the most sacred parts of the whole began to collapse.

Africa after World War II

Changing circumstances affected African countries in the aftermath of World War II. Independence movements gained momentum. Increased communication and actual contact with other parts of the world disturbed the relative isolation of even the remotest parts of the continent. The desire for a higher standard of living and for more widespread education came to the continent. The awareness of their country's natural resources developed among the masses; the exploitation of these by outside forces, together with a small minority of their own compatriots, aroused indignation. Outside entrepreneurs and a few within the country became wealthy at the expense of the mass of the population.

The attractions of socialism for a more equitable distribution of the developing wealth aroused the economic, sociological and political consciousness of ever increasing numbers of the population. The university and high school students became intensely conscientized and transmitted their concerns, their zeal, and enthusiasm to the ordinary villagers. The potential for wealth became a real, recognized, and stimulating influence. Socialism, with its attendant division of the world into two major power blocs, involved the African countries in high-powered internal politics and external world movements and confrontations. All these had an undermining effect on the African way of life. They stimulated a trend toward individualism, toward acquiring personal wealth and position, toward a progressive development upwards in the standard of living, toward the achievement and wielding of political power at national level. The old values became somewhat irrelevant, inadequate, and anachronistic in the engendered excitement. They came to be experienced as shackles holding down the nation and the individual, keeping them backward.

Aggressiveness, self-assertion, and arrogance replaced the cherished attitudes and etiquette of the old conservative societies. Maintaining the status quo, ideals of mutual help, knowing one's place and keeping to it, pride of family and concern for the preservation of prestige deriving from one's family rather than from one's own egoism, devotion and service to family members, especially at the cost of self-sacrifice, these fell into disregard and desuetude.

The amalgamation of a multiplicity of ethnic groups in these modern states intensified the quest for power and domination at the social level. Thus the dimension of new ethnic rivalries came on the scene. This was a rivalry of intense intra-ethnic loyalty with fierce, hostile competition between groups for the exercise of political power and the control of economic advantages. Thus the deep-rooted motivations for living and action that were temporarily in abeyance began to exert their influence again. The dynamics of the web of intra-group relationships reasserted itself in the functioning of the new governments. A switch was made from simple, subsistent societies to more complex, pluralistic, wealth-producing states without any change in attitudes, procedures, or goals. Notions of distributive justice and the common good never surfaced to consciousness.

Political and Social Cultures

African societies were attempting a leap from personalistic structures to societies based more on abstract principles and concepts. To date the attempts have not been successful. For example, the distinction between a person and the office he holds is not readily grasped or acknowledged. This fusion of the person with the office makes the temporary tenure of office not fully comprehensible, not necessarily required by the population, and not at all acceptable to the office holder. Naturally then, an identification of law with the arbitrary decisions of the one in power is almost instinctively accepted by both ruler and ruled. The governor and the governed tend to think in terms of absolutism, with all its attendant consequences. Constitutional and legal restrictions in the competence of office-holders are a stumbling block. Also, those higher-up on the hierarchial ladder subsume all the rights and authority and competency in all departments, even as regards the most minute details. The principle of subsidiarity scarcely functions at all.

The rule of law has not as yet taken root in the African political consciousness. It is intellectually known and understood, but its operation in practice is almost entirely frustrated. Exceptions to the law and modifications and mitigation of laws for personal reasons are quite common in political administration. Claiming privileges is a very pervasive feature of public life. The majesty of the law is acknowledged, for the most part, only when the selfish purposes of the law-enforcer are thereby served.

Worst of all, probably, this neglect of the principle of subsidiarity obliterates the lines of demarcation between the branches of government. The head of state becomes an absolute dictator, even though sometimes a benign one. In the executive, judicial, and legislative branches of government he becomes surrounded by a welter of sycophantic yes-men. Their positions have been denuded of real responsibility; they are constrained to accept their diminished and undignified roles or lose their positions. Their loyalty to party leaders, policies, and state officials is very superficial and very susceptible to change. Endurance in office for reasons of power and greed becomes paramount once an individual and his clique attain office. Politicians become hypocritical self-servers. Opposition is not and cannot be tolerated. It is equivalent to treason and sedition on the one hand, and personal envy, rivalry, and hostility on the other.

Governments become entrenched, a law unto themselves; suppression, oppression, and exploitation become the order of the day, even the main preoccupation of governments. Human rights vanish; they inhibit the selfish advantages of the ruling hegemony.

Human Rights

The infringement of human rights causes no embarrassment to the offenders; it can even endear the offender to the members of his own ethnic group or political clique. Society as a whole tends to accept this situation passively and is loathe or fearful to raise a finger in protest. In fact, fear is not the most frequent, nor the most persuasive motive for this passivity. It is rather the realization that there is greater value in accepting the system and becoming an expert manipulator of it. Flattery, feigning relationships of friendship, hypocrisy, undermining others are part of the technique of manipulation. Corruption becomes endemic; injustices of all kinds afflict the whole population in their persons and in their economic conditions. Crises keep mounting, dissatisfaction keeps intensifying, and there is no remedy at hand except a violent overthrow of the existing junta. The volcano erupts and the lava flows, wreaking destruction on people and property alike. And the pattern continues under new rulers.

Thus all over the continent dictators strive to preserve their domains, to the resentment of the vast majority of the citizens. Ethnic groups are locked in fatal opposition to each other; in the inevitable violent clashes, atrocities abound on all sides. Hatred dominates the minds and hearts of individuals and of entire communities. The situation is paradoxical. From cultures that enshrine appreciable values of human personhood, personal dignity, brotherhood, hospitality, and kindness there is emerging a continent of continual strife, heinous atrocities, uprooted refugee populations, starvation, utter poverty, and various other forms of human degradation.

The absence of profound reflection within African societies on what is happening to them, on the larger-than-life movements that are enveloping them, is a serious contributing cause to the perdurance of the chaotic state of affairs. There is no serious effort to identify the origin or source of the malady; much less does there exist a political will to eradicate the disease. Groups tend to use slogans culled from political science treatises, but they seem used only as rhetorical weapons in an effort to attain power, and they do not seem to be thoroughly understood or committed convictions.

Once a group gains power, a confusion in regard to political office takes over, a confusion resulting from an inadequate correlation and adjustment between cultural political processes and the requirements of a modern pluralistic, economically developing, complex state. A viable, sound, and just political philosophy for the modern state has not yet been worked out reflectively by us Africans. Or, in other words, the political philosophy of democracy has not as yet become inculturated in Africa. This is the tragic state of affairs in Africa at the close of the second millennium and the beginning of the third.

As it appears to me, our African societies are suffering from imperfection and incompleteness as to intellectual insights and volitional fortitude. It is not a question of abysmal ignorance nor a total lack of wholesome dispositions. Rather, Africans are faced with moving from military dictatorships to democracy without adequate preparation to undertake the necessary discipline and hardships. The African way of life presents the Church with an ideal instance for building the supernatural on the natural. She can provide that deepening and prolongation of insights for completing and perfecting an already appreciable system of values. This is an urgently experienced need in Africa today, already embarked on an irreversible movement toward modern nation statehood.

We in Africa are at fault in that our view of man's social nature and consequent commitments is limited to biological relationships and maybe a little beyond. Where the biological basis for relationship is not palpably obvious, we tend to ignore the possibility or even deny any relationship. We are somewhat blind to the unity of the whole human race. Not adverting to the individual status of each person, that he is a total, complete, entire, separate entity apart from his family, we fail to recognize the basic similarity of nature, the similarity in dignity, and the equality of all humans. We fail to recognize that the relationship sets up bonds and interpersonal obligations precisely because it establishes similar individuals, with similar claims to respect and not because of relationship alone.

We are also inexperienced both in theory and practice with regard to property, wealth, and the use and acquisition of material things. Our experience is limited and our view is confined to a system of inter-dependence, exclusively. Without the opportunity for improvement in our economic conditions we have neglected to develop a thorough and sound socio-economic philosophy. When, with the changed circumstances, the opportunity arises to acquire wealth, to improve the standard of living, we find ourselves without a guiding system, especially from the point of view of morality. We find ourselves abandoned to the untrammeled lure of material possessions.

Thus a greed that is absent at our subsistent level of living becomes glaringly and unjustly operative in the more affluent situation. To become rich at all costs, brooking no restraint, becomes the all-absorbing ambition of those who get the slightest exposure to the wider horizons. There is no concern for the morality of the methods of acquiring wealth; there is no respect for the rights of private ownership; and when one acquires wealth or property there is no acceptance of obligations and responsibilities attached thereto. Thieving, embezzlement and wholesale misappropriation of the national treasury, bribery, extortion, and exploitation have become part of our African way of life.

In short, the value of the African preoccupation with the social, relational aspect of man has to be acknowledged. But, likewise, its imperfections have to be taken into account. This working out of the correct balance of the social and individualistic concerns is a top priority for us Africans, at both theoretical and practical levels.

To summarize, the African experience during the last three decades and more is one of suffering. There is hardly a country that has been or is an exception to this suffering of our people, the suffering perpetrated by men and women who in one way or another govern us.

The Church as Sacrament of Justice and Peace

Fortunately, at this point in time, the Church occupies a position of respected moral influence throughout most of developing Africa. This gives the Church the opportunity to speak out, to assume leadership in the public forum for the eradication of injustice and hatred in the community.

The African Church, through her continental body, the Symposium of Episcopal Conferences of Africa and Madagascar (SECAM), or regional or national conferences or through individual bishops has from time to time called the attention of the powers that be to the inhumane situation that has existed and still exists in nearly all our countries. At its meeting in Kinshasa from July 15-22, 1984, ten years ago, SECAM issued a pastoral exhortation entitled "The Church and Human Promotion in Africa Today," which summarized the situation in Africa at that time and proposed ways of remedying it.

At a meeting in Kampala in 1969 we brought out a similar cry of anguish:

The problem of greatest priority of our times is the struggle for the development of peoples and for peace. The bishops of Africa and Madagascar would be failing in their mission if they were to ignore poverty, hunger, sickness, ignorance, the undermining of liberty, the tragic consequences of racial discrimination and the ravages of war and oppression which overwhelm so many of our fellow human beings in the Third World.

We have come back to this subject on several occasions to emphasize its urgency and gravity for Africa. As evidence of this we can cite other statements issued by the Church:

1. Declaration on Peace in Africa
2. Declaration on the Violation of Human Rights
3. Declaration on Justice and Peace
4. Co-responsible Evangelization
5. Declaration on Respect and Promotion of Human Life
6. Exhortation addressed to all apostolic workers on Justice and Evangelization in Africa
7. The decision to organize a Pan-African Conference on Justice and Peace.

In terms of declarations and exhortations, in terms of informing the African

Church of the situations existing at any given time in Africa, the bishops of Africa have carried out their mission; but unfortunately, all their good declarations and exhortations have not had entirely the desired effect for reasons I shall outline later on.

The Church has a very significant contribution to make to this ongoing African process. The Church has always taught the basic unity of the whole human race. She proclaims that all humans are made in the image and likeness of God, and in a very unique and noble way; all are children of God, and so the respect and regard due to the human person must not be determined or limited to human, biological parentage. This natural equality and unity within the race is infinitely enhanced by the redemption and the mystery of the incarnation. For, by his incarnation and his work of redemption, Christ has given us a participation in his divine nature. So, an infinitely more profound and pervasive similarity and unity is shared in and extended potentially to the whole human race.

Under the new headship of Christ we are all bound by infinitely closer links than those which we derive from biological origin. We are committed to ever stronger obligations to each other in terms of justice, respect, and love. The very nature and function of the Mystical Body of the People of God brings about this higher unity, this superior fraternity of man. This functioning requires that it be facilitated and explicated in the life and activities of the Church. In her evangelization it must be clearly preached and taught by the Church. Human minds and hearts need to be prepared for the fluctuation of the graces of redemption. In all her works and at all times the Church must be constantly reaching out to every nook and cranny of the world and be seen to be seeking to encompass all mankind in a community of love. The Church must always be seen to be the champion of the poor, the oppressed, and the down-trodden. The Church must make manifest that her charter and *raison d'être* derive from the Sermon on the Mount. She must make her members realize that "in Christ there is neither Jew nor Gentile." In these ways the Church will be functioning as the sacrament of justice, peace, and unity.

The Church can do much by enriching and enhancing the catechesis of her own members, developing a highly Christianized conscientization among them. The prospect of a more inculturated program of evangelization holds forth the promise and the hope of striking a more responsive chord in the African psyche.

Such a theology and spirituality, which fits in with our African mentality, is eminently Johannine. The discourse of our Lord to his disciples at the Last Supper narrated in St. John's gospel is very meaningful to us. It is steeped in the fatherhood of God, the unity and intimacy between the Father and the Son, obedience of the Son to the Father, the unity between Christ and his disciples, and the unity that must prevail among the disciples. "Be you perfect as your Heavenly Father is perfect"; "Love one another as I have loved you"; "If you love me, keep my commandments."

In this context, faith is not simply the acceptance of a proposition that may be the matrix of a series of commandments and prohibitions. Faith involves a commitment to a person, a vital union with a person from which there issues forth vital acts perfective of the person and of the union. They proceed from an inwardly experienced necessity that may or may not be already articulated in verbally expressed commands.

The life of the Christian is far richer than mere compliance with a set of decrees and laws. Union with Christ is the source of activity, and a more perfect union with Christ is the goal. It is vital activity in which the organism achieves and experiences its greatest perfection. This union with Christ involves a union with all other human beings who are either actually united with Christ through baptism or potentially united with him in virtue of the universal salvific will of God, manifested in the incarnation. Thus the desire to love and serve is directed to all mankind; it is universal, transcending all human boundaries.

Such a theology and spirituality of personal relationships is not without its dangers. Anthropomorphism on the one hand and animism on the other are extreme instances. It could also lapse easily into a religion of one-sided expectations from God and his Church and overplay the demand for the healing ministry. It could degenerate into a self-serving type of religion with no place for the disciplined self-sacrificial service of God and neighbor. Besides, the human condition being what it is, the question put to Jesus will constantly arise and will constantly have to be answered, "And who is my neighbor?"

While taking the necessary precautions to avoid any distortion of Christianity, it is obvious that only through some such inculturated approach to evangelization, to preaching the Good News, that a transformation of African thought and life-style will be accomplished. It is hoped that with renewed and inculturated evangelization the impact of the gospel in the areas of justice and peace will make itself manifest in the dealings of governments with their people and in the dealings of individual with individual. Our hope rests on a vigorous, courageous, fearless, consistent, inculturated proclamation of the Good News of the gospel.

It is one thing to tell our flocks what the problem is and what the seeming solutions are and another thing to be seen implementing these decisions. It seems to me that the Church in Africa has failed to be a leaven of justice, peace, and unity on our continent. In many African countries the Church in the past has not spoken up against the violations of the fundamental rights of its people. Some of us have either directly or indirectly encouraged despots in our countries, and individuals have collaborated with the powers that be in a way that has compromised them.

It must be noted, however that many bishops' conferences are addressing themselves to the problems that exist in their respective countries with fortitude and courage, regardless of the consequences. We had hoped that this would have been the case long ago, but better late than never.

Challenges Facing the Church

The Church in Africa needs to face these main challenges:

1. To contribute to the eradication of the negative aspects of tribalism: to contribute to the eradication of endemic corruption.

2. To stimulate, even in the wider community, intellectual inquiry into the nature

and destiny of man; to promote a thorough and complete appreciation of human rights; to bring about a correct understanding of political authority, its origin, purpose, and limitations; and to promote a sound philosophy of law and the rule of law.

3. To insert the Scriptures and a theological viewpoint into the ongoing national dialogue and debate.

4. To live up to her reality as a public institution possessed of a depth and breadth of information from revelation and from centuries of accumulated experience. To enter the public forum, fearlessly and unapologetically, never shrinking to being a private club of esoteric, eccentric believers. Always to project the image of an institution that is accredited from on high, with a message for the world and to transform the world.

Tasks that the Church should undertake to meet these challenges include:

1. making the social teaching of the Magisterium more available to the Christian people;

2. promoting the social responsibility of Christians and their full participation in public life;

3. catering to the new poor no longer catered for by the sagging extended family system;

4. networking and developing new strategies to respond to new situations of injustice and oppression in the world order;

5. using the moral weight of the Churches in bringing to a halt the situations of war in many places in Africa;

6. responding to the disarray in the fields of education and health;

7. taking initiatives in the promotion of the North-South dialogue; and

8. promoting the African women—transforming cultural and religious prejudices, new situations.

The Synod as Motive

The Synod bears testimony to the successes and failures, to the strengths and weaknesses of the Church in Africa: by highlighting the strengths the Synod will give added impetus to renewed evangelization; by giving serious reflective and penetrating consideration to the weaknesses, the Synod will develop a blueprint for the forms and procedures of the renewed evangelization.

Consideration must be given to the knowledge and evaluation of the African cultures lest our cultural influences distort the Christian message; but, more principally, in order that an inculturated presentation of the gospel may develop a richer, a more realistic, authentic, and life-influencing African Christianity. We must work toward a thorough Christian way of life, brilliant with the positive influences and contributions of African vitality.

Conclusions

In this paper we have endeavored to bring to the fore the problems of justice, peace, and unity as we see these on our continent. We have stated that the Church has responded, at least in her exhortations and declarations, but unfortunately the follow-up has been poor. We suggest the following for the discussion in the Synod:

1. The Synod must articulate in clear terms the Church's position on the violation of the fundamental rights of the African people, regardless of the consequences.

2. The Synod must condemn in no uncertain terms the treatment of our people, especially those who are suffering for religious reasons.

3. The Synod should reflect on the cooperation and non-cooperation of the African churches with regimes that are suppressive and oppressive to their people.

4. The Synod should state in its documents what the position of the local churches should be when faced with dictators.

5. The Church should be an example of justice, peace, and unity in her own institutions and life style. Those of us who shepherd our flock should be models of virtue, never giving the powers that be any chance to frustrate the work of Christ by blackmailing us.

6. The Church should be concerned with the whole person.

7. The Church should be a sacrament of unity, peace, and justice.

May true peace, justice, and unity reign in Africa.

18

The Church—Sacrament of Liberation

Jean-Marc Éla

I want to share my experience, my questions, and my attempts at reflection in order to learn to what extent the Church is called to become truly the sacrament of justice and liberation in Africa today. I would like to talk together, in African style, using several points of reference and taking time for an in-depth discussion of the questions that arise. First, I would like to consider the context in which this symposium is taking place. Next, I will introduce some conditions that oblige the Church to reexamine her positions in order to redefine herself for the third millennium. And, finally, I would like to ask whether, in order to be this sacrament of justice and liberation in Africa, the Church would not find it in her best interests to restore and renew the ministry of the theologian, or if you prefer, the teaching office of the Church.

Displacement of the Center of Gravity of Christianity

In order to understand our present situation, we must realize that, at the present time, we are in the midst of a great movement for change. In order to see how the Church will try to deal with it, we must first try to understand it. We are witnessing a displacement of the center of gravity of Christianity, which is moving from the center toward the South and, principally, toward Africa. For the Church, the African continent certainly plays a considerable role in this great movement toward the South. One might well ask whether this might not be, in a certain sense, a farewell to the West.

Jean-Marc Éla, a Cameroonian Jesuit theologian and sociologist, is the author of several books. He is a member of the faculty at the University of Yaoundé, Cameroon. He presented this paper at the symposium "Africa: The Kairos of a Synod," sponsored by SEDOS (Servizio di documenatzione e studi), Pax Christi, AFJN, and IDOC, and held in Rome at the time of the Synod.

I made this discovery while reading *The Coming of the Third Church*, written by missiologist Walter Buhlmann in 1978: "Our generation is experiencing the migration of the Church toward the Southern Hemisphere, of the displacement of the center of the Church toward the Third Church."

It is certain that Africa plays a considerable role in this movement, to the point where we could ask, "Is Africa not called today to become the new homeland of Christ?" When Pius XII, in his encyclical *Fidei Donum* drew the attention of the Catholic Church to the African continent, he had the clear insight that something was taking place there and that in order to think of the future of Christianity, it would be necessary henceforth to turn toward Africa. This is something that has happened and continues to happen. It is something that we must observe and consider carefully in order to understand the serious questions to which we must respond today.

A second observation is also verifiable. Since the last thirty or thirty-four years, we Africans have increasingly the feeling that our continent is no longer a stake or a pawn for the world powers. For them, Africa has ceased to matter. A new world order has moved into place, primarily since the breakdown of communism and the victory of capitalism, which has now become the sole model, with disastrous consequences in Africa. This new world order centers on the mechanisms of money, and in most of the regions of Africa, we are its direct victims.

No Longer Part of This World

On the one hand, we must acknowledge the powerlessness of socio-political projects that have not succeeded in finding concrete or credible answers to the vital questions and the great hopes of new African generations. On the other hand, it is true that we are witnessing the failure of all the models of development that have been imposed on us by the experts, to the degree that we are engulfed more and more in situations of suffering.

I feel that the most serious issue at the present time is that our African people risk crossing the dividing line between the material poverty of the Third World and that of total exclusion from consideration. From one point of view, we could say that today there is no longer a Third World. We are no longer "part of this world" to the extent that we no longer have any possibility for taking initiative or for making decisions in what concerns us. In large part, we are excluded from the great decisions around which the future of the world is planned and prepared. Today in Africa it seems that one could ask if there were not a certain number of peoples or states that are no longer needed on the geo-political and economic map of humanity.

The African Church and Liberation

What is certain, as was pointed out in the February 1994 issue of *Jeune Afrique*, is that we Africans are poorer than ever. And we have no problem in recognizing this fact. The outbreak of poverty is truly a public challenge hurled at Africa on the eve of the third millennium; the challenge comes from the poverty of the masses surrounding several islands of wealth. The challenge comes from the multitude oppressed by a small band of the elite that controls all the power. In this context the African people must cruelly submit all aspects of their lives to the programs of structural adjustment imposed by the international organizations. These organizations control their daily existence and even how they should live their relationship with God!

Not long ago, in a section of Yaoundé, a young woman said to me, "You want to go to Rome? What did the Pope say when they devalued the CFA franc?" I said to her, "Ask him." These are the realities with which we live at the present and which concern our relationship to God in the Church. This is why we should study how to take up the challenge, knowing that Africa calls upon the Christian conscience at a time when we are witnessing a renewal of structures of domination, and knowing that in spite of several declarations in principle for democracy, there is within our societies a return to dictatorships and a programmed recolonization of the continent. Are Africans aware that the abbreviation of the International Monetary Fund signifies Imperialism, Misery, and Famine? That is why the African continent appears to me today like an incontrovertible paradigm.

Because of our situation, Africa must be perceived at its heart to be one of the privileged poles of liberation. That is to say, one of the principle places where God will speak to the Church and to humanity.

What Have You Done to Your Brother?

The old question, "What have you done to your brother?" has been asked since the time of creation. This question probes deeper than ever into the very heart of our relationships with the rest of humanity. It is this question that we, in turn, are trying to ask when we place ourselves at the heart of our history, a history of suffering of entire nations, throughout the drama of colonization, of slavery, and of what I am calling a "high programmed" colonization of these later years.

We are tempted to ask how we truly can celebrate God in a world of oppression. How can we sing to the Lord in a world where we are without feeling? How do we announce the Lord of life to millions of men and women confined to situations of death, knowing that what kills in Africa is really the mechanism of poverty and oppression? If more and more people die in our African societies, it is because poverty is instituted in a structural manner. The IMF and the World Bank—as we know only too well—are not benevolent societies. To pay back those foreign debts (and we need to ask what these funds are being used for), we sacrifice the health of Africans and we must block all desire among the young for education. We must put aside all efforts to enter into modernity with more than just the wisdom of our fathers and all possibilities to appropriate technology and theory that would permit us to be really efficacious and operative in the direction of our lives and of our time.

These problems are serious. Because of our situation we must deepen our relationship with Jesus Christ. What does it mean to be Church in Africa today when we know that the Body of Christ, as it says in the canticle, is composed of "the sorrows of men crushed by injustice"?

The very focus of our reflection must be the African world where a great wind of liberation is blowing. We have to confront an Africa who wants to be freed from all forms of alienation. It is to that Africa that we must try to say the name of Jesus Christ. That is possible, in my opinion, only if the Church is truly the sacrament of justice and liberation.

It seems to me that only a Church which considers her duty to be the total liberation of the African will have meaning for tomorrow's generation of Africans. In looking back on the evangelization of our continent, we realize that the first evangelization preached a partial and incomplete gospel that centered uniquely on the salvation of souls and liberation from sin. The rest, all the consequences of sin in the world, in society, and in the institutions of human and social structures, was abandoned to secular powers, or, if you prefer, to charitable associations. They have neglected the important Gospel message of a total and integral salvation. The Church has come to us from outside, emanating from the dominant world at the center of a history of power and domination. Our exposure to this colonial Christianity has also exposed us to risks (and dangers) that we can verify.

What we are looking for today is a Church that is conscious of itself, a Church that begins with the world of the poor of our continent, of peoples, marginalized cultures, societies despised and in decline. It is necessary to reconsider the nature of the Church to see if it takes into account the situation of people in rags, people who are confined to a sort of geo-political and economic apartheid. This is the root of the problem. It is a question for the Church. The Church must initiate a radical rupture with the history of suffering, oppression, and exclusion; it must recognize that more than ever God's gambling stake is found outside the temple, in the sections of villages, in homes where the daily lives of men, women, and the young are a true calvary.

The Role of Faith Incarnate

We must understand that faith can no longer be proposed or lived on the fringes of the realities of life or in projects of society that call for the domination of some groups. It may be necessary to break with the Church of the Levites, the Church that passed by the man fallen into the hands of brigands. We Africans are in search of a Church that involves herself more and more with concrete questions, a Church that places in evidence the socio-political and economic dimensions of the goodness of liberation in Jesus Christ. In order to enter into the third millennium, the Church in Africa must resolutely leave the world of the Counter-Reformation, founded on the primary pillars of sin, grace, and the sacraments. In order to bring alive the memory of Jesus Christ, the Church must start with the hopes and struggles of those who refuse defeat and aspire to a new humanity. The Church must manifest its gospel foundations and nature where the poor and humble seek to remake their history by reversing the established order. We need to reappropriate the gospel of the Magnificat and call for our churches to return to the chant of Mary.

Throughout Mary's canticle, which we recite in our religious office without perhaps recognizing its real significance, God promises to overturn the powerful on their thrones and to lift up the humble. And for this it is necessary to detach oneself from all sorts of base compromises. We must rediscover the liberty of the gospel and the audacity of our faith in order to prepare for the birth of the Church of the third millennium. We must experience the gospel beginning with the "world outside," that real situation of our people. Second, we must hear again the appeal for in-depth conversion and renewal so we can place ourselves in a new school of faith and mission and so we can know how to be church in the midst of violence and torture. We must not let the dynamism of our faith exhaust itself through acts of worship.

Priorities of Mission

We must avoid casting our Church in Africa in a pious role; instead we should redefine the priorities of mission. I do not believe this is a departure from Catholic teaching, for several years ago before ordaining seminarians in Poland the Holy Father said to them: "You serve the dignity of man and his liberation, for the priesthood is a social sacrament" (*La Croix*, May 1, 1987).

Faced with tasks that challenge us, it seems to me that it is necessary to permit the Church in Africa to run the risk of being truly the Church of Christ, knowing that it has a specific mission. It is necessary to let this Church live, for the transformation of the world is a challenge to the Christian faith. Looking toward the year 2000, the Church must grow toward the totality of the creative initiatives and gospel practices that seek the socio-economic liberation of millions of men and women whose situation of economic, political, and social oppression is intolerable.

Given this perspective, we must insist on the necessity to rediscover the totality of liberation in a context both socio-economic and religious. This was stated after the Synod of Rome in 1971 and in the letter of Paul VI, *Evangelization in the Modern World*: "Churches must take into consideration the social dimensions of the Kingdom of God." The integral liberation of human persons will reveal that the signs and the seeds of a new world are inscribed in our African condition, a new world where there will be neither suffering nor crying, as it says in the Apocalypse.

To remake human beings in their totality according to the gospel is a project that God entrusts to the Church at the close of this century. In this moment, Africa is the place on the earth where creation groans loudest while waiting for its deliverance. This is why, in order to practice its ministries of justice and liberation, the church in Africa must really take upon itself the groaning of creation on African soil. This is how we shall become messengers of hope for many people who live in the expectation of the Messiah-Savior. As the Archbishop of Lumbashi remarked several years ago, "Our Church must achieve a real descent into hell. This means that we must carry the power of the cross of Jesus Christ to the heart of our society." In our reflections and our experience of faith, we need to return to the foot of the cross. We know that Christ has completely transformed our relationship with the world and with history. From an instrument of humiliation he has made an instrument of struggle for life that will triumph against the forces of death in the very atmosphere of the universe.

To Restore the Ministry of Theologian

In order to manifest the victorious power of the cross in Africa, I would like to insist on the need to restore and renew the ministry of theologian. I do not see how we can define a global point of view on evangelization in Africa without first listening to what the Spirit is saying to our communities. At the heart of our communities, men, women, youth, bishops, and religious are striving to reread the gospel.

We cannot receive our solutions from the exterior or from on high. How can there be a sector of the Church that claims sole possession of the truth and is content to give lessons to others? I think that the Church today must situate itself in the logic of this migration toward the South where one perceives that the future of the Church of tomorrow will be born. The Church must take note of this change and seek to understand itself through the problems and searching of the South. The Church must allow itself to develop in other areas in the South; this is where the future of the Church lies.

In order to try to rethink the mission of the Church, we must, as the French poet Paul Valéry said, try to turn ourselves "toward those who prophesy what the next day will be." It is certain that we will find the future of Christianity in Africa. We are the people of the future for God, for the Church of Christ. We must admit the reality, the existence, and the vitality of these churches. Catholicism has strengthened itself among us during the course of the last ten years, through research, the experiences of our pastors, theologians, small Christian communities, involved lay persons, and the young. It has started with our own experience, our struggles and the anguish of our brothers and sisters in a society where we feel ourselves really capable of sharing their lot. We must consider all this in order to speak for the Church—of God, of mission, or of evangelization. We need to realize that it is not possible to determine what the Church is in Africa or what the Church should be in the third millennium by clinging only to the general documents of the universal Church, as if nothing had been said or had happened in Africa.

Liberating Christianity

It seems to me that the Church needs to seriously consider the role of our five hundred bishops who are organized on both continental and regional levels. They have been a determining factor in the course of these last decades, not only in questions of inculturation, but also in problems of justice and liberation. One cannot lightly dismiss their contributions toward the mission of evangelization.

For more than twenty years many men and women have been dedicated to the development of an African and liberating Christianity. On the eve of Vatican II, well in advance of our brothers and sisters in Latin America, we were already involved in embracing liberation in the depths of our souls and in freeing those moving toward independence from all sorts of alienation. We thought that the entry of

Africa on the international scene would signify a resolute involvement to decolonize the Church as well. It seemed to me that we had to move from assistance to liberation. When the bishops assembled in Nairobi in 1989 they spoke quite precisely:

> Bishops of Catholic communities of all Africa and Madagascar, we would betray our mission and we would fail gravely in the love and service which we owe to the men of this land if we remain silent in the face of all these situations. For us, what is at stake in actual fact is man himself, whatever may be the color of his skin, his ethnicity, his social condition, his cultural and religious world.

Christ came to save and free humankind, their hopes, their aspirations, their struggles and sufferings, their successes and failures. Total liberation concerns man in all the dimensions of his being, of his existence. This liberation involves not only the spiritual and interior order, it has a direct effect on actual life, individually and collectively.

Christ liberated all men and all of man. In him and through him all have become fundamentally equal. We are each other's brothers. This is why the liberation of one man signifies "decolonization, development, social justice, respect for the inalienable and fundamental liberty of each person." I came across this text by chance when I was in Dar es Salaam in 1981.

I asked myself why such a text had not been able to bring about the radical decisions needed to bring about credible evangelization in Africa. The text certainly responds to our question of "What liberation?" and "For what Africa?"

What is remarkable is that throughout these last decades Christians—the laity as well as theologians and pastors throughout the religious world—have lived to some extent in a great communion around some of these fundamental choices. It is not necessary to invoke the famous text of Nyerere, who reminded us in 1970 that the Christian faith is a revolutionary faith. This text seemed to me to be a bearer of the future; it agrees completely with recent declarations of a group of laity who addressed the Holy Father in an open letter using these words:

> Holy Father, we have been made subject to and colonized by Lisbon, London and Paris; now we are brutalized by Washington and by the anonymous power in New York and Geneva. In spite of all that, the promise of total liberation brought by Christ has taken root in our hearts. Is this promise now going to fade and dry up under the severe and indifferent glance of the Church, which acts more like a master than a mother? (See page 66 above).

At this time all the African churches must in conscience profoundly reexamine themselves because they confront questions of the future. As SECAM reminded us in 1984, we need to reexamine our answer to the question: How will the Church contribute to the promotion of peoples who have been long oppressed by the dominations of sex, race, or class? This question requires a reconversion, a reorientation of the whole pastoral process, in order that in all the activities and occupations of its members the Church can appear truly as the sacrament of salvation, a sign that manifests and actualizes at the same time the love of God for humanity.

Faith and Liberation

This is our challenge. As the West has been struggling for centuries with the issue of synthesizing faith and reason (faith and intelligence), I feel that the biggest problem for Africa is to know how to link faith and liberation. This certainly requires us to respond to an almost Copernican revolution if we are truly convinced that the question of the poor *is* at the heart of Christian ministry.

In any event, it seems clear to me that, instead of severely attacking "deviations" or "interpretations," we need to rediscover the political dimensions of sin in the structures of our world; at the same time we need to discover the socio-economic demands of Christian sacramentalism.

In their pastoral exhortation of 1984 the bishops of Africa and Madagascar emphasized the impact of the eucharist in the struggles for liberation in Africa. They showed how in the most profound depth of our Christian life we feel ourselves called by the name of the eucharist as by the name of our baptism. We are called to make of our Church a Church that acts in history in favor of humankind, and principally on behalf of those who live in the prison of despair.

I ask myself how we can take up this challenge without giving our African theologians their proper and rightful place. The language we have received from the West is in crisis: it does not speak to us, it does not move our hearts, it does not communicate our thoughts. We feel the need to reinvent "our word of faith." Because true knowledge of God is needed to build the Church in Africa, we must recognize the special role of our theologians to penetrate this mystery. We need a language that can really speak to us of this God who reveals himself in Jesus Christ. This is the principal question of the future of the Church, even of Christianity. In Africa we cannot speak of faith without at the same time speaking of liberation.

The Church should move beyond the illusions of renewal, which risk that the Church might close in on herself. On the contrary, the Church ought to open herself to the urgent problems that confront African Christians. It is particularly necessary to be mindful of the young, because they are the Africa of tomorrow. In a Christian reflection group, the Malula Circle, which I organized in 1990 with students from the Cameroon, young people are aware that we cannot permit ourselves today to speak of the Church of the third millennium without taking seriously their concerns. For the young, these questions are serious. In the words of members of the Malula Circle, "If the Church does not listen to the young and their questions, doesn't she risk losing the Africa of the year 2000?"

If we are convinced that Africa's encounter with the faith is to succeed, it is necessary to reexamine *everything*, taking into account many urgent matters. One of the most urgent in today's Africa is retelling the Good News of Jesus Christ, that which reveals the God of the Exodus. Africa turns toward the Church to receive a message that will move her from servitude to suffering, to life and to resurrection.

19

On the Road toward an African Ecclesiology

Reflections on the Synod

Bénézet Bujo

African theology of the last decade has been intensively concerned with christology, and it has produced some concrete points of departure in diverse areas that can no longer be ignored. In contrast to this development, the formulation of an African ecclesiology has not proceeded apace, although even here different attempts have been made[1], timid though they be. Until now, theologians have devoted their attention to the transposition of practical models. Today there is a new type of ecclesial existence in Africa. Deserving of special mention are the so-called small Christian communities, which have lent the Black African Church a new vitality of its own. It is high time to explicate the theology that forms the background for practical ecclesiology in different African local churches and which could lead to an enrichment of the universal Church.

This article does not aim to develop such a theology; instead, it presents one of the models that are in need of a more profound examination for them to be of use to a genuine Black African ecclesiology. We could begin with various models, as has been done in the area of christology, including those of ancestor theology or initiation of healing. In what follows, the starting point will be a theology of ancestors made explicit by means of two examples: the ancestral tree and the council of elders.

Bénézet Bujo, a diocesan priest from Zaire, holds the chair of Moral Theology at the University of Freibourg, Switzerland. This essay was first published as *"Auf dem Weg zu einer afrikanischen Ekklesiologie"* in *Stimmen der Zeit* (April 1994). Translated by T. Allan Smith. It also appeared in *The Canadian Catholic Review*, November 1994. Revised and reprinted with author's permission.

The Theology of Ancestors as an Ecclesiological Nucleus

Numerous studies have made clear the deepest significance of the belief in ancestors for the life of Black African men and women. An ancestor is the main pillar on which a community or clan rests. The ancestor constitutes the unity of the community and represents the pivotal point from which all actions of the members of a clan take their dynamism and legitimacy. This observation is extremely important for an ecclesiological blueprint that strives to be at home in the Black African cultural heritage. In this article I attempt to trace the fundamental concept of ecclesiology back to Jesus Christ as Proto-Ancestor in such a way that the vitality of the community of believers will be visible in both a spiritual and organizational manner.

The Proto-Ancestor as Founder of a New Tribal Community

A genuinely African ecclesiology seems to rely on a correct understanding of community and family. As has already been intimated, the primordial ancestor, to whom the founding of the clan community may be attributed, plays an indispensable role. It is the primordial ancestor who is the sustaining force for later ancestors, who form a chain of unity and through whom the contemporary generation is able to trace its origins back to the first ancestor. One can say that a clan community is an assembly around one founding ancestor from whom all members are descended. It is self-evident that every member learns to conceive of his or her life as God's gift only via the primordial ancestor.

Such an understanding of community seems to be important for an African model of Church. It recalls in broad terms the Old Testament situation in which the assembly of Israel (*qehal Yahweh*) ultimately descends from a tribal organization. Siegfried Wiedenhofer rightly observes, "Israel's self-understanding as Yahweh's chosen people" is marked politically and socially by the different aspects of its history.

> Thus do such terms and concepts as "people of Yahweh" and "twelve tribes of Israel" (Gen. 49:1-28; Deut. 33) point back to the tribal organization of the pre-state period with its loose, decentralized alliance of tribes, clans, and families and their genealogically structured nature. Israel is here, so to speak, the clan, relatives, team, and combat troops of Yahweh.[2]

More precisely stated, all the tribes of Israel in their entirety can trace their origins back to a single tribal father, namely Abraham. Abraham is the first of those who believe in one God. He is the recipient of God's promises; with him God made the covenant by virtue of which Israel ultimately can be considered the people of God.[3] In the New Covenant, Jesus will call a tight circle of "Twelve" (*hoi dodeka*) "whom he wanted to keep with himself and then send out" (Mk. 3:14; Lk. 6:12f). The Twelve symbolically replace the twelve tribes of Israel. By restoring the symbolic People of the Twelve Tribes, Jesus lets it be known that he is the tribal father "of the eschatological Israel,"[4] the term that will ultimately encompass all peoples without distinction (cf. Lk. 10:1-20).[5] "Jesus's eschatological gathering-in movement happens in definite particular communities, but in such a way that they represent and intend the entirety of Israel and humanity."[6]

From a Black African perspective it is particularly important to connect this thought with the idea of Jesus as the tribal father of the eschatological Israel. As is known, the Black African founding ancestor is that tribal father from whom life in its many-sidedness circulates in all the members, not only biologically but also holistically. Anyone who does not remain in this vital union with the tribal father on the one hand, and with the other members of the clan community on the other, condemns himself or herself to death, because outside the community in its visible and invisible dimension no one can survive.

In this bipolar community of the living and the dead, including the primordial ancestor, no one lives for himself or herself alone. The life that has been received from God via the primordial ancestor must not be lived selfishly; rather, it must be placed by each member in the service of this bi-dimensional community.[7] In this connection the eschatological "gathering of Israel"[8] by Jesus as the eschatological tribal father can be further developed and deepened in the context of the Black African community. Thus Africans will be able to attain a better ecclesial life on their native continent.

In the light of the Black African community, Jesus Christ steps forward as the last Adam (cf. 1 Cor. 15:45) who has become the firstborn of the dead (Col. 1:18) and the first fruits of those who have fallen asleep (1 Cor. 15:20). Expressed in a Black African context, Jesus Christ is neither Adam the first human being and earthly creature (cf. 1 Cor. 15:45) nor is he the tribal father like Abraham, but this "ancestorship" and "tribal fatherhood" are infinitely fertile and eschatological. Jesus the Christ is thus not simply the primordial ancestor or primordial tribal father; rather, he is this by virtue of his surpassing this entire complex of ideas in an incomparable manner.

I have attempted to characterize this with the expression "Proto-Ancestor."[9] What this means is that although Jesus became part of this earth, and flesh of our flesh, as Christ the "vivifying Spirit" he is nonetheless the real life-giving source.[10] It is as the Proto-Ancestor that Jesus Christ establishes the new, eschatological clan community in its bipolar dimension of the living and the dead.

In many Black African ethnic groups the presence of the ancestors is visually represented by means of a special tree, the ancestor tree. The tree in question is an ever-verdant tree, such as the ficus, which symbolizes the life that never dies. Among the Bahema of eastern Zaire the ficus is planted on the grave of a family father. The father lying in the grave is not dead at all but shoots forth to new life as a ficus tree so that he now becomes shelter and vivifying "spirit." The branches and leaves of this tree symbolize the numerous descendants of the deceased. They owe to him their verdure. Separated from him they cannot survive.

Yet another characteristic of the ficus tree deserves to be mentioned. The ficus is rich in white resin, a symbol for the color of the afterlife on the one hand and for cow's milk, on the other, which is the staple food of the livestock-herding Bahema.

It is not out of place to transfer this fundamental reality to Jesus Christ. Primarily by means of his cross[11] the murdered Jesus becomes a green tree that dies no more. He owes this new life to God the Father, who raised him up in such a way that he definitively overcame death. The Father, however, operates together with the Holy Spirit, who is the inner vitality represented by the white resin of the ficus. The ficus tree or the cross as the tree of life thereby has a trinitarian dimension. Only if the branches and leaves of the ficus obtain its life-giving energy do they stay green. Similarly, as his members, Christ's disciples are guaranteed the life that never dies when they are rooted in the life of the Trinity through the very same Christ risen to life.

The tree of the ancestors, which is thus depicted in a trinitarian context with reference to Jesus Christ, opens a second ecclesiological dimension for the people of Black Africa. The ancestor tree is the sacrament of the encounter with God. As branches of the ficus tree, the faithful are members of the one body of the Lord and at the same time this tree is the place of assembly for the entire new clan community. In Black African tradition the tree of the ancestors is sacred and at the same time it is deemed the place where important events in life are played out. Beneath this tree thanksgiving, reconciliation, healing, and similar events take place. The tree of the ancestors promises the fullness of life and strengthens life in its all-embracing wholeness so that the community lives in healthy relationship.

From the perspective of Black Africans, the Church can no longer be thought of apart from this tree. The Church is the ever-verdant tree on the grave of Jesus Christ by which he is made visible. The Church as Proto-Ancestor tree is the sacrament par excellence in which the faithful encounter Christ as the sacrament of God. The Church initiates into life and each person who withdraws from her life-giving shade make a decision for death, because, according to Black African understanding, life is only possible in unity with the founding ancestor or tribal father. There is no question that this tree, identified as Church, also mirrors trinitarian life. The tree owes its verdure and life-giving shade—namely its sacramental and healing dimension—to the Crucified One who was raised by the Father through the power of the Holy Spirit. The faithful whose life is played out under the tree, which symbolizes the Risen One and the Church simultaneously, receive their vitality and sense of belonging in the Spirit through whom the Father raised the Son.

This sketch of ancestor ecclesiology is of profound importance for Black African men and women, for whom all events in life must be referred back to the community. Only in this context may all of life's problems be overcome.

The Council of Elders—The Beginning of an Ecclesiological Model

Within the framework of African christology it is necessary to draw attention to the problem of wisdom, which, for the most part, may be associated with the elders of a community. From the outset, we can attempt to interpret the concepts of wisdom and word christologically.[12] In the Black African context it is the word that holds the community together. The word of an older person acquires a special meaning because the older person customarily embodies wisdom. The one who listens to the word of an older person and takes it to heart is enabled to give the community a new vitality.

For the word is so mighty that, just as in the Old Testament, it accomplishes everything it was sent to achieve. Depending on whether it is uttered wisely or thoughtlessly the word can be either creative or destructive of community.

If we proceed from this understanding of the word, we then know that Jesus Christ himself is the real Word of God, and even more: he is "the power of God and the wisdom of God" (1 Cor. 1:24). On the other hand, we know that the God who makes the definitive promise can only do this in a Word that fosters wisdom. God's Spirit binds itself to the Word: "God's Word can never be so 'spiritless' that it would be bare information and pure assertion. It is rather a Deed-Word and a Word-Deed."[13]

In Isaiah the Word of God is compared with rain and snow that drench the earth and make it fruitful. The word that leaves the mouth of the Lord does not return to him empty, but accomplishes all that it was sent out to do (Is. 55:10-11). G. Sauter offers this interpretation: "Just as Jesus Christ, the Word of God, became flesh in order to live among human beings, so does the Spirit become word in order to establish community between God and human beings, indeed between humanity and the word, which likewise needs the redemption in order to live."[14]

From an African perspective the following interpretation seems to be even more appropriate: the Word that became flesh lived among us in order to make the world human. This happens not least by virtue of the Word's being the very Wisdom of the Father. In Africa people identify the word of an ancient (*mzee* in *Kiswahili*) with wisdom to such a degree that "to become old" and "wisdom" mean the same thing. In that case Jesus Christ is for us simply the *Mzee* of God because he not only possesses Wisdom but is and speaks Wisdom herself. Jesus Christ can therefore ultimately be designated as the genuine ancient who imbues all African ancients with their words of wisdom and makes them simultaneously experienced human beings. Only when they go to the school of the Proto-Ancient Jesus Christ can they be called children of God.

The explanation set forth here clearly contradicts the claim of many theologians who hold that the term Ancestor or Proto-Ancestor reduces Jesus Christ to an unattractive figure, particularly for young people. Jean Galot, for example, wonders whether or not today's youth in Africa feel particularly drawn to the term Ancestor. Galot proceeds primarily from a Western assessment of the term ancestor, and suggests that use of the word Ancestor with reference to Jesus Christ would arouse in many young people in the West the impression that religion belonged to the past or that it was good only for seniors. Galot fears a similar reaction in Africa, at least in those areas where young people are no longer so deeply rooted in the traditional cult of ancestors. He argues further that if it is inappropriate to name God the Father our ancestor, since God possesses perpetual youthfulness—after all, Jesus did not reveal an old man but a father—then it is even less suitable to give this name to the Son. For example, at Christmas no one would even think of calling the child lying in the manger an ancestor. Galot notes that Luke the Evangelist calls Jesus "Savior" and as such is entrusted with a mission that can be associated with the term ancestor only with difficulty.[15]

One could raise many objections to Galot's christological theory. The author knows well what a tortuous path christology has traveled in the West and what great variety of names it applied to Jesus Christ until a few proved their worth, none of which happened in a cultural void. This question, however, shall not be further explored here. At this point, it is important to inquire about the meaning of ancestor or Proto-Ancestor. It is astounding that Galot, as a non-specialist coming from a specific culture, permits himself such a clear-cut judgment. To all appearances he finds it unthinkable, for example, that the title of ancestor might be applied to small children, whence no doubt his inability to imagine speaking about the "Ancestor" at Christmas. An awareness of the fact that many ethnic groups (for example, the Lugbara of Zaire and Uganda) consider deceased infants to be their ancestors would have preserved Galot from such rash conclusions. In order correctly to interpret ancestor christology it would first of all be necessary to investigate what the word ancestor actually means in the Black African world. A further question would ask— even if one wished to limit the term ancestor to the circle of ancients—what position old people have in a Black African community. It would then be clear that old people are by no means unattractive in African traditional society, neither do they lack every and all vitality. Rather, the future of youth depends on the life-giving wisdom of the ancients. This means too, however, that a community without ancients soon dissipates.

If this is certain, African ecclesiology cannot help but rest on the model of the ancients. Here the Black African council of elders is of great significance. Proceeding from the classical terminology of *presbyteros* (elder), one would then have to adhere to a literal interpretation.[16] If priests are traditionally called *presbyteroi*, every priest, regardless of his age, is an ancient who belongs to the bishop's council of elders. The natural presumption then is that the priest disposes of experience and wisdom acquired during his years of formation. His bishop and congregation ought to consult him, for the simple reason that they may expect from him a word expressing wisdom and giving life.

For this to be successful, the priest must be so formed that he is equipped with an authentic worldly wisdom above and beyond intellectual knowledge that will suitably prepare him for his future tasks. The priest himself, no matter how young he might be, must show by his behavior that he is an ancient whose age expresses maturity and wisdom. If all of these pre-requisites are met, the bishop cannot help but take into account the experience and wisdom of his presbyter, since the advice coming from a priest has its origin in God's wisdom, Christ himself, in whose priesthood the priest participates.

At the same time, however, certain hierarchizing tendencies must be rejected, because even non-ordained men and women play an irreplaceable role in the life of the Church. By their baptism they participate in the priesthood of Jesus Christ. As baptized men and women they have died with Christ and have risen with him. They have "put on" wisdom and received the spirit of God to the benefit of the one community of the Church. They, too, are challenged to work together with bishops and presbyters in the building up of the one Church of Jesus Christ. This is the

reason they must have a share in the council of elders in parish and diocesan pala-
vers. The word which every member of the Church utters originates in Jesus Christ,
the Word and Wisdom of God, and is simultaneously spirit-given and spirit-filled.[17]
The Spirit of God does not remain "some impersonal, nameless and wordless energy, but enters into human language. The spirit may be heard in everyday words,
and in fact becomes the word which shapes human communication by providing a
foundation for, and building up human speech to and about God."[18]

So understood, an ecclesiology that takes Word and Wisdom for its starting
point functions in a trinitarian fashion. For, if the faithful participate in the creative
power of the Word and in the Wisdom of Jesus Christ, all of this in turn has its
origin in God the Father. On the other hand, the whole activity of those who believe
is consummated by the Holy Spirit in order to lead the Church into the eschatological
pleroma. All this should then be made explicit in the concretization of the Church
as the work of the triune God.

Some Practical Conclusions of Black-African Ecclesiology

All theories about the Church remain dead letters if they do not prove their
soundness and import through praxis. In other words, a given ecclesiology has
validity only when it promotes the community life of those who believe in Jesus
Christ so that they produce rich fruits. What is at risk is the salvation of human
beings, attainable only by means of a love for God and neighbor that is continually
growing. An ecclesiology hoping to be conducive to this salvation with regard to
love for God and neighbor will have to articulate itself concretely in a pluralistic
manner in keeping with a given cultural context. As Siegfried Wiedenhofer rightly
estimates:

> An ecclesiology in the context of inter-religious and intercultural dialogue will
> have to learn not only to avoid every type of absolutization of the Church but also
> to incorporate afresh in the understanding of Church those aspects which West-
> European developments have pushed into the background.[19]

Some questions are in order concerning the realization of the preceding
ecclesiological basis from a Black African perspective: the first is the problem of a
community being lived in praxis, and the second is the model of communication
between different Church members based on their particular field of activity.

Social Intercourse in a New Clan Community

The Black African sense of family must become the basis for ecclesial life in
Africa. This sense of family must see to it that community life does not become
colonialized through a type of anonymous subsystem, such as power or administration, to such an extent that healthy human relations are thereby made difficult or
even fail altogether. In this connection the small Christian communities in Africa
are to be considered as a blessing.[20] They seem to do better justice to the conditions

of Black African families. Their limited number of members in surveyable groups permits better cooperation and better solidarity in keeping with the sense of the African tradition. Such small groups do not permit anonymity but they do facilitate the transposition of traditional values into Christian ones. It is thus easier for the groups to converse in a palaver fashion. In the case of a conflict in the congregation, it is possible to proceed according to the traditional model, under consultation of the gospel, in order to achieve reconciliation motivated by Christian principles. As is the case in traditional African communities, the education of children could become a common duty of all members and not just of the parents.

The life of small communities must have consequences for parishes and dioceses and correct the hitherto existing, too rigidly institutionalized Church. Mention has been made of the council of elders, which encompasses all laymen and laywomen on the basis of their baptism.[21] At the parish level, men and women who bear responsibility in different villages and who live their Christian existence in small Christian communities are the people of wisdom to whom the parish priest should listen. These elders are often more experienced than their pastor, who perhaps disposes of great knowledge without much practical experience and wisdom.

What is valid for a parish congregation is to be extended to the diocesan level. As elders of the Christian community, non-clerics—men and women—can also advise their bishop, and not only through the institutionalized council of elders in a diocese. This can also happen informally in the manner of Black-African ancients: the elders of a community (priests and non-priests) have the responsibility of informing the bishop of what is called for with regard to the situation of the diocese. They even have the responsibility of correcting the bishop with wisdom and love.

There should be a similar relationship between the pope and bishops. Here African theology would prefer a model based on brotherly relations. The pope would then be considered the eldest son whose task it is to manage the common inheritance of the Lord together with his other brothers. "Big Brother" or "Big Sister" does not mean simply an authority with hierarchical overtones. Rather, it has to do with the type of responsibility shown in the way that a big brother or big sister is always available to their younger siblings. The one who has a responsibility in a family must care selflessly for orphans, the disenfranchised, and the like. This authority may never be misused, neither may siblings be affronted; instead, much effort must be invested in dialogue. In fact, wisdom is ascribed to the eldest brother only when and if he is also prepared to respect and listen to the wisdom of his sisters and brothers.

This is how the people of Black Africa imagine the pope. He it is who must strengthen his brothers and sisters in the faith and who never makes a decision without a palaver with other particular churches. This means that unless he dialogues with his brothers and sisters, he may not intervene in local church affairs. Those who advocate such an ecclesiological model have no desire to distort the mystery character of the Church. For, Christ as the sacrament of the encounter with God has incarnated himself profoundly in human reality in order to bring all of humanity ever closer to God. God takes human reality so seriously that he descends into the very depths of the non-divine in order to speak to humans in human form.

His Church is then indeed a mystery, but a mystery that is incarnated in a community with a human face.[22]

By the same token, however, this also means that the Church in Black Africa cannot help but become Black Africa. With some overstatement, Joseph Cardinal Malula once said justly that Africa was pregnant at the moment, that it was a matter of a very painful delivery that would happen one day. The expected child, that is, the local church, would definitely be born and it would be a *black* child.[23]

Should the expected church really be Black Africa, reference must be made to yet a wider dimension and that is the way in which siblings interact. Black African communities pay special attention to interpersonal relations. The illness of a member often originates in the worsening of interpersonal relations. The evil eye, unfriendly words, underhanded thoughts, oppressive exercises of power, and the like poison interpersonal relations and bring death upon both the individual and the whole community. A person can live soundly only in a community where everyone takes concern for healthy mutual relations.[24] The Apostle Paul understood this very well when he reprimanded the congregation in Corinth on account of the disorderly conduct among the members at the Lord's Supper. Paul traces sickness and cases of death in the Corinthian congregation back to the misuse of the body and blood of Christ (1 Cor. 11:28-30). The theological extrapolation of the importance of community for health reaches its pinnacle in the trinitarian community. The relation between the Father, the Son, and the Holy Spirit is so loving and healthy that there can be neither sickness nor death in this divine community. God cannot die (H. Zahrnt).

The Black African concept of community finds here an important support, which becomes its foundation. An ecclesiology that unfolds within the conceptual framework makes a contribution to a new understanding of Church that cannot be overlooked. A Church that proceeds from the idea of community and family can no longer tolerate anonymous power structures in its bosom which, instead of bringing the person to healing in a holistic sense, promote sickness and death. In this way it becomes clear that an ecclesiology based on the Black African notion of family could mean an enrichment and perhaps even a renovation of the entire Church.

For a New Model of Communication in the Church

The importance of the word for the existence of the Church has been mentioned earlier. From the view of Black Africans, if it is rooted in wisdom, the word is that reality which holds the community together. The word is creative or destructive. God, however, who has called all things into existence through his Word, wills that the power of the Word not be misused but that it bestow life. It is understandable then that even the Church is born and lives by God's Word. The Word makes the Church God's pilgrim people, as was brought out by the Second Vatican Council.[25] If the Church as the People of God lives from the Word of God, then this Word must so permeate each member that it becomes visible in his or her life.

According to African understanding, however, the word that penetrates into the depths of a person must be eaten and digested or processed. Only when it has been well digested can it play a communicative and community-building role. It is important, however, to stress that the individual may not hold a monopoly on the privately digested word. The other members of the community have the task of inquiring about the word of the individual. This happens by means of a palaver, in which the word that has been digested in the darkness of individuals must come out into the public sphere once more in order to prove its viability, for the benefit of the community.[26]

If the word in fact does mean life for everyone, it cannot and must not be controlled in private, but only in community. The words that are variably digested by individual members must be confronted with each other so that they may be verified against each other before being placed in the service of the community. It seems to me that the palaver process is extremely important for the life of the Church. The Church, who owes her existence to the Word and lives by it, must learn a new way of dealing with this Word. We know that it is principally contained in Scripture and tradition, and that this same Word is perceived, eaten, and digested by different members in various ways. A Word from Scripture and tradition that has been heard, eaten, and digested is destined for the good of the entire community of believers.

The question is how stewardship of the word ought to be exercised. According to the Black African palaver model, the word cannot be interpreted by some central authority but only by a community, that is, in the process of listening to one another. For in speaking and listening with and to each other, it is possible to repulse a fatal word and to confirm a life-promoting one, and to receive it into the service of the ecclesial community. Concretely, this would mean that it is not a solitary authority but this authority in concert with the community of all believers that explains Scripture and tradition for the good of the universal church. Not the individual but the Church community in her multifarious membership with its different functions and charisms is therefore the place for the exegesis of the Word of God.

This African palaver model even completes and corrects to some extent the individualistic view of Roman and Western ecclesiology that tends to ascribe the competence for decision-making and interpretation in many areas solely to the teaching magisterium of the Church. One ought to have recourse to the position of the eldest brother in the African context mentioned above. Sacred Scripture and tradition should be stewarded jointly by the head of the Church and all local churches. No important decision for the life of the faithful ought to be made without the local church. All members of this Church (bishops, priests, laymen and laywomen, rich, poor, illiterates, and so on) must have a say in a Christian palaver. Expressed concretely, this means that no document of the magisterium may be written without the participation of those affected by it. The production of such a document demands patience and speaking and listening to one another as brothers and sisters. The final text ought to document the life and faith experiences of all for the benefit of the entire community.

The goal of a Christian palaver must be to create peace in such a way that life attains its full growth in the Proto-Ancestor Jesus Christ. It is thus not a matter of pushing through one's own interests as an individual, nor the interests of a local church or central organ. A "palaver Church" from an African Christian perspective must always bear in mind the words of John the Baptist: "He must increase, but I must decrease" (Jn. 3:30). Only the one who decreases for the sake of the Lord can have life to the full.

If the goal of a Christian palaver is the growth of the life in Christ, it would be possible for a local church community or the individual believer to allow a consensus reached in mutual agreement with the head of the Church to stand, in the awareness that the unfolding of the life of the individual is only possible within the ecclesial community.[27] Conversely, this means that mutual agreement can lead even the supreme Church authority to endorse the opinion of the local church community so that peace and harmony among individual members reigns for the good of the whole. By decreasing, the supreme Church authority promotes the growth of Christ in all members and contributes at the same time to this same growth in itself.

The ecclesial dimension of the Black African palaver model leads to a better understanding of the ecclesial function of all of theology. To do theology does not at all mean to conduct victorious disputations. *To do theology is always a matter of creating ecclesial community.* The teaching authority and theology are in no way opponents who fight each other; they are participants in the palaver who ascertain the viability of the word that each member has eaten privately and digested in the dark of the "stomach" for the well-being of the entire Church because, as G. Sauter says, no one "can keep this word to himself or herself in order to get high on it and to bury it within."[28] Indeed, no one may pervert the creative Word of God and misuse it for the destruction of the Church as the community of those believing in God.

In Conclusion

The aim of these reflections was to make clear that the Church in Africa needs an ecclesiology that is truly rooted in indigenous culture. Many problems still find no adequate theological or organizational solutions because the African Church continues to reproduce a West-European model. As well, many of the misunderstandings between the African and the European Church can be traced back to the expectation that Black Africans should befriend a culturally conditioned concept of Church that arose in the West. The attempt fails because the West demands that Black Africans remain loyal without reservation to Western ecclesiology. It is, therefore, not surprising that the *Instrumentum Laboris* for the special bishops' synod on Africa passed over in complete silence the necessity of a genuinely African ecclesiology.[29]

Everyone knows, however, that the sometimes brutal and "unbrotherly" treatment of African Christian men, women, priests, and bishops can only be accounted by the shortcomings taken note of here. Had the cultural background of Black Africa been the starting point, it would have been impossible to let the aforesaid synod be prepared principally by a non-African. Instead, the whole thing could have arisen in Africa in cooperation with all levels of the Church. Only then would a dialogue with the responsible persons in Rome have been meaningful. In addition to this, the *Instrumentum Laboris* would have primarily abided by the studies published by African bishops and theologians, rather than citing almost exclusively papal documents alone.[30]

Had the "brother" model been taken seriously, the synod would not take place in Rome but in Africa. As is known, Rome was chosen as the site for the synod on the basis of communion theology: by assembling in Rome, the African bishops visibly and clearly emphasize their unity with the pope. Must a geographical interpretation of communion now be given precedence? Another objection pertaining to the difficult political situation in Africa was also advanced. Seen from the model of brotherly relations, communion with the pope would have been more credible had he come to Africa rather than ordering his brother to Rome. In keeping with the African model of brotherhood, it is the duty of the eldest brother himself to take time and undergo a risk by visiting his younger brothers at home, especially during difficult times. All the examples enumerated here aim to point out that an ecclesiology that does justice to the African situation remains one of the most pressing tasks of theology in Africa.

Notes

1. B. Bujo, "Ahnetheologie als Ansatzpunkt fur eine neue Ekklesiologie," in *Afrikanische Theologie in ihrem geschichtlichen Kontext* (Düsseldorf, 1986), 99-121. *The Church in African Christianity*, ed. J.N.K. Mugambi, L. Magesa (Nairobi, 1990); A. Losigo-Kulu, *Perspectives ecclésiologiques en Afrique francophone* (Rome, 1991).

2. S. Wiedenhofer, *Das Katholische Kirchenverstandnis* (Graz, 1992), 44-47.

3. R. Kohler, *Jesus der Proto-Ahne* (Dipl. arb. Tubingen, 1992), 44-47.

4. Wiedenhofer, 79.

5. See G. Lohfink, *Die Sammlung Israels* (Munich, 1975).

6. Wiedenhofer, 79.

7. B. Bujo, *Die ethische Dimension der Gemeinschaft* (Freiburg, 1993), 13f.

8. See Lohfink.

9. Bujo, *Afrikanische Theologie*, 79ff.

10. Cf. the misconception of C. Nyamiti, "The Church as Christ's Ancestral Mediation" in *The Church in African Christianity*, ed. Mugambi, Magesa, 169, n. 8.

11. B. Bujo, "*Auf der Suche nach einer afrikanischen Christologie,*" in *Der andere Christus*, ed. H. Dembowski, W. Greive (Erlangen, 1991), 94ff.

12. See Bujo, *Die ethische Dimension*, 193ff.

13. G. Sauter, in *Handbuch der Fundamental Theologie* (Freiburg, 1983), 207.

14. Sauter, 207f.

15. J. Galot, "*Le Christ, notre ancêtre?*" *Telema* 53 (1988), 32-34.

16. For the following see Bujo, *Die ethische Dimension*, 194ff.

17. Sauter, 208.

18. Ibid., 207.

19. Wiedenhofer, 39.

20. See C. Mwoleka, J. Healey, *Ujamaa and Christian Communities* (Eldoret, Kenya, 1976); B.Madefu-Kambuyi, *L'impact d'un discours anthropothéocentrique sur les communautés ecclésiales vivantes* (Rome, 1990); *Laien als Gemeindeleter*, ed. L. Bertsch (Freiburg, 1990).

21. Bujo, *Die ethische Dimension*, 193ff.

22. Ibid., 195f.

23. J. Malula, *L'Église à l'heure de l'Africanité* (Kinshasa, 1973), 12.

24. Bujo, *Die ethische Dimension*, 181ff.

25. *Lumen Gentium*, 9ff; Sauter, 206.

26. Bujo, *Die ethische Dimension*, 63-83.

27. Ibid., 79.

28. Sauter, 207.

29. This criticism is valid for the *Lineamenta* of 1990.

30. Cf. "Open Letter to the Holy Father. An African Synod without Africa?" in *New People* (March 1993), 1-4. (See pp. 61-67 above.)

20

Christians and Moslems in Africa

Challenges and Chances for a Genuine Relationship

Henri Teissier

The African Synod had as its objective a sharing among the churches on the continent to stimulate their witness. The relationship of the Christians on the continent with their Moslem counterparts came, in the course of the Synod, to be one of the important areas of witness. This article is a synthesis of the discussions of the Synod on this aspect of the mission of the Church in Africa today.

During the first ten days each member of the Synod (bishop or major superior) was asked to make an eight-minute presentation on the topic that appeared to him to be the most important for the particular church to which he belong. As it was necessary to choose among the multiplicity of facets of the mission, it was not surprising that the theme of the relationship with Islam and the Moslems was not the principal object of the interventions made in the general assembly. Only the bishops of North Africa (Mauritania, Morocco, Algeria, Tunisia, and Libya) and one or two bishops from Egypt placed their evangelical relationship with Islam at the center of their interventions.

However, in the other regions, several voices were raised on the same topic in the countries of the Sahel and of South Sahara (Senegal, Niger, Mali, Sierra Leone, Somalia, Djibouti, but particularly Sudan and Chad). In East Africa, Bishop Willigers of Uganda made it the theme of his entire intervention; an Ethiopian bishop (Mgr. Timotheos) and a bishop from Tanzania also addressed the topic. On the Gulf of Guinea, several reflections on this topic were proposed by a bishop of each one of the following countries: Nigeria, Ghana, Ivory Coast, and Guinea Bissau. To these

---

Henri Teissier, a White Father and the archbishop of Algiers, is author of numerous articles and two books in the area of Islamic-Christian dialogue. He is president of the Episcopal Conference of North Africa and a member of the Council of the Secretariat of the Synod.

interventions, it is necessary evidently to add that of Cardinal Arinze, President of the Pontifical Council for Interreligious Dialogue, and those of certain of the superiors general of missionary congregations (for example, Father Gotthard Rosner, Superior General of the White Fathers).

In short, out of 210 interventions, only 33 touched on this theme, with only 14 making it the center of the report. On the sole basis of these statistics, one might conclude that the question of relations with Islam was of secondary importance. But in reality, discussions in the informal gatherings showed that we were touching on a major dimension of our study of the Church's witness in Africa based on this testimony. What can we say now of the contents of these discussions?

The Church and Islam: The Challenges

All the bishops present at the Synod received a very interesting document prepared by Savino Palermo, SCJ, in two thick volumes entitled *Africa Pontificia*. This text gathers together all the official acts of the Holy See relating to Africa since the dawn of modern times. It suffices to leaf rapidly through the first pages of the first tome in order to meet the historical conflicts between the Church and Islam on the African continent, as shown, for example in Document 1 of April 14, 1419, of Martin V: "All the faithful are called to aid the king of Portugal during the war against the Saracens in Africa, in favor of the growth of the faith," or Document 4 of June 18, 1452, in which Pope Nicholas V grants to the king of Portugal "the right to conquer the Mohammedan kingdoms and territories for the triumph of the faith."

Most certainly Bishop Willigers of Uganda urged the bishops to forget the historical disputes that often arose from opposition that originated outside of Africa. However, several interventions in the general assembly did not fail to point out the disappearance of certain African churches under pressure from Islam (North Africa, Nubia), or their dramatic reduction (Egypt), or again the ancient threat against the Christian identity of one people (Ethiopia). Finally there were also expressions of a more general resentment. As Cardinal Otunga said: "For so long, we have been the infidels."

Actual Conflict

The Synod opened with the announcement of the absence of the Archbishop of Juba, detained at the airport of Khartoum by the Sudanese authorities. This brought to light, from the very beginning of our work, one of the most serious areas of conflict between a Moslem state (Sudan) and its African and Christian minority in the south of the country. There would be repeated references to this conflict during the course of the Synod. Certain bishops would have liked to have a joint resolution from the Synod, condemning the injustice done to the Christians in South Sudan. Yet, this idea was not pursued in order to avoid giving offense, which would have destroyed the atmosphere that they wanted the Synod to project.

Another intervention introduced us to the complex source of tension in Chad. In a very strong but very well-balanced text, Bishop Mathias N'Garteri of Moundou showed the multiform nature of these Islamic-Christian tensions in his country, including opposition between Arabic-speaking Chadians and Moslems in the North and African-speaking non-Moslem Chadians in the South, and between Christian farmers in the South and Moslems in the North occupying their lands with their troops because of the war and the drought.

In this context, it is necessary to identify the diversity of some branches of Islamic-Chadians. According to Bishop N'Garteri there are the traditional Muslims, essentially from the Tidjane Confrerie. They are tolerant and in the majority. There are also educated Muslims who master the two cultures, Arabic and French. And finally there are the new integrist groups who come from Sudan and who organize the conflict.

The bishop indicated the efforts made by the Church to save a relationship that has been positive, in particular, the joint efforts on behalf of human development.

The Development of Muslim Integrism in Africa

African Islam is traditionally tolerant. In many regions, African culture lies just below the surface of Christian or Muslim beliefs. Bishop John Olorunfemi Onaiyekan of Abuja remarked that in Nigeria, for example, a Yoruba is a Yoruba before being a Christian or Muslim. Bishop Willigers of Uganda expressed the need to develop the relationship between Christians and Muslims on the basis of this common African culture.

Unfortunately, for some time in several countries extremist elements from outside have been disturbing the relationships between Muslims and Christians, and even endangering the peace. Participants at the Synod described several examples. Without speaking of North Africa (notably Algeria) or of Egypt, they pointed out the development of such movements in other countries, such as Senegal, Niger, Chad, and Kenya.

Bishop Romano described the difficulties of dialogue and contact between Christians and Muslims who come from Muslim integrist movements, especially since the birth of the democracy four years ago in Niger.

Several integrist associations are actually operating in Niger. A religious movement with the name of Izala, born in Nigeria, is installing itself progressively and methodically in Niger. It already counts numerous followers. It makes much of religious formation, especially for women. The Tidjanes, the majority, are opposed to this movement, and can become violent. Recently a marabout had his throat cut during a scuffle. Just last week, the Tidjanes provoked trouble in a large village 160 kilometers north of the capital. Ten policemen died from blows with cudgels or arrows.

These are truly new developments in Niger.

These new movements have financial resources at their disposal that allow them to attain a disproportionate prestige in regions where the faithful of Islam are not numerous (for example in Zaire).

In this context, Father Giorgio Bertin of Somalia also mentioned integrism among the causes of recent disappearances from the Church in his country, and events such as the assassination of Bishop Colombo, the destruction of the cathedral, and so forth. Mauritania has also seen similar currents develop, which led last September to a serious attack against two priests. Bishop Ferrazzetta of Guinea Bissau also mentioned this. Bishop Salama of Egypt tied together these incidents as evidence of a global plan to penetrate all of Africa. Master Amin Fahim of Egypt expressed the wish that the Church define a global strategy to face the danger.

The report that synthesized the interventions (*relatio post disceptationem*) pointed out: "It is necessary, through dialogue with all people of good will, to identify these fanatics and confront them as enemies of peace and progress."

Islamic-Christian Encounters: The Chances

Areas Where Peaceful Interchange Is the Norm

The fear that certain Islamic trends will have adverse effects upon Islamic-Christian relations had an important place in the discussions of the Synod. However, this was not the only perspective expressed. Many who addressed this topic emphasized the traditional co-existence of Christian, Muslim, and Animist Africans. Bishop Sidibe of Mali spoke of the members of his family who are Muslims. Bishop Ganda of Sierra Leone remarked that three of the priests of his diocese are from Muslim families. The Greek Orthodox Patriarch Parthenios of Alexandria recalled his childhood relationships with Muslim playmates. Bishop Diouf of Senegal stressed the diversity of forms adopted by Islam in his country, placing in evidence the more open positions of the Islamic brotherhood.

Conditions for Peaceful Relationship

Several interventions stressed conditions to be implemented for peaceful relations with Muslim partners. The first condition stressed was the need to safeguard mutual respect for the rights of one another. No peace-making relationship can be established between Christian and Muslim partners if efforts are not made on both sides to respect the other community and, in particular, where one group is in the minority. In this context we have often spoken of "reciprocity." Muslims must understand that they cannot withhold from Christian minorities what they demand for their own minority communities.

The report that synthesized the interventions (*relatio post disceptationem*) pointed out that "As far as possible, we must insist on equity and reciprocity, often the best way to avoid the greatest crises. . . . Dialogue is difficult when there is no reciprocity, of course, and when freedom for religious conversion to Christianity is denied."

In his opening homily, John Paul II dedicated a long passage to Islam. He was thus the first witness to the openness in dialogue that respects the other. But at the same time he clearly affirmed the identity of Christianity.

To you, who believe and profess faith in the One God, we give witness to that ineffable mystery which God has willed to reveal to mankind in Jesus Christ, in Him who brings us justification by faith and the remission of sins. Jesus is the Son of Mary, the Virgin of Nazareth, as you, too, acknowledge. This Jesus, God-Man crucified and risen, is the hope of all humanity. He is also the hope of Africa!

In opening the Synod of Bishops of Africa, we beg you to pray to the One God, through Abraham, father of our faith, that one may be able to respond fully to the call that the People of Africa received from God, two thousand years ago, through Christ, in his Holy Church.

Spiritual Attitudes That Make Dialogue Possible

Several bishops have invited Christians and Muslims to a positive relationship by underlining the spiritual attitudes that make this possible. We can start with the suggestions of Bishop Romano of Niger:

It requires a great deal of modesty and humility to live as a minority in an Islamic country . . . The power of the risen Christ and the strength of the Spirit manifest themselves in littleness . . . but littleness does not mean weakness and still less subservience. It is necessary to invite Christians to "give an account" of the hope that is in them, but it must be done in friendship.

The sure road to dialogue and meeting, continued Bishop Romano, "passes first through humble service of people, especially the poorest . . . by working together for those great causes like the promotion of women . . . and the dialogue on life."

Bishop Martinelli of Libya noted in particular the direction that these spiritual attitudes take in the life and action of religious women.

The mystery of the Incarnation reminds us of Nazareth: the waiting. Something takes place gently . . . love penetrates the earth . . . one can refuse a doctrine, an idea, a preaching, one never refuses life given through love . . . That is the witness of the religious life. The experience of the Church in Libya shows us the importance of the presence of the religious women who live the spirit of service, of sisterly devotedness.

The report that synthesized the interventions included a statement of Bishop Romano who identified, among others, one of the motivations of dialogue. Bishop Romano noted the conviction that "Many Muslims, especially the poor and the lowly, live lives based on great evangelical values: like the gift of self, abandonment to God, pardon, generosity toward the others: these are the seeds of the Word. God is present in the history of men, of all men."

Bishop Taza of Egypt was even more precise: "The Muslims have the right to know that Christ loves them, that he died and rose for them, that the Christ remains the only means of salvation for each of them." This is why the Catholic Church has also in its heart a special love for each Muslim: dialogue is a means of communicating this love to each Muslim.

Theological Reflection on the Meaning of Islamic-Christian Encounter

Several of the interventions asked the Synod to encourage theological research on the meaning of Islamic-Christian dialogue. Bishop Gagnon (Algerian Sahara) said:

> The very existence of Islam, its vast differences and the number of its faithful (one billion) have not failed to raise theological problems of their own, such as the prophetic character of Mohammed, the place of Islam in the divine plan of salvation. All of that may be thought of as a stimulant to our own theological thinking and to our understanding of mission.

Father Gotthard Rosner, superior general of the White Fathers, contributed the following elements to this enlargement of the concept of mission:

> There is evangelization when Christians work together with men of good will in order to achieve God's design. Each time that the will of God is done, the Reign of God is realized. Where someone brings life, liberty and happiness to men, there is evangelization.

In my own intervention as archbishop of Algiers, I offered some similar remarks:

> It is a question of entering with our Muslim counterparts into the works of the Kingdom of God. It is in these that we continue the dialogue of salvation which Paul VI explained to us years ago . . . The tasks of the Kingdom are entrusted to all men, Christians or not. To join with Muslims who are laboring for the Kingdom—with the help of the Holy Spirit—and to work with them while living our own Christian fidelity, is the first stage of our mission in Muslim countries.

Bishop de Chevigny of Mauritania said the same thing: "The Church of Mauritania is aware of its missionary task, in willing to become, in many ways, a witness to the tenderness of God and an instrument in the building up of the Kingdom."

Several presenters of interventions strove to emphasize the theological meaning of the dialogue, for example, Monsignor Perron of Djibouti: "The spirit of dialogue is nothing more than the love of Christ for all men, and it should be a gift given to each baptized person through the anointing of the Holy Chrism."

Stimulating and Structuring Islamic-Christian Relationships

From the beginning of the Synod, Cardinal Arinze, president of the Pontifical Council for Interreligious Dialogue, insisted upon the need for the Church in Africa to devote itself to the means of stimulating the Islamic-Christian relationship, and of preparing itself to live it at a deeper level.

Cardinal Arinze emphasized that it is important "that each group of dioceses in a given region have a clear understanding of the Muslim presence there. It is necessary that Catholics be formed so that our relationship with Muslims may improve: to create commissions or a special Catholic center for Islamic studies in Africa, to enter into contact with Muslims and in particular with their directors," and so on.

The report that synthesized the interventions pointed out:

> The structures for dialogue with Muslims need to be put on a sure footing and tried on all levels—local, regional and national. As far as possible, these structures should be ecumenical, for the Muslims group all Christians together.
>
> There is a special place for women in the dialogue with the Muslims—they are the only ones who can approach Muslim women. They have sometimes succeeded where men have failed.

Bishop Michon, archbishop of Rabat, also stressed the role of Christian students from black Africa in Arab countries: "Their presence is significant in the dialogue with the Muslims and should be supported by Church authorities on both sides."

Conclusion

You will find the text of the final statement on Islam at the end of this article. It proposes a balanced synthesis of the different positions expressed at the synod.

Discussion began, often enough, with the awareness that extremist movements have endangered Islamic-Christian relations in Africa, and in consequence, the civil peace of the continent. But the testimony of the churches that have the experience of an Islamic-Christian relationship, willed as such, allowed them to move beyond fear. It is not a question of establishing a Christian front, which would deny freedom of movement to Islam. What is necessary is to find the means and the paths leading to an evangelical relationship with Muslims. It should make it possible to work together at the tasks that advance African people and African society. Islamic-Christian collaboration, at the approach of the third millennium, represents a major challenge to the fidelity of Christians and Muslims to respond to the call that God has addressed to them. This conviction has made progress during the Synod.

From the Final Message of the Synod: Islamic-Christian Relationships

We assure our Muslim brothers who freely dedicate themselves to the Faith of Abraham (*Nostra Aetate*, 3) that we want to develop with them, everywhere on the continent, the collaboration of Peace and Justice, which alone can glorify God.

The living God, creator of Heaven and Earth and Master of history, is the Father of the Great Human Family which we form. He wills that we give witness to him, to our faith, to the values and the religious traditions proper to each one. He wills that we work together to promote humanity and the development on all levels of service to the common good, while assuring mutual respect for religious freedom of persons and communities (cf. *NA*, 39). He does not will to be the idol in whose name others are killed. On the contrary, he wills that, in justice and in peace, we place ourselves at the service of life. As servants of his life in the hearts of men and in our human communities, we are in duty bound to share with one another the treasure of our faith in God, our common Father.

Part IV

The Future

21

The Future of the African Synod

Laurenti Magesa

In May 1994 the bishops' assembly of the African Synod ended in Rome. Just how "African" was the assembly in terms of motivation and commitment to the African ecclesial cause? How "African" was it with regard to content? In other words, did the assembly itself and the preparation leading to it measure up to the central theme of the Synod, that is, the task of building an inculturated Church in the African continent, an African Church?

Questions may still linger in some people's minds about one or the other of these issues, even at our present vantage point. Such questions must not be brushed aside or ignored if they can help, in any way whatsoever, to clarify the future orientation of the Church in Africa. But, at the same time, another perhaps more important warning must be sounded. We must be careful not to get stuck in unresolvable and fruitless misgivings about the Synod and what has taken place until now.

I think it is imperative at this point that we move forward and go beyond the somewhat cynical attitudes unfortunately fostered among many informed individuals by the inadequacies of the Synod process itself up to the time of the assembly. What I am suggesting is that criticism and critique of ecclesial events, such as the African Synod, must always be accompanied or followed by efforts toward positive construction. Some would refer to this effort as "lighting a candle" rather than simply "cursing the darkness." In the same way, others would describe it as considering the glass of water of the Synod not as "half empty" but as "half full." By whatever name it is called, however, we have to realize that perspective is important; it can be a powerful influence in how we do things.

At the time of my writing, the final redaction of the propositions of the Synod assembly has not yet been published. But judging from the published interventions

Laurenti Magesa, a Tanzanian diocesan priest, has served on the faculties at the Catholic University of Eastern Africa (CHIEA), the Jesuit School of Theology in Nairobi, and at the Maryknoll School of Theology in New York. He has also served parishes in Tanzania.

of the bishop delegates during the assembly, as well as from the Synod's final statement, there are some clear indications for positive pastoral action. One observes a considerably high degree of concern about important issues affecting the life of faith of African Christians. There is also an obvious measure of commitment to providing African answers to these African issues. Hopefully, this concern and commitment will come out even more explicitly in the apostolic exhortation expected to be published at the Pope's discretion, possibly some time next year (1995). (See Appendix 2).

Thus, once again, in spite of any reservations concerning the preparatory process and the Synod assembly, it now seems much more profitable to build upon and promote a serious commitment to changing the face of the African Church. Promoting such a commitment must occupy the most prominent place in this third and decisive phase of the African Synod. We hope that this spirit as well as pastoral plans for action will be encouraged and celebrated by the pope in those representative parts of the continent that he is expected to visit to promulgate the exhortation.

A deliberately positive outlook, clear planning, and firm action are the way to actualize the hope that the Synod process has engendered in the Church. In other words, positive planning and creative action are the road to construct an inculturated Church. What kind of Church is this? It is a Church whose faith is not considered by the people in their heart of hearts to be completely strange. It is a Church whose practice of faith does not estrange or alienate people from themselves and the world around them. It is, on the contrary, a Church and a faith that help to integrate people, to make them whole in every way. It is a Church that, after the manner of Jesus Christ himself, comes to offer life in abundance at all levels.

Isn't this always and everywhere the call of the Church? This vocation seems more intensively required in Africa after the recent assembly of African bishops. As someone expressed it, "The assembly has ended but the Synod has begun." There can be no better expression of the tasks that lie ahead for our Church. For the bishop-delegates, getting to know one another was an obvious achievement of the assembly, as was sharing the pains and appreciating the hopes of their people. What now faces the entire African Church is how to ease those pains and realize those hopes in a concrete way. After all, it was for the ultimate purpose of changing the alienating (that is, painful and hopeless) aspects of the Church in Africa—insofar as it was not a truly incarnated Church—that the African bishops held their month-long palaver in Rome.

I shall not dwell here on the specific issues that arose during the assembly discussions. These issues are spelled out in the *Lineamenta* and *Instrumentum Laboris*. The most pressing issues are not theological but pastoral. They involve a concern for and commitment to a contextualized way for the Church to live authentically in the African environment. How can the word of God be proclaimed understandably and be accepted maturely in Africa? How can the African Church fulfill the universal Christian mandate of being missionary? In an address, Father Joseph Healey posed the problem as involving "a new way of being Church" rather than merely "a new way for the Church to be."

The published documents also exhibit a realization that the African Church is charged by Christ himself, as are all other Churches, to transform the world, to turn it into the Reign of God. Thus all the documents speak about the use of modern means of social communications for this purpose. They decry the situation of injustice, lack of peace, and the presence of numerous instances of murderous violence in the region. They call for respect and understanding between and among religions and faiths. Above all, they call for a "model" of Church that will enable the realization of these aspirations. This is by no means an easy agenda.

Due to its complexity and uncertainty, there is a real danger, then, that this agenda may in reality—or even in name—be shelved and forgotten after the "celebrative" phase of the Synod. It is, therefore, very encouraging to note that some bishop-delegates to the Synod have already spoken publicly about it since their return. Some have even organized seminars and workshops to discuss the hopes of the assembly and have projected more in the near future. I refer to places like Nigeria, Kenya, Zimbabwe, and Zambia, where some work has already been done. This is not true, however, for most of the continent. What is happening in the latter case? Where is their pastoral strategy?

To begin with, there was never widespread popular enthusiasm about the procedure of the Synod in many parts of Africa before the assembly. Given that fact, it would now seem obvious and necessary to maintain and promote whatever popular interest there is by immediately reporting on the assembly. "Keep the conversation going!" should be central to any pastoral plan. If a conversation about the assembly is not ongoing in any place, it needs to start immediately.

I would like to propose a way which, I think, will ensure that conversation about the Synod occurs throughout the African Church and that interest in the African Synod is kept alive in all our countries. Indeed, the Church must come to grips with the fact that in reality the African Synod is just beginning. Its success or failure will be determined most decisively now on African soil, long after the assembly in Rome has ended.

The Beginning of the Synod

There has to be a mechanism, a plan, a strategy—call it what you will—designed to ensure that the concern and commitments of the Synod assembly are widely known, and that the interest and enthusiasm of all the faithful are maintained in order to analyze and implement them. Enthusiasm is an indispensable quality or virtue in evangelization. Enthusiasm for the Word is a fundamental aspect of the missionary nature of the Church. It is also obviously essential to the task of transforming the Church in Africa after the Synod assembly.

Lack of enthusiasm about the future of the Synod would be a sure way of removing it from our active consciousness. We all want to live "normal" lives, and unless the concerns of the Synod are made part and parcel of our normal lives—that is to say everyday, routine—as soon as possible, they will be relegated to the subconscious, or even expelled from our memory altogether.

Fortunately some structures and substructures already exist that can be used to maintain and promote the enthusiasm already generated by the process of the Synod.

The main structure is the diocese. While the substructures may not be very prominent in some areas, they exist in most areas in Africa. These are the small communities of the faithful and other similar associations that are indispensable to the
work of the Church.

To my mind, the project of transforming the Church in Africa will depend on
these units and how they are used. This is not to say, obviously, that new ways to
implement the commitments of the Synod may not be created. I am simply saying
that for the time being these are the available structures. At the same time, I feel the
need to warn that if we try to find entirely new structures, we may risk spreading
our energies too thin and thus lose sight of the central aspirations of the Synod.
Moreover, given the dominant mood of a good number of leaders and members of
the African Church today, the wiser approach toward change seems to be the revitalization of existing structures.

The question now is clear. By using these existing structures, what can be done
to promote, in practice, the success of the aspirations of the Synod?

The first step is communication, open and honest communication. As I have
indicated, the way to keep interest about the Synod alive is through conversation.
People need information concerning the Synod assembly. What went on there?
What were the predominant concerns expressed on the assembly floor? Did voices
differ on issues due to different circumstances? On what questions was there agreement or near agreement, and on which ones was there no consensus? What aspects
of disagreement were part of the general agreements? Conversely, what aspects of
agreement were there in the general disagreements?

In addition, people need to know whether or not their own particular concerns
were expressed by their delegates. What information did the delegates receive before they left? A sense of pride is not completely foreign to the nature of a local
church, nor is it necessarily wrong. Those who worked for almost five years preparing for the Synod assembly should gain a good feeling of achievement, a feeling
that is important also for spiritual growth, to know that their work was considered.
It also encourages among the community a sense of the importance of participating
in the affairs of the church, and a desire to do so.

Let it be said right away that withholding information about the Synod *in any
way* is tantamount to declaring it irrelevant and destroying any popular interest in
it. Once again, without popular interest, the Synod will not be able to influence
change in people's lives. And the African Church has already expended too much
prayer, time, money and emotional energy since 1989 to allow this to happen. Let
us not mock God by inaction (cf. Gal. 6:7). Given our structures, the dissemination
of information has to begin, then, with the African bishops.

All bishop-delegates to the Synod assembly must see themselves as morally
accountable. They are first of all accountable to their episcopal conferences. This
means that they must report back to them in a very thorough way what they brought
back from the assembly. This will best be done in conversation, as has been the
case in Nigeria (according to Archbishop John Onaiyekan of Abuja) with all bishop-
delegates present before the entire conference. The conversation may, of course, be

supplemented by a written report, a joint work of the delegates; but it ought not to substitute for it.

Each bishop, in turn, must see himself, in the same way, as morally accountable to the faithful in his diocese. The conversation begun at the episcopal conference level has to be realized on the diocesan level as well. This can, for the time being, be done through diocesan synods and Christian community meetings. The purpose in this procedure must, of course, not be to *control* but to *empower* the people through *knowledge*. Empowerment through information and knowledge should be the ultimate aim of keeping people informed.

The type of *skills* used in organizing and conducting diocesan meetings on the African Synod will be relevant to maintain enthusiasm for the African Synod. Two different types of skills can be employed in this task: those that are primarily hierarchical and those that are more egalitarian in nature. As a Church in Africa we are very much accustomed to hierarchical skills which, in a sense, are easier to apply than the egalitarian ones. Hierarchical skills are also tempting to use as a direct means of imparting information and knowledge. But what is called for now is much more than the mere imparting of information.

What we are talking about here is, once again, *empowerment*, which is achieved through people's reception and digestion of information and their acquisition of true knowledge. The goal is to transform people's lives to appreciate their own dignity as children of God. The use of hierarchical skills will be detrimental to this cause. What is likely to produce beneficial results will be the use, on both structural levels, of egalitarian skills. These were hinted at by the Synod assembly.

Archbishop Monsengwo Pasinya of Kisangani, Zaire, underlined the fact, which was also mentioned in the Synod's final message, that the assembly paid attention to the theme of the Church as family. Evangelization was seen in the context of humanity being the "family of God." "The family takes a central position in African society. African culture is a culture of the family."[1]

Touching on the practicalities of the value of family in the context of the Synod, Archbishop Monsengwo explained:

> The Synod can be summarized as follows: The Church in Africa seeks to become more and more the family of God. The Church wants African families to become more and more Church themselves. This Church-family should transform the society in which it finds itself into the kind of family-society where there is more fellowship, more equality and more love. To achieve this, we have to be ready to share with the entire Church the faith we ourselves have received. This is inculturation.[2]

Those who attended the Synod assembly, as well as those who have otherwise acquired and digested information about the Synod, "have to be ready to share with the entire Church" that gift. This is the archbishop's characterization not only of the Church, but also of the Synod and of the entire task of inculturation.

In practical terms, any diocesan synods must be designed as genuinely participatory affairs. They have to ensure that besides the obvious and necessary presence of the bishop, clergy, and religious in each diocese, there is real and "full participation of the laity," the "equitable and full participation of women," and the "loyal and faithful participation of the theologians." A group of African theologians in Rome pointed out that this includes an atmosphere of "openness to all, unprejudiced dialogue and fraternal communion."[3]

Historian and theologian John Mary Waliggo from Uganda is fond of pointing out the danger of using the image of family uncritically to describe the reality of the Church in Africa. He likes the image, but he cautions that "family" should not be understood only as an entity that consists of the father with the rest regarded as children. No, the authentic family, he says, consists of father, mother, brothers and sisters, aunts and uncles, and so on, and so should the authentic Church-family. It is not constituted only of the bishop but is made up of all the faithful in the diocese.

These African theologians identified exclusiveness as another serious and dangerous obstacle to the realization of the concerns and commitments of the Synod. As they explained:

> We want to point out three dangers of exclusiveness within the church of today: the exclusiveness of the clergy against the laity; the exclusiveness of the magisterium over against the theologians, both male and female; the exclusiveness of the male hierarchy over against women and their ministries in the church.[4]

What has to be taken seriously into account in spirit, word, and deed is the fact that the whole community of believers is led by the Spirit. Within the Church everyone must be allowed to prophesy and to dream dreams. The most often mentioned dream for the Church in Africa is inculturation. Justice and peace, the theme mentioned most frequently during the assembly (forty times), is certainly part of the entire process of inculturation.

Presence of Contours of the Dream

The main outlines that can make the dream of inculturation real and tangible already exist among us. They have existed for a long time. In this respect, the African church is truly blessed. But there has been and continues to be one major problem. It is that these contours have been often wrongly analyzed by the leadership of the church and thus proscribed.

For the majority of Christians in Africa, however, these contours indicate, in the most existential way possible, their expression of faith in Christ. A diocesan synod can therefore be the means for a conversation with African believers, particularly those who manifest what, for lack of a better term, is called "popular Christianity."

Popular Christianity or popular Catholicism describes how the faithful have assimilated and live out the demands of the faith. It is distinguished from "official" Christianity, the reception and expression of the faith fostered by Church leaders. It would be correct to characterize the former as the *sensus fidelium*, the faith of the Church, and the latter more narrowly as the *magisterium*, that is, the segment in the

Church charged with the responsibility of collating, purifying, and articulating the *sensus fidelium*. It seems obvious that the *magisterium* and the *sensus fidelium* rely on one another. Obviously, the *sensus fidelium* is the base, but dialogue between it and the *magisterium* is essential.

Sidbe Semporé, a theologian from Burkina Faso, explains accurately this need for dialogue:

> Popular Catholicism is for pastors and the Church of Africa a leaven of conversation and questioning. For the Church in a state of Synod, it represents a necessary passage. The African Synod can bear fruits only if it listens to the "ordinary" Christians, taking into consideration that the part of the Gospel lived by the majority of Catholics forms the basis, as well as the profound interrogation of the African milieu. The path already covered in Africa since a century of Christianity is a way of the Gospel strewn with snares. For this way to lead to the Sources of Life, the Church, in Africa, must cast off its old borrowed cloak in order to put on an Easter "African gown," with a real Pentecost "loincloth"![5]

Popular Christianity, on which—to a great extent—the success of inculturation and therefore of the African Synod is dependent, finds justification in the universal work of the Spirit. During this "state of synod," the Spirit may invert the hierarchical structure of the Church to some degree, and this may threaten some people in leadership positions. Yet, it is central to the realization of dialogue and authentic conversation during the diocesan synods. For this purpose we must accept, as Leonardo Boff has put it, that:

> The Church must be thought of not so much as beginning with the risen Christ, now in the form of the Spirit, but rather as beginning with the Holy Spirit, as the force and means by which the Lord remains present in history and so continues his work of inaugurating a new world.[6]

Engaging popular Christianity seriously in dialogue with official Christianity does not constitute a diminution or removal of the true authority of Church leaders. On the contrary, it promotes its enhancement, extension, and authentic realization. This should assuage any fear that some bishops and priests in Africa might harbor about the process of diocesan synods in which egalitarian principles predominate.

The fact is that leadership of the official Church is primarily *de jure. De facto*, on the other hand, as far as the practical expression of Christian life, six days a week, is concerned, the official Church exerts little influence among the great majority of the faithful. Whether we choose to admit it or not, there are in reality two parallel Churches, the juridical Church and the Church of the Spirit. They are destined not to converge unless and until they can converse with understanding and mutuality. If they meet on those terms and integrate, the authority of the official Church will extend naturally over the entire Church of Christ.

It must not be forgotten that the Synod process is not meant to be an exclusively intra-Catholic affair. To begin with, interreligious or interfaith dialogue is one of its significant themes. Observers from other faiths were invited to the Synod as observers. Moreover, the freedom of the work of the Spirit mandates that we observe how people of other religions and faiths respond positively to the Spirit of God who is in them. This means that some of the contours for realizing the aspirations of the Synod are to be found among non-Catholic faith groups. They must be approached not primarily as adversaries but as sources (*loci*) of revelation.

As concerns the shifts affecting the mission and ministry of the Church today, the missiologist Anthony Bellagamba has recently written:

> If the felt need for religious experience is a megatrend in the world, then, in the Church's mission to the world, *dialogue* is the response that is needed at present. To make direct conversion the chief object of mission among peoples who are searching, under the influence of the Spirit, to kindle their own faith, deepen their own religiosity, may be an anachronistic attempt, perhaps even contrary to the movement of the Spirit. There is certainly a place for direct proselytism, direct conversion in every soul whom the Spirit may choose from among the people. These will gladly follow the Lord Jesus. But one of the major objects of mission may very well be dialogue among religions, rather than proselytism.[7]

With reference to the diocesan synods and local Christian associations that we are proposing as ways of continuing the African Synod, one thinks of the independent churches, indigenous churches, and African religions. What are the characteristics of their organization and what is the theological justification for it? What are their forms of ministry and worship, and why? There is no lack of literature today on all of these questions. If diocesan synods plan to continue the work of the African Synod, face-to-face encounters with these communities will be fruitful. They will indicate more clearly the orientation the Church ought to follow toward genuine inculturation.

Conclusion

I suspect many readers are now asking: Will all this happen? Indeed, I am asking the same question myself. As I see it, the very question indicates the possible danger confronting the future process of the Synod. It means that the process has not yet been able to show concrete signs of change in the life of the African Church. A related question should be: What must we do to implement these and other progressive steps toward inculturation.

Here is where each one of us becomes an apostle of and for the Synod in our own way. Are you a bishop, chancellor or vicar general, sister, catechist, priest? Do whatever you can to show to everyone who cares to listen the importance of the above strategies for the Church, for the growth of your diocese, parish, and community. Are you a teacher, musician, counselor? Do the same with your students, listeners, and clients. Are you involved in Christian associations at any level? Engage them democratically in discussions about the Synod.

The point is simple and clear. Whoever you are, wherever you may be, initiate, insist on, and sustain dialogue about the implementation of the Synod. In dialogue lies the hope that the whole process has not, and will not, be in vain.

Notes

1. *ANB-BIA (African News Bulletin-Bulletin d'Information Africaine)* Supplement, 15 May 1994, p. iv.

2. ANB-BIA Supplement, 15 May, 1994, p. v.

3. *ANB-BIA*, No. 259, 1 June, 1994, p. 6.

4. *ANB-BIA*, No. 259, 1 June, 1994, p. 6.

5. See P. Turkson and F. Wijsen, eds., *Inculturation* (Kampen: KOK, 1994), p. 46.

6. Leonardo Boff, *Church, Charism, Power,* NY: Crossroad, 1985, p. 150.

7. *Mission and Ministry in the Global Church* (Maryknoll, N.Y.: Orbis Books, 1992), p. 3.

22

Message of the AMECEA and IMBISA Bishops

To the Catholic Faithful and all people of good will in these Regions,

Formation for Justice

Many times in the course of the Synod, the bishops called for a much deeper formation of the laity in the Bible and in the social teaching of the Church, which has been so amply developed by recent popes, John XXIII, Paul VI, and John Paul II. At the center of both the Bible and the Church's social teaching is respect for every human person as a child of God, deeply loved by God. A better knowledge of the Church's social teaching will permit the whole Church to play its role of awakening the moral conscience of all in view of healing the ills which afflict African societies. This will be done by the only means proper to the Church: the teaching and courageous stand of the pastors, the living witness of the lay faithful, and the prayer of the whole Church. Lay people, knowing the call of the Synod, must be prepared to ask, even demand, the formation they need. When it is provided, they must be faithful in following it. The Synod asked that the Bible should be in the hands of every Catholic from his/her earliest years.

The Synod recalled that direct involvement in the political arena is the proper duty of the lay members of the Church and repeatedly called for their involvement. If they are to respond, the Church owes them a deeper formation than has hitherto been offered in both the Bible and the social teaching of the Church. Individuals are powerless to change society but Catholics together—better still, all Christians together—could have a profound effect over a number of years. Working through small Christian communities in every parish, well-prepared Christians could begin to call for and work for improvements in the neighborhood and slowly extend this to the whole country. The Synod reminded Catholics that poverty, hunger, illit-

---

AMECEA is the Association of Member Episcopal Conferences of Eastern Africa. IMBISA is the Inter-regional Meeting of the Bishops of Southern Africa.

eracy, denial of human rights and all other ills in their area must become their concern, if they are to live rather than just profess the Christian faith. To many this is a hard saying especially as most have a hard enough time providing for themselves and their own families. Jesus' story of the man who fell into the hands of brigands on the road from Jerusalem to Jericho and was beaten, robbed and left half dead, was recalled many times during the Synod. He was seen to be the figure of so many people in our societies.

Justice within the Church

The bishops recognized that if the Church is to speak of justice, it must itself be just. It must pay just salaries to all those who serve in a salaried capacity and provide retirement benefits. It must recognize the rights and dignity of each individual and be open to dialogue and collaborative ministry in which the gifts of each and of all are recognized. Laity must share in decision making in the Church. Considerable attention was given to the situation of women both in the Church and in society.

The condition of African women was lamented by a number of bishops. In some areas there is still female circumcision, the dispossession of widows and their children by the late husband's family, widowhood rites and wife inheritance, and the general tendency to treat women and girls as inferior. Mrs. Kathryn Hauwa Hoomkwap, a lay woman from Nigeria who spoke eloquently to the Synod assembly, complained that: "Childlessness, the fear of evil spirits, witchcraft are real concerns which are very often laughed at, dismissed as imaginary and non-existent in our Church circles. But to the suffering African women these problems are real." Bishop De Jong of Kitwe, Zambia, drew attention to the fact that social change has often benefited men at the expense of women and this has contributed to the emergence of "the apartheid of gender," in which the status of women has been maintained inferior to that of men. Other bishops pointed out that today there are new forms of abuse and oppression which were not typical in traditional societies: prostitution, concubinage, abandoned mothers, forced abortion, and sexual abuse of girls in schools by their teachers.

Each episcopal conference was called on to champion the rights of women especially with regard to education, widowhood, brideprice, pregnancy, delivery, single mothers, justice in marriage, and adequate remuneration for their work. There was a call, too, for further study of the role and place of women in Church and society, to be carried out in cooperation with government agencies where possible. Besides, adequate spiritual assistance should be given to women who play an indispensable role in family, Church, and society.

Conclusion

Time does not permit me to deal with many other aspects of justice which the Synod considered. What was remarkable was the absolute conviction of the bishops that unless the Church commits itself to the struggle for justice, it is failing in its mission of evangelization. We would have wished to share with you also some of the things said about communication and the means of social communication but we must conclude. The word *synod* comes from two Greek words, *syn* and *hodos*, a journey with or a journey together. The journey is not over. In a sense, it has just begun. There were five years of preparation and the Synod has now been celebrated. The pope has yet to come to Africa to encourage us to put into practice in life what has been decided. He will write a document gathering together all that has been reflected and pointing the way for the future.

We need not wait for these events, however important. Share the good news of the Synod among yourselves and be ready to cooperate with the bishops who will now try to bring its fruits to every diocese, every parish, every small Christian community. It is there that Christian life is lived, and it is there we must change and open ourselves to the new things the Holy Spirit is saying to the churches in Africa. The bishops have done what they could. They have done it well. Now they must take up again a journey together with the people, priests, and religious. They cannot continue the journey alone. The fruit of the Synod will perish on the tree unless Catholics join now in the harvesting.

In their final message from the Synod, the bishops declared:

In thanksgiving for the faith that we have received, and inspired by great joy, we turn toward the year 2000 which is approaching. We are filled with hope and determination to share the good news of salvation in Jesus Christ with every man and woman. That is our prayer and we invite the whole Family of God to pray with us and with Mary for a new Pentecost.

23

Women in the Churches in Africa

Possibilities for Presence and Promises

Bernadette Mbuy-Beya

I want to consider how African women have been living their experience of God and how they have expressed this experience. I speak of churches in the plural, since Africa contains many cultures and many forms of the Church. The churches of Africa are committing themselves more and more to the struggle for justice and freedom and are even involved in the process of democratization. It is then all the more surprising that these churches are silent—if not complicitous—when it comes to the question of women.

The position of women in African societies is not a pretty picture. The Circle of African Woman Theologians has already condemned the deplorable situation of women. The group has been working tirelessly so that each woman and each man might be recognized as a child of God, sharing equally in human dignity. Women do not lead this fight alone; more and more men are supporting them. Moreover, what these women are fighting for is not uniformity between themselves and men; rather, they want to be fully women in society as well as in the Church. As African women theologians we firmly hope that as a result of this Synod the churches of Africa will enter a new phase of maturity and will begin to act boldly, particularly with respect to Christian marriage and the role of women in ecclesial communities.

In his letter on the dignity and vocation of women, the Holy Father has already sounded an alarm, taking up the message of Vatican II to women, a message that makes a strong call to our churches:

The moment is coming, the moment has come, when woman's vocation is fully

Bernadette Mbuy-Beya, a religious sister from Zaire, is Mother Superior of the Ursuline Sisters and Director of the Institut Supérieur des Sciences Réligieuses in Lubumbashi, Zaire.

realized; the moment when woman takes on in the world an influence, a radiance, a power until now unattained. That is why at this time when humanity is undergoing so many changes women filled with the spirit of the Gospel can do so much to help humanity not to fail.[1]

We women theologians call upon the consciences of all the churches of Africa to bring about a radical change of mentality and to redefine the man-woman relationship in society and in the Church. Furthermore, we hope that this appeal will bring the Good News of the African Synod to Africa's women.

The Place of Women in African Society

It is impossible to discuss the issue of women in the Church without first of all examining the cruelty that women experience in society. The Church, generally speaking, does not perceive women any differently than does society at large; that is to say, the Church itself does not escape the temptation to discriminate against women, although perhaps never quite so overtly as the rest of society.

For the past two years the Zairean section of the Circle of African Woman Theologians has been studying closely the violence that victimizes African women in order to find non-violent ways of actively combating it.[2] Violence inflicted on women may be physical, psychological, or moral, including ten types of physical violence that negatively affect women's health: beatings and wounds, rape, venereal diseases, premarital pregnancy, abortion, too frequent pregnancies, bodily disfiguration, sexual mutilation, purification rites, and prostitution.

In each case our analysis has responded to the following questions:

—What? (Nature of the damage)
—By whom? (Individual or society)
—Against whom? (Women in general, the young, the elderly)
—Why? (Situations leading to violence)
—Consequences? (Effects on persons and on society)
—What to do? (Outline of solutions)
—By whom? (Who is responsible for change?)
—When? (Time frame to achieve specific objectives)

We concluded that a woman is the victim of violence from all sides and in her many roles: first in her family as a child and then a young woman; in her marriage as wife and mother; and finally in her social environment as worker or colleague. She suffers violence at the hands of man or because of man, and especially when there is a gulf between the aspirations of society and individuals. Violence affects both her body and her spirit.

We have defined psychological and mental violence as acts against a woman by another person that alter or deprive her of her thought, her will, or her behavior. They can range from an insult to the complete negation of a woman's personality. Considering the nature and forms of such violence, we have noted six types of acts: insulting or humiliating words; taboos and prohibitions; infidelity of the husband, which is accepted by tradition; incest; repudiation of the wife; and refusal of a wife's right to child custody. Such forms of violence seriously harm a woman because they destroy her inner life, shatter her personality, and throw her life off balance. Responsibility for such violence falls upon African society as a whole, for this is where the violence occurs. This state of affairs cries out to our collective conscience and requires a redefinition of our cultural and social values and the way we socialize individuals.

The Circle of African Woman Theologians addressed a letter to the chairman of Zaire's Sovereign National Conference, Archbishop Monsengwo, in which it raised a voice against the systematic destruction of the family.[3] Some of the sad observations made in the letter included:

1. Prostitution has become virtually institutionalized. No law either prohibits debauchery or takes any measures to protect the population from this curse that spares no family.

2. Even very young children have been tainted by moral, material, and intellectual corruption.

3. The concentration of wealth in the hands of an affluent minority plunges the rest of the population into misery and gives rise to a class of merchant women whose children are left on the streets.

4. The harmful intrusion of the extended family into the affairs of the nuclear family is a source of conflict and separation whose principal victims are the wife and children.

5. To the detriment of woman's dignity, the dowry has become a source of important income for men.

6. Tribalism has been chosen as a strategy to democracy, producing ethnic conflicts that plunge Zaire into a senseless bloodbath; the children suffer most.

7. The confiscation of the media by the ruling powers favors disinformation and estranges the people from the management of the commonwealth.

8. The deterioration of school and health facilities severely compromises the future of our children.

While not exhaustive, this list of social ills is a useful barometer indicating the state of health of Zairean society. It can be generalized to apply to most African societies today.

Women in the Church

Now we turn briefly to the role women play in the Church in Africa, as well as the role they could play if the churches in Africa were to agree to participate in their liberation. Much is at stake.

Are women truly present in the Church in Africa? Sister Justine Kahungu says that woman is indeed present in God's Church in Zaire. Her activity is seen in the liturgy; she devotes her talents to the choir; she directs and guides the young; she proclaims the Word of God; and at the offertory, alongside man, she offers to God "the fruit of the earth and the work of human hands." Sister Justine speaks also of the women involved in Catholic Action movements, in charismatic renewal as shepherdesses, as leaders of "living ecclesial communities" (CEV), or as the wives of

Bakambi, lay parish administrators. She notes also the increasing number of religious women who take on the duties of assistant pastors in parishes.[4] We have met some of these women, and heard their testimonies.

Mama Emerence Mbuyi is 54 years old, a widowed mother of several children. She has sung in the Cathedral's Swahili choir for many years. Here is what she told us:

> I love to sing for the Lord and I've been doing it since the age of nine. I was married to a man who loved the Lord and who accepted my vocation in the Church. In the choir I come into contact with a great many young people whom I help prepare for marriage or guide on the path of a priestly or religious vocation. My vocation includes lots of joy but also pain. I have seen many young people whom I thought well-rooted in Christ turn to the sects. The Christian community is my second family. It strongly supported me when I lost my husband a few years ago.

Mama Régine, Mama Prudence, and Mama Rose run a nutritional program in their parish. This is their way of participating in the development of their CEV. We started with forty-seven malnourished children, who were examined by a nutritional specialist. They received a ration of soybean porridge every day. Their number grew steadily as more children were recommended by the leaders of the CEVs of the different neighborhoods.

> At the time of the second visit by the nutritionist, seventy children were examined; she noted among them thirty-seven cases to be fed every day, and thirty-three to be treated three times a week. Most of the children began by being treated for worms; in one case special medical care was needed. We watch over attendance by the children, visit homes in case of illness or prolonged absence, and give nutritional advice to parents. We're very happy to come together each morning and do this work for God.

These Christian women play an important role in the CEVs, particularly in view of the serious economic crisis in Zaire, which hits the poorest of the poor the hardest. Mama Léonie Kaj, a catechist in her parish, shares her experience with us:

> I am the mother of two children but I have seven at home. I am in the Magnificat community as "a woman alone with Jesus," a movement for single women. I am a math teacher at Maadini Institute, a school of the Gecamines (the local mining company). In the parish of St. John in Kamalondo I've been in charge of the religious education program for both children and adults for five years. My first term has just ended and been renewed.
>
> As a catechist in my CEV I work with catechumens and sometimes with first communicants. My work as a teacher overflows into my work as a catechist. In each case it's a matter of deepening both the human and the spiritual. I'm thrilled by this work. In the evening at 5 o'clock, I'm at the parish. Before Christmas and Easter we prepare the catechumens or the first communicants more intensively for the sacraments of baptism, reconciliation, or the Eucharist. It's demanding, but for God nothing is too much! When I was put in charge of the catechetical

ministry the Christian community accepted me and helped me to improve.

The priests of my parish have accepted me, despite differences about admitting people to the sacraments. The catechists teach and form and try to explain Christian doctrine. Our priests take little interest in our catechetics. They don't know how, what or where we teach. They're there to administer the sacraments, and sometimes we have to beg them to do that. The biggest problem in my parish concerns when to admit children or any young people to the sacrament of reconciliation. Our priests prefer communal penance. But then when will our children and young people overcome their fear of confession?

Religious education is at the heart of parish life, and the contact with our priests has to be on-going to deepen the Christian knowledge of the catechists. All too often one gets the idea that catechetics is the affair of the laity alone. As a woman involved in the church at the parish level, I feel at ease since I participate in committee meetings and parish council meetings where decisions about the running of the parish are made. I also participate once a month in a sector meeting which groups several parishes together.

Mama Léonie concludes by noting that while women are very often involved in catechetical ministry, few of them are engaged in pastoral ministry. She believes women are afraid of working face to face with adults, particularly men. She would like to see a greater involvement in pastoral ministry.

Mama Marie-Louise Kasongo Mujinga Kinyembo is in charge of charismatic renewal in the archdiocese. A married woman, she is mother of six children. She recounts her adventure with God as a series of calls at different moments of her life. Mama Marie-Louise has known joyful times, but has also suffered a lot, feeling unaccepted because she is a woman.

The first call from God came to me when I was twelve, after my confirmation. In the silence of my soul I felt God's passing and I realized that I was a Christian and saw that my life was changing. I loved to attend the eucharistic celebration every day, to receive communion, to contemplate and to meditate. I heard the second call at the age of thirteen. Without knowing that another way was to open up before me, I thought of consecrating myself in religious life. It wasn't hard for me to give up the idea of religious life and consecrate myself in married life at the age of nineteen.

The Lord has helped me through the trials of married life and in times of sickness. I've been operated on nine times. The Lord has never stopped showing me his love and his hand is on me.

I was filled with the Holy Spirit in 1979 when the Lord chose me for his service. Guided by my bishop, I started the prayer group called Light of the World. Things went well and the members used their gifts to answer the appeals of God's people through prayer and healing. My husband encouraged me in this new ministry, and my children prayed with me, especially the older girls, who continue to be very active.

In 1984 my pastor asked me to coordinate the groups active in the parish and to belong to the parish council. This was not at all easy for my male brethren. Although the pastor had entrusted the organization of all the groups to me, my brothers could not accept his decision and clearly showed their preference to be guided by a man and not a woman. I was deeply hurt. Even now it is impossible to find unanimity in these groups and to provide any kind of real organization. I'm not ready to resign and I trust in the Lord.

In 1985 the Lord gave me another sign and called me to visit prisoners to share the Word with them and be for them a sign of his presence. We go regularly to the very large Kasapa Prison to bring food, to do first aid for those in need, and also to lead a prayer group with our brothers and sisters in detention.

In 1991 I was elected chairperson of charismatic renewal in the archdiocese. The first woman named to the post, I found it no small task! In this position I had to organize the first Congress of Charismatic Renewal. The Congress was a success, but the editing of the minutes was assigned to some male intellectuals who never did it, in spite of numerous reminders. Is this a way of protesting against my nomination? In any case, it shows that we have a long way to go to be converted.

As I've already told you, I keep struggling in prayer for wisdom. The bishop and his vicar general continue to encourage me, advising me to be patient. I'm not looking for glory, but as a mother I'd like to keep giving life in the Church through a ministry of prayer and reconciliation. The Lord has done great things for me. I have witnessed the most unexpected conversions. How I wish for my whole life to be praise! As long as the Lord needs me, I'm there and available.

Mama Véronique Kyabu Kabila, married and mother of seven children, devotes herself fully to the Children of Light (*Bilenga ya Mwinda*). With emotion she shares her great devotion to the Virgin Mary. Mama Véronique tells us that it was in 1981 that she felt deep desire to serve the Lord, following Mary's example.

I wanted to be a handmaid of the Lord, to bring Jesus into the world through works that manifest him (Jn. 4:21-23), be converted myself and help others to be converted. This deep desire was for me a call which I had to answer with an unconditional YES. Ever since, I've been working to serve the Lord my Creator anywhere he wants to use me.

Mama Véronique is currently a member of the Youth Commission of her CEV (small Christian community) and is a very active member of the Circle of African Woman Theologians. She is also a mother and her motherhood has taken on a new meaning because of all the children her ministry has brought to the Church. Mama Véronique would like the clergy to trust and allow greater freedom for the laity involved in the Church. The Spirit breathes on them and on the whole church community as well.

Sister Générose is a Daughter of St. Paul in Zaire. Her religious vocation has something of the miraculous about it, given the military milieu in which she was born and brought up. She calls us to share her joy as a consecrated woman.

Those in the military are the first victims of the drop in standard of living which Zaireans have been living through. For example, a Zairean soldier—if and when paid—earns less than 100 Belgian francs (53) a month. However, a minimum of 1,000 BF is required to meet essential monthly expenses. How in such conditions can one feed a family and pay for the children's schooling? In consequence, the military steal, pillage, etc. And even if they don't, public opinion automatically brands them as thieves.

A lot of things happen in a military camp: robberies, rapes, rows among the wives, violence among the children, and so on. It's in this setting that I was born and grew up. My name is Generose Sibay and for several years I've belonged to the Pauline family in the Congregation of the Daughters of St. Paul.

I had the good fortune to have as a father a soldier who is a Christian and who understood the importance of education and good upbringing for his eleven children. My father tilled the soil very hard so as to raise us with dignity.

My vocation was born when I saw the enormity of ignorance in the military camps, especially among the girls, and when I saw old people abused as sorcerers. The Lord was calling me to announce the Good News and console his people. "The Spirit of God has chosen me to extend the reign of Christ among the nations, to console the hearts worn down by suffering."

Today I am a consecrated woman in the Church and it's a great joy for me to be able to share all that the Lord has given me. Our congregation has made a preferential option for women, and we are working hard for the advancement of women in the mass media. The liberation of the African woman is an urgent concern for our society and our church. Action must be quick if Africa is to be saved.

As a religious I don't feel any complex as far as men are concerned. Our Mother Thecla (Merlo), co-foundress of our congregation, has taught me how to live in complementarity so that the Word of God may spread quickly and be received with honor (2 Thess. 3:1).

These few testimonies don't give us a complete picture of the lives of women active in the churches, but they do give us an idea of the different possibilities of presence.

The picture of women in the Church also offers some rays of hope. Ten years ago, at the opening of his diocese's synod, the Archbishop of Lubumbashi declared: "Africa needs a Gospel and a faith to save us from the sinful situations that make up our daily life . . . Let us then be prophets of now and not cantors of a bourgeois gospel."[5]

However, looking at the facts, we strongly fear that the situation of women is not considered to be one of these sinful situations. Moreover, the minutes of that diocesan synod made no allusion to women, although women had been invited to it. In fact, lay people and religious men and women were invited so as to widen the circle of priests around the bishops during the synod. I remember with great pleasure the evening when the lay people decided to walk out of the synod because the Church was making so little room for them. Women religious, with tears in their eyes, told the bishops that they too were fully members of the Church. In response, a moving eucharist was celebrated to close the synod.

Five years later, at Easter 1989, the archbishop published a pastoral letter on women, entitled "I Am a Human and Not Your Doormat." It elicited diverse reactions and revealed an image that many still have of women—that women are not truly human beings.[6] In this letter the archbishop showed a deeper consciousness of the status of women; he denounced the status quo and invited all to review their conduct. He noted that women appeared to be of no use to the Church beyond giving birth in the sacrament of matrimony to become good mothers of families or by religious profession, to become "good sisters," as they say.

One encouraging sign occurred in January 1992, during the Third General Assembly of the Ecumenical Association of Third World Theologians (EATWOT) in Nairobi. It had been decided to hold an outdoor ecumenical celebration. During the ceremony those present were called upon to ask pardon for the sins of our respective continents and to make a gesture of reparation for the benefit of the poor in Nairobi. One by one, Africans, Asians, Latin Americans, and the ethnic minorities of the United States expressed repentance in his or her own way. Then, totally unexpectedly, a Catholic priest, a white Latin-American, knelt down in the middle of the circle, inviting all the men to do likewise. He asked the women present to pardon the concrete sins that men had committed against them. The women were overwhelmed. One woman was then designated to receive the demand for pardon and grant the pardon in the name of all the others. She was an African religious, superior general of her congregation. She in turn knelt in an attitude of welcoming life and prayed to God that peace might come between men and women of the Third World.

The next day at the five-year election, women were elected to four of the seven places on EATWOT's executive committee. Clearly, the men were ready to run the association together with the women, whereas at its foundation in 1976 one lone woman had been admitted and only as an observer.[7] African churches should fall into step with EATWOT's example, for women might just be "the stone the builders rejected," which could become the cornerstone of tomorrow's church.

The gifts of God are distributed without discrimination to all in the Church, which needs all talents to be a credible sign of God's presence in the African world. Let us recall here Paul's message to the Church at Corinth:

> I never stop thanking God for all the graces you have received through Jesus Christ. I thank him that you have been enriched in so many ways, especially in your teachers and preachers; the witness to Christ has been strong among you so that you will not be without any of the gifts of the Spirit while you are waiting for our Lord Jesus Christ to be revealed (1 Cor. 1:4-7).

We must all then go beyond the Holy Father's beautiful meditation on the dignity and vocation of woman in the Church and in the world, and move to the effective recognition of this particular treasure through the sharing of ecclesial authority.

Vatican II, in its *Dogmatic Constitution on the Church* (No. 32), says there is but one chosen people of God, having the same filial grace and the same vocation to perfection; one salvation, one hope, and one undivided charity. The Council's declaration is very clear: in Christ and in the Church there is no inequality on the basis of race or nationality, social condition or sex. "For you are all one in Christ" (Gal. 3:28; Col. 3:11). Are our churches aware that they must lead the fight against structures that oppress women in the same way that they led the fight against structures that oppressed blacks in South Africa? This is one and the same struggle.

We have mentioned prostitution as a social evil, but we have not spoken explicitly of AIDS, which is decimating Africa. It is believed that there may soon be as many as ten million children orphaned by AIDS. Is it too much to ask the churches to appeal vigorously to the consciences of all people? It is not too late, for example, to issue a pastoral letter on AIDS, considering the extent of the plague and its grave consequences for the peoples of Africa.

African Women and Theology

Theology by African women does exist. Since 1986, African women have expressed both their experience of being discriminated against as women and their struggle for the right to life and the respect of their dignity. They have published *The Will to Arise: Women, Tradition, and the Church in Africa*,[8] a book that breaks the silence and speaks about their lives and their hopes. Women's theology in Africa concerns the whole life of every woman, regardless of education or social status; through it, women assert their belonging to the Church.

Africa is struggling to be freed from fear, hunger, racism, and oppression, be it economic, political, or religious. But the answers won't come from theological treatises on liberation alone. The Gospel—a message of liberation—will take root in African soil only because women and men aren't afraid of dirtying their hands in the earth or of risking their lives in the defense of the poor and helpless.

The difficulty for women's theology lies in the limitations imposed by poverty and the demands of daily life. It's hard to think about writing with a baby on your back crying from hunger, or with a child weakened by an attack of sickle-cell anemia. A second obstacle is the lack of funds to support women's theology, which has often prevented our work from being published. Such is the case with the report of the Yaoundé Colloquium on Theology from the Perspective of African Women, and the French translation of *The Will to Arise*, to cite but two instances. Another limitation, no less important, is the rate of illiteracy, which is rising in countries like Zaire because of the destruction of the school system, or in countries like Angola because of war. As a consequence the gap in the level of schooling between girls and boys continues to widen.

In Africa we want to live decently and to be able to express or experience God in our human communities. We do theology in our own fashion with women such as Teresa Okure, Teresia Hinga, Bette Ekeya, and Margaret Umeagudosu, to cite just a few, who work in academia, but our theological reflection is also based on wisdom and feeling. It is done not only in the head, but in the heart and the gut. In the

Bible we meet women who, like ourselves, fought for the right to life, like the midwives at the time of Moses; women like Miriam, Deborah, Ruth, Esther, Judith; later Mary the Mother of Jesus, the prophetess Anne, Martha, and Mary. By their deeds these women were instruments of God's favor.

At the present time, one group of women playing an important role in the Church is women religious. The late Cardinal Malula, founder of the Sisters of Ste. Therese of the Child Jesus of Kinshasa, summed up his works: "My whole effort can be summed up in three key words: form girls who are fully women, authentically African, and authentically religious."[9] The consecrated life of women is a gift of God to the churches of Africa. With a view to survival, many international congregations have opened their doors to African girls.[10] In order to ensure a smoother collaboration with diocesan religious women, many bishops have discovered for themselves the charism of "Father Founder." But often these religious are treated like the personal housekeepers of the bishop and of the local clergy.

Even if religious women are willing to serve the Church in the most humble tasks, it remains clear that the meaning of consecrated life lies elsewhere. Called first of all "to be with the Lord" (Mark 3:14), the African woman religious says "Yes" to the Lord so that life may spring forth in Africa. For her the meaning of religious life is a question of fidelity to God and to the cultural values of life-giving, of family solidarity, of a sense of responsibility, and of integration into the milieu.

In Shaba, a region of Zaire particularly infected with xenophobia, religious women have broken the silence, coming out of their convents to call upon the political authority. They expressed themselves in this way:

Governor,

Those of us working in the field of health care deplore the lack of medicine, the lack of money, and the severity of illnesses whose principal cause is malnutrition. To go to the fields would be a solution: we have land and rain; but many people have given up farming because of insecurity.

This is what we ask of you: that you make use of the media to encourage the people to farm; that you publicly ask the military and others at your service and who should be at the service of the population to help people farm in peace.

We believe that you are hearing—through us—the cry of our people that we want to be heard and which we are determined to have heard fully.

As far as the agricultural campaign is concerned, we for our part are committing our efforts in the zones where we are present so as to organize collective work and do all in our power to make the project succeed.

One of the tasks of religious life in Africa is the Christianizing of the various rites of passage that affect the lives of women, and that is not an easy thing to do. Thus, the Circle of African Woman Theologians aims for a new conception of the feminine being within current society. This new conception entails a change in mentality, which must take place first of all in each woman herself. She must first of all accept herself as a human being, loved and wanted as she is by God (Gen. 1:27-28). The Circle of African Woman Theologians has decided to undertake a number of activities to equip women to raise their consciousness and be mobilized:

—Organize educational conferences with secondary school seniors (already begun).

—Help women participate in the mass media to inform, educate, and communicate (made possible thanks to the Daughters of St. Paul).

—Launch a campaign to sensitize people to the rights of women, calling upon all powers that be (action made difficult by the current economic crisis).

—Use health care facilities to provide basic health education (difficult to get started).

—Promote the participation of women in the CEVs (action already going on).

—Promote and work for agricultural development (practically impossible because of insecurity).

—Awaken the consciousness of the people to protect the land of our ancestors by fighting against deforestation and the dumping of toxic waste.

—Promote and work in the struggle against illiteracy (action to be encouraged).

—Favor the economic independence of women by establishing cooperatives (impossible because of the current economic crisis).

The Archbishop of Lubumbashi is right in asserting that it is not sufficient to pray or lament; women must be committed from now on to helping our people improve their lot.[11] Thus he calls upon women to cease waiting and to cease acting like defeated victims, but rather to take full charge of themselves. The liberation of women is in the hands of woman herself and she must fight for it. Consequently, the Roman Catholic Church in Africa must cease being a masculinized Church and become a Church for both men and women.

The priesthood of women is a difficult topic to address in the Catholic Church, still more so in Africa! Yet it would be good to study it in the light of certain African traditions that have given woman an important place in the life of the community.[12] The fact that so many women spontaneously emerge as "spiritual leaders" is a sign of the times that must be reckoned with. The current proliferation of different kinds of spirituality gives proof of the anguished search of our people, who are crushed by suffering and yet hungry for God. Many different forms of spirituality are a challenge to the structures of our institutional churches.[13] Many people marginalized by church law feel more at ease in prayer groups outside the churches, and it is often women shepherdesses who take on these ministries of welcome and of God's mercy.

Women's Ministries in the African Church

Before speaking of women's ministries, the Church must first work to guarantee women the possibility of adequate theological training so that they can effectively participate in the whole life of the Church. In Africa, at least in the Catholic Church, sacred studies hold no great importance in the eyes of families. Parents do not want to spend their money in such studies for girls. It is therefore incumbent upon the religious congregations to provide sisters with a solid spiritual and theological formation. The fight for the liberation of women must find strength in a great inner freedom acquired through prayer and through a spirit of sacrifice, in a deep and intimate relationship with Jesus Christ. Only this relationship can reveal woman to herself and prepare her for the role of mother, giving and bearing life.

It must not be forgotten that we are invited all together, women and men, to seek a new way of being Church today. There are certain women, shepherdesses of prayer groups and religious in parish or hospital ministries, for example, who have close contact with the life of the community and with people in search of God. It would be desirable for them to take on certain sacramental ministries such as baptism, the sacrament of the sick, the sacrament of reconciliation, and the role of official Church witness at weddings.[14] One need not even mention the roles of lector or homilist, which are already required. I myself have assumed the responsibilities of pastoral assistant in two different parishes. Until now, in our diocese, at least, only women religious may distribute communion alongside the priest and laymen. Any woman with a real responsibility in the Church should be able to be called to this ministry.

Recommendations

In conclusion, we offer several recommendations to guide reflections after the Synod.

1. The Church of Africa has already devoted much effort to the education and advancement of women. To battle against the silence of women themselves and silence about the lives of women, we recommend that the Church encourage women to undertake sacred studies.

2. The Church of Africa has made great efforts in the liturgy so that God can dwell amidst the people. We recommend therefore that women, especially, be given the task of creating new symbols that touch the hearts of the faithful.

3. Because of increasingly high illiteracy, access to the media is essential in Africa. Since virtually all Africans listen to the radio, we recommend that the Church encourage educational broadcasts hosted by women.

4. The struggle for the liberation of women and for the protection of creation concerns us all. Let the Church spare no effort to preach against all forms of exploitation of women and children and against the destruction of the environment.

5. "In the world and not of it." Let the Church of Africa hold on to its freedom in the face of political power, let it defend the rights of the poor and the helpless, and let it protect the people from any form of segregation.

6. "Arise, shine out, for your light has come." Let African women take their place in the Church without waiting for a handout and take real responsibility in important decision-making that affects the life of the community.

7. We are aware of major gaps in the formation of our shepherdesses and in their discernment. May the Church give them direction.

8. If on one hand women ask the Church to recognize their feminine ministries, on the other hand they must show their spirit of initiative and make bold strides in the vineyard.

9. To encourage greater solidarity among women, we recommend that Zaire's Movement of Catholic Women be extended throughout Africa.

To conclude, we would like to express all the faith we have in the African Synod for a better future in Africa by citing this text from the Apocalypse:

Then I saw a new heaven and a new earth; the first heaven and the first earth had disappeared now, and there was no longer any sea. I saw the holy city, and the new Jerusalem, coming down from God out of heaven, as beautiful as a bride dressed for her husband. Then I heard a loud voice call from the throne. "You see this city? Here God lives among men. He will make his home among them; they shall be his people, and he will be their God; his name is God-with-them. He will wipe away all tears from their eyes; there will be no more death, and no more mourning or sadness. The world of the past has gone." Then the One sitting on the throne spoke: "Now I am making the whole of creation new" (Rev. 21:1-5).

Notes

1. *Mulieris Dignitatem*, John Paul II, August 15, 1988.

2. "La Femme, La Société, L'Église," Bureau Diocésain de Catechèse, Mbegu, *Dossiers Jeunes*, No. 37, pp. 1-8.

3. Ibid., p. 6.

4. Sr. Justine Kahungu, "La Femme dans L'Église" in *Faire la Théologie dans la Perspective des Femmes Africaines*. Unpublished document (Yaoundé, August 1986).

5. *Voies Nouvelles pour L'Évangelization: Actes du Synode de Loishia, août 19-29, 1984*. Archdiocese du Lubumbashi, p. 5.

6. "Je suis un homme et pas votre natte," Pastoral Letter of Monseigneur Kabanga, Easter 1989, 4.

7. "A Movement Named EATWOT" in Virginia Fabella, ed. *Beyond Bonding: A Third World Women's Theological Journey* (EATWOT and Institute of Women's Studies, 1993), p. 7.

8. Mercy Oduyoye and Musumbi R. A. Kanyoro, *The Will to Arise: Women, Tradition, and the Church in Africa* (Maryknoll, N.Y.: Orbis Books, 1992).

9. Bernadette Mbuy-Beya, *"Mes ton plus jolie pagne,"* article prepared for the Global Forum on Religious Life, Manila, August 21-31, 1993.

10. Ibid.

11. *Je suis un homme*, Pastoral Letter of Mgr. Kabanga, Lent 1976.

12. Ibid.

13. *"Expérience féminine de Dieu dans la Renouveau Charismatique à Lubumbashi"* in *Faire la Théologie dans la Perspective des Femmes Africaines*. Unpublished document (Yaoundé, August 1986).

14. Ibid.

24

Mass Media and the Shaping of Modern African Cultures

Renato Kizito Sesana

If anyone still had any doubt about the influence that modern mass media can have in Africa, the happenings of April 1994 in Rwanda should have been convincing. The incitement to ethnic violence and the calculated misinformation of RTLM (Radio Télévision Libre Mille Collines) was the single major factor in the creation of the climate of mass hysteria that unleashed the massacre of the Tutsi. On the other side, the information system of the Rwanda Patriotic Front (RPF), competently run by western-trained professionals, made its version of the facts the only acceptable one in the eyes of the western world. Each side craftily used their knowledge of the culture of their audience in order to sell their truth and to reach their purpose.[1]

In the midst of such a propaganda war, the Church relied on personal contacts, sermons, and some outdated printed material (pastoral letters, bulletins). No wonder that the courage, dedication, and witness of the thousands of lay people, who worked to save the lives of the brethren of any ethnic group and often paid with their own lives, did not succeed in having any significant impact on the ferocity of the war; their courage went unnoticed by the local and international mass media.

This is not to say that the presence of a church radio or press would have solved the Rwanda problem, but certainly what happened is a sign of the dangerous gap existing between Church and mass media. Even where Church media exist, there is little mass media mentality, or the ability to use them effectively. This is nothing new; it is not limited to Africa but is widespread in the church. A peaceful reciprocal acceptance of Church and mass media has not been achieved even in the tradi-

Renato Kizito Sesana, an Italian Comboni Missionary, was the founding editor of *New People* magazine in Nairobi, Kenya. At present he is responsible for media in the Rumbek diocese in Southern Sudan.

tionally Christian countries that invented the mass media. We cannot ignore the fact that in 1832 in the encyclical *Mirari Vos,* Gregory XVI defined the freedom of press as "evil, and never enough abhorred and detested." Today, in spite of the Second Vatican Council and the words of *Communio et Progressio* (the 1971 pastoral instruction published by the Pontifical Commission for Social Communication as mandated by the Council Fathers) about the need for public opinion in the Church, it is a fact that most church leaders are ill at ease when dealing with the media; a free public opinion in the Church is hardly tolerated; and any systematic pastoral program in this field is lacking.

Successes and Failures

In Africa this inadequate use of the media in the Church's pastoral and missionary activities is particularly evident. Catholic mass media have not been able to keep up with the pace of demographic growth, the progress of technology, or the fast changing culture. From its prestigious, if not influential, position of a few decades ago, the Catholic press is now marginalized, if not totally irrelevant. For example, some prestigious newspapers disappeared, including *Afrique Nouvelle,* which was published in Dakar (Senegal) and used to reach almost all Francophone Africa. Because of external factors, such as lack of electricity or telephone, others lost importance or incisiveness—such as *DIA* of Kinshasa (Zaire), the only Catholic News Agency in Africa. Others had difficulties with politics or finances, such as Uganda's *Munno,* an influential Catholic daily newspaper that had to close a year ago. In Zambia the weekly ecumenical *National Mirror* plugs along with a very limited circulation.

These problems are not specific to the Catholic press. The All Africa Press Service (APS), an English news agency of the All African Conference of Churches (AACC), also has difficulty in becoming an effective means of information and public opinion formation. There are some remarkable exceptions in the print media. *Icengelo,* published in the Chibemba language at Ndola (Zambia), with a circulation of 80,000 copies, truly represents a point of reference in the battle for democratization that still continues in Zambia. Zimbabwe's *Moto* is a rare example of freedom of the press, both in the civilian and in the ecclesiastical context, and it presents important discussions of the concrete problems of Zimbabwe. *Renaître,* born three years ago in Kinshasa (Zaire), has become a popular fortnightly magazine on the problems of Church and society. *New People,* started in 1989 in Nairobi (Kenya) and distributed throughout English-speaking Africa, has played an important role in popularizing the issues of the African Synod. Because of its interest in the Synod, *New People* has drawn the attention of the Vatican.

Since independence, Catholic broadcasting stations, both radio and television, have practically disappeared. They have been nationalized or simply closed down by the military and dictatorial regimes that took over. For example, Télestar, the radio/TV production center founded in 1963 by the diocese of Kinshasa, was nationalized in 1974. Today the trend is changing: at the beginning of 1995 Africa had at least fourteen Catholic radio stations functioning, and many other Catholic institutions are in the process of applying for permission or of preparing for operation. These courageous initiatives are still too new to be properly appreciated and evaluated.

It is easy to detect the causes of this situation. The general poverty of Africa makes it difficult for the African Church to manage any means of mass communication that require large investments. The financial resources of dioceses and of episcopal conferences are very limited. Where can the necessary capital be found to set up newspapers, recording studios, or radio and television stations? The international agencies that generously provided such financing in the past now show less interest. International Catholic agencies can be convinced to restart a press or radio and television stations only when they become aware that a new political and economic climate is in place in Africa and that the Church should be part of this struggle. Such agencies usually expect that funds will be well administered, something that has not always happened in the past. The deterioration of African economies makes it difficult not only to raise local funds, but even to sell products. In almost all African countries, a catechism or a school textbook is often a luxury.

Moreover, the freedom of the press is far from being a given in most African countries. There is still reluctance to license new broadcasting stations or register new magazines. African politicians understand very well that all means of communications—roads, railways, airways as well as newspapers and broadcasting stations—are powerful instruments that influence opinion and they want to manage them directly. The press has not escaped this control. A cynical joke says that "News is what the powerful don't want people to know." Numerous African journalists who have tried to inform people about significant events have been imprisoned and tortured. Occasionally, as in the case of the Ugandan priest, Clement Kiggundu, editor of *Munno*, they have been simply eliminated.

Yet the most important reasons for the failure of the Church in the field of the media are internal. The basis for a meaningful communication does not exist. There is no participatory and democratic mentality and there is no internal freedom. In a Church where unchecked authority and secrecy are the unquestioned pillars of every communication, it is not possible to develop or encourage a desire for well-informed public opinion. Calls for freedom of the press seem to carry no serious moral authority. The hope is that the winds of democratic change blowing throughout the continent will allow a free public opinion to emerge and to express itself through the media. This will have repercussions in the Church: people will no longer accept a passive role as mere receivers of communication. The African Church must make a great effort to rebuild its credibility and its presence in the world of social communications.

Africa: A Cultural Battleground

Since independence, in most African countries the mass media have been used primarily for two purposes. The first is dissemination of the official truth, which often means disinformation or even outright lies. This has created a skepticism among the most educated population. Mass media are seen as the "master's" voice.

In Kinshasa, for example, people, wanting to identify someone as a liar would say "He speaks like a radio." The second use of media is for entertainment, most of which is of American or European origin, resulting in alienation from the local reality. European and American films, videos, television shows, music, and magazines are flooding into Africa. While some of this may be of quality and stimulate local creativity (but where is the money for local productions?), most is not, and has an eroding effect on traditional cultural values.

This western influence promotes a spirit of consumerism, individualism, materialism, and competition, without communicating any positive human values. Moreover it confirms, at every level, the heavy dependency of Africa. As a result, too often mass media in Africa are not a means of communication but of domination, manipulation, and oppression. In no way do they promote understanding and communion, which should ideally be the aim of any real communication process.

Africa is a playground—or a battleground—of many different and often conflicting cultures: African or traditional cultures that still shape the mind and soul of every African; modern culture, imported from the West and heavily influenced by individualism; the mass media culture, a development of modern culture; Christian culture, whose main frame of reference is defined by the Bible and Church tradition; Arab-Islamic culture, referring to the Qur'an and all the richness of the Arab tradition.

Media and Culture

In this context of rapid political and social change, of cultural confrontation, mass media plays a highly significant role by shaping the Africans of tomorrow. If the media are used to enforce a dehumanized vision of the modern African, they form people who accept all information given them from the top, without courage or ambition for self-growth and self-liberation, helpless in front of imported technologies, people who can only choose to repeat models and examples of the developed countries. This is worse than slavery.

Mass media offer an open frontier for the Church to present, amid much noise and ephemeral seductions, the only Word that truly saves. Catholic newspapers, magazines, and broadcasting stations have a role to play, but let us not delude ourselves, they can reach only a small part of the audience. The real game is played in the commercial media. The presence there of Catholic lay professionals is the key to influencing our modern culture.

The number of young Africans who wish to translate their faith into the language of the mass media continues to increase. The growth in membership of UCAP (Union Catholique Africaine de la Presse) and its members' readiness to face challenges indicates that in a few years the Church could have many lay people both committed and professionally skilled. Hopefully, these young African journalists will rediscover and revalue the richness of traditional African communication as well as the communicative force of the Gospel and of the Christian community.

Preparing for the African Synod

Abundant documents and resolutions on the theme of "Means of Social Communication" were part of the preparation for the Synod. The most important meeting on this topic, the Pan-African Meeting of Episcopal Commissions for Social
Communications, was held in Ibadan in 1973. At its meeting in 1990, the Symposium of Episcopal Conferences of Africa and Madagascar (SECAM), which meets
every three years, concentrated on the theme of "Evangelization in Africa through
the Means of Communication." These two meetings took place in extremely different contexts in the Church and the civil society and expressed quite different moods.
While the Ibadan document is affirmative and indicates actions, the Lomé document of SECAM is more reflective and exhortative and words like "encourage,"
"insist," and "recommend" abound.

While these two meetings expressed the commitment of the African Church to
become more involved in the mass media, the gap between the planning of 1973,
the wishes of 1990, and the reality is painfully evident. Goodwill is not sufficient.
A reading of the final resolutions of the Ibadan document is a nostalgic trip through
a list of unfulfilled dreams.[2] The *Instrumentum Laboris* for the African Synod did
not seem to take into consideration much of the previous work done in Africa. Its
section on "Means of Social Communication" simply synthesizes Vatican documents on the theme, with some attempts at contextualization. Sometimes this effort
to make the document sound African becomes pathetic, as when it speaks of the
"The Talking Drum" (135). Yet, there are some good points, particularly the need
for a pastoral plan and recognition of the "impact that both the traditional and the
modern media exert on the life of society today [that] create what is in fact a new
culture" (138).

The Message and the Propositions from the Synod

The four weeks reserved for the Synod proved to be too short a time to face all
the issues present in the *Instrumentum Laboris*. From the beginning, the two major
topics of justice and peace and inculturation attracted most of the attention of the
Fathers. The means of social communication received scant attention. There was
no reference to social communication in the summary of the bishops' interventions
of the first two weeks.[3] At the end the African Synod produced two documents: the
"Message of the Synod" addressed to the Family of God in Africa and to the Family of God all over the world, and a list of sixty-four "Propositions" submitted to
the Holy Father.

A comparison between the two texts reveals a different approach to the means
of social communication. The Message dedicates four of seventy-one paragraphs
to this theme. It highlights two aspects as important and complementary: "a new
and emerging cultural universe" and "a series of means serving communication."
This recognizes that the media form a new culture with specific values and counter-
values and need to be evangelized. This represents a new Areopagus for the mod-

ern age, to use an expression of John Paul II in *Redemptoris Missio*. This is, then, a clear awareness of a challenge, of the need to open up to a new world, to enter into it with courage and creativity. The text also emphasizes the need for formation of those who use the media. All in all, the text of the Message is inspiring; it represents a rather sharp departure from the simplistic traditional way of looking to the means of communication as an extension of the pulpit.

In the Propositions, seven of the sixty-four are on the theme of social communication. The approach is rather different from that of the Message: "In faithfulness to Christ who is the Communicator *par excellence*, the Church is aware of her duty of fostering social communications *ad intra et ad extra*." This duty leads to the need to promote communication from within through a better diffusion of information, the use of a full range of traditional and modern techniques, the development of pastoral plans, the need to guarantee access to the media to every person without exception, the formation of Christian communicators, the setting up of radio stations, the securing of a satellite channel, the opening of libraries and audiovisual centers, and the creation of commissions for communications at all levels in the church structure. This approach is similar to the traditional use of the mass media to make the voice of the pastors heard everywhere, a communication from the top to the bottom, from the center to the periphery, rather than a bold call to face the challenge of a new culture, of a new Areopagus. Neither document explicitly mentioned a well-informed public opinion inside the Church, contrary to the ample space given to it in the *Communio et Progressio* (115-121).

Communication and Life

Communication is not a technique disconnected from life or reserved for highly trained technicians and sophisticated intellectuals. Communication is life. And the life-context of communication is as important as the message. I received the news that the location of the African Synod was to be Rome just after my return from the annual meeting of the New Sudan Council of Churches in southern Sudan. Forty church people from different denominations attended, including bishops, moderators, and pastors. It was held in Kaya, a large village with a few brick houses. The participants met in a church built with mud and dry grass, and their sleeping quarters were tents continually beaten by the wind. Food was simple and scarce, though much better than that eaten by the local people.

The contrast between this meeting and the logistical reasons cited by some for holding the Synod in Rome (accommodation, communication) was shocking. Without advocating that the Synod should have been celebrated in Kaya, many decent and suitable places could have been found in Africa. A Synod held in Africa would have communicated a drastically different symbolic value and vision. And if the Synod had been interrupted by civil disturbances or by logistical shortcomings, that would have been a sign to Africans that the Church was close to their life situation, that of a suffering exploited people. This message would have been more meaningful than any well-worded statement sent by electronic mail from Rome.

The Experience of Communication in Africa

After a class at Tangaza Theological College in Nairobi, a young African who was completing his pastoral experience in a shantytown on the outskirts of Nairobi said:

> I have realized that the single most important factor in my relationship with our people is the time I take to communicate with them. Before going there I felt embarrassed by my rich clothes, by the fact that I have three good meals a day, that I have plenty of time for study and prayer, which they can hardly imagine. Yet people did not question me on these issues. What people want is that I take time to communicate. They want to know me as a person. What people demand from me is to be more available to them.

This student is on his way toward reappropriating the inheritance of his ancestors. In Africa, establishing relationships is more important than action. People feel more human when they "communicate" rather than when they "do." The very act of communication has value, regardless of the message.

Any serious reflection on how to communicate the Good News in Africa should develop from the richness of the African communicative experience rather than from the technical aspect, the "means of social communication." Communication in Africa, as anywhere else, is the establishment of relationships, the creation of meaning, the building of understanding and communion. In fact, this is perhaps stronger here in Africa than elsewhere. So the problem is not simply how to use modern means of social communication, but how to draw the African communicative experience into the life of the Church.

I think that the first step is to liberate our African gift for communication and for building up human relationships. At the beginning of my ministry in Africa, I was lucky to be initiated into pastoral work by an experienced priest, a White Father. In our area, it was expected that priests would help solve family and village conflicts. I was always afraid of making mistakes, due in part to my poor knowledge of the local language. One day when I was particularly nervous about going alone to assist in solving a rather important conflict, the older priest told me:

> What you have to do is to listen with patience, kindness, understanding and respect. Even after you think you have fully understood the case, never try to speed up the process, or say that you are in a hurry to go back to the mission. Listen to every single person who wants to speak. If after doing this you still pass a wrong judgment, the elders will help you to correct it. What is important is not the judgment, since everybody in the village knows already who is wrong and who is right! What is important is the process, the sitting together, the reciprocal listening, the building of relationship.

In the same way, I would say that what is important at this moment of change and growth for the Church in Africa is to put communication at the center of the internal life of the Church and of the relationship of the Church with the world. This means listening with respect, understanding, and love to what the people have to say. This means allowing people to express their faith with freedom and joy, without any restraint other than their love for Jesus. Jesus adopted a model of a shared communication. His identification with his listeners, particularly the poor and the marginalized, was total.

The Church needs to devise new ways to put the means of communication at the service of the Gospel. There is still a need to decolonize both models and means of communication. Small Christian Communities (SCCs) are the natural environment for a process of rediscovering authentic forms of African communication. They are the place where traditional culture, the Gospel, and modern culture meet and give new shape to peoples' lives. Working together, new and old African models of communication can revive communication inside the Church and make it not only more vital, more African, but more human!

The reflections of Bénézet Bujo (see pages 139-151 herewith) are an outstanding example. Africa must discover that Christian communication lies not only in spreading information, in exchanging ideas or moral teaching. These dimensions should be present, of course, but the first purpose of communication is to make visible Christ's presence in today's history. It is to uncover God's action and cooperate with it. A conversion is needed.

By rediscovering how Africans communicate, the Church will reach the poor, the marginalized, the ordinary worker and housewife. Such communication will be based on the spoken language of daily life and the communicator will be in empathy with the listeners. The old one-way communication model from top to bottom—from bishop to priest to religious to faithful—should be replaced by a dialogue in which the particular functions, responsibilities, duties, rights of each member are taken into proper consideration.

Inculturation and Communication

The challenge is formidable. Scientists tell us that the media not only transmit messages, but also shape and create a new culture. Or, in Western society, the media are the culture. As Cardinal Martini wrote:

> The media are no longer screens we watch or radios we listen to. They are an atmosphere in which we are immersed. We live in this world of sounds, images, colors, impulses, and vibrations as our ancestors were once immersed in the forest, like fish in water. It is our environment and the media are a new way of being alive. But alive in what way? . . . Just as an ideology dispenses us from thinking and a bureaucracy frees us from acting, so the media frees us from feeling. Superficial feelings drive out deeper ones.[4]

For a large portion of the human race, the media have become the primary socializing force, replacing family, school, and Church. Now the task of the African

Church is apparently two-fold and contradictory. On the one side is the need for African cultures to inculturate the Gospel. On the other side is the need to inculturate the mass media culture. I can foresee two possible future scenarios. First, modern mass media will flatten out all cultural diversity throughout the world and Africa will become a peripheral part of an empire based in North America and the Pacific Rim. We will speak the same language, watch the same TV programs, and express our dreams in the same way. This scenario is too sad to contemplate, and it would make any talk of inculturation in Africa superfluous!

The second scenario is that the traditional cultures will creatively meet the challenges of modernity and of the mass media culture and through an undoubtedly painful process of transformation and integration give rise to new African cultures. In this scenario, if the Church wants to communicate the Gospel, it will have to do so with courage and boldness or risk becoming irrelevant.

The link between inculturation and communication is essential. It is not possible to imagine a deep inculturation that will not pass through African forms of communication. And the media will have to be inculturated, used in an African way. This interaction between inculturation and communication is the inevitable focal point from which the new African modern culture will emerge.

Hope for the Future

A new vision is needed. Christian communicators should emphasize faith and creativity rather than techniques. We need to communicate compelling images. Modern Africans cannot avoid the eternal question: "Does God exist? And, if God exists, how is God present in human history?" Turning this question (and the search for an answer) into a challenging and engaging newspaper article or TV program is no easy task. It requires a profoundly personal spiritual experience, high professionalism, immersion into the cultural environment of the audience, and bold imagination—all things that too often are sadly missing from the Catholic media.

Pastoral plans calling for more personnel, more money for the Catholic press and for radio and TV stations will not necessarily solve the problem of communicating the Gospel in Africa. The communicator must be an artist who sings a new song, gives life to new symbols, interprets and re-expresses the African experience of poverty and dependence, while opening it at the same time to new horizons. Communication is how we pray and the way we build our churches.

To communicate is to be present, although not necessarily physically, in the market, at the well, at dances and festivities, in the beer hall, at funerals. Communication is the constant re-creation of a culture. What better way to summarize the path ahead than the following quote from a talk given by a young Catholic Kenyan journalist during the 1994 UCAP meeting in Dakar? After describing the parallel between the freedom proclaimed by Jesus and the practice of freedom in the field of the media, Albert Mori indicated some paths to increase freedom in the society and in the church:

> We have to nurture the taste for truth and freedom in ourselves first, and then in our listener or reader (audience). Everything we write or say should somehow

advance and promote the thirst for truth and freedom. We should create practical avenues for freedom. We have to open spaces for it to be exercised. We have the talents, knowledge and ability to do this. If there is no room for freedom in our working environment, we have to start from outside.

[We have to] put our professionalism at the service of small groups, of people printing newsletters, organizing group discussions. One of our roles is to provoke a spark of freedom which could light a huge fire. We can in many ways challenge our national leaders to take a greater interest and show greater concern for the poor other than at election time.

Whenever possible, we should try to become owners of the media. In many countries, lack of freedom is caused by the fact that media ownership is concentrated in the hands of the governments or businessmen with other interests. I do not think of becoming owners of mass media empires, but of alternative media like newsletters, monthly information services, etc. It is not a dream, it is possible, and some of us here have already done it. In some countries, like Uganda, people with very limited economic means have started radio broadcasting, feeling that the time was ripe and the government would not risk to go against the public feeling . . . Facts proved them to be right. Some of our members may have the creativity and the courage to try something similar.

We have to look at our work not simply as transmission of information, but as evangelization of the new culture emerging in Africa. We are on the spot where, according to the words of the African Synod, "a new culture that has its own language and its own specific values and counter-values" is created. It is also up to us if this new emerging culture is going to be imbued with evangelical values like reconciliation, peace, solidarity, non-violence, tolerance, respect for human dignity.

Let's take the example of the so-called "mob justice" in Kenya. People are sometimes killed on the spot by members of the public because they are caught stealing. In general they are poor people stealing something to survive, and an average of five or six per week are killed in this inhuman way in Nairobi alone. (Incidentally, it never happens that the rich and powerful, who do steal on a grand scale, are victims of mob justice). Mob justice has become fashionable also because of the press, which gives it a high profile. If we were able, as Catholic journalists, to report about mob justice in a way which highlights its degrading barbarity for all who take part in it, we would have helped in the evangelization of society.

All this will be facilitated and achieved if we have strong media associations, unions and cooperatives to support each other, even across borders. We should, however, be careful that the unions we form do not become another way of being elitist, and oppress the poor, but always evaluate if our work is of real service to the poor.[5]

Notes

1. See W. Schonecke, "What Does the Rwanda Tragedy Say to AMECEA Churches?" *Amecea Documentation Service*, No. 424.

2. For a complete collection of Catholic and ecumenical documents produced in Africa on

the media, see *The African Church in the Communications Era*, edited by M. Phillipart (Nairobi: St. Paul Publications, 1992).

3. See *Synodus Episcoporum Bulletin* (Holy See Press Office, 26 April 1994).

4. *Il lembo del mantello*, Pastoral Letter on Communication, 1992.

5. Albert Odhiambo Mori, "African Press and Freedom," intervention at the UCAP Conference in Dakar, Senegal, 1994.

25

"The Synod of Hope" at a Time of Crisis in Africa

John Mary Waliggo

Part 1

The Special Assembly for Africa of the Synod of Bishops met in Rome from April 10 to May 8 in 1994. In their concluding message, the Synod Fathers referred to their encounter as "the Synod of hope." Were they too optimistic of what they had achieved or were they being realistic? In using the word hope, were they referring to the church in Africa, to the African continent as a whole, or to both? And what exactly did they mean by hope?

In the opinion of some participants and observers, the Synod had shortcomings. I want to touch on these areas of disappointment in order to show that what was achieved by the Synod can be transformed into liberative action only if these shortcomings are overcome. My evaluation touches on the preparation of the Synod, its composition, methodology, duration, and concluding message. Then I will identify some areas of hope.

Preparation

It needs to be said, and loudly too, that the preparation of the Synod, despite affirmations to the contrary, was inadequate, primarily because it failed to actively involve the very people who make up the Church in Africa—the laity. Yet the impact of the Synod depends on their participation. In their concluding message, the Synod Fathers recognized the importance of legitimizing what they had to say by

John Mary Waliggo, a Ugandan priest, was formerly on the faculty at the Catholic University of Eastern Africa in Nairobi, Kenya. He presently works in the Catholic Secretariat in Kampala, Uganda. He is a member of the Ugandan Constitutional Commission.

acknowledging the people of God in Africa, Madagascar and the Islands: "You prepared this Synod actively and with enlightened zeal through your responses to the questionnaire contained in the *Lineamenta* and through your reflection on the *Instrumentum Laboris* (5)." But did African Christians actively participate in the preparation of the Synod? The answer is—No.

We can test the truth of that answer in almost any African country. In Uganda, for example, thirteen of the sixteen Catholic dioceses responded. Some were responses to a questionnaire submitted by diocesan pastoral coordinators alone or assisted by a few priests and immediate co-workers. Few of the many Catholic bodies responded: only the two major seminaries at Ggaba and Katigondo, the Association of Religious Women, the Brothers of the Christian Instruction and, at the very last moment, a group of Catholic youth. There were two national meetings of pastoral coordinators and theologians to discuss the *Lineamenta* and what participants felt should be the themes of the Synod. At the end of October 1991, the bishops then met to prepare joint memoranda to the Synod Secretariat. The date for the Synod was announced in Lubaga Cathedral, Kampala, by the pope on February 9, 1993, and the *Instrumentum Laboris* was launched that same day. From that day until the Synod was held in Rome, I am not aware of any group meeting (apart from the youth of Kampala) to discuss that document or to offer further views to the bishops.

When we talk of involving the people of God in the process, we certainly do not intend to limit ourselves to bishops, priests and perhaps religious. The people of God includes all the baptized and all men and women in our society. If the family is the most basic unit of the Church (indeed, the domestic Church), the entire process should have began there and moved upwards to the diocesan, national, regional, and continental levels.

The Catholic Church takes pride, and legitimately so, in the fact that it has an outstanding organizational structure. But we fail miserably when we try to utilize it fully for a process like the Synod. We praised thousands of catechists for their commitment, yet left them out. We also ignored numerous apostolic movements of the laity and the many Catholic intellectuals and professionals. Women, in their various movements and associations, were not listened to. Youth, millions of children, workers, rural farmers, the urban poor, refugees, the sick, the old—none were helped to voice their real concerns in their own words and sentiments. Neither were the priests, as individuals or through their associations, nor the many indigenous religious congregations empowered to speak their deep-felt sentiments and views.

The Church exists in society. The best way to discover its true image is to involve society in its self-evaluation and self-criticism. Christians of other denominations, Muslims, members of other religious bodies, and the traditionalists have much to offer in evaluating the Church's presence in Africa. Nowhere were any of these actively involved in the process. Even political leaders and politicians, economic leaders and business people, cultural leaders and grassroots communities would have had a lot to offer on the theme of evangelization chosen by the pope. But they were not asked.

I emphasize this point for five basic reasons. First, we must change from a clerical notion of Church to an understanding of Church as a communion, a people of God in which every member has both rights and duties and is entitled to full respect and involvement in what goes on in the Church. It is only then that we can become a Church-as-Family, as the bishops' concluding message clearly stated.

Second, it is only by encouraging the participation of each and every baptized person in the identification of issues to be discussed, in the decision-making itself, and in its implementation that the active role of the laity can be enhanced. It is one thing to talk about the need for lay participation in the Church and quite another to effect that invitation through concrete processes.

Third, the coinciding of the African Synod with the current democratization process in Africa should have taught us an important lesson. In Uganda, the Synod process began at the same time as our constitution-making exercise. Ugandans contributed almost 30,000 memoranda to the constitutional process, with perhaps more than 10,000 of them coming from Catholics. As stated above, the Synod received no more than 25 memoranda from Uganda. Obviously, people were not motivated to participate in the Synod process. This indicates the Church's failure to read correctly the "signs of the times."

The fourth reason is dictated by common sense. People participate more in activities they have contributed to from the beginning. Their involvement develops a sense of love and concern and responsibility. To involve people now in implementing the Synod message—when they did not even know the Synod was taking place—is difficult. We must begin with convincing explanations about why they were left out from the beginning.

Fifth, and intimately linked with the fourth reason, we must learn to involve people if we want to make a real difference in the Church in Africa. In all future processes, we should always take the model of Church as a communion in which each person matters and has something unique to contribute. There is, therefore, a genuine need to develop an ecclesiology of communion in the true African sense. We need to focus on democratization, consultation, and deliberations within the Church to strengthen its structures and institutions.

There are at least four causes for the inadequate involvement of people. First, the identification of the theme and its priorities was done from above. The five sub-themes did not touch on all the major worries of the laity at the grassroots. The questionnaires also came from above; this by itself stifled a possible wider debate. Many people simply responded to those questions rather than express their innermost feelings, joy or anxieties. Once people were excluded from the agenda, they found themselves already stifled from the very beginning.

Two, involving people requires an effective methodology that can excite people at many levels. Several such methodologies have been developed, based primarily on the approach of Paolo Freire. Such methodologies make it possible for children and the illiterate to participate fully in analyzing their situation and in determining causes and remedies. Neither the *Lineamenta* nor the *Instrumentum Laboris*—nor any other document produced locally for the Synod process—suggested any such methodology.

Three, any involvement of people requires money and personnel. Simply asking people to contribute their views on the Synod was not sufficient. Each country, each diocese, and in fact, each parish could have used full-time personnel to animate the exercise, to travel among the people, explaining, creating interest, and answering initial questions. Such teams would have required sufficient financial support. Given that money is often found to put up buildings, to acquire transport, and so on, certainly both money and personnel could have been found for an exercise of this magnitude, one that happens only once in two thousand years! The *Lineamenta* and the *Instrumentum Laboris* should have been illustrated, translated into the thousands of African languages, and then widely disseminated. Other booklets and posters should have appeared to animate people. All of these were missing and missed.

Finally, at its heart the failure was ecclesiological. Deep down, many of us still continue to define the Church in terms of the clergy. The bishop and the clergy become the local Church, especially in terms of decision-making. This may be why many dioceses in Africa have so far resisted holding fully representative diocesan synods. These stumbling blocks must be removed as we begin to implement the Synod.

Social Analysis of Church and Society

One other important aspect neglected in the preparation for the African Synod was a serious and scientific social analysis of the African Church and the African society. This was needed in order to evaluate critically the pastoral methods used and the areas of success and failure in evangelization. Such an analysis would have examined the social and cultural milieu in which evangelization has been taking place, the process of conversion, the interaction, the response, the spirituality, and the maturity of African Christians. Such a study should have yielded relevant and significant themes for the Synod.

A similar study of African society could have revealed the main areas for deeper evangelization and the nature of dialogue and relationship demanded today of the Church in Africa. Such studies would have provided a rich historical and contextual background for the Synod. Even if this process of social analysis was lacking in the preparation, it is not too late to undertake it in order to confront the real issues of Church and society during the implementation phase.

Composition of the Synod

In both Church and society today, there is general support for strategies that include rather than exclude any section of community and that aspire to empower those marginalized to speak for themselves rather than always be spoken for. Unfortunately, the Synod did not make use of such strategies. Indeed, this was a bishops' Synod. That is accepted. But even a bishops' Synod can make ample room for including other sections. As we know, the Synod was composed of bishop delegates from the national episcopal conferences of Africa and Madagascar, some theologians, the heads of the Roman Curia as well as some of its members, some representatives from continental and regional conferences outside Africa, several superiors general of missionary congregations working in Africa, a few lay African Christian observers, and at least five representatives of the All African Conference of Churches.

Having excluded the largest majority of the African laity from participating in the preparatory stage, the Synod should have been more sensitive to their representation within its deliberations, even as mere observers. The few lay observers who were invited went to the Synod in their private and individual capacity. They did not have an official mandate to consult the bodies they belong to and they had no special preparation. One wonders what their presence added to the Synod and what message they took back to their fellow African laity. Certainly, with a meaningful, effective representation, African catechists, lay men and women, youth, intellectuals and professionals, indigenous congregations of women and men, and so forth, could have contributed significantly to the Synod's understanding of the theology of Church-as-family. If superiors general of international congregations were found worthy to participate, why were superiors of locally founded congregations not also invited? The theology of communion, of Church as people of God, and of Church-as-family must be visible in all that the Church does and plans. This is a major challenge for us.

The Methodology

The methodology for any major endeavor, such as the recently concluded Synod, is as important as the content itself. The methodology greatly affects the content and the outcome. As an observer from outside the Synod, I need only indicate a few aspects of the methodology that I found lacking. First, most bishop delegates came with prepared, written interventions. These were not available before the Synod. The first two weeks were spent listening to these interventions, which were often repetitive. It was difficult logistically for a delegate to modify his already prepared intervention. Thus, instead, several delegates speaking on inculturation might emphasize the same or similar points, rather than supplementing what previous speakers had already said.

Second, the identification of only five sub-themes under that all embracing theme of evangelization tended to stifle free discussion in other areas, equally important and relevant. Selection of these five sub-themes tended to limit the discussion of the very theme of evangelization. Evangelization includes proclamation (*kerygma*), service (*diakonia*), witness (*martiria*), worship (*leiturgia*), and building community and solidarity (*koinonia*).

But evangelization should be considered in relation to all human dimensions: religious and spiritual, moral and ethical, cultural and educational, political and economic, physical and environmental. Evangelization extends from each individual person to the family, community, nation, and the global human family. Evangelization includes the message, the pastoral methods, the animating theologies, the interaction, the special situations, and the vision for the future. Evangelization means concrete plans and strategies to share the Good News with children, youth, adults, men and women, the old, the sick, workers and unemployed, leaders and public servants, refugees and displaced people, the poor, prisoners, rural farmers, and the handicapped and disabled. In a word, evangelization is all-embracing. To reduce it to five sub-themes without first allowing a free and general discussion of the general theme certainly affected the content and conclusions of the Synod itself.

Third, a Synod of this nature and at this time did not need to be as secretive and closed in as it was. One of the sub-themes was the means of social communications. Having realized the importance of media in our present world, the Synod should have been more sensitive to the media. It would have been helpful to have had a daily press briefing for the media. Some media people, carefully selected, should have been given access to the discussions to observe fully the atmosphere, the enthusiasm and emotions—or the lack thereof—of the delegates. In the end, what we have are statements and the concluding message. These important words would have had greater meaning if we had known more about the discussion and the emphasis they had been given.

Fourth, the one-month schedule was restrictive for such a unique meeting of such importance. Since this was the first Synod in two thousand years of evangelization to deal with the Church in Africa, it would have been more prudent not to have a fixed schedule. Vatican II is a relevant example. One month was almost needed for delegates to get to know each other, share ideas and views, plan for the work, gradually enter the spirit of the Synod, discover where more consultation was needed, and then forge ahead. It was only after the first session of Vatican II in 1963 when the Council Fathers were in recess that they began to reflect fully on what was desired, to consult more extensively, and then later to come back determined to do a better and lasting job. The timetable of the African Synod was too tight, too short to allow a wider discussion on evangelization or, above all, to develop an adequate theology to support the rich pastoral sharing.

Finally, according to African cultural values and traditions, every significant event involves everyone, whether invited or not. People attend weddings, funerals, and societal events to participate and to give both moral and physical support. In this tradition, groups of Africans and Africanists who were not part of the Synodal assembly gathered in Rome to give African support to this important and unique event. In my view, the group of African theologians gathered at SEDOS (Servizio di Documentazione e Studi in Rome) fulfilled a very important mission. They united their efforts with those of the bishop delegates. They also provided relevant information on Africa, the Church in Africa, the Synod itself and what African Christians were expecting from it for the many journalists, missionaries who had worked in Africa, Africans living in Rome and elsewhere, and non-Africans who wanted to witness this event.

This supportive group met a much felt need, similar to many groups whose positive contributions to the Vatican II message should never be underestimated. It therefore was unexpected when some of the organizing members of the Synod and some bishop delegates took an initial negative view of their presence. The theology of Church-as-family proposed by the Synod is developed around the sharing of roles by all members of the family. It is based on the understanding that each member, however young or feeble, has a specific contribution to make.

The process and theology of inculturation that was unanimously called for by the Synod Fathers includes promoting positive societal values, which include support groups, in all activities carried out by Church leaders. It is only when we become a secretive, closed-in Church that we fear the contributions of well-intended supportive groups. As we embark on implementing the Synod, it is necessary to develop attitudes that appreciate pluralism and the unique contribution of every group.

Part 2

Evaluation of the Synod Message

Having talked to several Synod Fathers and studied their concluding message, it is my view that it is both correct and appropriate to call this encounter "the Synod of hope." I shall identify ten topics that clearly show that the African church is moving forward. Hope and optimism are realistic if we plan carefully for the implementation of the Synod, if we develop theologically what has been provided and then translate it into liberative pastoral action.

The first achievement of the Synod, which was shared by almost every delegate, was the atmosphere of friendliness and freedom of expression that dominated the Synod. Bishops got to know one another. They shared ideas and experiences, and gradually came to discover they had a lot in common. Geographical and linguistic barriers began to disappear, revealing a strong unity of purpose for the common task.

Unlike Vatican II, the African Synod did not witness a sharp division between "progressives" and "conservatives." The delegates moved rather toward an African sense of consensus in which the middle position provided a unifying element. They had not come to introduce innovations in the Church, but neither did they seem to feel it was desirable to oppose the liberative movement of Vatican II and post-Vatican II. Their mission was to emphasize those elements in the universal teaching of the Church that are most urgently needed by the Church in Africa. Thus, the Synod was pastoral in its orientation and content. The delegates were pleased with their achievements, and united in purpose to implement the Synod. This in itself was no mean achievement. Their unity of purpose can become a powerful incentive for African theologians and pastoral agents.

A second and more tangible achievement is contained in the concluding message of the Synod. Drawing from this document, I will highlight ten contributions of the Synod.

Inculturation

After talking about inculturation for the last forty years, after developing several theologies of inculturation and initiating several experiments in inculturation, the Synod Fathers gave clear and full support to the process and theology of inculturation.

Evangelization consists of proclamation *and* inculturation, they said. The domain of inculturation "is the entire Christian life." The Synod Fathers strongly recommended dialogue with African traditional religion and with African cultural values and the guardians of those values.

From now on, the movement and process of inculturation have official approval and support. Those few bishops, members of the clergy, and pastoral agents who, in the name of orthodoxy and defence of the faith, have been either opposed or indifferent to the movement need now to undergo a fundamental *metanoia*, a conversion, to join the consensus of the African Synod. African theologians and the many non-Africans who have been highly suspicious of the inculturation movement, alleging false motives to it, need a fundamental change in their attitudes. Those African Christians, especially among the elite and lay leaders, who prefer the status quo (*semper idem*) need to seriously rethink their position; they must learn to view Christianity as a message of life that changes in order to be relevant to all times, cultures, and peoples. Those African theologians who have restricted inculturation to liturgy and other externals need the humility to accept that all aspects of Christian life must be inculturated. This enormous task must be undertaken in solidarity with one another.

Commitment to Justice and Peace

The theme of justice and peace, human rights and reconciliation, democratization and stability was undoubtedly most highlighted at the Synod. It is important to remember the context of the Synod: the tragedy in Rwanda happened just before it began, and it continued throughout the month of the Synod. None of the bishops from Rwanda managed to attend the Synod. With this sad context in mind, the delegates gave a lot of time and thought to justice and peace in Africa. Bishops fully recognized the great omission of the African church: "We have not always done what we could in order to form the laity for life in society, to a Christian vision of politics and economics. A protracted absence of the lay faithful from this field has led them to believe that the faith has nothing to do with politics."

This admission has vital importance. If the politics and economics of Africa are to change fundamentally, it is necessary to realize what has not yet been accomplished and to make urgent plans to rectify the situation. The bishops called on all Christians without exception to educate themselves on democracy. A lay Christian who participates in the democratic process becomes the sign of a church that promotes justice and peace.

To achieve peace, we are called to work for justice, for there cannot be genuine peace without justice. "Democracy should become one of the principal routes along which the Church travels together with the people. There is need for prophets for our times, and the whole Church should become prophetic." If these powerful statements are translated into action, they will have the power to transform the Church and society in Africa.

In the past, it was not easy to know or even guess whether African church leaders wanted "prophets" in their communities. To challenge the church in Africa to be prophetic has been often interpreted as an unwarranted challenge of its leadership.

Conformity and uniformity seemed to be the only accepted norms, even in Africa's Catholic universities. Nonetheless, the Synod has committed the Church in Africa to travel with the people along the road of democracy. This means the Church itself should become more democratic and an example of democratization.

The Synod clearly rejected the inferiority complex that has been forced on the African black people, the injustice of the North to the South, the northern world view that maintains a structural inequality, the unjust terms of trade, the unjust price system, the massive sale of arms to Africa so that Africans may kill one another, and the unjust external debt that oppresses Africa and its people. This was a powerful message indeed, especially coming from the African bishops who in the past have been known to be timid in their condemnation of the North. Such a message is a good starting point for genuine dialogue with the North, for both Church and society.

The message to African political leaders, the military, and all those who embezzle public funds and carry out institutionalized corruption can be used to effectively challenge any future dictator in Africa. The Synod's support to the current democratization process in Africa and to its consolidation should arouse every Christian and African of goodwill to play his or her active part. As a continent we must say No to war, oppression, racism, ethnic rivalry, inferiority complex, injustices, dictatorship, and corruption.

Commitment to Dialogue and Ecumenism

Vatican II was based on a very strong commitment to ecumenism, religious dialogue, and cooperation. Forty years after the Second Vatican Council, the Church in Africa has not progressed enough in this area. Many of the ecumenical unions formed in the 1960s disintegrated long ago. Fundamentalism has taken over in many churches, including the Catholic Church in Africa. Relations with Muslims have not been friendly, especially since the birth of Islamic fundamentalism in the Sudan and Nigeria and in most of the countries in North Africa. This is part of our context. The Synod called for dialogue with African traditional religion, with the Coptic churches of Egypt and Ethiopia, the Anglican church, the Protestant churches, the Muslims, and members of other religions. There was no specific mention of the thousands of African indigenous churches or the breakaway churches from the Catholic communion.

Ecumenism and religious dialogue have faced many obstacles in Africa because the introducers of the various religious traditions have often been fundamentalist in approach. In wanting to emphasize the difference between one tradition and another, they stressed the aspects that divide rather than those that unite. Poorly educated pastoral agents may fear the challenge and exposure to ecumenism and sincere religious dialogue. The economic poverty of the continent has also caused some religious traditions to oppose dialogue for fear of losing the little they have. The "politics of religion" has also been a hindrance to dialogue, as some religions feel favored and others discriminated against by the political system.

Yet without a culture of religious pluralism and peaceful coexistence, Africa can never be stable. Hopefully, this initial challenge of the bishops will be developed in the final text so that the Church in Africa can reflect on these issues and take the necessary action.

Church-as-Family

The Synod messages show clearly that the theme of Church-as-family was central to the bishops' thinking. The concept is repeated several times to underscore its importance and it is made clear that the Church-as-family must always be at the service of the entire community in Africa. African theologians should reflect on this theme. The bishops could have chosen the well-developed Vatican II concept, the Church as a communion or *communio* or as people of God; they purposely chose Church-as-family. It would be interesting to learn how that theme gathered such overwhelming support.

Obviously, the bishops wanted to use the African family as a model or the model for being and living Church. This model includes everyone, baptized and non-baptized. It is the basis of unity and solidarity because it means sharing roles and involving every member. It emphasizes small communities and fits the ecclesiologies developed by several African theologians based on the African family, clan, and tribe. Some theologians have gone further to develop the model of African blood brotherhood (and sisterhood). As the bishops pointed out, they owed much to African theological reflections on this point.

However, this does not hide the fact that the model of Church-as-family has some very fundamental problems that need clarification, if it is to serve the purpose for which it is recommended. First, we need to be clear about the type of family being envisaged. Is it the African traditional family, or the contemporary one? In any case, the African family, whether traditional or contemporary, is still very hierarchical. The father figure is still much feared by the other members of the family. The wife is not yet given full rights of equality, and for this reason the women's movement in Africa is very powerful. The rights of children are only beginning to be realized and respected. Therefore, when the Church-as-family model is recommended, it is important to agree that this does *not* mean any of the families that are not yet fully liberated. We must create a vision of an African family where equality is guaranteed, clear sharing of responsibility is accepted, the clear option for the disadvantaged members is made, and deadly tensions are eliminated.

The theology of Church-as-family is a double-edged sword. It can be profitably used but it may also lead to benign paternalism. We must be careful not to end up again with a pyramid structure of the Church instead of the circular one of communion. We African theologians must take on the challenge of this theme and show how it can be used positively to create a new understanding of the African Church and society.

Commitment to Theological Research and the Role of African Theologians

One of the most positive elements in the message is the bishops' clear recognition of the role of the African theologians and of theological research. African theologians were praised for their contribution to evangelization:

> The Synod knows that without the conscientious and devoted exercise of your function something essential would be lacking. The Synod expresses its gratitude and its encouragement to you to continue working with your distinctive role certainly, but in communion with your pastors.

The bishops acknowledged the importance of doing theology and theological research. They called on all major seminaries and higher institutions of learning to define with vigor and transmit effectively "our cultures in all that they have that is viable and transmissible, being always careful to find the possible meeting points with other cultures."

It would be most useful to know how the bishops reached this consensus, given the fact that not a few of them have viewed African theologians with some suspicion in the past. African theologians the Synod had requested, through the powerful words of Jean-Marc Éla, to recognize their service as a distinctive ministry within the Church. It is now a challenge to all of us to respond to the call, beginning with the very text of the bishops.

Active Participation of the Laity

The theology of active lay participation and of the family as the domestic Church obviously influenced the bishops. The United Nations Conference on the Family about to take place in Cairo (September 1994) also greatly influenced what the bishops had to say on family values. They agreed that the African Christian family should be evangelizing, mature in faith, educative of all its members, and serve as the active living cell of the local Church. The laity were challenged to evangelize all strata of society and especially the political and economic sectors. The Synod expressed the need for "holy" politicians and political leaders. In sum, the laity must find its legitimate role in the Church-as-family and fill it.

Relevant Formation of Pastoral Agents

The challenges of the Synod can only be realized if the future and present pastoral agents are fully and properly trained. There is a need to rethink the syllabi of our institutions to form pastoral agents. Inculturation, justice and peace, genuine dialogue and ecumenism, and effective methods of communication ought to be treated as core issues for serious study and reflection rather than as appendices.

Church Support for Liberation of Women

The Synod emphasized the liberation and support of all the formerly marginalized groups: women, youth, the poor, the sick, the victims of AIDS, refugees, and displaced people. There was a greater emphasis, however, on women. The oppression of and discrimination against women were identified as one of the major forms of the structure of sin engulfing our African societies. To educate a woman is to educate a people. Your bishops and all those who participated in this holy Synod are determined to take every measure to see your dignity fully respected.

These were powerful words, and if I were an African woman, I would certainly test my local Church to see how serious it is in translating those words into real liberative action! One thing is clear, African women can look to the Church for support in their struggle for equality and equal opportunities. They can demand their distinctive roles in the Church and they can powerfully articulate their aspirations in Church and society. Should any Church leader let them down, they should know it is the individual and not the Church as a whole that has done so.

Optimism for the Future of Africa

Despite the many sad predictions for Africa and the present catastrophes in some parts of our continent, the bishops were optimistic for the future. This optimism is meant to challenge us to do whatever we can to save Africa, to liberate Africa, to develop Africa and love it.

An Exemplary Church

It took courage for the bishops to fully recognize publicly that the African Church needs to make a critical examination of conscience. Justice and respect for human rights have sometimes been lacking within its internal structures, institutions, and decisions. If the Church gives witness to justice, she recognizes that whoever dares to speak to others about justice should also strive to be just in their eyes. It is necessary therefore to examine with care the procedures, the possessions, and the life style of the Church.

Conclusion

In conclusion I cannot help asking the following questions: Was the Synod in Rome the climax of the entire process or simply one of the important stages? Will the Church in Africa establish an efficient organization to widely discuss the outcome of the Synod, or will it continue its usual way as it did during the preparatory stage? Will there be a real commitment by all Church leaders in Africa to implement the message or are we to read beautiful words that will remain on paper? Above all, will the African Church enjoy the freedom it needs to develop its unique identity and contribute richly to the world Church? It is too early to respond adequately to any of these questions, but the sooner we consider them the better. Fearlessly, let us confront the challenges presented and begin a new evangelization of the African society.

26

The Church in Africa Today

Reflections on the African Synod

John Olorunfemi Onaiyekan

My country, Nigeria, began existence as an independent nation in 1960 with great hopes and expectations. The tragic thirty-month civil war heightened rather than diminished these hopes. In the mid-seventies, we were planning big: big airports and seaports; big industrial installations especially in the iron, steel and petroleum sectors; big universities; even a brand new big federal capital to be constructed on empty land. We were the giant of Africa, ready to take off to join the orbit of the great world powers. My generation grew up with that exhilarating mood of optimism. And indeed many of these giant projects actually took off and went a long way.

Then somewhere along the line, around the 1980s, things began to turn sour. One after the other, many hopes of previous decades were postponed and eventually abandoned, thanks to a tragic collusion between mismanagement and corruption at home, and a hostile and merciless economic atmosphere abroad. Thus hopes became mere dreams and even dreams became an act of faith possible only for the most optimistic. One had the feeling of being in a jet plane speeding down a runway but unable to take off and unable to stop.

In December 1993, the Nigerian bishops went to Rome on their Ad Limina visit. From Rome they took the unprecedented step of issuing a Christmas message to the nation with the significant title, "Let not our dreams die!" The Christmas message of the bishops was a cry of anguish to our rulers to keep our dreams of greatness alive, and a call of encouragement to all our people not to give up.

John Olorunfemi Onaiyekan, co-adjutor bishop of Abuja and apostolic administrator of Ilorin, Nigeria, was a member of the council for the preparation of the Synod and is a member of the Permanent Council for the Synod of Bishops.

I have briefly recounted this recent history of Nigeria because the experience of Nigeria is the experience of the rest of Africa—except that it is still worse in many places. The Special Assembly for Africa of the Synod of Bishops gave us an opportunity to compare notes, to listen to one another's stories, and to reflect together. In this reflection, the sad fact emerged that to look to the future of Africa is anything but cheerful. But we did, and we refused to despair. We were even able to disperse on a note of joy and hope, having reinforced our solidarity, renewed our commitment to integral evangelization, and rededicated ourselves to the Risen Lord of history.

I am not going to review the proceedings of the Synod, as this has been done elsewhere in these pages. Instead, I want to focus this reflection on the message of the Synod for two categories of Christ's faithful, namely, the priests and the laity, who together constitute a major core of the church. Effective implementation of the Synod demands that every segment of the Church be aware of what the Synod expects of it and take appropriate action to respond effectively.

The Synod Views the Priest in Africa

In a sense, everything that was discussed at the Synod concerns the priests, since they are a key agent of evangelization, especially at the grassroots level. The effective apostolate of other segments of Christ's faithful, especially the laity, greatly depends on an adequate number of priests who are properly formed, live a faithful priestly life, and have the ability to work in fruitful collaboration with other segments of Christ's faithful, especially the religious and the laity.

This was undoubtedly one reason why the Synod paid so much attention to promoting vocations to the priesthood and to ensuring proper formation for all candidates, taking note of the needs and conditions of our local churches. It is interesting that no one suggested less stringent requirements in order to make up for the lack of workers in the vineyard. Rather, the appreciable increase in number of candidates was seen as a proof that it is necessary to continue along the same general lines of careful recruitment and serious formation. With the regrettable decline in vocations in the traditional missionary-sending lands of the North, it becomes ever more necessary to promote local vocations, not only for local needs, but also for mission *ad gentes*, especially within Africa.

Inculturation

The theological basis of inculturation was clarified in terms of such fundamental theological concepts as Trinity, Incarnation, and the Paschal Mystery. The unity in diversity that characterizes the Blessed Trinity is reflected in the unity of the Church with its diversity that must necessarily entail diversity of cultures. The aim of inculturation, it was stressed, is to bridge the gap between faith and life; not to offer a cheap and easy form of Christianity. Pastoral attention, serious studies, and the courageous exploitation of existing areas of freedom in experimentation were strongly recommended.

The Synod insisted that the process of inculturation must be handled with extreme care and seriousness. The priest has a most important role to play in this. He must be the first to understand the nature, objective, methods, and scope of true inculturation and then he must help the lay faithful to follow his example. In many cases, there is need for a real conversion of spirit and a change of attitude in order to achieve the desired goals of the Church and the African Synod.

The Synod emphasized the need for serious studies of our cultures and their relationship with the principles of the Christian faith. Priests are expected to be in the forefront of this research and experimentation. However, they also ought to find ways of involving enlightened and interested laity who are often at the cutting edge of the dilemmas of the conflicts and tensions between our faith and culture.

In the area of experimentation, priests are to show both the courage to be creative as well as the prudence to work within established parameters. Even the greatest expert should be open to dialogue with his priestly confreres and to directives from the appropriate ecclesiastical authorities. We must have the humility to abandon or suspend experiments that are not considered acceptable, even though we may feel quite sure of what we are doing. The rejection of some suggestions or proposals should be considered as a challenge to pursue our research in other directions, rather than as a source of discouragement or annoyance. This is an area that demands sincere collaboration between experts and, on the one hand, those with pastoral responsibility to decide what is acceptable or prudent, and on the other hand, those with pastoral experience of the realities.

Dialogue within and without the Church

The Synod stressed the need to cultivate a spirit of dialogue by promoting sincere dialogue within the Church. This touches priests in a special way since they are at the crossroads between the hierarchy and the lay faithful, and their lives intersect that of the religious. A good relationship among priests also demands a *spirit* of dialogue: of listening to others and being ready to respect their positions. Priests should not remain behind the times; they should learn the authentic language and spirit of Vatican II to promote true ecumenism.

The same goes for the more problematic area of dialogue with Muslims. Islam is a major factor in many places, with different types of relationships with the Church, ranging from "very good" in Senegal to a delicate equilibrium of forces in Nigeria, a tolerated minority in the Maghreb, a precarious survival in Egypt, and an outright policy of extermination of Christians in the Sudan.

There have been and are serious problems of relationship in many places where intolerance, oppression, and at times, even violence and killing are perpetrated by people who claim to be defending or promoting Islam. Such problems become challenges to be faced in faith, humility and love. Remembering that priests may not always find clerical counterparts in Islam with whom to relate authoritatively, we reflected together on how to respond in an evangelical way to provocation and violence. In spite of our diversity of experiences, there was nevertheless a deep sense of solidarity and unity permeating the whole Synod Assembly. As one bishop from Sudan rightly pointed out: "It requires a lot of faith and grace to be able to dialogue with someone who is killing your brothers and sisters and denies you the right to exist."

There is need for prayer and the dialogue of love and life. But there is also need for effective action at all levels: religious, political, diplomatic. The bottom line is that the Synod rejected violence. In limited cases, the principles of legitimate self-defense and the disarming of the unjust aggressor were evoked. How these principles, valid in themselves, are to be translated into practical action will depend a lot on the actual conditions of things. In any case, we should continue to stress that freedom of religion is a fundamental human right and challenge all governments, including Islamic nations, to respect this right.

Turning to African Traditional Religion, it can be said that the Synod finally rehabilitated the religion of our forebears, giving full recognition to the genuine religious values it contains. It was stressed that it is such values that make the African so open to the Gospel message. The authoritative exponents and devout followers of these religions therefore deserve as much respect as their counterparts in the so-called "world religions." Establishing a dialogue with followers of African Traditional Religion is highly dependent on the theological signals coming from the parish priest. In any case, at the grassroots level, if anything is going to happen in dialogue with others, the priest, especially the parish priest, must supply a vigorous and well informed leadership.

Justice and Peace

The Church's exercise of her prophetic role of denouncing injustice in society will be in great part through the voice and action of the priest. The priest cannot join those who idly sit by and ask "What is the Church doing?" As an agent of development in the rural and urban communities, the priest is a positive promoter of justice and peace.

In the political arena, the priest ought to know his true role and play it fully and courageously. This he can and must do without going against the rules of the Church. Making people aware of their rights, encouraging and empowering them to insist on those rights, reminding them of their duties as citizens—all these are eminently political roles, often more important and lasting than vying for political office in partisan elections.

Social Communication

Some priests have both the aptitude and the training for the professional apostolate of social communication. It is good to give such people the opportunity to exercise their talents to spread the kingdom. Priests who are experts in communications have an important role to play in helping their lay professional colleagues to establish the vital and necessary link between the Christian faith and the practice of their profession. They can also direct diocesan offices and programs for social communication. Such positions need not necessarily be held by priests or religious; in some cases, a lay professional could even be more effective.

The vast majority of priests, however, will not be experts in social communication. But every priest, by the nature of his calling, has to be a communicator of the Good News. He must learn how to communicate, using all the means that are available. A minimum of familiarity with the modern means of communication has to be part and parcel of the training program for all priests.

The Synod stressed the continued importance of our traditional means of social communications, such as proverbs and stories, singing and dancing, music and drama. We can no longer presume that every young seminarian will be familiar with these as many of them are far removed from their traditional environments. There is, therefore, need for a conscious effort to inculcate the skills and knowledge required for being able to make effective use of those means.

The Laity in the African Synod

Now I want to highlight a few points about the role that the Synod expects the laity to play in the Church in Africa toward the year 2000. In the first place, I believe it is important to remember the great lesson of the 1987 Synod on the Laity: that the normal way of being a Christian is the lay state, and that the Church is first of all the people of God gathered together in faith by Christ through baptism and confirmation, and nourished by the eucharist. Although the clergy and religious occupy special places in the Church, whatever roles they play are a function of the people of God.

Therefore, whatever the synod may say about what the Church in Africa should be or do will depend above all on the response of the huge army of the lay faithful. A greater awareness of this fact by both clergy and laity will impact the Christian message on the world around us.

Proclamation

The Synod praised the Lord for the impressive success of evangelization in Africa in the past one hundred years. The Synod acknowledged the heroic efforts of the foreign missionaries who blazed the trail and also acknowledged the part played by the laity, even in the pioneering years. In many places, the missionary priest arrived after the lay people had already prepared the ground. Catechists, village teachers, community leaders, male and female, all form an army of so far largely nameless missionary heroes, whose full story is still waiting to be told.

It is necessary for the Church to improve the formation and organization of the laity in order to sustain and improve their participation in the task of proclaiming the Gospel message. The lay apostolate organizations deserve to be promoted and challenged to be bold and zealous proclaimers of the Gospel. It is here that the witness of life as a powerful means of evangelization comes to mind. Everyone has a role to play.

The catechists received special recognition for their past record for the excellent work they are doing today. In many cases, they bear the burden of the heat of the day, exercising their ministry in all kinds of places and for minimal remuneration. They are to be given due respect and care, as well as adequate training to make them ever more effective.

Finally, there is the serious issue of how to finance our missionary programs, especially those directed to the poorest parts of Africa. Just as it is the duty of the laity to maintain their pastors and church structures, so they must provide for the missionaries that the local church sends abroad. If this matter is not courageously addressed, we may find ourselves sending our missionaries only to rich nations that can look after them well. They may then run the risk of becoming, or of being seen as, mercenaries. Those who first sent missionaries to us were not very rich people, but they gave generously out of their poverty. Now we must be generous too, even in our poverty.

Inculturation

Bridging the gap between culture and faith, which is what inculturation is mainly about, concerns the laity in a most direct way. Whether in marriage or burial, in chieftaincy titles or village festivals, the laity often find themselves on the cutting edge of dilemmas that inevitably arise. There are usually no ready-made answers to these problems, although church teaching supplies adequate principles. But Christians, enlightened by the Spirit, must play their own part in seeking practical solutions that are compatible with Christian principles. A good Christian ought to have a spiritual instinct to be able to determine what is acceptable and what is not.

Perhaps in the past there was too much of a tendency to condemn things as "pagan" when they were simply cultural. We are now in a position to set the records straight in a way that those who went before us could not do. However, it is not possible to canonize everything done in our culture. All cultures, including our own, stand under the judgment of the Gospel message.

Dialogue

The Synod showed concern for dialogue first within the Church. This is where we develop the spirit of dialogue. If we cannot relate well with one another within the Church, how can we manage with those outside the Church? Every segment of the Church, including the laity, is challenged to examine itself in this regard. This means a readiness to acknowledge whatever is good in others and to allow them to be different, while promoting all those things that unite. A laity council, as an umbrella organization for all church groups, is a good forum for such intra-church dialogue.

In dealing with dialogue with followers of other religions, the Synod greatly stressed the importance of a "dialogue of life" by which people of different faiths live and act together in matters of common concern. This precedes religious dialogue in the strict sense, and in many cases, it may be the only kind of dialogue possible. The laity are best placed for this as they meet followers of other religions in the marketplaces of life: in the offices, in business and professions, in political organizations and village meetings, in social clubs and cultural societies. They can witness together to the good things we share and our common concern to improve the world. While any opportunity to identify ourselves as followers of Christ should not be missed, by the same token, we should respect the religious convictions of those who do not share our faith.

The Synod presented dialogue with Islam as a challenge that we must all take on, doing all in our power to live in peace with Muslims in our society. Since Islam is basically a lay religious organization, it may be that the laity may succeed where clergy have failed. The interesting experience of the Catholic Women's Organization (CWO) working in some places with Muslim women organizations has been quite instructive in this regard.

The Synod urges us to respect the honest followers and authentic leaders of our African Traditional Religion. There is a special problem in relating with those who have their legs in both camps, with some even claiming to be members of our Church. It is recognized that this kind of dialogue is still difficult for us. But we must start somewhere.

Justice and Peace

The Synod emphasized the political arena, showing its conviction that most of the problems facing our continent result from inept or corrupt governments. Effective government is essential to tackle poverty and disease, civil wars and social unrest, rampant corruption, and blatant abuse of human rights. This is a direct challenge to the laity, whose role it is to make the Gospel values present in these areas.

The Synod recognized that many children of the Church in positions of authority have not lived according to the principles of their faith. This is a call for a serious rededication of the African lay Christian to the service of God and of neighbor, guided by a careful reading of the social teachings of the Church. Many countries, including our own, are caught in the vicious circle of successive bad governments, building up an oppressive system of endemic corruption and the breakdown of the rule of law. To challenge and break through this vicious circle will require not only sustained prayer but also a generous spirit of involvement, with all the risks that go with it. To overcome pervasive injustice with truth and peace requires that a price be paid, otherwise nothing will happen. Since justice and peace embrace all facets of life, the whole society must accept responsibility for the state of the nation, and each one must play his or her part.

All the above do not reduce the importance of the social welfare activities of the Church, whether directly or through her members. In a situation of grave misery, such programs cushion the pains of austerity and keep hope alive in those who have no where else to turn. However, the first and best "charity" is to help people obtain their rights to a decent life of human dignity. This is why Church leaders must continue to denounce bad government, corruption, and institutionalized injustice. The laity are expected to support their shepherds in this crusade and to get directly and personally involved in it.

Social Communication

The modern means of social communications have become all pervasive. Powerful, they can be used for good or for evil, so it is important to know how to make good use of them. The Synod also stressed the responsibility of the family to protect children and youth against cultural pollution from the mass media. This concerns all the laity as families.

The Synod outlined a special task for lay people in the media, whether public or private: they are to practice their profession in such a way that they serve truth and good at all times. This means not only the technical experts but also those who formulate policies and administer media houses. Where the Church owns and runs its own media, she should be able to count on her members to make their expertise available for this apostolate. Catholic lay media professionals need to be given adequate pastoral and spiritual assistance as well as doctrinal formation at an appropriate level. Organizations of Catholic media practitioners would be a useful forum to develop such a program.

The reference to the traditional means of social communication, such as stories, proverbs, drama, dance, and music, raises the question of how to rescue and preserve these fast-fading cultural values. Today's social conditions interfere with the role of parents in handing down such values to the next generation. However, continuing effort is needed in that direction.

Conclusion

As has been pointed out, the word *synod* is derived from two Greek words: *syn* and *hodos*, meaning with and way or journey. This highlights two important aspects of the concept of synod. First, as a way or journey, the Synod is a dynamic and progressive process. In a true sense, the Synod began that day of Epiphany 1989 when the pope announced its convocation. Since then, the whole Church of God has been on a journey of faith with the Church of Africa. This journey had a high point during the month-long assembly in Rome, but it did not end there. The journey continues, as we all try to implement the fruits of the Synod discussion. This will continue well beyond the year 2000.

The second aspect is that of togetherness, walking hand in hand, supporting one another, seeking unity of mind and heart. The role of the pope as the focus of this unity is very crucial. His visit to Africa during 1995 is intended to celebrate the fruits of the Synod. The Post-Synodal Apostolic Exhortation of the pope (see Appendix 2) will be a final record of the Synod.

The Synod's "Message" also captures the general mood and thrust of the Synod for the people of God and the general public. A Synod, however, and especially an African Synod, cannot have its abundant fruits adequately wrapped up in a document, no matter how carefully prepared. The Synod is an experience of grace: to celebrate, to share, to live by. For a month, we had the experience of living in a Church that is a Family of God, united in love across boundaries of nations, race and social conditions. Our collegial reflection enriched each one of us. The most important fruit is what we have all taken back—our convictions, ideas, and inspirations for the future. It is important to share this fruit first with the other members of the African hierarchy who remained at home, and then with the members of Christ's faithful in our respective nations and dioceses.

This Synod, in my opinion, experienced an admirable degree of common mind, despite the great diversity on the African continent. On matters of principle, in particular, whether in faith or morality, there were no sharp divisions. Even on the level of pastoral perceptions and concrete suggestions for action, differences of positions were accommodated as representing different responses to different challenges. The principal aim, to promote evangelization in the different circumstances of the Church in Africa, united us all in a common chorus singing in harmony with different voices and instruments.

I was personally edified at the palpable sense of solidarity and empathy for churches undergoing dramatic difficulties: war in Rwanda; religious persecution in Sudan, the Church of mere presence in Islamic nations. Perhaps because we were truly challenged to share one another's burdens and pains, the Synod was such a joyful celebration of the Risen Lord reigning in the Church and in the world.

Conclusion

Peter K. Sarpong

Expectations of the Synod

Much was said about what the ope christened the Special Assembly for Africa of the Synod of Bishops, but which, in fact, came to be appropriately known and referred to briefly as the African Synod. Much was done in preparation for it and much was expected from it. But one can realistically and honestly ask what the Synod was actually expected to achieve for a society as huge, complex, complicated and varied as the African society. Africa is not a dot on the map; it is a continent, the second largest in the world, and contains more than 500 million people. Racially, it radically embraces the three major stocks of *homo sapiens*—the Mongoloid, Caucasoid and the Negroid. The diversity and number of its cultures is simply bewildering. How could a single occurrence over the course of only one month expect to influence or impact such a situation, especially since the Catholic Church is in terms of population only 12 to 15 percent of Africa? What kind of impact was actually expected?

I suppose a Synod has three broad objectives. The first is to take stock of what has happened in the past: to assess mistakes, omissions, achievements, and determine the current direction. Second, when it is found that things could have been done better or changed or even omitted completely, a Synod is meant to propose appropriate substitutes or emendations. In the past this role of a Synod has led to condemnations of errors and to anathemas directed against heretics. Finally, at its conclusion, a Synod should lead to the formulation of a vision. A Synod should be able to indicate directions to which the Church should turn in the hope of a better performance and, in some cases, its future survival. Without a vision, one gropes in the dark aimlessly.

Whereas a local or regional Synod would be expected to achieve a measure of success in these areas because it is dealing with a more or less homogenous reality, it is obvious that such expectations for the complex continent of Africa were rather idealistic. Any vision deemed appropriate would also have to be somewhat nebu-

Peter K. Sarpong, the bishop of Kumasi, Ghana, is a well-known theologian of inculturation and the author of several books.

lous, as it must by the very nature of Africa be a conclusion drawn from completely divergent and sometimes unrelated circumstances.

Outcomes of the Synod

This view seems to have been confirmed at the African Synod. We were going to deal with the Church in Africa as if we had a united voice or experience, and as if we even had a consensus understanding of what the Church is.

Proclamation

Under the heading of Proclamation, we stressed the importance of the centrality of the Word of God in evangelization. The Bible need not be presented to the African as something important; it already is. Everywhere on the African continent people are so eager for the Word of God that new religious movements calling themselves Christian are springing up like mushrooms. Everywhere on the continent, people are seen daily with the Bible under their arms, going from town to town, street to street, proclaiming the Word of God and calling people to conversion of heart.

To talk to the African of the centrality of the Word of God is to carry coals to Newcastle. Africans believe in the power of the word. Ideally, they will never disobey the word of a dying person. Given their strong belief in a unique God and their conviction that God has spoken to us through the Bible, they have no problem making that word in the Bible central to their lives.

What we should have stressed—but did not so much as mention—is the danger that lies in fundamentalist approaches to the interpretation of the Bible. Such readings fan the flames of bigotry and intolerance everywhere in Africa and in many cases cause a great deal of havoc. The Word of God is truth itself and truth cannot contradict itself. Yet, we have a situation in Africa where the same Word of God is so differently understood and interpreted as to pitch various Christian religious camps against one another, resulting in bitter recriminations.

In such a situation, it is a mockery of justice for us to condemn other forms of religious conflicts, such as those existing between Christians and Muslims. Nonetheless, we talked about dialogue. One problem we Christians face, though, is the problem of how to dialogue with people who stop at nothing to destroy you, people who think that you have no right to exist, such as the situation described by the bishops of the Sudan.

The problem in cases of conflict between Christians and Christians or between Muslims and Christians (or, sometimes, between Muslims and Muslims) is that of religious militancy, intolerance, bigotry, and fundamentalism. Yet, in any camp normal orthodox followers of any trend tend to be reasonable.It is this diversity of experiences that made it difficult to arrive at what could be called a vision for Africa.

The Association of Episcopal Conferences of Anglophone West Africa (AECAWA) met in Nigeria in 1986 to deliberate on Christian-Muslim relationships. Muslims were invited to send observers to the triennial meeting, yet no Muslims attended. Also in 1986, at the invitation of the pope, Nigerian Muslims failed to send a representative to Assisi to attend the international meeting to pray for peace. (In 1982 the pope prepared a speech to be delivered to Muslims in Kano, Nigeria, but when he arrived at the Kano stadium it was completely empty. Undoubtedly, the *Guinness Book of Records* could record this as the first time a pope prepared a speech with no audience to deliver it to.)

When the conclusions of the 1986 meeting in Lagos were being drawn up, the bishops of Sierra Leone and The Gambia objected to some proposals (which, by no means, were offensive or radical) on the grounds that they might alienate friendly Muslims in their parts of Africa. They saw no point in such formulations that in essence and in details might not apply to other parts of West Africa or even to Ghana. The key seemed to be differences of experiences.

Inculturation

The next topic scheduled for discussion was inculturation. Some of us are of the opinion that inculturation should not have been a topic at all; instead, it should have been the leaven to permeate the totality of the discussions at the Synod. Inculturation is not something different, apart from, or opposed to the other topics—justice and peace, proclamation, dialogue, and social communications. A proper understanding of inculturation is essential to the relevance and meaning of all these other topics.

Those who know and respect African culture also know that an integral part of it is the idea of a Supreme Being, a God of total perfection, perhaps even more perfect than Christianity's teaching about God. A good understanding of inculturation exposes acts of exploitation and injustice as culturally condemnable, deplorable, and indefensible. Properly understood, inculturation can teach us how to make use of the gifts God has given us through tremendous advances in social communication to proclaim God's word. Inculturation should point the way to dialogue, harmonious existence, and understanding. As it is natural that even in the same African household, a father may owe allegiance to one god, the mother to another, and the children to yet another, without any confrontation or lack of harmony, so should the larger family of African cultures live in harmony with one another.

One African bishop who remarked that we were wasting time discussing dancing instead of talking about justice and peace demonstrated a lamentable misunderstanding of the meaning of inculturation. If inculturation means no more than dancing, clapping hands, or drumming, then I feel I am experiencing a totally different Church. Indeed, inculturation is intended precisely to prevent the sort of injustices that the prelate thought should be stressed instead of dancing.

Dancing, joy, and excitement are important to Christianity and to Catholicism *if* they are well understood; otherwise they are useless. They must not simply be looked upon as entertainment, a manner of making the worship "enjoyable," as it were. On the contrary, they must either be a reflection of the internalized deep relationship of love between the worshipper and God, our dear Father, that creates an atmosphere of joy or lead to that internalized relationship. Peace comes about only through this internalized relationship, not through learned talks about peace at meetings. As St. Augustine said: "My soul is restless until it rests in the Lord."

That remark of an African bishop reflected the stand on inculturation of many in the Synod, which was a pity in my opinion. Inculturation deals with the totality of the Christian reality—faith, morality, liturgy, the organization of the Church, the nature of religious life, catechesis, everything and anything in the Christian tradition.

At the end of a discussion, one priest remarked: "As for me, I do not see what this whole thing is about. I have received the faith and I do not see why I should change it." I explained in my workshop that probably one of the reasons why African bishops looked negatively at the concept of inculturation was that we had a wrong view of African religion and African life. Our ample use of such words as polygamy, paganism, heathenism, fetishism, animism, idolatry, and primitive to describe African Traditional Religion demonstrates this. I went on to explain that these were not just misnomers, but that it was totally unjust to use such words to describe a reality that in essence is as good as any religious experience. These words, therefore, should be dropped once and for all.

I made it clear that today no serious anthropologist would use such words to describe African Traditional Religion. African Traditional Religion incorporates the loftiest ideas about God, eternity, goodness, dynamic morality, and so on. One prelate countered with the ferocity of a boxer who realizes that his opponent has collected so many points that the only way he can win the fight is with a knock-out: "Let the anthropologists use what words they want, because we are here talking about religion and not anthropology!"

A second synod bishop also warned against inculturation, saying that if strangers in Rome were to adapt to Rome's careless driving, such strangers would be well-inculturated, but that such inculturation would not bring them holiness! I realized the gigantic task ahead of us.

Inculturation is not indiscriminate imitation even of what is good. Inculturation in the Church is meant to bring about a new creation in Christ. It is meant to correct that habit of reckless driving in Rome, which clearly demonstrates the lack of appreciation for the dignity of the human person.

Achievements of the Synod

During the discussions, it was clear that there could be no consensus on anything, let alone a single vision for the future. In a way, this was natural. We are all conditioned by what we experience. It was obvious to us that the bishops of Liberia, Rwanda, and Sudan would stress atrocities being committed in their countries. Other bishops had preoccupations that made little impression on other representatives.

In the end, however, when the inevitability of our lack of unanimity or even of consensus (not to talk about unavoidable conflicts and serious divergences of opinion) was taken into account, the Synod was a healthy and salvific exercise for the Church, a resoundingly successful event. We listened to one another and appreciated each other's points of view, even if we did not agree with them. We became aware of each other's problems and more sensitive to issues that were far from us. In certain areas such as justice and social communication, we agreed with one another. There was unanimity in our insistence on quality formation of evangelizers.

Undoubtedly the most important consensus we reached is that all Christ's faithful should be involved in evangelization, from the bishop to the housewife, from the teacher to the farmer. Moreover, prominence was given to what we may call the structural agents of evangelization. Schools were singled out for mention along with novitiates. Although priests and some bishops have tended to play down the almost indispensable role of higher institutes of ecclesiastical learning in Africa, it was heartening to see that the role of these institutes was also stressed.

Self-Sufficiency

The need for the Church to be self-supporting was, for me, a controversial point. Although it is true that the Church cannot be said to be mature if it depends entirely on outside help to exist (whether for personnel, equipment or money), it is equally true that the Church in Africa is dependent on very poor people who barely have the means for survival. The insistence on self-sufficiency, which in the last analysis depends upon the contribution of these poor people, creates a sense of insensitivity to their plight. (I want to note that in my opinion too little was said about the fact that priests and religious of Africa should be more self-sacrificing and respect their commitments to their vows.)

This stress on self-sufficiency may also give the impression that we are not grateful to the older Churches that have been helping us or that they have no obligation to help us. Given the universality of the Church, it is my view that the Church should not diminish the responsibility of those who have an abundance to support those who have not. Help should always be given non-paternalistically and with charity and concern.

The Church Family

The Synod came up with the beautiful concept of "Church Family" to describe what the Christian community should be on our continent. It is important though to stress that while such concepts are wonderful and indeed must be borrowed from African culture, they risk negating what they are supposed to affirm if they are not carefully handled. The African extended family system demonstrates caring, a sharing of problems and blessings, concern, and love. People mobilize themselves to achieve a good or to expel an evil. All these are good, but often within the same community, the person outside the group is regarded as if he or she was a nonperson. Identifying outsiders as strangers has been the cause of some of the worst atrocities in Africa and has led to the negative aspects of tribalism and ethnicity.

The love of Christ is unrestricted and universal. Without boundaries, it embraces even the enemy. Within the family of Christ, there is no black or white, slave or free person, Greek or Roman, man or woman. The universal problem of Africa is that most societies do not practice nor accept this view of Christian love. It is hard to love an enemy. Thus, we need a vision that will take into account the vision of Christ—that of universal reconciliation. This is the vision that can turn the Church into a family that does not exclude any person from its ambient. Alas, in Africa—and even in some bishops' conferences—there are signs of *restricted* love.

International Dimension

Through the Synod, we were able to voice our dissent about occurrences in Africa that are evil. We described for the international community the disastrous consequences to Africans of some of its monetary policies in the Third World. We told the international community that if it is serious about lifting Africans from poverty, then it must adjust the prices of Africa's raw commodities and reduce the huge debts Africa owes the industrialized world. One Synod representative, speaking for the Synod, appealed so passionately to the conscience of the international community to reduce foreign debt that he received the only ovation of the first two weeks. Although aid with strings attached may not have been given the emphasis it needed, it was indirectly referred to in a negative way.

The Media

The need to evangelize the media in order to make them a means of evangelization was discussed. In many cases, the media are used to poison the minds of Africans and to propagate crime, violence, falsehoods, and immorality. What is more, only rarely do news items that are not derogatory to Africa appear in the media in Europe or North America. For the media in North America or Europe, Africa is the place of tribal wars, refugees, hunger, poverty, disease and ignorance. If they are to promote the dignity of the human person, created in the image and likeness of God, the media must balance their presentation of Africa so that those who have never been to Africa can have an accurate image of Africa.

Science and Technology

While science and technology may be the hallmark of the industrialized world, humanity, friendship, forgiveness (shown in the remarkable way Africans live peacefully with their one-time oppressive colonizers) form part of African life and must be given the prominence they deserve. It should not be forgotten that science without humanity is terrorizing even as humanity without science is sterile.

Conclusion

The very fact that the bishops of Africa—with their different backgrounds, mentalities, convictions and preoccupations—could come together and express themselves in a common forum, agreeing from time to time and on other occasions agreeing to disagree, was indeed a great achievement. I am not worried because the Synod took place in Rome. Given the incredible diversity in Africa, perhaps it was best to meet on neutral ground.

One thing that the Synod made clear was that Africa cannot survive relying solely on human ingenuity. Even if the effects and benefits of religious conviction cannot be quantified, they have a power that has endured throughout the ages to promote human fulfillment.

Appendix 1

Lineamenta Questions

Proclamation of the Good News of Salvation

1. What lessons can be learned from the history of the Church in Africa in view of the Church's evangelizing mission in that continent today?

2. What are the signs of the times which indicate or underline the urgency of a new period or stage of the evangelization of Africa today? How can an awareness be fostered concerning the arrival of a *kairos*, or "Africa's hour," in which Africa can be won over for Christ?

3. What are the concrete forms or ways through which the Church in Africa must carry out its missionary obligation towards Herself?

4. What are the possible concrete ways by which the Church in Africa could express Her missionary obligation and commitment beyond the confines of the African continent?

5. How is the pastoral [fostering] of vocations concretely carried out in your particular church [diocese]?

6. What do you think about the level and situation of formation in African major seminaries (spiritual formation, intellectual, ascetical, disciplinary, pastoral, human, etc.)? What are the criteria followed in particular churches for the selection and admission of candidates into major seminaries?

7. In practical ways how can the ongoing formation of diocesan priests be fostered?

8. In what concrete ways does your particular church provide for the formation of catechists?

9. Is any concrete action taken in particular churches for the formation of Christ's lay faithful, such as:

   —courses for the promotion of religious culture
   —the social teaching of the Church
   —biblical apostolate?

10. What do you think about the mutual relations between bishops and religious congregations in particular churches in Africa?

11. "Various forms of religious life should be cultivated in a young Church, so that they can display different aspects of Christ's mission and the Church's life, can devote themselves to various pastoral works, and can prepare their members to exercise them rightly. Still, bishops in their conference should take care that congregations pursuing the same apostolic aims are not multiplied to the detriment of the religious life and the apostolate" (*Ad Gentes*, n. 18). In the light of the above conciliar statement, what do you think about the multiplicity of religious congregations of diocesan right in Africa?

12. What evangelizing role is played in your particular church by the following: the family, the school, small communities, movements?

13. In the light of the mystery of the Church as communion, what do you think of racial or tribal

divisions and oppositions in your country? What role do the agents of evangelization play in your country in favor of Church-communion?

14. The Vatican Council's *Decree on the Missionary Activity of the Church* says that "from the very start, the Christian Community should be so formed that it can provide for its own necessities in so far as this is possible" (*Ad Gentes*, n. 15). In the light of this conciliar directive, is there a sufficient awareness in particular churches about the necessity and urgency of achieving financial self-reliance? What initiatives, strategies and efforts does your particular church undertake in view of the attainment of financial self-reliance?

Inculturation

15. Do you consider inculturation as urgent and necessary, *hic et nunc*, for the Church in Africa? Please give reasons for your position.

16. Has your particular church already embarked on any efforts aimed at promoting inculturation? If so, please specify the areas concerned, mentioning as well the agents involved (bishops, priests, men and women religious, theologians, the lay faithful).

17. Either before or during this experimentation in inculturation, was any explanation given to the clergy and to the lay faithful concerning what it meant (or what it entailed)? Have they been involved in the entire process of inculturation?

18. What are the reactions of the faithful towards these attempts at inculturation? Were they favorable or not? Did you consider it necessary to offer explanations to the faithful before starting any experiments? Please give reasons for your position.

19. What do you consider as the most urgent fields/areas of inculturation in Africa today: theological, liturgical, moral, social, pastoral or catechetical?

20. What are the fruits of your efforts in inculturation, judging them by the following criteria:
   (a) contribution to the glory of God, the Creator;
   (b) greater participation in the salvific action of the Redeemer;
   (c) better organization of the Christian life;
   (d) compatibility of local traditions and cultural *mores* with the Gospel;
   (e) communion with the universal Church?

21. Are you aware of any abuses in efforts towards inculturation? Please give some examples.

22. Have efforts in inculturation helped to foster communion within the particular church? In what sense?

[Inter-religious] Dialogue

23. To what extent have the modern means of transport and social communications affected closer interaction between adherents of different religions in your area? How has this affected the Church's mission of evangelization?

24. How do people in your area generally see the relationship between dialogue and evangelization in the mission of the Church? Is there a tendency to neglect one in favor of the other? Are the official directives of the Church on these matters available to and properly understood by the generality of your people? What steps are being taken to ensure this?

25. What are the major difficulties of religious dialogue in general in your area? What special opportunities does your social situation offer for dialogue?

26. Would you see the Catholic Church as playing a leadership role in inter-religious dialogue in your country? If so, in what ways.

27. According to Vatican II, what are the objectives and importance of ecumenical dialogue with non-Catholic churches and ecclesial communities?

28. In what ways and to what extent has the ecumenical spirit blowing in the Catholic Church affected the Church in your land in its relationship with other Christians?

29. Do you have the phenomenon of proliferation of sects in your country? How does this affect ecumenical dialogue?

30. Has a formal ecumenical dialogue been launched in your country, between the Catholic Church and other Christian communities? If so, since when? At what level? How consistent? And with what result?

31. What effort is being made in your country, diocese and parishes, to promote the unity of Christians?

32. What are the main areas of possible collaboration between Christians of different confessions, in view of closer ecumenical relationship, e.g., political, social, cultural, Bible apostolate, religious education?

33. How much ecumenical collaboration is there in the following areas: political, social, cultural, religious, Bible apostolate, prayers?

34. What are the dangers to avoid and the obstacles to overcome in ecumenical dialogue in your area? For example, intransigence or indifference?

35. What form of training in ecumenism do you give to your priests, seminarians, religious and laity in order to prepare them for a fruitful dialogue?

36. Is there a sizable Orthodox community in your country? If so, how far and fast is dialogue with them moving?

37. How strong is the presence of Islam in your country, and how does this compare to Catholic and [overall] Christian presence? Are there reliable official figures on the relative numerical strengths of the different religious groups?

38. Do you think being a Christian or [a] Muslim affect[s] one's access to key positions in your country's political life? Can you illustrate this with examples?

39. Does Islam have an official or privileged status in your country? If so, how does this affect dialogue? In particular, how do government policies on religion promote or hinder dialogue with Islam?

40. What is the impact of international Islamic organizations on Islam in your country, and how does this affect dialogue? Which of these are most active in your area?

41. Have you noticed an intensification of Islamic propagation in your country in recent years? What are the main external sources of support for such programs? How do they affect the chances of Christian evangelization on the one hand, and the opportunities for dialogue on the other?

42. At what stage is the dialogue between Christians and Muslims? How far is the principle of reciprocity respected in Christian-Muslim relations? Are there any difficulties? If so, mention the most important ones.

43. What steps have been taken in the particular church to prepare for dialogue? What possibilities for formation exist? What attitudes are inculcated in schools, in colleges of teacher training, in seminaries and in catechetical centers?

44. To what extent is African Traditional Religion [ATR] still surviving in our area? How is it coping with the impact of modern science and technology and, in the political context, of modern state structures?

45. What efforts have been made in your diocese, ethnic area, region or country to study the African Traditional Religion prevalent in your area? Are there scientific academic research works produced on them from the theological, anthropological, sociological, canonical, liturgical or other perspectives?

46. What theological or other Church faculties or agencies in your area study African Traditional Religion?

47. Is a course on African Traditional Religion taught in your major seminaries and houses of religious or pastoral formation?

48. Is there any commission on African Traditional Religion formed by your bishops' conference?

49. Are there any directives or documents of bishops on African Traditional Religion?

50. What are the positive elements of African Traditional Religion which the Church could or should adopt or retouch?

51. Are there any liturgical rites or other initiatives already introduced in your area as a result of pastoral attention to African Traditional Religion?

52. What are the negative elements [of ATR] which will have to be rejected?

53. Are there syncretistic developments from African Traditional Religion in your area, and if so, what action is the Church taking to meet such challenges?

54. How much and how effectively is the laity involved in the pastoral attention of your particular church to African Traditional Religion?

55. What is the extent of the presence of sects and new religious movements in your country?

56. Is there a fairly comprehensive inventory of such sects, including their different characteristics?

57. Have you any way of monitoring their influence on Catholics? Which groups of Catholics are influenced by them and become their followers?

58. What do these sects have that attract some Catholics?

59. Has your particular church any clear pastoral program in light of these sects and movements?

60. Can you identify in your country any groups who will fall under the heading treated in this section? Among such groups, are there any that are anti-Catholic or anti-Christian in their policies and methods? If so, what are the prospects for dialogue?

61. How much are Catholic lay persons involved in and contributing to the formulation and propagation of state ideologies in your country? What influence, if any, does Catholic social and political doctrine have on such ideologies?

62. Has your particular church any commission for dialogue with local cultural and ideological groups?

Justice and Peace

63. Describe the awareness of the Church in Africa—particular, regional and continental—to the vital link between the Church's mission of evangelization and action on behalf of human promotion justice and peace? What programs of formation exist in this regard, particularly towards the lay faithful's active participation in civil life and politics.

64. There are many papal documents, and those of national, regional and continental episcopal bodies, which express the appeal of the Church in this area. How well is the Church's message known and put into practice at the various levels of African society? How can it be improved?

65. What is the present situation in your diocese, region or country concerning:

(a) Human promotion: health, education, social structures, respect for the human person, the situation of prisoners, torture, etc.

(b) Justice: violations of human rights, recognition of political rights, the right of association and free expression (of one's opinions), etc.

(c) Peace: relations between ethnic, racial, religious and ideological groups; situations of armed conflict and war; refugees, etc.

66. What are the root causes of situations of various disorders in the area of the promotion of human dignity, justice and peace?

67. What are the main efforts aimed at changing these situations which have been already undertaken in your country or region by

—Churches or ecclesial communities?

—the State or by other groups?

68. How can the Church at Her various levels contribute to help improve these situations through a renewed effort in evangelization?

Means of Social Communications

69. After the promulgation of the document of Vatican Council II *Inter Mirifica* (4 December 1963), in your opinion which official texts of the Church on the means of social communications ought to be given more attention in the evangelizing mission of the Church in Africa?

70. What are the means of evangelization which ought to be given the benefit of attention and reflection today in the particular churches, especially according to the official documents, *Inter Mirifica* and *Communio et Progressio* [29 January 1971]?

71. In this "era of communication," have Church leaders and the faithful in your area been concretely aware of the phenomenon both in the world and in Africa—[of] how social communications affect people's ideas of the world and others, in their collective and individual behavior?

72. Does announcing Jesus Christ, deepening one's faith and fostering the overall total development of the person, through use of the means of social communications, appear to you as a valuable and urgent pastoral project?

73. Would it be desirable to make an objective inventory of those *modern* means of communication more widely used in your area by politicians, traders and people?

74. Do groups of young people and adults show any preference for certain kinds of mass media? What percentage of the population in your area makes use of the following: radio, press, cinema, television and video?

75. Is it possible to do a research study on the kind of films usually available in the video-clubs which are opening in your area? Cannot the Church offer an alternative to families and young people by providing better, or even religious, films?

76. How can the *traditional* means of social communications be assessed and used to proclaim the Gospel and advance human promotion?

77. Is the Church discourse on the means of social communications in your country constructive and a source of motivation for communicators and [their] users? Please give examples.

78. How are the leaders and faithful concretely engaged in the ministry of communication? Has there been any effort to develop sharing of communication resources between the African Churches? (South-South cooperation).

79. Does a concerted and effective *strategy* exist in your Church for the *training* of Christian communicators (priests, religious, lay men and women)?

80. Is there a listing available of all those who have been locally trained and those trained abroad? Are they employed in the communication ministry? If yes, in what area of competence are they working and what are the conditions under which they work?

81. What links exist between your particular church and those in charge of social communication in the area, as well as the professionals who work in the industry? What pastoral activity is envisioned towards those persons, Christian or not, involved in the various areas of social communications?

VATICAN CITY, 1990

Appendix 2

Post-Synodal Apostolic Exhortation

John Paul II

1. THE CHURCH WHICH IS IN AFRICA celebrated with joy and hope its faith in the Risen Christ during the four weeks of the Special Assembly for Africa of the Synod of Bishops. Memories of this event are still fresh in the minds of the whole Ecclesial Community.

Faithful to the tradition of the first centuries of Christianity in Africa, the Pastors of this Continent, in communion with the Successor of the Apostle Peter and members of the Episcopal College from other parts of the world, held a Synod which was intended to be an occasion of hope and resurrection, at the very moment when human events seemed to be tempting Africa to discouragement and despair.

The Synod Fathers, assisted by qualified representatives of the clergy, religious and laity, subjected to a detailed and realistic study the lights and shadows, the challenges and future prospects of evangelization in Africa on the threshold of the Third Millennium of the Christian faith.

The members of the Synodal Assembly asked me to bring to the attention of the whole Church the results of their reflections and prayers, discussions and exchanges.[1] With joy and gratitude to the Lord I accepted this request and today, at the very moment when, in communion with the Pastors and faithful of the Catholic Church in Africa, I begin the celebration phase of the Special Assembly for Africa, I am promulgating the text of this Post-Synodal Apostolic Exhortation, the result of an intense and prolonged collegial endeavor.

But before describing what developed in the course of the Synod, I consider it helpful to go back, if only briefly, over the various stages of an event of such decisive importance for the Church in Africa.

The Council
2. The Second Vatican Ecumenical Council can certainly be considered, from the point of view of the history of salvation, as the cornerstone of the present century which is now rapidly approaching the Third Millennium. In the context of that great event, the Church of God in Africa experienced true moments of grace. Indeed, the idea of some form of meeting of the African Bishops to discuss the evangelization of the Continent dates back to the time of the Council. That historic event was truly the crucible of collegiality and a specific expression of the *affective* and *effective* communion of the worldwide Episcopate. At the Council, the Bishops sought to identify

233

appropriate means of better sharing and making more effective their care for all the Churches (cf. 2 Cor 11:28), and for this purpose they began to plan suitable structures at the national, regional and continental level.

The Symposium of Episcopal Conferences of Africa and Madagascar

3. It is in such a climate that the Bishops of Africa and Madagascar present at the Council decided to establish their own General Secretariat with the task of coordinating their interventions, in order to present to the Council Fathers, as far as possible, a common point of view. This initial cooperation among the Bishops of Africa later became permanent in the creation in Kampala of the *Symposium of Episcopal Conferences of Africa and Madagascar* (SECAM). This took place in July-August 1969, during the visit of Pope Paul VI to Uganda—the first of a Pope to Africa in modern times.

The Convocation of the Special Assembly for Africa of the Synod of Bishops

4. The General Assemblies of the Synod of Bishops, held regularly from 1967 onwards, offered valuable opportunities for the Church in Africa to make its voice heard in the Church throughout the world. Thus, at the Second Ordinary General Assembly (1971), the Synod Fathers from Africa happily took the occasion offered them to appeal for greater justice in the world. The Third Ordinary General Assembly (1974), evangelization in the modern world, made possible a special study of the problems of evangelization in Africa. It was then that the Bishops of the Continent present at the Synod issued an important message entitled *Promoting Evangelization in Co-Responsibility*.[2] Shortly afterwards, during the Holy Year of 1975, SECAM convoked its own plenary meeting in Rome, in order to examine the subject of evangelization.

5. Subsequently, from 1977 to 1983, some Bishops, priests, consecrated persons, theologians and lay people expressed a desire for an *African Council* or *African Synod*, which would have the task of evaluating evangelization in Africa vis-à-vis the great choices to be made regarding the Continent's future. I gladly welcomed and encouraged the idea of the "working together, in one form or another," of the whole African Episcopate in order "to study the religious problems that concern the whole Continent."[3] SECAM thus studied ways and means of planning a continental meeting of this kind. A consultation of the Episcopal Conferences and of each Bishop of Africa and Madagascar was organized, after which I was able to convoke a Special Assembly for Africa of the Synod of Bishops. On 6 January 1989, the Solemnity of the Epiphany—the liturgical commemoration on which the Church renews her awareness of the universality of her mission and her consequent duty to bring the light of Christ to all peoples—I announced this "initiative of great importance for the Church," welcoming, as I said, the petitions often expressed for some time by the Bishops of Africa, priests, theologians and representatives of the laity, "in order to promote an *organic pastoral solidarity* within the entire African territory and nearby Islands."[4]

An event of grace

6. The Special Assembly for Africa of the Synod of Bishops was *an historic moment of grace*: the Lord *visited* his people in Africa. Indeed, this Continent is today experiencing what we can call a *sign of the times*, an *acceptable time*, a *day of salvation*. It seems that the "hour of Africa" has come, a favorable time which urgently invites Christ's messengers to launch out into the deep and to cast their nets for the catch (cf. Lk 5:4). Just as at Christianity's beginning the minister of Candace, Queen of Ethiopia, rejoiced at having received the faith through Baptism and went on his way bearing witness to Christ (cf. Acts 8:27-39), so today the Church in Africa, joyful and grateful for having received the faith, must pursue its evangelizing mission, in order to bring the peoples of the Continent to the Lord, teaching them to observe all that he has commanded (cf. Mt 28:20).

From the opening Solemn Eucharistic Liturgy which on 10 April 1994 I celebrated in Saint Peter's Basilica with thirty-five Cardinals, one Patriarch, thirty-nine Archbishops, one hundred forty-six Bishops and ninety priests, the Church, which is the Family of God[5] and the community of believers, gathered about the Tomb of Peter. Africa was present there, in its various rites, with the entire People of God: it rejoiced, expressing its faith in life to the sound of drums and other African musical instruments. On that occasion Africa felt that it was, in the words of Pope Paul VI, "a new homeland for Christ,"[6] a land loved by the Eternal Father.[7] That is why I myself greeted that moment of grace in the words of the Psalmist: "This is the day which the Lord has made; let us rejoice and be glad in it" (Ps 118:24).

Recipients of the Exhortation

7. In communion with the Special Assembly for Africa of the Synod of Bishops, I wish to address this Post-Synodal Apostolic Exhortation in the first place to Pastors and lay Catholics, and then to our brothers and sisters of other Christian Confessions, to those who profess the great monotheistic religions, in particular the followers of African traditional religion, and to all people of good will who in one way or another have at heart Africa's spiritual and material development or who hold in their hands the destiny of this great Continent.

First of all my thoughts naturally turn to the Africans themselves and to all who live on the Continent; I think especially of the sons and daughters of the Catholic Church: Bishops, priests, deacons, seminarians, members of Institutes of Consecrated Life and Societies of Apostolic Life, catechists and all those who make service of their brothers and sisters the ideal of their life. I wish to confirm them in their faith (cf. Lk 22:32) and to urge them to persevere in the hope which the Risen Christ gives, overcoming every temptation to discouragement.

Outline of the Exhortation

8. The Special Assembly for Africa of the Synod of Bishops examined thoroughly the topic which had been placed before it: "The Church in Africa and her evangelizing mission towards the Year 2000: 'You shall be my witnesses' (Acts 1:8)." This Exhortation will therefore endeavor to follow closely the same thematic framework. It will begin from the historic moment, a true *kairos*, in which the Synod was held, examining its objectives, preparation and celebration. It will consider the current situation of the *Church in Africa*, recalling the different phases of missionary commitment. It will then examine the various aspects of the *evangelizing* mission which the Church must take into account at the present time: evangelization, inculturation, dialogue, justice and peace, and the means of social communication. A mention of the *urgent tasks* and *challenges* facing the Church in Africa *on the eve of the Year 2000* will enable us to sketch out the tasks of Christ's witnesses in Africa, so that they will make a more effective contribution to the building up of God's Kingdom. It will thus be possible at the end to describe the responsibilities of the Church in Africa as a missionary Church: a Church of mission which itself becomes missionary: "You shall be my witnesses to the ends of the earth" (Acts 1:8).

CHAPTER I
AN HISTORIC MOMENT OF GRACE

9. "This Special Assembly for Africa of the Synod of Bishops is a *providential event of grace*, for which we must give praise and thanks to the Almighty and Merciful Father through the Son in the Holy Spirit."[8] It is with these words that the Fathers solemnly opened the discussion of the Synod's theme during the first General Congregation. On an earlier occasion, I had expressed a similar conviction, recognizing that "the Special Assembly is an ecclesial event of fundamental importance for Africa, a *kairos, a moment of grace*, in which God manifests his salvation. The whole Church is invited to live fully this time of grace, to accept and spread the Good News. The effort expended in preparation for the Synod will not only benefit the celebration of the Synod itself, but from this time on will work *in favor of the local Churches which make their pilgrim way in*

Africa, whose faith and witness are being strengthened and are becoming increasingly mature."[9]

Profession of faith

10. This moment of grace was in the first place manifested in a solemn profession of faith. Gathered about the Tomb of Peter for the opening of the Special Assembly, the Synod Fathers proclaimed their faith, the faith of Peter who, in answer to Christ's question, "Do you also wish to go away?" replied: "Lord, to whom shall we go? You have the words of eternal life; and we have believed, and have come to know, that you are the Holy One of God" (Jn 6:67-69). The Bishops of Africa, in whom the Catholic Church during those days found herself expressed in a special way at the Tomb of the Apostle, confirmed their steadfast belief that the greatness and mercy of the one God were manifested above all in the Redemptive Incarnation of the Son of God, the Son who is consubstantial with the Father in the unity of the Holy Spirit and who, in this Trinitarian unity, receives the fullness of honor and glory. This—the Fathers affirmed—is our faith; this is the faith of the Church; this is the faith of all the local Churches which everywhere in Africa are on pilgrimage towards the House of God.

This faith in Jesus Christ was manifested unceasingly, forcefully and unanimously in the interventions of the Synod Fathers throughout the meeting of the Special Assembly. In the strength of this faith, the Bishops of Africa entrusted their Continent to Christ the Lord, convinced that he alone, through his Gospel and his Church, can save Africa from its present difficulties and heal its many ills.[10]

11. At the same time, at the solemn opening of the Special Assembly, the Bishops of Africa publicly proclaimed their faith in the "unique Church of Christ, which in the Creed we avow as one, holy, catholic and apostolic."[11] These characteristics indicate essential features of the Church and her mission. She "does not possess them of herself; it is Christ who, through the Holy Spirit, makes his Church one, holy, catholic and apostolic, and it is he who calls her to realize each of these qualities."[12]

All those privileged to be present at the celebration of the Special Assembly for Africa rejoiced to see how African Catholics are assuming ever greater responsibility in their local Churches and are seeking a deeper understanding of what it means to be both Catholic and African. The celebration of the Special Assembly showed to the whole world that the local Churches of Africa hold a rightful place in the communion of the Church, that they are entitled to preserve and to develop "their own traditions, without in any way lessening the primacy of the Chair of Peter. This Chair presides over the whole assembly of charity and protects legitimate differences, while at the same time it sees that such differences do not hinder unity but rather contribute towards it."[13]

Synod of resurrection, synod of hope

12. By a singular design of Providence, the solemn inauguration of the Special Assembly for Africa of the Synod of Bishops took place on the Second Sunday of Easter, at the end of the Easter Octave. The Synod Fathers, assembled in Saint Peter's Basilica on that day, were well aware that the joy of their Church flowed from the same event which had gladdened the Apostles' hearts on Easter Day (cf. Lk 24:40-41): the Resurrection of the Lord Jesus. They were deeply aware of the presence in their midst of the Risen Lord, who said to them as he had to his Apostles: "Peace be with you" (Jn 20:21,26). They were also aware of his promise to remain with his Church for ever (cf. Mt 28:20), and therefore also throughout the duration of the Synodal Assembly. The Easter spirit in which the Special Assembly began its work, with its members united in celebrating their faith in the Risen Lord, spontaneously brought to mind the words which Jesus addressed to the Apostle Thomas: "Blessed are those who have not seen and yet believe" (Jn 20:29).

13. This was indeed a Synod of Resurrection and Hope, as the Synod Fathers joyfully and enthusiastically declared in the opening words of their *Message* to the People of God. They are words which I willingly make my own: "Like Mary Magdalene on the morning of the Resurrection, like the disciples at Emmaus with burning hearts and enlightened minds, the Special Synod for

Africa, Madagascar and the Islands proclaims: *Christ, our Hope, is risen. He has met us, has walked along with us.* He has explained the Scriptures to us. Here is what he said to us: 'I am the First and the Last, I am the Living One; I was dead, and behold, I am alive for ever and ever and I hold the keys of death and of the abode of the dead' (Rev 1:17-18)... And as Saint John at Patmos during particularly difficult times received prophecies of hope for the People of God, we also announce a message of hope. At this time when so much fratricidal hate inspired by political interests is tearing our peoples apart, when the burden of the international debt and currency devaluation is crushing them, we, the Bishops of Africa, together with all the participants in this holy Synod, united with the Holy Father and with all our Brothers in the Episcopate who elected us, we want to say a word of hope and encouragement to you, Family of God in Africa, to you, the Family of God all over the world: *Christ our Hope is alive; we shall live!*"[14]

14. I exhort all God's People in Africa to accept with open hearts the message of hope addressed to them by the Synodal Assembly. During their discussions the Synod Fathers, fully aware that they were expressing the expectations not only of African Catholics but also those of all the men and women of the Continent, squarely faced the many evils which oppress Africa today. The Fathers explored at length and in all its complexity what the Church is called to do in order to bring about the desired changes, but they did so with an attitude free from pessimism or despair. Despite the mainly negative picture which today characterizes numerous parts of Africa, and despite the sad situations being experienced in many countries, the Church has the duty to affirm vigorously that these difficulties can be overcome. She must strengthen in all Africans hope of genuine liberation. In the final analysis, this confidence is based on the Church's awareness of God's promise, which assures us that history is not closed in upon itself but is open to God's Kingdom. This is why there is no justification for despair or pessimism when we think about the future of both Africa and any other part of the world.

Affective and effective collegiality

15. Before dealing with the different themes, I would like to state that the Synod of Bishops is an extremely beneficial instrument for fostering ecclesial communion. When towards the end of the Second Vatican Council Pope Paul VI established the Synod, he clearly indicated that one of its essential tasks would be to express and foster, under the guidance of the Successor of Peter, mutual communion between Bishops throughout the world.[15] The principle underlying the setting up of the Synod of Bishops is straightforward: the more the communion of the Bishops among themselves is strengthened, the more the communion of the Church as a whole is enriched. The Church in Africa testifies to the truth of these words, for it has experienced the enthusiasm and practical results which accompanied the preparations for the Assembly of the Synod of Bishops devoted to it.

16. At my first meeting with the Council of the General Secretariat of the Synod of Bishops, gathered to discuss the Special Assembly for Africa, I indicated the reason why it seemed appropriate to convoke this Assembly: the promotion of "an organic pastoral solidarity throughout Africa and the adjacent Islands."[16] With these words I wished to include the main goals and objectives which that Assembly would have to pursue. In order to clarify my expectations further, I added that the reflections in preparation for the Assembly "should cover all the important aspects of the life of the Church in Africa, and in particular should include evangelization, inculturation, dialogue, pastoral care in social areas and the means of social communication."[17]

17. During my Pastoral Visits in Africa, I frequently referred to the Special Assembly for Africa and to the principal aims for which it had been convoked. When I took part for the first time on African soil at a meeting of the Council of the Synod, I did not fail to emphasize my conviction that a Synodal Assembly cannot be reduced to a consultation on practical matters. Its true *raison d'être* is the fact that the Church can move forward only by strengthening communion among her members, beginning with her Pastors.[18]

Every Synodal Assembly manifests and develops solidarity between the heads of particular

Churches in carrying out their mission beyond the boundaries of their respective Dioceses. The Second Vatican Council taught: "As lawful Successors of the Apostles and as members of the Episcopal College, Bishops should always realize that they are linked one to the other, and should show concern for all the Churches. For by divine institution and the requirement of their apostolic office, each one in concert with his fellow Bishops is responsible for the Church."[19]

18. The theme assigned to the Special Assembly—"The Church in Africa and her evangelizing mission towards the Year 2000. 'You shall be my witnesses' (Acts 1:8)"—expresses my desire that this Church should live the time leading up to the Great Jubilee as "a new Advent," a time of expectation and preparation. In fact I consider preparations for the Year 2000 as one of the keys for interpreting my Pontificate.[20]

The series of Synodal Assemblies which have taken place in the course of nearly thirty years— General Assemblies and Special Assemblies on a continental, regional or national level—are all part of preparing for the Great Jubilee. The fact that evangelization is the theme of all these Synodal Assemblies is meant to indicate how alive today is the Church's awareness of the salvific mission which she has received from Christ. This awareness is especially evident in the Post-Synodal Apostolic Exhortations devoted to evangelization, catechesis, the family, reconciliation and penance in the life of the Church and of all humanity, the vocation and mission of the lay faithful and the formation of priests.

In full communion with the universal church

19. Right from the beginning of the preparations for the Special Assembly, it was my heartfelt desire, fully shared by the Council of the General Secretariat, to ensure that this Synod would be authentically and unequivocally African. At the same time, it was of fundamental importance that the Special Assembly should be celebrated *in full communion with the universal Church*. Indeed, the Assembly always kept in mind the needs of the universal Church. Likewise, when the time came to publish the *Lineamenta*, I invited my Brothers in the Episcopate and the whole People of God throughout the world to pray for the Special Assembly for Africa, and to feel that they were part of the activities being promoted in preparation for that event.

This Assembly, as I have often had occasion to say, was of profound significance for the universal Church, not only because of the great interest raised everywhere by its convocation, but also because of the very nature of ecclesial communion which transcends all boundaries of time and space. In fact the Special Assembly inspired many prayers and good works through which individuals and communities of the Church in the other continents accompanied the Synodal process. And how can we doubt that through the mystery of ecclesial communion the Synod was also supported by the prayers of the Saints in heaven?

When I directed that the first working session of the Special Assembly should take place in Rome, I did so in order to express even more clearly the communion which links the Church in Africa with the universal Church, and in order to emphasize the commitment of *all the faithful* to Africa.

20. The solemn Eucharistic concelebration for the opening of the Synod at which I presided in Saint Peter's Basilica highlighted the universality of the Church in a striking and deeply moving way. This universality, "which is not uniformity but rather communion in a diversity compatible with the Gospel,"[21] was experienced by all the Bishops. They were aware of having been consecrated as members of the Body of Bishops which succeeds the College of the Apostles, not only for one Diocese but for the salvation of the whole world.[22]

I give thanks to Almighty God for the opportunity which he gave us to experience, through the Special Assembly, what genuine catholicity implies. "In virtue of this catholicity each individual part of the Church contributes through its special gifts to the good of the other parts and of the whole Church."[23]

A relevant and credible message

21. According to the Synod Fathers, the main question facing the Church in Africa consists in delineating as clearly as possible what it is and what it must fully carry out, in order that its message

may be relevant and credible.[24] All the discussions at the Assembly referred to this truly essential and fundamental need, which is *a real challenge for the Church in Africa.*

It is of course true "that the Holy Spirit is the principal agent of evangelization: it is he who impels each individual to proclaim the Gospel, and it is he who in the depths of consciences causes the word of salvation to be accepted and stood."[25] After reaffirming this truth, the Special Assembly rightly went on to add that evangelization is also a mission which the Lord Jesus entrusted to his Church under the guidance and in the power of the Holy Spirit. Our cooperation is necessary through fervent prayer, serious reflection, suitable planning and the mobilization of resources.[26]

The Synod's debate on the *relevance* and *credibility* of the Church's message in Africa inescapably entailed consideration of the *very credibility of the proclaimers of this message.* The Synod Fathers faced the question directly, with genuine frankness and devoid of any complacency. Pope Paul VI had already addressed this question in memorable words when he stated: "It is often said nowadays that the present century thirsts for authenticity. Especially in regard to young people, it is said that they have a horror of the artificial or false and that they are searching above all for truth and honesty. These *signs of the times* should find us vigilant. Either tacitly or aloud— but always forcefully—we are being asked: Do you really believe what you are proclaiming? Do you live what you believe? Do you really preach what you live? The witness of life has become more than ever an essential condition for real effectiveness in preaching. Precisely because of this we are, to a certain extent, responsible for the progress of the Gospel that we proclaim."[27]

That is why, with reference to the Church's evangelizing mission in the field of justice and peace, I have said: "Today more than ever, the Church is aware that her social doctrine will gain credibility more immediately from *witness of action* than as a result of its internal logic and consistency."[28]

22. How can I fail to recall here that the Eighth Plenary Assembly of SECAM held in Lagos, Nigeria, in 1987, had already considered with remarkable clarity the question of the credibility and relevance of the Church's message in Africa? That same Assembly had declared that the credibility of the Church in Africa depended upon Bishops and priests who followed Christ's example and could give witness of an exemplary life; upon truly faithful men and women religious, authentic witnesses by their way of living the evangelical counsels; upon a dynamic laity, with deeply believing parents, educators conscious of their responsibilities and political leaders animated by a profound sense of morality.[29]

The Family of God in the synodal process

23. Speaking to the members of the Council of the General Secretariat on 23 June 1989, I laid special emphasis on the involvement of the whole People of God, at all levels and especially in Africa, in the preparations for the Special Assembly. "If this Synod is prepared well," I said, "it will be able to involve all levels of the Christian Community: individuals, small communities, parishes, Dioceses, and local, national and international bodies."[30]

Between the beginning of my Pontificate and the solemn inauguration of the Special Assembly for Africa of the Synod of Bishops, I paid a total of ten Pastoral visits to Africa and Madagascar, going to thirty-six countries. On my Apostolic Visits after the convocation of the Special Assembly, the theme of the Synod and the need for all the faithful to prepare for the Synodal Assembly always figured prominently in my meetings with the People of God in Africa. I also took advantage of the *ad Limina* Visits of the Continent's Bishops in order to ask for the cooperation of everyone in the preparation of the Special Synod for Africa. In addition, on three separate occasions I held working sessions with the Council of the General Secretariat of the Synod *on African soil*: at Yamoussoukro, Ivory Coast (1990); at Luanda, Angola (1992); and at Kampala, Uganda (1993). All this was done in order to mobilize an active and harmonious participation by Africans in the preparation of the Synodal Assembly.

24. The presentation of the *Lineamenta* at the Ninth Plenary Assembly of SECAM in Lomé, Togo, on 25 July 1990, was undoubtedly a new and significant stage in the preparation of the Special Assembly. It can be said that with the publication of the *Lineamenta* preparations for the

Synod began in earnest in all the particular Churches of Africa. The Assembly of SECAM in Lomé approved a *Prayer for the Special Assembly* and requested that it be recited both publicly and privately in every African parish until the actual celebration of the Synod. This initiative of SECAM was truly felicitous and did not pass unnoticed by the universal Church.

In order to make the *Lineamenta* more available, many Episcopal Conferences and Dioceses translated the document into their own languages, for example into Swahili, Arabic, Malagasy, etc. "Publications, conferences and symposia on the themes of the Synod were organized by various Episcopal Conferences, Institutes of Theology and Seminaries, Associations of Institutes of Consecrated Life, Dioceses, some important journals and periodicals, individual Bishops and theologians."[31]

25. I fervently thank Almighty God for the meticulous care with which the Synod's *Lineamenta* and the *Instrumentum Laboris*[32] were drawn up. It was a task accepted and carried out by Africans—Bishops and experts—beginning with the Ante-Preparatory Commission of the Synod which met in January and March 1989. This Commission was then replaced by the Council of the General Secretariat of the Special Assembly for Africa of the Synod of Bishops, established on 20 June 1989.

I am also deeply grateful to the working group which so carefully prepared the Eucharistic Liturgies for the opening and closing of the Synod. The group, which included theologians, liturgists and experts in African chants and musical instruments, ensured, in keeping with my wishes, that these celebrations would have a distinctly African character.

26. I must now add that the response of the African peoples to my appeal to them to share in the preparation of the Synod was truly admirable. The replies given to the *Lineamenta*, both within and beyond the African Ecclesial Communities, far exceeded every expectation. Many local Churches used the *Lineamenta* in order to mobilize the faithful and, from that time onwards, we can say that the results of the Synod were beginning to appear in a fresh commitment and renewed awareness among African Christians.[33]

Throughout the various phases of the preparation for the Special Assembly, many members of the Church in Africa—clergy, religious and laity—entered with exemplary dedication into the Synodal process, "walking together," placing their individual talents at the service of the Church, and fervently praying together for the Synod's success. More than once the Synod Fathers themselves noted, during the actual Synodal Assembly, that their work was made easier precisely by the "careful and meticulous preparation of the Synod, and the active involvement of the entire Church in Africa at all levels."[34]

God wills to save Africa

27. The Apostle of the Gentiles tells us that God "desires all men to be saved and to come to the knowledge of the truth. For there is one God, and there is one mediator between God and men, the man Christ Jesus, who gave himself as a ransom for all" (1 Tim 2:4-6). Since God, in fact, calls all people to one and the same divine destiny, "we ought to believe that the Holy Spirit in a manner known only to God offers to everyone the possibility of being associated with this Paschal Mystery."[35] God's redeeming love embraces the whole of humanity, every race, tribe and nation: thus it also embraces all the peoples of Africa. Divine Providence willed that Africa should be present during the Passion of Christ in the person of Simon of Cyrene, forced by the Roman soldiers to help the Lord to carry the Cross (cf. Mk 15:21).

28. The Liturgy of the Sixth Sunday of Easter in 1994, at the Solemn Eucharistic Celebration for the closing of the working session of the Special Assembly, provided me with the occasion to develop a meditation upon God's salvific plan for Africa. One of the Scriptural readings, taken from the Acts of the Apostles, recalled an event which can be understood as *the first step in the Church's mission "ad gentes"*: it is the account of the visit made by Peter, at the bidding of the Holy Spirit, to the home of a Gentile, the centurion Cornelius. Until that time the Gospel had been proclaimed mainly to the Jews. After considerable hesitation, Peter, enlightened by the Spirit,

decided to go to the house of a Gentile. When he arrived, he discovered to his joyful surprise that the centurion was awaiting Christ and Baptism. The Acts of the Apostles says: "the believers from among the circumcised who came with Peter were amazed, because the gift of the Holy Spirit had been poured out even on the Gentiles. For they heard them speaking in tongues and extolling God" (10:45-46).

In the house of Cornelius the miracle of Pentecost was in a sense repeated. Peter then said: "Truly I perceive that God shows no partiality, but in every nation any one who fears him and does what is right is acceptable to him . . . Can anyone forbid water for baptizing these people who have received the Holy Spirit just as we have?" (Acts 10:34-35,47).

Thus began the Church's mission *ad gentes*, of which Paul of Tarsus would become the principal herald. The first missionaries who reached the heart of Africa undoubtedly felt an astonishment similar to that experienced by the Christians of the Apostolic age at the outpouring of the Holy Spirit.

29. God's salvific plan for Africa is at the origin of the growth of the Church on the African Continent. But since by Christ's will the Church is by her nature missionary, it follows that the Church in Africa is itself called to play an active role in God's plan of salvation. For this reason I have often said that "the Church in Africa is a missionary Church and a mission Church."[36]

The Special Assembly for Africa of the Synod of Bishops had the task of examining appropriate ways and means whereby Africans would be better able to implement the mandate which the Risen Lord gave to his disciples: "Go therefore and make disciples of all nations" (Mt 28:19).

CHAPTER II
THE CHURCH IN AFRICA

I. BRIEF HISTORY OF THE CONTINENT'S EVANGELIZATION

30. On the opening day of the Special Assembly for Africa of the Synod of Bishops, the first meeting of this kind in history, the Synod Fathers recalled some of the marvels wrought by God in the course of Africa's evangelization. It is a history which goes back to the period of the Church's very birth. The spread of the Gospel has taken place in different phases. The first centuries of Christianity saw the evangelization of Egypt and North Africa. A second phase, involving the parts of the Continent south of the Sahara, took place in the fifteenth and sixteenth centuries. A third phase, marked by an extraordinary missionary effort, began in the nineteenth century.

First phase
31. In a message to the Bishops and to all the peoples of Africa concerning the promotion of the religious, civil and social well-being of the Continent, my venerable Predecessor Paul VI recalled in memorable words the glorious splendor of Africa's Christian past: "We think of the Christian Churches of Africa whose origins go back to the times of the Apostles and are traditionally associated with the name and teaching of Mark the Evangelist. We think of their countless Saints, Martyrs, Confessors, and Virgins, and recall the fact that from the second to the fourth centuries Christian life in the North of Africa was most vigorous and had a leading place in theological study and literary production. The names of the great doctors and writers come to mind, men like Origen, Saint Athanasius, and Saint Cyril, leaders of the Alexandrian school, and at the other end of the North African coastline, Tertullian, Saint Cyprian and above all Saint Augustine, one of the most brilliant lights of the Christian world. We shall mention the great Saints of the desert, Paul, Anthony, and Pachomius, the first founders of the monastic life, which later spread through their example in both the East and the West. And among many others we want also to mention Saint Frumentius, known by the name of Abba Salama, who was consecrated Bishop by Saint Athanasius and became the first Apostle of Ethiopia."[37] During these first centuries of the Church in Africa,

certain women also bore their own witness to Christ. Among them Saints Perpetua and Felicitas, Saint Monica and Saint Thecla are particularly deserving of mention.

"These noble examples, as also the saintly African Popes, Victor I, Melchiades and Gelasius I, belong to the common heritage of the Church, and the Christian writers of Africa remain today a basic source for deepening our knowledge of the history of salvation in the light of the Word of God. In recalling the ancient glories of Christian Africa, we wish to express our profound respect for the Churches with which we are not in full communion: the Greek Church of the Patriarchate of Alexandria, the Coptic Church of Egypt and the Church of Ethiopia, which share with the Catholic Church a common origin and the doctrinal and spiritual heritage of the great Fathers and Saints, not only of their own land, but of all the early Church. They have labored much and suffered much to keep the Christian name alive in Africa through all the vicissitudes of history."[38] These Churches continue to give evidence down to our own times of the Christian vitality which flows from their Apostolic origins. This is especially true in Egypt, in Ethiopia and, until the seventeenth century, in Nubia. At that time a new phase of evangelization was beginning on the rest of the Continent.

Second phase

32. In the fifteenth and sixteenth centuries, the exploration of the African coast by the Portuguese was soon accompanied by the evangelization of the regions of Sub-Saharan Africa. That endeavor included the regions of present-day Benin, São Tomé, Angola, Mozambique and Madagascar.

On Pentecost Sunday, 7 June 1992, for the commemoration of the five hundred years of the evangelization of Angola, I said in Luanda: "The Acts of the Apostles indicate by name the inhabitants of the places who participated directly in the birth of the Church and the work of the breath of the Holy Spirit. They all said: 'We hear them telling in our own tongues the mighty works of God' (Acts 2:11). Five hundred years ago the people of Angola were added to this chorus of languages. In that moment, in your African homeland the Pentecost of Jerusalem was renewed. Your ancestors heard the message of the Good News which is the language of the Spirit. Their hearts accepted this message for the first time, and they bowed their heads to the waters of the baptismal font in which, by the power of the Holy Spirit, a person dies with Christ and is born again to new life in his Resurrection . . . It was certainly the same Spirit who moved those men of faith, the first missionaries, who in 1491 sailed into the mouth of the Zaire River, at Pinda, beginning a genuine missionary saga. It was the Holy Spirit, who works as he wills in people's hearts, who moved the great King of the Congo, Nzinga-a-Nkuwu, to ask for missionaries to proclaim the Gospel. It was the Holy Spirit who sustained the life of those four first Angolan Christians who, returning from Europe, testified to the Christian faith. After the first missionaries, many others came from Portugal and other European countries to continue, expand and strengthen the work that had been begun."[39]

A certain number of Episcopal Sees were erected during this period, and one of the first fruits of that missionary endeavor was the consecration in Rome, by Pope Leo X in 1518, of Don Henrique, the son of Don Alfonso I, King of the Congo, as Titular Bishop of Utica. Don Henrique thus became the first native Bishop of Black Africa.

It was during this period, in 1622, that my Predecessor Pope Gregory XV permanently erected the Congregation *de Propaganda Fide* for the purpose of better organizing and expanding the missions.

Because of various difficulties, the second phase of the evangelization of Africa came to an end in the eighteenth century with the disappearance of practically all the missions south of the Sahara.

Third phase

33. The third phase of Africa's systematic evangelization began in the nineteenth century, a period marked by an extraordinary effort organized by the great apostles and promoters of the African mission. It was a period of rapid growth, as the statistics presented to the Synodal Assembly by the Congregation for the Evangelization of Peoples clearly demonstrate.[40] Africa has responded

with great generosity to Christ's call. In recent decades many African countries have celebrated the first centenary of the beginning of their evangelization. Indeed, the growth of the Church in Africa over the last hundred years is a marvelous work of divine grace.

The glory and splendor of the present period of Africa's evangelization are illustrated in a truly admirable way by the Saints whom modern Africa has given to the Church. Pope Paul VI eloquently expressed this when he canonized the Ugandan Martyrs in Saint Peter's Basilica on World Mission Day, 1964: "These African Martyrs add a new page to that list of victorious men and women that we call the martyrology, in which we find the most magnificent as well as the most tragic stories. The page that they add is worthy to take its place alongside those wonderful stories of ancient Africa . . . For from the Africa that was sprinkled with the blood of these Martyrs, the first of this new age (and, God willing, the last, so sublime, so precious was their sacrifice), there is emerging a free and redeemed Africa."[41]

34. The list of Saints that Africa gives to the Church, the list that is its greatest title of honor, continues to grow. How could we fail to mention, among the most recent, Blessed Clementine Anwarite, Virgin and Martyr of Zaire, whom I beatified on African soil in 1985, Blessed Victoria Rasoamanarivo of Madagascar, and Blessed Josephine Bakhita of the Sudan, also beatified during my Pontificate? And how can we not recall Blessed Isidore Bakanja, Martyr of Zaire, whom I had the privilege of raising to the honors of the altar in the course of the Special Assembly for Africa? "Other causes are reaching their final stages. *The Church in Africa must furnish and write her own Martyrology*, adding to the outstanding figures of the first centuries . . . the Martyrs and Saints of our own day."[42]

Faced with the tremendous growth of the Church in Africa over the last hundred years and the fruits of holiness that it has borne, there is only one possible explanation: all this is a gift of God, for no human effort alone could have performed this work in the course of such a relatively short period of time. There is however no reason for worldly triumphalism. In recalling the glorious splendor of the Church in Africa, the Synod Fathers only wished to celebrate God's marvelous deeds for Africa's liberation and salvation.

"This is the Lord's doing;
      it is marvelous in our eyes" (Ps 118:23).
"He who is mighty has done great things for me,
      and holy is his name" (Lk 1:49).

Homage to missionaries

35. The splendid growth and achievements of the Church in Africa are due largely to the heroic and selfless dedication of generations of missionaries. This fact is acknowledged by everyone. The hallowed soil of Africa is truly sown with the tombs of courageous heralds of the Gospel.

When the Bishops of Africa met in Rome for the Special Assembly, they were well aware of the debt of gratitude which their Continent owes to its ancestors in the faith.

In his Address to the inaugural Assembly of SECAM at Kampala, on 31 July 1969, Pope Paul VI spoke about this debt of gratitude: "By now, you Africans are missionaries to yourselves. The Church of Christ is well and truly planted in this blessed soil (cf. *Ad Gentes*, 6). One duty, however, remains to be fulfilled: we must remember those who, before you, and even today with you, have preached the Gospel in Africa; for Sacred Scripture admonishes us to 'Remember your leaders, those who spoke to you the word of God; consider the outcome of their life; and imitate their faith' (Heb 13:7). That is a history which we must not forget; it confers on the local Church the mark of its authenticity and nobility, its mark as 'apostolic. ' That history is a drama of charity, heroism and sacrifice which makes the African Church great and holy from its very origins."[43]

36. The Special Assembly worthily fulfilled this debt of gratitude at its first General Congregation when it declared: "It is appropriate at this point to pay profound homage to the *missionaries*, men and women of all the Religious and Secular Institutes, as well as to all the countries which, during the almost two thousand years of the evangelization of the African Continent, devoted

themselves, without counting the cost, to the task of transmitting the torch of the Christian faith . . . That is why we, the happy inheritors of this marvelous adventure, joyfully pay our debt of thanks to God on this solemn occasion."[44]

The Synod Fathers strongly reiterated their homage to the missionaries in their *Message* to the People of God, but they did not forget to pay tribute to the sons and daughters of Africa who served as co-workers of the missionaries, especially catechists and translators.[45]

37. It is thanks to the great missionary epic which took place on the African Continent, especially during the last two centuries, that we were able to meet in Rome in order to celebrate the Special Assembly for Africa. The seed sown at that time has borne much fruit. My Brothers in the Episcopate, who are sons of the peoples of Africa, are eloquent witnesses to this. Together with their priests, they now carry on their shoulders the major part of the work of evangelization. Signs of this fruitfulness are also the many sons and daughters of Africa who enter the older missionary Congregations or the new Institutes founded on African soil, taking into their own hands the torch of total consecration to the service of God and the Gospel.

Deeper roots and growth of the Church

38. The fact that in the course of almost two centuries the number of African Catholics has grown quickly is an outstanding achievement by any standard. In particular, the building up of the Church on the Continent is confirmed by facts such as the noteworthy and rapid increase in the number of ecclesiastical circumscriptions, the growth of a native clergy, of seminarians and candidates for Institutes of Consecrated Life, and the steady increase in the network of catechists, whose contribution to the spread of the Gospel among the African peoples is well known. Finally, of fundamental importance is the high percentage of indigenous Bishops who now make up the Hierarchy on the Continent.

The Synod Fathers identified many very significant accomplishments of the Church in Africa in the areas of inculturation and ecumenical dialogue.[46] The outstanding and meritorious achievements in the field of education are universally acknowledged.

Although Catholics constitute only fourteen per cent of the population of Africa, Catholic health facilities make up seventeen per cent of the health-care institutions of the entire Continent.

The initiatives boldly undertaken by the young Churches of Africa in order to bring the Gospel "to the ends of the earth" (Acts 1:8) are certainly worthy of note. The missionary Institutes founded in Africa have grown in number, and have begun to supply missionaries not only for the countries of the Continent but also for other areas of the world. A slowly increasing number of African diocesan priests are beginning to make themselves available, for limited periods, as *fidei donum* priests in other needy Dioceses—in their own countries or abroad. The African provinces of Religious Institutes of pontifical right, both of men and of women, have also recorded a growth in membership. In this way the Church offers her ministry to the peoples of Africa; but she also accepts involvement in the "exchange of gifts" with other particular Churches which make up the People of God. All this manifests, in a tangible way, the maturity which the Church in Africa has attained: this is what made possible the celebration of the Special Assembly of the Synod of Bishops.

What has become of Africa?

39. A little less than thirty years ago many African countries gained their independence from the colonial powers. This gave rise to great hopes with regard to the political, economic, social and cultural development of the African peoples. However, "in some countries the internal situation has unfortunately not yet been consolidated, and violence has had, or in some cases still has, the upper hand. But this does not justify a general condemnation involving a whole people or a whole nation or, even worse, a whole continent."[47]

40. But what is the true overall situation of the African Continent today, especially from the point of view of the Church's evangelizing mission? In this regard the Synod Fathers first of all asked:

"In a Continent full of bad news, how is the Christian message 'Good News' for our people? In the midst of an all-pervading despair, where lie the hope and optimism which the Gospel brings? Evangelization stands for many of those essential values which our Continent very much lacks: hope, peace, joy, harmony, love and unity."[48]

After correctly noting that Africa is a huge Continent where very diverse situations are found, and that it is necessary to avoid generalizations both in evaluating problems and suggesting solutions, the Synodal Assembly sadly had to say: "One common situation, without any doubt, is that Africa is full of problems. In almost all our nations, there is abject poverty, tragic mismanagement of available scarce resources, political instability and social disorientation. The results stare us in the face: misery, wars, despair. In a world controlled by rich and powerful nations, Africa has practically become an irrelevant appendix, often forgotten and neglected."[49]

41. For many Synod Fathers contemporary Africa can be compared to the man who went down from Jerusalem to Jericho; he fell among robbers who stripped him, beat him and departed, leaving him half dead (cf. Lk 10:30-37). Africa is a Continent where countless human beings—men and women, children and young people—are lying, as it were, on the edge of the road, sick, injured, disabled, marginalized and abandoned. They are in dire need of Good Samaritans who will come to their aid.

For my part, I express the hope that the Church will continue patiently and tirelessly its work as a Good Samaritan. Indeed, for a long period certain regimes, which have now come to an end, were a great trial for Africans and weakened their ability to respond to situations: an injured person has to rediscover all the resources of his own humanity. The sons and daughters of Africa need an understanding presence and pastoral concern. They need to be helped to recoup their energies so as to put them at the service of the common good.

Positive values of African culture

42. Although Africa is very rich in natural resources, it remains economically poor. At the same time, it is endowed with a wealth of cultural values and priceless human qualities which it can offer to the Churches and to humanity as a whole. The Synod Fathers highlighted some of these cultural values, which are truly a providential preparation for the transmission of the Gospel. They are values which can contribute to an effective reversal of the Continent's dramatic situation and facilitate that worldwide revival on which the desired development of individual nations depends.

Africans have a profound religious sense, a sense of the sacred, of the existence of God the Creator and of a spiritual world. The reality of sin in its individual and social forms is very much present in the consciousness of these peoples, as is also the need for rites of purification and expiation.

43. In African culture and tradition the role of the family is everywhere held to be fundamental. Open to this sense of the family, of love and respect for life, the African loves children, who are joyfully welcomed as gifts of God. *"The sons and daughters of Africa love life.* It is precisely this love for life that leads them to give such great importance to the veneration of their ancestors. They believe intuitively that the dead continue to live and remain in communion with them. Is this not in some way *a preparation for belief in the Communion of the Saints?* The peoples of Africa respect the life which is conceived and born. They rejoice in this life. They reject the idea that it can be destroyed, even when the so-called 'progressive civilizations' would like to lead them in this direction. And practices hostile to life are imposed on them by means of economic systems which serve the selfishness of the rich."[50] Africans show their respect for human life until its natural end, and keep elderly parents and relatives within the family.

African cultures have an acute sense of solidarity and community life. In Africa it is unthinkable to celebrate a feast without the participation of the whole village. Indeed, community life in African societies expresses the extended family. It is my ardent hope and prayer that Africa will always preserve this priceless cultural heritage and never succumb to the temptation to individualism, which is so alien to its best traditions.

Some choices of the African peoples

44. While the shadows and the dark side of the African situation described above can in no way be minimized, it is worth recalling here a number of positive achievements of the peoples of the Continent which deserve to be praised and encouraged. For example, the Synod Fathers in their *Message* to the People of God were pleased to mention the beginning of the democratic process in many African countries, expressing the hope that this process would be consolidated, and that all obstacles and resistance to the establishment of the rule of law would be promptly removed through the concerted action of all those involved and through their sense of the common good.[51]

The "winds of change" are blowing strongly in many parts of Africa, and people are demanding ever more insistently the recognition and promotion of human rights and freedoms. In this regard I note with satisfaction that the Church in Africa, faithful to its vocation, stands resolutely on the side of the oppressed and of voiceless and marginalized peoples. I strongly encourage it to continue to bear this witness. *The preferential option for the poor* is "a special form of primacy in the exercise of Christian charity, to which the whole Tradition of the Church bears witness . . . The motivating concern for the poor—who are in the very meaning of the term 'the Lord's poor'—must be translated at all levels into concrete actions, until it decisively attains a series of necessary reforms."[52]

45. In spite of its poverty and the meager means at its disposal, the Church in Africa plays a leading role in what touches upon integral human development. Its remarkable achievements in this regard are often recognized by governments and international experts.

The Special Assembly for Africa expressed deep gratitude "to all Christians and to all men and women of good will who are working in the fields of assistance and health-care with *Caritas* and other development organizations."[53] The assistance which they, as Good Samaritans, give to the African victims of wars and disasters, to refugees and displaced persons, deserves the admiration, gratitude and support of all.

I feel it my duty to express heartfelt thanks to the Church in Africa for the role which it has played over the years as a promoter of peace and reconciliation in many situations of conflict, political turmoil and civil war.

II. Ppresent-Day Problems of the Church in Africa

46. The Bishops of Africa are faced with two fundamental questions. How must the Church carry out her evangelizing mission as the Year 2000 approaches? How can African Christians become ever more faithful witnesses to the Lord Jesus? In order to provide adequate responses to these questions the Bishops, both before and during the Special Assembly, examined the major challenges that the Ecclesial Community in Africa must face today.

More profound evangelization

47. The primary and most fundamental fact noted by the Synod Fathers is the thirst for God felt by the peoples of Africa. In order not to disappoint this expectation, the members of the Church must first of all deepen their faith.[54] Indeed, precisely because she evangelizes, the Church must "begin by being evangelized herself."[55] She needs to meet the challenge raised by "this theme of the Church which is evangelized by constant conversion and renewal, in order to evangelize the world with credibility."[56]

The Synod recognized the urgency of proclaiming the Good News to the millions of people in Africa who are not yet evangelized. The Church certainly respects and esteems the non-Christian religions professed by very many Africans, for these religions are the living expression of the soul of vast groups of people. However, "neither respect and esteem for these religions nor the complexity of the questions raised is an invitation to the Church to withhold from these non-Christians the proclamation of Jesus Christ. On the contrary the Church holds that these multitudes have the right to know the riches of the mystery of Christ (cf. Eph 3:8)—riches in which we believe that the whole of humanity can find, in unsuspected fullness, everything that it is gropingly searching for concerning God, man and his destiny, life and death, and truth."[57]

48. The Synod Fathers rightly affirmed that "a serious concern for a true and balanced inculturation is necessary in order to avoid cultural confusion and alienation in our fast evolving society."[58] During my visit to Malawi I made the same point: "I put before you today a challenge— a challenge to reject a way of living which does not correspond to the best of your traditions, and your Christian faith. Many people in Africa look beyond Africa for the so-called 'freedom of the modern way of life'. Today I urge you to look inside yourselves. Look to the riches of your own traditions, look to the faith which we are celebrating in this assembly. Here you will find genuine freedom—here you will find Christ who will lead you to the truth."[59]

Overcoming divisions

49. Another challenge identified by the Synod Fathers concerns the various forms of division which need to be healed through honest dialogue.[60] It has been rightly noted that, within the borders left behind by the colonial powers, the co-existence of ethnic groups with different traditions, languages, and even religions often meets obstacles arising from serious mutual hostility. "*Tribal oppositions* at times endanger if not peace, at least the pursuit of the common good of the society. They also create difficulties for the life of the Churches and the acceptance of Pastors from other ethnic groups."[61] This is why the Church in Africa feels challenged by the specific responsibility of healing these divisions. For the same reason the Special Assembly emphasized the importance of ecumenical dialogue with other Churches and Ecclesial Communities, and of dialogue with African traditional religion and Islam. The Fathers also considered the means to be used to achieve this goal.

Marriage and vocations

50. A major challenge emphasized almost unanimously by the Episcopal Conferences of Africa in their replies to the *Lineamenta* concerned Christian marriage and family life.[62] What is at stake is extremely serious: truly "the future of the world and of the Church passes through the family."[63]

Another fundamental responsibility which the Special Assembly highlighted is concern for vocations to the priesthood and consecrated life. It is necessary to discern them wisely, to provide competent directors and to oversee the quality of the formation offered. The fulfillment of the hope for a flowering of African missionary vocations depends on the attention given to the solution of this problem, a flowering that is required if the Gospel is to be proclaimed in every part of the Continent and beyond.

Social and political difficulties

51. "In Africa, the need to apply the Gospel to concrete life is felt strongly. How could one proclaim Christ on that immense Continent while forgetting that it is one of the world's poorest regions? How could one fail to take into account the anguished history of a land where many nations are still in the grip of famine, war, racial and tribal tensions, political instability and the violation of human rights? This is all a challenge to evangelization."[64]

All the preparatory documents of the Synod, as well as the discussions in the Assembly, clearly showed that issues in Africa such as increasing poverty, urbanization, the international debt, the arms trade, the problem of refugees and displaced persons, demographic concerns and threats to the family, the liberation of women, the spread of AIDS, the survival of the practice of slavery in some places, ethnocentricity and tribal opposition figure among the fundamental challenges addressed by the Synod.

Intrusiveness of the mass media

52. Finally, the Special Assembly addressed the means of social communication, an issue which is of the greatest importance because it concerns both the instruments of evangelization and the

means of spreading a new culture which needs to be evangelized.[65] The Synod Fathers were thus faced with the sad fact that "the developing nations, instead of becoming *autonomous nations* concerned with their own progress towards a just sharing in the goods and services meant for all, become parts of a machine, cogs on a gigantic wheel. This is often true also in the field of social communications which, being run by centers mostly in the northern hemisphere, do not always give due consideration to the priorities and problems of such countries or respect their cultural make-up. They frequently impose a distorted vision of life and of man, and thus fail to respond to the demands of true development."[66]

III. FORMATION OF THE AGENTS OF EVANGELIZATION

53. With what resources will the Church in Africa succeed in meeting the challenges just mentioned? "The most important [resource], after the grace of Christ, is the people. The whole People of God in the theological understanding of *Lumen Gentium*—this People, which comprises the members of the Body of Christ in its entirety—has received the mandate, which is both an honor and a duty, to proclaim the Gospel . . . The whole community needs to be trained, motivated and empowered for evangelization, each according to his or her specific role within the Church."[67] For this reason the Synod strongly emphasized the training of the agents of evangelization in Africa. I have already referred to the necessity of formation for candidates to the priesthood and those called to the consecrated life. The Assembly also paid due attention to the formation of the lay faithful, appropriately recognizing their indispensable role in the evangelization of Africa. In particular, the training of lay catechists received the emphasis which it rightly deserves.

54. A last question must be asked: Has the Church in Africa sufficiently formed the lay faithful, enabling them to assume competently their civic responsibilities and to consider socio-political problems in the light of the Gospel and of faith in God? This is certainly a task belonging to Christians: to bring to bear upon the social fabric an influence aimed at changing not only ways of thinking but also the very structures of society, so that they will better reflect God's plan for the human family. Consequently I have called for the thorough formation of the lay faithful, a formation which will help them to lead a fully integrated life. Faith, hope and charity must influence the actions of the true follower of Christ in every activity, situation and responsibility. Since "evangelizing means bringing the Good News into all the strata of humanity, and through its influence transforming humanity from within and making it new,"[68] Christians must be formed to live the social implications of the Gospel in such a way that their witness will become a prophetic challenge to whatever hinders the true good of the men and women of Africa and of every other continent.

CHAPTER III
EVANGELIZATION AND INCULTURATION

The Church's mission

55. "Go into all the world and preach the Gospel to the whole creation" (Mk 16:15). Such is the mandate that the Risen Christ, before returning to his Father, gave to his Apostles: "And they went forth and preached everywhere" (Mk 16:20).

"The task of evangelizing all people constitutes the essential mission of the Church . . . Evangelizing is in fact *the grace and vocation proper to the Church*, her deepest identity. She *exists in order to evangelize.*"[69] Born of the evangelizing mission of Jesus and the Twelve, she is in turn sent forth. "Depositary of the Good News to be proclaimed . . . having been sent and evangelized, the Church herself sends out evangelizers. She puts on their lips the saving Word."[70] Like the Apostle to the Gentiles, the Church can say: "I preach the Gospel . . . For necessity is laid upon me. Woe to me if I do not preach the Gospel!" (1 Cor 9:16).

The Church proclaims the Good News of Christ not only by the *proclamation of the Word* which she has received from the Lord, but also by the *witness of life*, thanks to which Christ's disciples bear witness to the faith, hope and love which dwell in them (cf. 1 Pet 2:15).

This testimony which the Christian bears to Christ and the Gospel can lead even to the supreme sacrifice: martyrdom (cf. Mk 8:35). For the Church and the Christian proclaim the One who is "a sign of contradiction" (cf. Lk 2:34). They preach "Christ crucified, a stumbling block to Jews and folly to Gentiles" (1 Cor 1:23). As I said earlier, besides honoring the illustrious Martyrs of the first centuries, Africa can glory in its Martyrs and Saints of the modern age.

The purpose of evangelization is "transforming humanity from within and making it new."[71] In and through the Only Son the relations of people with God, one another and all creation will be renewed. For this reason the proclamation of the Gospel can contribute to the interior transformation of all people of good will whose hearts are open to the Holy Spirit's action.

56. To bear witness to the Gospel in word and deed: this is the task which the Special Assembly for Africa of the Synod of Bishops received and which it now passes on to the Church of the Continent. "You shall be my witnesses" (Acts 1:8): this is the challenge. In Africa these should be the fruits of the Synod in every area of people's lives.

Born of the preaching of valiant missionary Bishops and priests, effectively assisted by "the ranks of men and women catechists, to whom missionary work among the nations owes so very much,"[72] the Church in Africa, having become "a new homeland for Christ,"[73] is now responsible for the evangelization of the Continent and the world. As my Predecessor Pope Paul VI said in Kampala: "Africans, you are now your own missionaries."[74] Because the vast majority of Africans have not yet heard the Good News of salvation, the Synod recommends that missionary vocations should be encouraged and asks that prayer, sacrifice and effective solidarity for the Church's missionary work be favored and actively supported.[75]

Proclamation

57. "The Synod recalls that to evangelize is to proclaim by word and witness of life the Good News of Jesus Christ, crucified, died and risen, the Way, the Truth and the Life."[76] To Africa, which is menaced on all sides by outbreaks of hatred and violence, by conflicts and wars, evangelizers must proclaim *the hope of life rooted in the Paschal Mystery*. It was precisely when, humanly speaking, Jesus' life seemed doomed to failure that he instituted the Eucharist, "the pledge of eternal glory,"[77] in order to perpetuate in time and space his victory over death. That is why at a time when the African Continent is in some ways in a critical situation the Special Assembly for Africa wished to be "the *Synod of Resurrection, the Synod of Hope . . . Christ our Hope is alive; we shall live!*"[78] Africa is not destined for death, but for life!

It is therefore essential that "the new evangelization should be centered on a transforming encounter with *the living person of Christ*."[79] "The first proclamation ought to bring about this overwhelming and exhilarating experience of Jesus Christ who calls each one to follow him in an adventure of faith."[80] This task is made all the easier because "the African believes in God the Creator from his traditional life and religion and thus is also open to the full and definitive revelation of God in Jesus Christ, God with us, Word made flesh. Jesus, the Good News, is God who saves the African . . . from oppression and slavery."[81]

Evangelization must reach "individual human beings and society in every aspect of their existence. It is therefore expressed in various activities, and particularly in those which the Synod examined: proclamation, inculturation, dialogue, justice and peace and the means of social communication."[82]

For the full success of this mission, it must be ensured that "in evangelization prayer to the Holy Spirit will be stressed for a continuing Pentecost, where Mary, as at the first Pentecost, will have her place."[83] The power of the Holy Spirit guides the Church into all truth (cf. Jn 16:13), enabling her to go into the world in order to bear witness to Christ with confident resolve.

58. The Word that comes from the mouth of God is living and active, and never returns to him

in vain (cf. Is 55:11; Heb 4:12-13). We must therefore proclaim that Word tirelessly, exhorting "in season and out of season . . . unfailing in patience and in teaching" (2 Tim 4:2). Entrusted first of all to the Church, the written Word of God is not "a matter of one's own interpretation" (2 Pet 1:20), but is to be authentically interpreted by the Church.[84]

In order that the Word of God may be known, loved, pondered and preserved in the hearts of the faithful (cf. Lk 2:19,51), greater efforts must be made to provide access to the Sacred Scriptures, especially through full or partial translations of the Bible, prepared as far as possible in cooperation with other Churches and Ecclesial Communities and accompanied by study guides for use in prayer and for study in the family and community. Also to be encouraged is the scriptural formation of clergy, religious, catechists and the laity in general; careful preparation of celebrations of the Word; promotion of the biblical apostolate with the help of the Biblical Center for Africa and Madagascar and the encouragement of other similar structures at all levels. In brief, efforts must be made to try to put the Sacred Scriptures into the hands of all the faithful right from their earliest years.[85]

Urgent need for inculturation

59. On several occasions the Synod Fathers stressed the particular importance for evangelization of inculturation, the process by which "catechesis '*takes flesh*' in the various cultures."[86] Inculturation includes two dimensions: on the one hand, "the intimate transformation of authentic cultural values through their integration in Christianity" and, on the other, "the insertion of Christianity in the various human cultures."[87] The Synod considers inculturation an urgent priority in the life of the particular Churches, for a firm rooting of the Gospel in Africa.[88] It is "a requirement for evangelization,"[89] "a path towards full evangelization,"[90] and one of the greatest challenges for the Church on the Continent on the eve of the Third Millennium.[91]

Theological foundations

60. "But when the time had fully come" (Gal 4:4), the Word, the Second Person of the Blessed Trinity, the Only Son of God, "by the power of the Holy Spirit he became incarnate from the Virgin Mary, and was made man."[92] This is the sublime mystery of the Incarnation of the Word, a mystery which took place *in history*: in clearly defined circumstances of time and space, amidst a people with its own culture, a people that God had chosen and accompanied throughout the entire history of salvation, in order to show through what he did for them what he intended to do for the whole human race.

Jesus Christ is the unmistakable proof of God's love for humanity (cf. Rom 5:8). By his life, his preaching of the Good News to the poor, his Passion, Death and glorious Resurrection, he brought about the remission of our sins and our reconciliation with God, his Father and, thanks to him, our Father too. The Word that the Church proclaims is precisely the Word of God made man, who is himself the subject and object of this Word. *The Good News is Jesus Christ.*

Just as "the Word became flesh and dwelt among us" (Jn 1:14), so too the Good News, the Word of Jesus Christ proclaimed to the nations, *must take root* in the life-situation of the hearers of the Word. Inculturation is precisely this insertion of the Gospel message into cultures.[93] For the Incarnation of the Son of God, precisely because it was complete and concrete,[94] was also an incarnation in a particular culture.

61. Given the close and organic relationship that exists between Jesus Christ and the Word that the Church proclaims, the inculturation of the revealed message cannot but follow the "logic" proper to the *Mystery of the Redemption*. Indeed, the Incarnation of the Word is not an isolated moment but tends towards Jesus' "Hour" and the Paschal Mystery: "Unless a grain of wheat falls into the earth and dies, it remains alone; but if it dies, it bears much fruit" (Jn 12:24). Jesus says: "And I, when I am lifted up from the earth, will draw all men to myself" (Jn 12:32). This emptying of self, this *kenosis* necessary for exaltation, which is the way of Christ and of each of his disciples (cf. Phil 2:6-9), sheds light on the encounter of cultures with Christ and his *Gospel*. "Every culture

needs to be transformed by Gospel values in the light of the Paschal Mystery."[95]

It is by looking at the Mystery of the Incarnation and of the Redemption that the values and counter-values of cultures are to be discerned. Just as the Word of God became like us in everything but sin, so too the inculturation of the Good News takes on all authentic human values, purifying them from sin and restoring to them their full meaning.

Inculturation also has profound links with the *Mystery of Pentecost*. Thanks to the outpouring and action of the Spirit, who draws gifts and talents into unity, all the peoples of the earth when they enter the Church live a new Pentecost, profess in their own tongue the one faith in Jesus, and proclaim the marvels that the Lord has done for them. The Spirit, who on the natural level is the true source of the wisdom of peoples, leads the Church with a supernatural light into knowledge of the whole truth. In her turn the Church takes on the values of different cultures, becoming the "*sponsa ornata monilibus suis*," "the bride who adorns herself with her jewels" (cf. Is 61:10).

Criteria and areas of inculturation

62. Inculturation is a difficult and delicate task, since it raises the question of the Church's fidelity to the Gospel and the Apostolic Tradition amidst the constant evolution of cultures. Rightly therefore the Synod Fathers observed: "Considering the rapid changes in the cultural, social, economic and political domains, our local Churches must be involved in the process of inculturation in an ongoing manner, respecting the two following criteria: compatibility with the Christian message and communion with the universal Church . . . In all cases, care must be taken to avoid syncretism."[96]

"Inculturation is a movement towards full evangelization. It seeks to dispose people to receive Jesus Christ in an integral manner. It touches them on the personal, cultural, economic and political levels so that they can live a holy life in total union with God the Father, through the action of the Holy Spirit."[97]

Thanking God for the fruits which the efforts at inculturation have already brought forth in the life of the Churches of the Continent, notably in the ancient Eastern Churches of Africa, the Synod recommended "to the Bishops and to the Episcopal Conferences to take note that inculturation includes the whole life of the Church and the whole process of evangelization. It includes theology, liturgy, the Church's life and structures. All this underlines the need for research in the field of African cultures in all their complexity." Precisely for this reason the Synod invited Pastors "to exploit to the maximum the numerous possibilities which the Church's present discipline provides in this matter."[98]

The Church as God's Family

63. Not only did the Synod speak of inculturation, but it also made use of it, taking the *Church as God's Family* as its guiding idea for the evangelization of Africa.[99] The Synod Fathers acknowledged it as an expression of the Church's nature particularly appropriate for Africa. For this image emphasizes care for others, solidarity, warmth in human relationships, acceptance, dialogue and trust.[100] The new evangelization will thus aim at *building up the Church as Family*, avoiding all ethnocentrism and excessive particularism, trying instead to encourage reconciliation and true communion between different ethnic groups, favoring solidarity and the sharing of personnel and resources among the particular Churches, without undue ethnic considerations.[101] "It is earnestly to be hoped that theologians in Africa will work out the theology of the Church as Family with all the riches contained in this concept, showing its complementarity with other images of the Church."[102]

All this presupposes a profound study of the heritage of Scripture and Tradition which the Second Vatican Council presented in the Dogmatic Constitution *Lumen Gentium*. This admirable text expounds the doctrine on the Church using images drawn from Sacred Scripture such as the Mystical Body, People of God, Temple of the Holy Spirit, Flock and Sheepfold, the House in which God dwells with man. According to the Council, the Church is the Bride of Christ, our Mother, the

Holy City and the first fruits of the coming Kingdom. These images will have to be taken into account when developing, according to the Synod's recommendation, an ecclesiology focused on the idea of the Church as the Family of God.[103] It will then be possible to appreciate in all its richness and depth the statement which is the Dogmatic Constitution's point of departure: "By her relationship with Christ, the Church is a kind of sacrament or sign of intimate union with God, and of the unity of all mankind."[104]

Areas of application

64. In practice, and without any prejudice to the traditions proper to either the Latin or Eastern Church, "inculturation of the *liturgy*, provided it does not change the essential elements, should be carried out so that the faithful can better understand and live liturgical celebrations."[105]

The Synod also reaffirmed that, when doctrine is hard to assimilate even after a long period of evangelization, or when its practice poses serious pastoral problems, especially in the sacramental life, fidelity to the Church's teaching must be maintained. At the same time, people must be treated with justice and true pastoral charity. Bearing this in mind, the Synod expressed the hope that the Episcopal Conferences, in cooperation with Universities and Catholic Institutes, would set up study commissions, especially for matters concerning marriage, the veneration of ancestors, and the spirit world, in order to examine in depth all the cultural aspects of problems from the theological, sacramental, liturgical and canonical points of view.[106]

Dialogue

65. "Openness to dialogue is the Christian's attitude inside the community as well as with other believers and with men and women of good will."[107] *Dialogue is to be practiced first of all within the family of the Church* at all levels: between Bishops, Episcopal Conferences or Hierarchical Assemblies and the Apostolic See, between Conferences or Episcopal Assemblies of the different nations of the same continent and those of other continents, and within each particular Church between the Bishop, the presbyterate, consecrated persons, pastoral workers and the lay faithful; and also between different rites within the same Church. SECAM is to establish "structures and means which will ensure the exercise of this dialogue,"[108] especially in order to foster an organic pastoral solidarity.

"United to Jesus Christ by their witness in Africa, Catholics are invited to develop an *ecumenical dialogue* with all their baptized brothers and sisters of other Christian denominations, in order that the unity for which Christ prayed may be achieved, and in order that their service to the peoples of the Continent may make the Gospel more credible in the eyes of those who are searching for God."[109] Such dialogue can be conducted through initiatives such as ecumenical translations of the Bible, theological study of various dimensions of the Christian faith or by bearing common evangelical witness to justice, peace and respect for human dignity. For this purpose care will be taken to set up national and diocesan commissions for ecumenism.[110] Together Christians are responsible for the witness to be borne to the Gospel on the Continent. Advances in ecumenism are also aimed at making this witness more effective.

66. "Commitment to dialogue must also embrace all Muslims of good will. Christians cannot forget that many Muslims try to imitate the faith of Abraham and to live the demands of the Decalogue."[111] In this regard the *Message of the Synod* emphasizes that the Living God, Creator of heaven and earth and the Lord of history, is the Father of the one great human family to which we all belong. As such, he wants us to bear witness to him through our respect for the values and religious traditions of each person, working together for human progress and development at all levels. Far from wishing to be the one in whose name a person would kill other people, he requires believers to join together in the service of life in justice and peace.[112] Particular care will therefore be taken so that Islamic-Christian dialogue respects on both sides the principle of religious freedom with all that this involves, also including external and public manifestations of faith.[113] Christians and Muslims are called to commit themselves to promoting a dialogue free from the risks of false

irenicism or militant fundamentalism, and to raising their voices against unfair policies and practices, as well as against the lack of reciprocity in matters of religious freedom. [114]

67. With regard to African traditional religion, a serene and prudent dialogue will be able, on the one hand, to protect Catholics from negative influences which condition the way of life of many of them and, on the other hand, to foster the assimilation of positive values such as belief in a Supreme Being who is Eternal, Creator, Provident and Just Judge, values which are readily harmonized with the content of the faith. They can even be seen as a *preparation for the Gospel*, because they contain precious *semina Verbi* which can lead, as already happened in the past, a great number of people "to be open to the fullness of Revelation in Jesus Christ through the proclamation of the Gospel." [115]

The adherents of African traditional religion should therefore be treated with great respect and esteem, and all inaccurate and disrespectful language should be avoided. For this purpose, suitable courses in African traditional religion should be given in houses of formation for priests and religious. [116]

Integral human development

68. Integral human development—the development of every person and of the whole person, especially of the poorest and most neglected in the community—is at the very heart of evangelization. "Between evangelization and human advancement—development and liberation—there are in fact profound links. These include links of an anthropological order, because the man who is to be evangelized is not an abstract being but is subject to social and economic questions. They also include links in the theological order, since one cannot dissociate the plan of creation from the plan of Redemption. The latter plan touches the very concrete situations of injustice to be combatted and of justice to be restored. They include links of the eminently evangelical order, which is that of charity: how in fact can one proclaim the new commandment of love without promoting in justice and peace the true, authentic advancement of man?" [117]

When the Lord Jesus began his public ministry in the synagogue at Nazareth, he chose the Messianic text of the Book of the Prophet Isaiah in order to shed light on his mission: "The Spirit of the Lord God is upon me, because he has anointed me to preach good news to the poor. He has sent me to proclaim release to the captives and recovering of sight to the blind, to set at liberty those who are oppressed, to proclaim the acceptable year of the Lord" (Lk 4:18-19; cf. Is 61:1-2).

The Lord thus considers himself as sent to relieve human misery and combat every kind of neglect. He came to *liberate* humanity; he came to take upon himself our infirmities and diseases. "The entire ministry of Jesus is marked by the concern he showed to all those around him who were affected by suffering: persons in mourning, paralytics, lepers, the blind, the deaf, the mute (cf. Mt 8:17)." [118] "It is impossible to accept that in evangelization one could or should ignore the importance of the problems so much discussed today, concerning justice, liberation, development and peace in the world." [119] The liberation that evangelization proclaims "cannot be contained in the simple and restricted dimension of economics, politics, social or cultural life; it must envisage the whole man, in all his aspects, right up to and including his openness to the absolute, even the Divine Absolute." [120]

The Second Vatican Council says so well: "Pursuing the saving purpose which is proper to her, the Church does not only communicate divine life to men but in some way casts the reflected light of that life over the entire earth, most of all by its healing and elevating impact on the dignity of the person, by the way in which it strengthens the seams of human society and imbues the everyday activity of men with a deeper meaning and importance. Thus through her individual members and her whole community, the Church believes she can contribute greatly towards making the family of man and its history more human." [121] The Church proclaims and begins to bring about the Kingdom of God after the example of Jesus, because "the Kingdom's nature . . . is one of communion among all human beings—with one another and with God." [122] Thus "the Kingdom is the source of full liberation and total salvation for all people: with this in mind then, the Church walks and lives intimately bound in a real sense to their history."[123]

69. Human history finds its true meaning in the Incarnation of the Word of God, who is the foundation of restored *human dignity*. It is through Christ, the "image of the invisible God, the first-born of all creation" (Col 1:15), that man is redeemed. "For by his Incarnation the Son of God has united himself in some fashion with every man."[124] How can we fail to exclaim with Saint Leo the Great: "Christian, recognize your dignity"?[125]

To proclaim Jesus Christ is therefore to *reveal to people their inalienable dignity*, received from God through the Incarnation of his Only Son. "Since it has been entrusted to the Church to reveal the mystery of God, who is the ultimate goal of man," continues the Second Vatican Council, "she opens up to man at the same time the meaning of his own existence, that is, the innermost truth about himself."[126]

Endowed with this extraordinary dignity, people should not live in sub-human social, economic, cultural and political conditions. This is the theological foundation of the struggle for the defense of personal dignity, for justice and social peace, for the promotion, liberation and integral human development of all people and of every individual. It is also for this reason that the development of peoples—within each nation and among nations—must be achieved *in solidarity*, as my Predecessor Pope Paul VI so well observed.[127] Precisely for this reason he could affirm: "The new name for peace is development."[128] It can thus rightly be stated that "integral development implies respect for human dignity and this can only be achieved in justice and peace."[129]

Becoming the voice of the voiceless

70. Strengthened by faith and hope in the saving power of Jesus, the Synod Fathers concluded their work by renewing their commitment to accept the challenge of being instruments of salvation in every area of the life of the peoples of Africa. "The Church," they declared, "must continue to exercise her prophetic role and be the voice of the voiceless,"[130] so that everywhere the human dignity of every individual will be acknowledged, and that people will always be at the center of all government programs. The Synod "challenges the consciences of Heads of State and those responsible for the public domain to guarantee ever more the liberation and development of their peoples."[131] Only at this price is peace established between nations.

Evangelization must promote initiatives which contribute to the development and *ennoblement* of individuals in their spiritual and material existence. This involves the development of every person and of the whole person, considered not only individually but also and especially in the context of the common and harmonious development of all the members of a nation and of all the peoples of the world.[132]

Finally, evangelization must denounce and combat all that degrades and destroys the person. "The condemnation of evils and injustices is also part of that *ministry of evangelization* in the social field which is an aspect of the Church's *prophetic role*. But it should be made clear that proclamation is always more important than condemnation, and the latter cannot ignore the former, which gives it true solidity and the force of higher motivation."[133]

Means of social communication

71. "From the beginning it has been a characteristic of God to want to communicate. This he does by various means. He has bestowed being upon every created thing, animate or inanimate. He enters into relationships with human beings in a very special way. 'In many and various ways God spoke of old to our fathers by the prophets; but in these last days he has spoken to us by a Son' (Heb 1:1-2)."[134] The Word of God is by nature word, dialogue and communication. He came to restore on the one hand communication and relations between God and humanity, and on the other hand those of people with one another.

The Synod paid great attention to the mass media under two important and complementary aspects: as a new and emerging cultural world and as a series of means serving communication. First of all, they constitute a new culture that has its own language and above all its own specific values and counter-values. For this reason, like any culture, the mass media need to be evangelized.[135]

Today in fact the mass media constitute not only a world but also a culture and civilization. And it is also to this world that the Church is sent to bring the Good News of salvation. The heralds of the Gospel must therefore *enter this world* in order to *allow themselves to be permeated* by this new civilization and culture for the purpose of learning how to make good *use* of them. "The first Areopagus of the modern age is the world of communications, which is unifying humanity and turning it into what is known as a 'global village. ' The means of social communication have become so important as to be for many the chief means of information and education, of guidance and inspiration in their behavior as individuals, families and within society at large."[136]

Training in the use of the mass media is therefore a necessity not only *for the preacher* of the Gospel, who must master, among other things, the media *style* of communication but also for the *reader*, the *listener* and the *viewer*. Trained to understand this kind of communication, they must be able to make use of its contributions with discernment and a critical mind.

In Africa, where *oral transmission* is one of the characteristics of culture, such training is of capital importance. This same kind of communication must remind pastors, especially Bishops and priests, that the Church is sent to *speak*, to preach the Gospel in words and deeds. Thus she *cannot remain silent*, at the risk of failing in her mission, except in cases where silence itself would be a way of speaking and bearing witness. We must therefore always preach in season and out of season (cf. 2 Tim 4:2), in order to build up, in charity and truth.

CHAPTER IV
IN THE LIGHT OF THE THIRD CHRISTIAN MILLENNIUM

I. PRESENT-DAY CHALLENGES

72. The Special Assembly for Africa of the Synod of Bishops was convoked so that the whole Church of God on the Continent might reflect on its evangelizing mission in the light of the Third Millennium and prepare, as I have said, "an organic pastoral solidarity within the entire African territory and nearby Islands."[137] Such a mission includes, as already mentioned, *urgent tasks and challenges, due to the profound and rapid changes in African societies* and to the effects of the emergence of a global civilization.

Need for Baptism

73. The first urgent task is of course evangelization itself. On the one hand, the Church must assimilate and live ever more fully the message which the Lord has entrusted to her. On the other hand, she must bear witness to this message and proclaim it to all who do not yet know Jesus Christ. It is indeed for them that the Lord said to the Apostles: "*Go therefore and make disciples of all nations*" (Mt 28:19).

Just as at Pentecost, the goal of preaching the *kerygma* is to bring the hearer to *metanoia* and *Baptism*: "The proclamation of the word of God has *Christian conversion* as its aim: a complete and sincere adherence to Christ and his Gospel through faith."[138] Conversion to Christ moreover "is joined to Baptism not only because of the Church's practice, but also by the will of Christ himself, who sent the Apostles to make disciples of all nations and to baptize them (cf. Mt 28:19). Conversion is also joined to Baptism because of the intrinsic need to receive the fullness of new life in Christ. As Jesus says to Nicodemus: '*Truly, truly, I say to you, unless one is born of water and the Spirit, he cannot enter the Kingdom of God*' (Jn 3:5). In Baptism, in fact, we are born anew to the life of God's children, united to Jesus Christ and anointed in the Holy Spirit. Baptism is not simply a seal of conversion, a kind of *external sign* indicating conversion and attesting to it. Rather, it is a *Sacrament which signifies and effects* rebirth from the Spirit, establishes real and unbreakable bonds with the Blessed Trinity, and makes us members of the Body of Christ, which is the Church."[139] Therefore a journey of conversion that did not culminate in Baptism would stop half-way.

It is true that people of upright heart who, through no fault of their own have not been reached by the proclamation of the Gospel but who live in harmony with their conscience according to God's law, will be saved by Christ and in Christ. For every human being there is always an actual call from God, which is waiting to be acknowledged and received (cf. 1 Tim 2:4). It is precisely in order to facilitate this recognition and acceptance that Christ's disciples are required not to rest until the Good News of salvation has been brought to all.

Urgency of evangelization

74. The Name of Jesus Christ is the only one by which it has been decreed that we can be saved (cf. Acts 4:12). Because in Africa there are millions who are not yet evangelized, the Church is faced with the necessary and urgent task of *proclaiming the Good News to all, and leading those who hear it to Baptism and the Christian life*. "The urgency of missionary activity derives from the *radical newness of life* brought by Christ and lived by his followers. This new life is a gift from God, and people are asked to accept and develop it, if they wish to realize the fullness of their vocation in conformity to Christ."[140] This new life in the radical newness of the Gospel also involves certain breaks from the customs and culture of whatever people in the world, because the Gospel is never an internal product of a particular country but always comes "from outside," from on high. For the baptized the great challenge will always be that of leading a Christian life in conformity with the commitments of Baptism, the Sacrament which signifies death to sin and daily resurrection to new life (cf. Rom 6:4-5). Without this conformity, it will be difficult for Christ's disciples to be the "*salt of the earth*" and "*light of the world*" (Mt 5:13,14). If the Church in Africa makes a vigorous and unhesitating commitment to this path, the Cross can be planted in every part of the Continent for the salvation of peoples not afraid to open their doors to the Redeemer.

Importance of formation

75. In all areas of Church life formation is of primary importance. People who have never had the chance to learn cannot really know the truths of faith, nor can they perform actions which they have never been taught. For this reason "the whole community needs to be trained, motivated and empowered for evangelization, each according to his or her specific role within the Church."[141] This includes Bishops, priests, members of Institutes of Consecrated Life and Societies of Apostolic Life, members of Secular Institutes and all the lay faithful.

Missionary training has to have a special place. It is "the task of the local Church, assisted by missionaries and their Institutes, and by the personnel from the young Churches. This work must be seen not as peripheral but as central to the Christian life."[142]

The formation program will especially include the training of the lay faithful, so that they will fully exercise their role of inspiring the temporal order—political, cultural, economic and social—with Christian principles, which is the specific task of the laity's vocation in the world. For this purpose competent and well motivated lay people need to be encouraged to enter politics.[143] By worthily carrying out the duties of public office they will be able to "advance the common good and prepare the way for the Gospel."[144]

Deepening the faith

76. The Church in Africa, in order to evangelize, must begin "by being evangelized herself . . . She needs to listen unceasingly to what she must believe, to her reasons for hoping, to the new commandment of love. She is the People of God immersed in the world, and often tempted by idols, and she always needs to hear the proclamation of the 'mighty works of God'."[145]

In Africa today "formation in the faith . . . too often stops at the elementary stage, and the sects easily profit from this ignorance."[146] A serious deepening of the faith is thus urgently needed, because the rapid evolution of society has given rise to new challenges linked to the phenomena notably of family uprooting, urbanization, unemployment, materialistic seductions of all kinds, a certain secularization and an intellectual upheaval caused by the avalanche of insufficiently critical ideas spread by the media.[147]

The power of witness

77. Formation must aim to provide Christians not only with technical expertise in passing on more dearly the content of the faith but also with a profound personal conviction enabling them to bear effective witness to it in daily life. All those called to proclaim the Gospel will therefore seek to act with total docility to the Spirit, who "today, just as at the beginning of the Church, acts in every evangelizer who allows himself to be possessed and led by him."[148] "Techniques of evangelization are good, but even the most advanced ones could not replace the gentle action of the Spirit. Even the most thorough preparation of the evangelizer has no effect without the Holy Spirit. Without the Holy Spirit the most convincing dialectic has no power over the human heart. Without him the most highly developed schemes on a sociological or psychological basis are quickly seen to be quite valueless."[149]

Genuine witness by believers is essential to the authentic proclamation of the faith in Africa today. In particular they should show the witness of sincere mutual love. "'This is eternal life, that they know you the only true God, and Jesus Christ whom you have sent' (Jn 17:3). The ultimate purpose of mission is to enable people to share in the communion which exists between the Father and the Son. The disciples are to live in unity with one another, remaining in the Father and the Son, so that the world may know and believe (cf. Jn 17:21-23). This is a very important missionary text. It makes us understand that we are missionaries above all because of *what we are*, a Church whose innermost life is unity in love, even before we become missionaries *in word and deed*."[150]

Inculturating the faith

78. By reason of its deep conviction that "*the synthesis between culture and faith is not only a demand of culture but also of faith,*" because "a faith that does not become culture is not fully accepted, not entirely thought out, not faithfully lived,"[151] the Special Assembly for Africa of the Synod of Bishops considered inculturation a priority and an urgent task in the life of Africa's particular Churches. Only in this way can the Gospel be firmly implanted in the Continent's Christian communities. Following in the footsteps of the Second Vatican Council,[152] the Synod Fathers interpreted inculturation as a process that includes the whole of Christian existence— theology, liturgy, customs, structures—without of course compromising what is of divine right and the great discipline of the Church, confirmed in the course of centuries by remarkable fruits of virtue and heroism.[153]

The challenge of inculturation in Africa consists in ensuring that the followers of Christ will ever more fully assimilate the Gospel message, while remaining faithful to all authentic African values. Inculturation of the faith in every area of Christian and human life is an arduous task which can only be carried out with the help of the Spirit of the Lord who leads the Church to the whole truth (cf. Jn 16:13).

A reconciled community

79. The challenge of dialogue is fundamentally the challenge of transforming relationships between individuals, nations and peoples in religious, political, economic, social and cultural life. It is the challenge of Christ's love for all people, a love that the disciple must reproduce in his own life: "By this all men will know that you are my disciples, if you have love for one another" (Jn 13:35).

"Evangelization continues the dialogue of God with humanity and reaches its apex in the person of Jesus Christ."[154] Through the Cross he brought an end in himself to the hostility which divides people and keeps them apart (cf. Eph 2:16).

Despite the modern civilization of the "global village," in Africa as elsewhere in the world the spirit of dialogue, peace and reconciliation is far from dwelling in the hearts of everyone. Wars, conflicts and racist and xenophobic attitudes still play too large a role in the world of human relations.

The Church in Africa is aware that it has to become for all, through the witness borne by its own sons and daughters, a place of true reconciliation. Forgiven and mutually reconciled, these sons and daughters will thus be able to bring to the world the forgiveness and reconciliation which Christ our Peace (cf. Eph 2:14) offers to humanity through his Church. Otherwise the world will look more and more like a battlefield, where only selfish interests count and the *law of force* prevails, the law which fatally distances humanity from the hoped-for *civilization of love*.

II. THE FAMILY

Evangelizing the family

80. "The future of the world and of the Church passes through the family."[155] Not only is the Christian family the first cell of the living ecclesial community, it is also the fundamental cell of society. In Africa in particular, the family is the foundation on which the social edifice is built. This is why the Synod considered the evangelization of the African family a major priority, if the family is to assume in its turn the role of *active subject* in view of the evangelization of families through families.

From the pastoral point of view, this is a real challenge, given the political, economic, social and cultural difficulties which African families must face as a result of the great changes which characterize contemporary society. While adopting the positive values of modernity, the African family must preserve its own essential values.

The Holy Family as a model

81. In this regard the Holy Family, which according to the Gospel (cf. Mt 2:14-15) lived for a time in Africa, is the "*prototype and example for all Christian families*"[156] and the *model and spiritual source* for every Christian family.[157]

To repeat the words of Pope Paul VI, pilgrim to the Holy Land: "The home of Nazareth is the school where we begin to understand the life of Jesus—the school of the *Gospel* . . . Here, in this school, one learns why it is necessary to have a spiritual rule of life, if one wishes to follow the teaching of the Gospel and become a disciple of Christ."[158] In his profound meditation on the mystery of Nazareth, Pope Paul VI invites us to learn a threefold lesson: of *silence*, of *family life* and of *work*. In the home of Nazareth each one lives his or her own mission in perfect harmony with the other members of the Holy Family.

Dignity and role of man and woman

82. The dignity of man and woman derives from the fact that when God created man, "*in the image of God* he created him, male and female he created them*" (Gen 1:27). Both man and woman are created "in the image of God," that is, endowed with intelligence and will and therefore with freedom. The account of our first parents' sin confirms this (cf. Gen 3). The Psalmist sings of man's incomparable dignity: "Yet you have made him little less than a god; with glory and honor you crowned him, gave him power over the works of your hand, put all things under his feet" (Ps 8:6-7).

Having both been created in the image of God, man and woman, although different, are essentially equal from the point of view of their humanity. "From the very beginning, both are persons, unlike the other living beings in the world about them. The woman is another 'I' in a common humanity,"[159] and each is a help for the other (cf. Gen 2:18-25).

"In creating the human race 'male and female,' God gives man and woman an equal personal dignity, endowing them with inalienable rights and responsibilities proper to the human person."[160]

The Synod deplored those African customs and practices "which deprive women of their rights and the respect due to them"[161] and asked the Church on the Continent to make every effort to foster the safeguarding of these rights.

Dignity and role of Marriage

83. God—Father, Son and Holy Spirit—is love (cf. 1 Jn 4:8). "The communion between God and his people finds its definitive fulfillment in Jesus Christ, the Bridegroom who loves and gives himself as the Savior of humanity, uniting it to himself as his Body. He reveals the original truth of marriage, the truth of the 'beginning,' and, freeing man from his hardness of heart, he makes man capable of realizing this truth in its entirety. This revelation reaches its definitive fullness in the gift of love which the Word of God makes to humanity in assuming a human nature, and in the sacrifice which Jesus Christ makes of himself on the Cross for his Bride, the Church. In this sacrifice there is entirely revealed that plan which God has imprinted on the humanity of man and woman since their creation (cf. Eph 5:32-33); the Marriage of baptized persons thus becomes a *real symbol of that new and eternal Covenant* sanctioned in the Blood of Christ."[162]

The mutual love of baptized spouses makes present the love of Christ for his Church. As a sign of this love of Christ, Marriage is a *Sacrament of the New Covenant*: "Spouses are therefore the *permanent reminder* to the Church of what happened on the Cross; they are for one another and for the children *witnesses* to the salvation in which the Sacrament makes them sharers. Of this salvation event Marriage, like every sacrament, is a memorial, actuation and prophecy."[163]

Marriage is therefore a state of life, a way of Christian holiness, a vocation which is meant to lead to the glorious resurrection and to the Kingdom, where "they neither marry nor are given in marriage" (Mt 22:30). Marriage thus demands an indissoluble love; thanks to this stability it can contribute effectively to the complete fulfillment of the spouses' baptismal vocation.

Saving the African family

84. Many interventions in the Synod Hall highlighted present-day threats to the African family. The concerns of the Synod Fathers were all the more justified in that the preparatory document of a United Nations Conference held in September 1994 in Cairo—on African soil—clearly seemed to wish to adopt resolutions contradicting many values of the African family. The Synod Fathers, accepting my concerns previously expressed to the Conference and to all the world's Heads of State,[164] launched an urgent appeal to safeguard the family. They pleaded: "Do not allow the African family to be ridiculed on its own soil! Do not allow the International Year of the Family to become the year of the destruction of the family!"[165]

The family as open to society

85. By its nature marriage, which has the special mission of perpetuating humanity, transcends the couple. In the same way, by its nature, the family extends beyond the individual household: it is oriented towards society. "The family has vital and organic links with society, since it is its foundation and nourishes it continually through its role of service to life: it is from the family that citizens come to birth and it is within the family that they find the first school of the social virtues that are the animating principle of the existence and development of society itself. Thus, far from being closed in on itself, the family is by nature and vocation open to other families and to society, and undertakes its social role."[166]

Along these lines, the Special Assembly for Africa affirmed that the goal of evangelization is to build up the Church as the Family of God, an anticipation on earth, though imperfect, of the Kingdom. The Christian families of Africa will thus become true "domestic churches," contributing to society's progress towards a more fraternal life. This is how African societies will be transformed through the Gospel!

CHAPTER V
"YOU SHALL BE MY WITNESSES" IN AFRICA

Witness and holiness

86. The challenges mentioned show how opportune the Special Assembly for Africa of the Synod of Bishops was: the Church's task in Africa is immense; in order to face it everyone's cooperation is necessary. *Witness* is an essential element of this cooperation. Christ challenges his disciples in Africa and gives them the mandate which he gave to the Apostles on the day of his Ascension: "You shall be my witnesses" (Acts 1:8) in Africa.

87. The proclamation of the Good News by word and deed opens people's hearts to the desire for *holiness*, for being configured to Christ. In his First Letter to the Corinthians, Saint Paul addresses "those sanctified in Christ Jesus, called to be saints, together with all those who in every place call on the name of our Lord Jesus Christ" (1:2). Preaching the Gospel also aims to build up the Church of God, in the light of the coming of the Kingdom, which Christ will hand over to the Father at the end of time (cf. 1 Cor 15:24).

"Entrance into the Kingdom of God demands a change of mentality (*metanoia*) and behavior and a life of witness in word and deed, a life nourished in the Church by the reception of the sacraments, particularly the Eucharist, the Sacrament of salvation."[167]

Inculturation, through which the faith penetrates the life of individuals and their primary communities, is also a path to holiness. Just as in the Incarnation Christ assumed human nature in everything but sin, analogously through inculturation the Christian message assimilates the values of the society to which it is proclaimed, rejecting whatever is marked by sin. To the extent that an ecclesial community can integrate the positive values of a specific culture, inculturation becomes an instrument by which the community opens itself to the riches of Christian holiness. An inculturation wisely carried out purifies and elevates the cultures of the various peoples.

From this point of view the *liturgy* is called to play an important role. As an effective way of proclaiming and living the mysteries of salvation, the liturgy can make a valid contribution towards the elevation and enrichment of specific manifestations of the culture of a people. It will therefore be the task of competent authority to see to the inculturation of those liturgical elements which, following artistically worthy models, can be changed in the light of current norms.[168]

I. AGENTS OF EVANGELIZATION

88. Evangelization needs agents. For "how are men to call upon him [the Lord] in whom they have not believed? And how are they to believe in him of whom they have never heard? And how are they to hear without a preacher? And how can men preach unless they are sent?" (Rom 10:14-15). The proclamation of the Gospel can be fully carried out only through the contribution of all believers at every level of the universal and local Church.

It is especially the concern of the local Church, entrusted to the responsibility of the Bishop, to coordinate the commitment to evangelization by gathering the faithful together, confirming them in the faith through the work of the priests and catechists, and supporting them in the fulfillment of their respective tasks. In order to accomplish this, the Diocese is to establish the necessary structures for getting together, dialogue and planning. By making use of these structures the Bishop will be able to guide in a suitable manner the work of priests, religious and laity, welcoming the gifts and charisms of each one, in order to put them at the service of an updated and nearsighted plan of pastoral action. The different Councils provided for by the current norms of Canon Law are to be considered a great help in contributing to this end.

Vital Christian communities

89. Right from the beginning, the Synod Fathers recognized that the Church as Family cannot

reach her full potential as Church unless she is divided into communities small enough to foster close human relationships. The Assembly described the characteristics of such communities as follows: primarily they should be places engaged in evangelizing themselves, so that subsequently they can bring the Good News to others; they should moreover be communities which pray and listen to God's Word, encourage the members themselves to take on responsibility, learn to live an ecclesial life, and reflect on different human problems in the light of the Gospel. Above all, these communities are to be committed to living Christ's love for everybody, a love which transcends the limits of the natural solidarity of clans, tribes or other interest groups.[169]

Laity

90. The laity are to be helped to become increasingly aware of their role in the Church, thereby fulfilling their particular mission as baptized and confirmed persons, according to the teaching of the Post-Synodal Apostolic Exhortation *Christifideles Laici*[170] and the Encyclical Letter *Redemptoris Missio*.[171] Lay people are to be trained for their mission through suitable centers and schools of biblical and pastoral formation. Similarly, Christians who occupy positions of responsibility are to be carefully prepared for political, economic and social tasks by means of a solid formation in the Church's social doctrine, so that in their places of work they will be faithful witnesses to the Gospel.[172]

Catechists

91. "The role of the catechist has been and remains a determinative force in the implantation and expansion of the Church in Africa. The Synod recommends that catechists not only receive a sound initial formation . . . but that they continue to receive doctrinal formation as well as moral and spiritual support."[173] Both Bishops and priests are to have their catechists at heart, seeing to it that they are guaranteed suitable living and working conditions so that they carry out their mission properly. In the midst of the Christian community the catechists' responsibility is to be acknowledged and held in respect.

The family

92. The Synod launched an explicit appeal for each African Christian family to become "a privileged place for evangelical witness,"[174] a true "domestic church,"[175] a community which believes and evangelizes,[176] a community in dialogue with God[177] and generously open to the service of humanity.[178] "It is in the heart of the family that parents are by word and example . . . the first heralds of the faith with regard to their children."[179] "It is here that the father of the family, the mother, children, and all members of the family exercise the *priesthood of the baptized* in a privileged way 'by the reception of the sacraments, prayer and thanksgiving, the witness of a holy life and self denial and active charity.' Thus the home is the first school of Christian life and 'a school for human enrichment.' "[180]

Parents are to see to the Christian education of their children. With the practical help offered by strong, serene and committed Christian families, Dioceses will develop a program for the family apostolate as part of their overall pastoral plan. The Christian family, as a "domestic Church" built on the solid cultural pillars and noble values of the African tradition of the family, is called upon to be a powerful nucleus of Christian witness in a society undergoing rapid and profound changes. The Synod felt this challenge with a particular urgency because the Church was then celebrating the Year of the Family with the rest of the international community.

Young people

93. The Church in Africa knows well that youth are not only the present but above all the future of humanity. It is thus necessary to help young people to overcome the obstacles thwarting their development: illiteracy, idleness, hunger, drugs.[181] In order to meet these challenges, young people themselves should be called upon to become the evangelizers of their peers. No one can do this

better than they. The *pastoral care of youth* must clearly be a part of the overall pastoral plan of Dioceses and parishes, so that young people will be enabled to discover very early on the value of the gift of self, an essential means for the person to reach maturity.[182] In this regard, the celebration of World Youth Day is a privileged instrument for the pastoral care of youth, which favors their formation through prayer, study and reflection.

Consecrated men and women

94. "In the Church understood as the Family of God, *consecrated life* has the particular function not only of indicating to all the call to holiness but also of witnessing to fraternal life in community. Therefore, all who live the consecrated life are called to respond to their vocation in a spirit of communion and cooperation with the respective Bishops, clergy and laity."[183]

In the present-day circumstances of the mission in Africa, it is necessary to foster religious vocations to the contemplative and active life, above all choosing them with great discernment, and then seeing that they receive an integral human formation, as well as one which is solid in its spiritual and doctrinal, apostolic and missionary, biblical and theological dimensions. This formation is to be faithfully and regularly updated down through the years. With regard to the foundation of new Religious Institutes, great prudence and enlightened discernment are needed, and the criteria laid down by the Second Vatican Council and the canonical norms now in force are to be followed.[184] Once established, these Institutes are to be helped in acquiring juridical status and becoming autonomous in the management both of their own works and of their respective sources of income.

The Synodal Assembly, having stated that "Religious Institutes that do not have houses in Africa" are not authorized "to come seeking new vocations without prior dialogue with the local Ordinary,"[185] then urged the leaders of the local Churches and of the Institutes of Consecrated Life and the Societies of Apostolic Life to foster dialogue among themselves, in order to create, in the spirit of the Church as Family, mixed groups for consultation which would serve as a witness to fraternity and as a sign of unity in the service of a common mission.[186] In this light, I have also accepted the request of the Synod Fathers to revise, if necessary, some points in the document *Mutuae Relationes*,[187] in order to define better the role of religious life in the local Church.[188]

Future priests

95. The Synod Fathers affirmed that "today more than ever there is need to form *future priests* in the true cultural values of their country, in a sense of honesty, responsibility and integrity. They shall be formed in such a manner that they will have the qualities of the representatives of Christ, of true servants and animators of the Christian community . . . solidly spiritual, ready to serve, dedicated to evangelization, capable of administering the goods of the Church efficiently and openly, and of living a simple life as befits their milieu."[189] While respecting the traditions proper to the Eastern Churches, seminarians "should acquire affective maturity and should be both clear in their minds and deeply convinced that for the priest celibacy is inseparable from chastity."[190] Moreover "they should receive adequate formation on the meaning and place of consecration to Christ in the priesthood."[191]

Deacons

96. Where pastoral conditions lend themselves to respect and understanding of this ancient ministry in the Church, Episcopal Conferences and Assemblies are to study the most suitable ways of promoting and encouraging the permanent diaconate "as an ordained ministry and also as an instrument of evangelization."[192] Where deacons already exist they should be provided with an integrated and thorough program of permanent formation.

Priests

97. Deeply grateful to all the priests—diocesan and members of Institutes—for the apostolic

work they are doing and aware of the demands made by the evangelization of the peoples of Africa and Madagascar, the Synodal Assembly urged priests to live their "faithfulness to their vocation in the total gift of self to their mission and in full communion with their Bishop."[193] As for the Bishops, they are to see to the ongoing formation of priests, especially in the first years of their ministry,[194] helping them especially to deepen their understanding of sacred celibacy and to persevere in living it faithfully, recognizing "this surpassing gift which the Father has given them, and which the Lord praised so openly. Let them keep in mind the great mysteries which are signified and fulfilled in it."[195] This formation program is also to give particular attention to the wholesome values present in the priests' surroundings. It is appropriate moreover to mention that the Second Vatican Council encouraged among priests "a certain common life," that is some kind of community life in the different forms suggested by real personal and pastoral needs. This will contribute towards the growth of the spiritual and intellectual life, of apostolic and pastoral ministry, of charity and mutual support, especially with regard to priests who are elderly, sick or in difficulty.[196]

Bishops

98. The Bishops themselves will carefully pastor the Church which God obtained with the Blood of his own Son, fulfilling the responsibility entrusted to them by the Holy Spirit (cf. Acts 20:28). According to the recommendation of the Second Vatican Council, Bishops dedicated to carrying out "their Apostolic office as witnesses of Christ before all people"[197] are to exercise personally, in a spirit of trusting cooperation with the presbyterate and other pastoral workers, an irreplaceable service of unity in charity, carefully fulfilling their responsibilities of teaching, sanctifying and governing. Moreover they are regularly to update themselves theologically and to foster their spiritual life, taking part as much as possible in the sessions of renewal and formation organized by the Episcopal Conferences or the Apostolic See.[198] In particular, they should never forget the admonition of Pope Saint Gregory the Great, according to whom the Pastor is the light of his faithful above all through an exemplary moral conduct marked by holiness.[199]

II. STRUCTURES OF EVANGELIZATION

99. It is a source of joy and comfort to note that "the laity are more and more engaged in the mission of the Church in Africa and Madagascar," thanks especially "to the dynamism of Catholic Action movements, apostolic associations and new spiritual movements."[200] The Synod Fathers requested that this thrust be pursued and developed among all the laity: adults, youth and children.

Parishes

100. By its nature the parish is the ordinary place where the faithful worship and live their Christian life. In it they can express and practice the initiatives which faith and Christian charity bring to the attention of the community of believers. The parish is the place which manifests the *communion of various groups and movements*, which find in it spiritual sustenance and material support. Priests and lay people will see to it that parish life is harmonious, expressing the Church as Family, where all devote "themselves to the Apostles' teaching and fellowship, to the breaking of bread and the prayers" (Acts 2:42).

Movements and associations

101. A fraternal harmony which bears living witness to the Gospel will also be the goal of apostolic movements and religious associations. In them the lay faithful truly find a privileged opportunity to be the "leaven in the dough" (cf. Mt 13:33), especially in areas concerned with the administration of temporal goods according to God's plan and the struggle for the promotion of human dignity, justice and peace.

Schools

102. "Catholic schools are at one and the same time places of evangelization, well-rounded education, inculturation and initiation to the dialogue of life among young people of different religions and social backgrounds."[201] The Church in Africa and Madagascar should therefore make its own contribution to the fostering of "education for all"[202] in Catholic schools, without neglecting "the Christian education of pupils in non-Catholic schools. For university students there will be a program of religious formation which corresponds to the level of studies."[203] These contributions presuppose the human, cultural and religious formation of the educators themselves.

Universities and Higher Institutes

103. "The Catholic Universities and Higher Institutes in Africa have a prominent role to play in the proclamation of the salvific Word of God. They are a sign of the growth of the Church insofar as their research integrates the truths and experiences of the faith and helps to internalize them. They serve the Church by providing trained personnel, by studying important theological and social questions for the benefit of the Church, by developing an African theology, by promoting the work of inculturation especially in liturgical celebration, by publishing books and publicizing Catholic truth, by undertaking assignments given by the Bishops and by contributing to a scientific study of cultures."[204]

In this time of generalized social upheaval on the Continent, the Christian faith can shed helpful light on African society. "*Catholic cultural centers* offer to the Church the possibility of presence and action in the field of cultural change. They constitute in effect public *forums* which allow the Church to make widely known, in creative dialogue, Christian convictions about man, woman, family, work, economy, society, politics, international life, the environment."[205] Thus they are places of listening, respect and tolerance.

Material means

104. Precisely in this context the Synod Fathers emphasized how necessary it is for each Christian community to be organized so that as far as possible it can provide for its own needs.[206] Besides qualified personnel, evangelization requires material and financial means, and Dioceses are often far from possessing them in sufficient measure. It is therefore urgent that the particular Churches in Africa have the objective of providing for their own needs as soon as possible, thereby assuring their self-sufficiency. Consequently, I earnestly invite the Episcopal Conferences, Dioceses and all the Christian communities of the Continent's Churches, insofar as it is within their competence, to see to it that this self-sufficiency becomes increasingly evident. At the same time, I call on sister Churches all over the world to be more generous to the Pontifical Mission Aid Societies so that, through their structures of assistance, they will be able to offer to poorer Dioceses economic assistance dedicated to projects that will generate resources, with a view to increasing the financial self-reliance of the Churches.[207] Lastly, we cannot forget that a Church is able to reach material and financial independence only if the people entrusted to it do not live in conditions of extreme poverty.

CHAPTER VI
BUILDING THE KINGDOM OF GOD

Kingdom of justice and peace

105. The mandate that Jesus gave to his disciples at the moment of his Ascension into heaven is addressed to the Church of God in all times and places. The Church as the Family of God in Africa must bear witness to Christ also by promoting justice and peace on the Continent and throughout the world. The Lord says: "Blessed are the peacemakers, for they shall be called sons of God. Blessed are those who are persecuted for righteousness' sake, for theirs is the Kingdom of heaven"

(Mt 5:9-10). The Church's witness must be accompanied by a firm commitment to justice and solidarity by each member of God's People. This is especially important for the lay faithful who hold public office, because such witness demands an abiding spiritual attitude and a way of life consistent with the Christian faith.

Ecclesial dimension of witness

106. The Synod Fathers drew attention to the ecclesial dimension of this witness and solemnly declared: "The Church must continue to play her prophetic role and be the voice of the voiceless."[208]

But to achieve this effectively, the Church, as a community of faith, must be an energetic witness to justice and peace in her structures and in the relationships among her members. The Message of the Synod courageously states: "The Churches in Africa are also aware that, insofar as their own internal affairs are concerned, justice is not always respected with regard to those men and women who are at their service. If the Church is to give witness to justice, she recognizes that whoever dares to speak to others about justice should also strive to be just in their eyes. It is necessary therefore to examine with care the procedures, the possessions and the life style of the Church."[209]

In what concerns the promotion of justice and especially the defense of fundamental human rights, the Church's apostolate cannot be improvised. Aware that in many African countries gross violations of human dignity and rights are being perpetrated, I ask the Episcopal Conferences to establish, where they do not yet exist, Justice and Peace Commissions at various levels. These will awaken Christian communities to their evangelical responsibilities in the defense of human rights.[210]

107. If the proclamation of justice and peace is an integral part of the task of evangelization, it follows that the promotion of these values should also be a part of the pastoral program of each Christian community. That is why I urge that all pastoral agents are to be adequately trained for this apostolate. "The formation of clergy, religious and laity, imparted in the areas of their apostolate, should lay emphasis on the social teaching of the Church. Each person, according to his state of life, should be specially trained to know his rights and duties, the meaning and service of the common good, honest management of public goods and the proper manner of participating in political life, in order to be able to act in a credible manner in the face of social injustices."[211]

As a body organized within the community and the nation, the Church has both the right and the duty to participate fully in building a just and peaceful society with all the means at her disposal. Here we must mention the Church's apostolate in the areas of education, health care, social awareness and in other programs of assistance. In the measure that these activities help to reduce ignorance, improve public health and promote a greater participation of all in solving the problems of society in a spirit of freedom and co-responsibility, the Church creates conditions for the progress of justice and peace.

The salt of the earth

108. In the pluralistic societies of our day, it is especially due to the commitment of Catholics in public life that the Church can exercise a positive influence. Whether they be professionals or teachers, businessmen or civil servants, law enforcement agents or politicians, Catholics are expected to bear witness to goodness, truth, justice and love of God in their daily life. "The task of the faithful lay person . . . is to be the salt of the earth and light of the world, especially in those places where only a lay person is able to render the Church present."[212]

Cooperation with other believers

109. The obligation to commit oneself to the development of peoples is not just an *individual* duty, and still less an *individualistic* one, as if it were possible to achieve this development through the isolated efforts of each person. It is a responsibility which obliges *each and every man and woman*, as well as *societies and nations*. In particular, it obliges the Catholic Church and the other Churches and Ecclesial Communities, with which Catholics are willing to cooperate in this field.[213]

In this sense just as Catholics invite their Christian brothers and sisters to share in their initiatives, so, when they accept invitations offered to them, Catholics show that they are ready to cooperate in projects undertaken by other Christians. In the promotion of integral human development Catholics can also cooperate with the believers of other religions, as in fact they are already doing in various places. [214]

Good administration of public affairs

110. The Synod Fathers were unanimous in acknowledging that the greatest challenge for bringing about justice and peace in Africa consists in a good administration of public affairs in the two interrelated areas of politics and the economy. Certain problems have their roots outside the Continent and therefore are not entirely under the control of those in power or of national leaders. But the Synodal Assembly acknowledged that many of the Continent's problems are the result of a manner of governing often stained by corruption. A serious reawakening of conscience linked to a firm determination of will is necessary, in order to put into effect solutions which can no longer be put off.

Building the nation

111. On the political front, the arduous process of building national unity encounters particular problems in the Continent where most of the States are relatively young political entities. To reconcile profound differences, overcome longstanding ethnic animosities and become integrated into international life demands a high degree of competence in the art of governing. That is why the Synod prayed fervently to the Lord that there would arise in Africa *holy politicians*—both men and women—and that there would be saintly Heads of State, who profoundly love their own people and wish to serve rather than be served.[215]

The rule of law

112. The foundation of good government must be established on the sound basis of laws which protect the rights and define the obligations of the citizens.[216] I must note with great sadness that many African nations still labor under authoritarian and oppressive regimes which deny their subjects personal freedom and fundamental human rights, especially the freedom of association and of political expression, as well as the right to choose their governments by free and honest elections. Such political injustices provoke tensions which often degenerate into armed conflicts and internal wars, bringing with them serious consequences such as famine, epidemics and destruction, not to mention massacres and the scandal and tragedy of refugees. That is why the Synod rightly considered that an authentic democracy, which respects pluralism, "is one of the principal routes along which the Church travels together with the people . . . The lay Christian, engaged in the democratic struggle according to the spirit of the Gospel, is the sign of a Church which participates in the promotion of the rule of law everywhere in Africa."[217]

Administering the common patrimony

113. The Synod also called on African governments to establish the appropriate policies needed to increase economic growth and investment in order to create new jobs.[218] This involves the commitment to pursue sound economic policies, adopting the right priorities for the exploitation and distribution of often scarce national resources in such a way as to provide for people's basic needs, and to ensure an honest and equitable sharing of benefits and burdens. In particular, governments have the binding duty to protect the *common patrimony* against all forms of waste and embezzlement by citizens lacking public spirit or by unscrupulous foreigners. It is also the duty of governments to undertake suitable initiatives to improve the conditions of international commerce.

Africa's economic problems are compounded by the dishonesty of corrupt government leaders who, in connivance with domestic or foreign private interests, divert national resources for their own profit and transfer public funds to private accounts in foreign banks. This is plain theft, whatever the legal camouflage may be. I earnestly hope that international bodies and people of integrity in Africa and elsewhere will be able to investigate suitable legal ways of having these embezzled funds returned. In the granting of loans, it is important to make sure of the responsibility and forthrightness of the beneficiaries.[219]

The international dimension

114. As an Assembly of Bishops of the universal Church presided over by the Successor of Peter, the Synod furnished a providential occasion to evaluate positively the place and role of Africa in the universal Church and the world community. Since we live in a world that is increasingly interdependent, the destinies and problems of the different regions are linked together. As God's Family on earth, the Church should be the living sign and efficacious instrument of universal solidarity for building a world-wide community of justice and peace. A better world will come about only if it is built on the solid foundation of sound ethical and spiritual principles.

In the present world order, the African nations are among the most disadvantaged. Rich countries must become clearly aware of their duty to support the efforts of the countries struggling to rise from their poverty and misery. In fact, it is in the interest of the rich countries to choose the path of solidarity, for only in this way can lasting peace and harmony for humanity be ensured. Moreover, the Church in the developed countries cannot ignore the added responsibility arising from the Christian commitment to justice and charity. Because all men and women bear God's image and are called to belong to the same family redeemed by Christ's Blood, each individual should be guaranteed just access to the world's resources which God has put at everyone's disposal.[220]

It is not hard to see the many practical implications of this. In the first place it involves working for improved socio-political relations among nations, ensuring greater justice and dignity for those countries which, after gaining independence, have been members of the international community for less time. A compassionate ear must also be lent to the anguished cries of the poor nations asking for help in areas of particular importance: malnutrition, the widespread deterioration in the standard of living, the insufficiency of means for educating the young, the lack of elementary health and social services with the resulting persistence of endemic diseases, the spread of the terrible scourge of AIDS, the heavy and often unbearable burden of international debt, the horror of fratricidal wars fomented by unscrupulous arms trafficking, the shameful and pitiable spectacle of refugees and displaced persons. These are some of the areas where prompt interventions are necessary and expedient, even if in the overall situation they seem to be inadequate.

I. SOME WORRISOME PROBLEMS

Restoring hope to youth

115. The economic situation of poverty has a particularly negative impact on the young. They embark on adult life with very little enthusiasm for a present riddled with frustrations and they look with still less hope to a future which to them seems sad and somber. That is why they tend to flee the neglected rural areas and gather in cities which in fact do not have much more to offer them. Many of them go to foreign countries where, as if in exile, they live a precarious existence as economic refugees. With the Synod Fathers I feel the duty to plead their cause: it is urgently necessary to find a solution for their impatience to take part in the life of the nation and of the Church.[221]

But at the same time I also wish to appeal to the youth: Dear young people, the Synod asks you to take in hand the development of your countries, to love the culture of your people, and to work for its renewal with fidelity to your cultural heritage, through a sharpening of your scientific and technical expertise, and above all through the witness of your Christian faith.[222]

The scourge of AIDS

116. Against the background of widespread poverty and inadequate medical services the Synod considered the tragic scourge of AIDS which is sowing suffering and death in many parts of Africa. It noted the role played in the spread of this disease by irresponsible sexual behavior and drafted this strong recommendation: "The companionship, joy, happiness and peace which Christian marriage and fidelity provide, and the safeguard which chastity gives, must be continuously presented to the faithful, particularly the young."[223]

The battle against AIDS ought to be everyone's battle. Echoing the voice of the Synod Fathers, I too ask pastoral workers to bring to their brothers and sisters affected by AIDS all possible material, moral and spiritual comfort. I urgently ask the world's scientists and political leaders, moved by the love and respect due to every human person, to use every means available in order to put an end to this scourge.

"Beat your swords into ploughshares" (Is 2:4): no more wars!

117. The Synod incisively described the tragedy of wars which are tearing Africa apart: "For some decades now Africa has been the theater of fratricidal wars which are decimating peoples and destroying their natural and cultural resources."[224] This very sad situation, in addition to causes external to Africa, also has internal causes such as "tribalism, nepotism, racism, religious intolerance and the thirst for power taken to the extreme by totalitarian regimes which trample with impunity the rights and dignity of the person. Peoples crushed and reduced to silence suffer as innocent and resigned victims all these situations of injustice."[225]

I cannot fail to join my voice to that of the members of the Synodal Assembly in order to deplore the situations of unspeakable suffering caused by so many conflicts now taking place or about to break out, and to ask all those who can do so to make every effort to put an end to such tragedies.

Together with the Synod Fathers, I likewise urge a serious commitment to foster on the Continent conditions of greater social justice and good government, in order thereby to prepare the ground for peace. "If you want peace, work for justice."[226] It is much better—and also easier—to prevent wars than to try to stop them after they have broken out. It is time that peoples beat their swords into ploughshares, and their spears into pruning hooks (cf. Is 2:4).

118. The Church in Africa—especially through some of its leaders—has been in the front line of the search for negotiated solutions to the armed conflicts in many parts of the Continent. This mission of pacification must continue, encouraged by the Lord's promise in the Beatitudes: "Blessed are the peacemakers, they shall be called sons of God" (Mt 5:9).

Those who foment wars in Africa by the arms trade are accomplices in abominable crimes against humanity. I make my own the Synod's recommendations on this subject. Having said that "the sale of arms is a scandal since it sows the seed of death," the Synod appealed to all countries that sell arms to Africa to stop doing so, and it asked African governments "to move away from huge military expenditures and put the emphasis on the education, health and well-being of their people."[227]

Africa must continue to seek peaceful and effective means so that military regimes will transfer authority to civilians. But it is also true that the military are called to play a distinctive role in the nation. Thus, while the Synod praised the "brothers in the military for the service that they assume in the name of our countries,"[228] it immediately warned them forcefully that "they will have to answer before God for every act of violence against the lives of innocent people."[229]

Refugees and displaced persons

119. One of the most bitter fruits of wars and economic hardships is the sad phenomenon of refugees and displaced persons, a phenomenon which, as the Synod mentioned, has reached tragic dimensions. The ideal solution is the re-establishment of a just peace, reconciliation and economic development. It is therefore urgent that national, regional and international organizations should find equitable and long-lasting solutions to the problems of refugees and displaced persons.[230] In the meantime, since the Continent continues to suffer from the massive displacement of refugees,

I make a pressing appeal that these people be given material help and offered pastoral support wherever they may be, whether in Africa or on other Continents.

The burden of the international debt

120. The question of the indebtedness of poor nations towards rich ones is a matter of great concern for the Church, as expressed in many official documents and interventions of the Holy See.[231]

Taking up the words of the Synod Fathers, I particularly feel it is my duty to urge "the Heads of State and their governments in Africa not to crush their peoples with internal and external debts."[232] I also make a pressing appeal to "the International Monetary Fund and the World Bank and all foreign creditors to alleviate the crushing debts of the African nations."[233] Finally, I earnestly ask "the Episcopal Conferences of the industrialized countries to present this issue consistently to their governments and to the organizations concerned."[234] The situation of many African countries is so serious as to leave no room for attitudes of indifference and complacency.

Dignity of the African woman

121. One of the characteristic signs of our times is the growing awareness of women's dignity and of their specific role in the Church and in society at large. "So God created man in his own image, in the image of God he created him; male and female he created them" (Gen 1:27).

I have repeatedly affirmed the fundamental equality and enriching complementarity that exist between man and woman.[235] The Synod applied these principles to the condition of women in Africa. Their rights and duties in building up the family and in taking full part in the development of the Church and society were strongly affirmed. With specific regard to the Church, women should be properly trained so that they can participate at appropriate levels in her apostolic activity.

The Church deplores and condemns, to the extent that they are still found in some African societies, all "the customs and practices which deprive women of their rights and the respect due to them."[236] It is recommended that Episcopal Conferences establish special commissions to study further women's problems in cooperation with interested government agencies, wherever this is possible.[237]

II. COMMUNICATING THE GOOD NEWS

Following Christ, the Communicator "par excellence"

122. The Synod had much to say about social communications in the context of the evangelization of Africa, carefully taking into account present circumstances. The theological point of departure is Christ, the Communicator *par excellence* who shares with those who believe in him the truth, the life and the love which he shares with his Heavenly Father and the Holy Spirit. That is why "the Church is aware of her duty of fostering social communications *ad intra* and *ad extra*. The Church should promote communication from within through a better diffusion of information among her members."[238] This will put her in a more advantageous position to communicate to the world the Good News of the love of God revealed in Jesus Christ.

Traditional forms of communication

123. The traditional forms of social communication must never be underestimated. In many places in Africa they are still very useful and effective. Moreover, they are "less costly and more accessible."[239] These forms include songs and music, mimes and the theater, proverbs and fables. As vehicles of the wisdom and soul of the people, they are a precious source of material and of inspiration for the modern media.

Evangelization of the world of the media

124. The modern mass media are not only instruments of communication, but also a world to

be evangelized. In terms of the message they transmit, it is necessary to ensure that they propagate the good, the true and the beautiful. Echoing the preoccupation of the Synod Fathers I express my deep concern about the moral content of very many programs with which the media flood the African Continent. In particular I warn against the pornography and violence which are inundating poor countries. In addition, the Synod rightly deplored "the very negative portrayal of the African in the media and called for its immediate cessation."[240]

Every Christian should be concerned that the communications media are a vehicle of evangelization. But Christians who are professionals in this sector have a special part to play. It is their duty to ensure that Christian principles influence the practice of the profession, including the technical and administrative sector. To enable them to exercise this role properly, they need to be provided with a wholesome human, religious and spiritual training.

Using the means of social communication

125. Today the Church has at her disposal a variety of means of social communication, traditional as well as modern. It is her duty to make the best possible use of them in order to spread the message of salvation. In the Church in Africa many obstacles impede easy access to these means, not the least of which is their high cost. Moreover, in many places government regulations impose undue control on them. Every possible effort should be made to remove these obstacles. The media, whether private or public, should serve all people without exception. Therefore I invite the particular Churches of Africa to do everything in their power to meet this objective.[241]

Cooperation and coordination in the mass media

126. The media, especially in their most modern forms, have a wide-ranging impact. Consequently, closer cooperation is needed in this area, in order to ensure more effective coordination at all levels: diocesan, national, continental and worldwide. In Africa, the Church has a great need for solidarity with sister Churches in the richer and technologically more advanced countries. Programs of continental cooperation which already exist in Africa, such as the Pan African Episcopal Committee for Social Communications, should be encouraged and revitalized. As the Synod suggested, it is necessary to establish closer cooperation in other areas, such as professional training, structures of radio and television production and stations that transmit to the whole Continent.[242]

CHAPTER VII
"YOU SHALL BE MY WITNESSES TO THE ENDS OF THE EARTH"

127. During the Special Assembly, the Synod Fathers thoroughly explored the overall situation in Africa, in order to encourage an ever more effective and credible witness to Christ in every local Church, every nation, every region, and in the entire African Continent. In all the discussions and recommendations made by the Special Assembly the overriding concern was to *bear witness to Christ*. I found in them the spirit of what I had said in Africa to a group of Bishops: "By respecting, preserving and fostering the particular values and riches of your people's cultural heritage, you will be in a position to lead them to a better understanding of the mystery of Christ, which is also to be lived in the noble, concrete and daily experiences of African life. There is no question of adulterating the word of God, or of emptying the Cross of its power (cf. 1 Cor 1:17), but rather of bringing Christ into the very center of African life and of lifting up all African life to Christ. Thus not only is Christianity relevant to Africa, but Christ, in the members of his Body, is himself African."[243]

Open to mission

128. The Church in Africa is not called to bear witness to Christ only on the Continent; for to it the Risen Lord also says: "You shall be my witnesses to the ends of the earth" (Acts 1:8). For this very reason, during their discussions of the Synod's theme, the Fathers carefully avoided every tendency to isolationism by the Church in Africa. At all times the Special Assembly kept in view the missionary mandate which the Church received from Christ: to bear witness to him in the whole world.[244] The Synod Fathers acknowledged God's call to Africa to play its full part, at the world level, in his plan for the salvation of the human race (cf. 1 Tim 2:4).

129. It is on account of this commitment to the Church's catholicity that the *Lineamenta* of the Special Assembly for Africa declared: "No particular Church, not even the poorest, can ever be dispensed from the obligation of sharing its personnel as well as its spiritual and temporal resources with other particular Churches and with the universal Church (cf. Acts 2:44-45)."[245] For its part, the Special Assembly strongly stressed Africa's responsibility for mission "to the ends of the earth" in the following words: "The prophetic phrase of Paul VI, 'You Africans are missionaries to yourselves,' is to be understood as 'missionaries to the whole world' . . . An appeal is launched to the particular Churches of Africa for mission outside the confines of their own Dioceses."[246]

130. In gladly and gratefully endorsing this declaration of the Special Assembly, I wish to repeat to all my Brother Bishops in Africa what I said a few years ago: "The Church in Africa's obligation to be missionary to itself and to evangelize the Continent entails cooperation among the particular Churches in the context of each African country, among the various nations of the Continent and also of other continents. In this way Africa will be fully integrated in missionary activity."[247] In an earlier appeal addressed to all the particular Churches, both young and old, I already said that "the world is steadily growing more united, and the Gospel spirit must lead us to overcome cultural and nationalistic barriers, avoiding all isolationism."[248]

The bold determination manifested by the Special Assembly to engage the young Churches of Africa in mission "to the ends of the earth" reflects the desire to implement, as generously as possible, one of the important directives of the Second Vatican Council: "In order that this missionary zeal may flourish among their native members, it very fitting that the young Churches should participate as soon as possible in the universal missionary work of the Church. Let them send their own missionaries to proclaim the Gospel all over the world, even though they themselves are suffering from a shortage of clergy. For their communion with the universal Church reaches a certain measure of perfection when they themselves take an active part in missionary zeal towards other nations."[249]

Organic pastoral solidarity

131. At the beginning of this Exhortation I pointed out that in announcing the convocation of the Special Assembly for Africa of the Synod of Bishops I had in mind the promotion of "an organic pastoral solidarity within the entire African territory and nearby Islands."[250] I am pleased to say that the Assembly kept this objective firmly in view. Discussions at the Synod revealed the Bishops' readiness and generosity for this pastoral solidarity and for sharing their resources with others, even when they themselves needed missionaries.

132. Specifically to my brother Bishops, who "are directly responsible, together with me, for the evangelization of the world, both as members of the College of Bishops and as Pastors of the particular Churches,"[251] I wish to address a special word in this regard. In their daily ministry to the flock entrusted to them, they must never lose sight of the needs of the Church as a whole. As *Catholic* Bishops, they must feel the concern for all the Churches which burned in the Apostle's heart (cf. 2 Cor 11:28). Nor can they fail to express this concern, especially when they deliberate and decide *together* as members of their respective Episcopal Conferences. Through liaison bodies at the regional and continental levels, they are in a better position to discern and evaluate the pastoral needs surfacing in other parts of the world. The Bishops express their apostolic solidarity

in a pre-eminent way through the Synod of Bishops: "among its affairs of general concern, it should give special consideration to missionary activity. For this is a supremely great and sacred task of the Church."[252]

133. The Special Assembly also rightly pointed out that, in order to achieve an overall pastoral solidarity in Africa, it is necessary to promote the renewal of priestly formation. The words of the Second Vatican Council can never be pondered enough: "The spiritual gift which priests received at their Ordination prepares them not for any limited and narrow mission but for the widest scope of the universal mission 'even to the very ends of the earth' (Acts 1:8)."[253]

That is why I have urged priests "to make themselves readily available to the Holy Spirit and the Bishop, to be sent to preach the Gospel beyond the borders of their own country. This will demand of them not only maturity in their vocation, but also an uncommon readiness to detach themselves from their own homeland, culture and family, and a special ability to adapt to other cultures, with understanding and respect for them."[254]

I am deeply grateful to God to learn that a growing number of African priests have been responding to the call to bear witness "to the ends of the earth." It is my ardent hope that this trend will be encouraged and strengthened in all the particular Churches of Africa.

134. It is also a source of great comfort to know that the Missionary Institutes which have been present in Africa for a long time are now "receiving more and more candidates from the young Churches which they founded,"[255] thus enabling these same Churches to take part in the missionary activity of the universal Church. Similarly, I give thanks for the new Missionary Institutes which have been established on the Continent and are now sending their members *ad gentes*. This is a providential and marvelous development which shows the maturity and dynamism of the Church in Africa.

135. In a special way I would like to endorse the specific recommendation of the Synod Fathers that the four Pontifical Mission Aid Societies be established in every particular Church and in every country as a means of achieving an *organic pastoral solidarity* in favor of the mission "to the ends of the earth." These Societies, because they are under the auspices of the Pope and the Episcopal College, rightly have the first place, "since they are the means of imbuing Catholics from their very infancy with a genuinely universal and missionary outlook. They are the means for undertaking an effective collection of funds to subsidize all the missions, each according to its needs."[256] A significant result of their activity "is the fostering of lifelong vocations *ad gentes*, in both the older and younger Churches. I earnestly recommend that their promotional work be increasingly directed to this goal."[257]

Holiness and mission

136. The Synod reaffirmed that all the sons and daughters of Africa are called to holiness and to be witnesses to Christ throughout the world. "The lesson of history confirms that by the action of the Holy Spirit evangelization takes place above all through the witness of charity, the *witness of holiness*."[258] I therefore wish to repeat to all Christians in Africa what I wrote some years ago: "A missionary is really such only if he commits himself to the way of holiness . . . Every member of the faithful is called to holiness and to mission . . . The renewed impulse to the mission *ad gentes* demands holy missionaries. It is not enough to update pastoral techniques, organize and coordinate ecclesial resources, or delve deeply into the biblical and theological foundations of faith. What is needed is the encouragement of a new 'ardor for holiness' among missionaries and throughout the Christian community."[259]

As I did then, so again I address myself to the Christians of the young Churches in order to remind them of their responsibilities: "Today, you are the hope of this two-thousand-year-old Church of ours: being young in faith, you must be like the first Christians and radiate enthusiasm and courage. In a word, you must set yourselves on the path of holiness. Only thus can you be a sign of God in the world and re-live in your own countries the missionary epic of the early Church. You will also be a leaven of missionary spirit for the older Churches."[260]

137. The Church in Africa shares with the universal Church "the sublime vocation of realizing, first of all within herself, the unity of humankind over and above any ethnic, cultural, national, social or other divisions in order to signify precisely that such divisions are now obsolete, having been abolished by the Cross of Christ."[261] By responding to her vocation to be a redeemed and reconciled people in the midst of the world, the Church contributes to promoting the fraternal coexistence of all peoples, since she transcends the distinctions of race and nationality.

In view of the specific vocation entrusted to the Church by her Divine Founder, I earnestly call upon the Catholic Community in Africa to bear authentic witness before all humanity to the Christian universalism which has its source in the fatherhood of God. "All persons created by God have the same *origin*. Whatever may, throughout history, have been their dispersion or the accentuation of their differences, they are *destined* to form one sole family according to God's plan established 'in the beginning.'"[262] The Church in Africa is called to reach out in love to every human being, firmly believing that "by his Incarnation the Son of God has united himself in some fashion with every man."[263]

In particular, Africa ought to make its own special contribution to the ecumenical movement, an urgent task which, on the threshold of the Third Millennium, I have emphasized once more in my Encyclical Letter *Ut Unum Sint*.[264] Certainly the Church on the Continent can also play an important role in interreligious dialogue, above all by fostering close relations with Muslims and by promoting respect for the values of African traditional religion.

Putting solidarity into practice

138. In bearing witness to Christ "to the ends of the earth," the Church in Africa will no doubt be assisted by the conviction of the *"positive* and *moral value* of the growing awareness of *interdependence* among individuals and nations. The fact that men and women in various parts of the world feel personally affected by the injustices and violations of human rights committed in distant countries, countries which perhaps they will never visit, is a further sign of a reality transformed into *awareness*, thus acquiring a *moral* connotation."[265]

It is my desire that Christians in Africa will become ever more aware of this interdependence among individuals and nations, and will be ready to respond to it by practicing the virtue of *solidarity*. The fruit of solidarity is peace, an inestimable good for peoples and nations in every part of the world. For it is precisely by means of fostering and strengthening solidarity that the Church can make a specific and decisive contribution to a true culture of peace.

139. By entering into contact with all the peoples of the world through her dialogue with the various cultures, the Church brings them closer to one another, enabling each people to assume, in faith, the authentic values of others.

Ready to cooperate with all people of good will and with the international community, the Church in Africa does not seek advantages for itself. The solidarity which it expresses "seeks to go beyond itself, to take on the *specifically Christian* dimensions of total gratuity, forgiveness and reconciliation."[266] The Church seeks to contribute to humanity's conversion, leading it to acceptance of God's salvific plan through her witness to the Gospel, accompanied by charitable work on behalf of the poor and the neediest. In so doing she never loses sight of the primacy of the transcendent and of those spiritual realities which are the first fruits of man's eternal salvation.

In their discussion on the Church's solidarity with peoples and nations, the Synod Fathers were at all times fully aware that "earthly progress must be carefully distinguished from the growth of Christ's Kingdom. Nevertheless, to the extent that the former can contribute to the better ordering of human society, it is of vital concern to the Kingdom of God."[267] Precisely for this reason the Church in Africa is convinced—as the work of the Special Assembly clearly demonstrated—that waiting for Christ's final return "can never be an excuse for lack of concern for people in their concrete personal situations and in their social, national and international life,"[268] since these earthly conditions have a bearing upon humanity's pilgrimage towards eternity.

CONCLUSION

Towards the new Christian millennium

140. Gathered around the Virgin Mary as at a new Pentecost, the members of the Special Assembly examined in depth the evangelizing mission of the Church in Africa *on the threshold of the Third Millennium*. At the conclusion of this Post Synodal Apostolic Exhortation in which I present the fruits of this Assembly to the Church in Africa, Madagascar and the adjacent Islands and to the whole Catholic Church, I give thanks to God—Father, Son and Holy Spirit—who granted us the privilege of living the genuine "moment of grace" which the Synod was. I am deeply grateful to the People of God in Africa for all that they did for the Special Assembly. This Synod was prepared with zeal and enthusiasm, as can be seen from the answers to the questionnaire attached to the outline document (*Lineamenta*) and from the reflections gathered in the working document (*Instrumentum Laboris*). The Christian communities of Africa ardently prayed for the success of the work of the Special Synod, and it was abundantly blessed by the Lord.

141. Since the Synod was convoked in order to enable the Church in Africa to assume its evangelizing mission as effectively as possible in preparation for the Third Christian Millennium, with the present Exhortation I invite God's People in Africa—Bishops, priests, consecrated persons and lay faithful—to set their faces resolutely towards the Great Jubilee which we shall celebrate a few years hence. For all the peoples of Africa the best preparation for the new Millennium must consist in a firm commitment to implement with great fidelity the decisions and orientations which, with the Apostolic authority of the Successor of Peter, I present in this Exhortation. They are decisions and orientations which can be traced back to the genuine heritage of the Church's teaching and discipline and in particular to the Second Vatican Council, the main source of inspiration for the Special Assembly for Africa.

142. My invitation to God's People in Africa to prepare themselves for the Great Jubilee of the Year 2000 is also meant to be a *clarion call to Christian joy*. "The great joy announced by the angel on Christmas night is truly for all the people (cf. Lk 2:10) . . . The Blessed Virgin Mary was the first to have received its announcement, from the Angel Gabriel, and her *Magnificat* was already the exultant hymn of all the humble. Whenever we say the Rosary, the joyful mysteries thus place us once more before the inexpressible event which is the center and summit of history: the coming on earth of Emmanuel, God with us."[269]

It is the two thousandth Anniversary of that event of great joy which we are preparing to celebrate with the coming Great Jubilee. And so Africa, which "is also in a sense the 'second homeland' of Jesus, since as a small child, it was there that he sought refuge from Herod's cruelty,"[270] is called to joy. At the same time, "everything ought to focus on the primary objective of the Jubilee: *the strengthening of faith and of the witness of Christians*."[271]

143. On account of the many difficulties, crises and conflicts which bring about so much suffering and misery on the Continent, some Africans are at times tempted to think that the Lord has abandoned them, that he has forgotten them (cf. Is 49:14)! "And God answers with the words of the great Prophet: 'Can a woman forget her own baby and not love the child she bore? Even if a mother should forget a child, I will never forget you. I have written your names on the palms of my hands' (Is 49:15-16). Yes, on the palms of Christ, pierced by the nails of the Crucifixion. The names of each one of you [Africans] is written on those palms. Therefore with full confidence we cry out: 'The Lord is our help and our shield. In him do our hearts find joy. We trust in his holy name' (Ps 28:7)."[272]

Prayer to Mary, Mother of the Church

144. In thanksgiving for the grace of this Synod, I appeal to Mary, Star of Evangelization and, as the Third Millennium draws near, to her I entrust Africa and its evangelizing mission. I turn to her with the thoughts and sentiments expressed in the prayer which my Brother Bishops composed

at the close of the working session of the Synod in Rome:

O Mary, Mother of God
and Mother of the Church,
thanks to you, on the day of the Annunciation,
at the dawn of the new era,
the whole human race with its cultures
rejoiced in recognizing itself
ready for the Gospel.
On the eve of a new Pentecost
for the Church in Africa, Madagascar
and the adjacent Islands,
the People of God with its Pastors
turns to you and with you fervently prays:
May the outpouring of the Holy Spirit
make of the cultures of Africa
places of communion in diversity,
fashioning the peoples
of this great Continent
into generous sons and daughters
of the Church
which is the Family of the Father,
the Brotherhood of the Son,
the Image of the Trinity,
the seed and beginning on earth
of the eternal Kingdom
which will come to its perfection
in the City that has God as its Builder:
the City of justice, love and peace.

Given at Yaoundé, in Cameroon, on 14 September, Feast of the Triumph of the Cross, in the year 1995, the seventeenth of my Pontificate.

Joannes Paulus II

NOTES

1. Cf. *Propositio* 1.

2. Declaration of the Bishops of Africa and Madagascar present at the Third Ordinary General Assembly of the Synod of Bishops (20 October 1974): *La Documentation catholique* 71 (1974), 995-996.

3. Address to a group of Bishops of Zaire during their *ad Limina* visit (21 April 1983), 9: *AAS* 75 (1983), 634-635.

4. Angelus (6 January 1989), 2: *Insegnamenti* XII/1 (1989), 40.

5. Cf. Second Vatican Ecumenical Council, Dogmatic Constitution on the Church *Lumen Gentium*, 6.

6. Homily at the Canonization of Blessed Charles Lwanga, Matthias Molumba Kalemba and Twenty Companion Martyrs (18 October 1964): *AAS* 56 (1964), 907-908.

7. Cf. John Paul II, Homily at the Closing Liturgy of the Special Assembly for Africa of the Synod of Bishops (8 May 1994), 6: *L'Osservatore Romano* (English-language edition), 11 May 1994, 2.

8. *Relatio ante disceptationem* (11 April 1994), 1: *L'Osservatore Romano*, 13 April 1994, 4.

9. Address at the Third Meeting of the Council of the General Secretariat for the Special Assembly for Africa of the Synod of Bishops, Luanda (9 June 1992), 5: *AAS* 85 (1993), 523.

10. Cf. *Relatio post disceptationem* (22 April 1994), 2: *L'Osservatore Romano*, 24 April 1994, 8.

11. Second Vatican Ecumenical Council, Dogmatic Constitution on the Church *Lumen Gentium*, 8.

12. *Catechism of the Catholic Church*, No. 811.

13. Second Vatican Ecumenical Council, Dogmatic Constitution on the Church *Lumen Gentium*, 13.

14. *Message of the Synod* (6 May 1994), 1-2: *L'Osservatore Romano* (English-language edition), 11 May 1994, 6.

15. Cf. Motu Proprio *Apostolica Sollicitudo* (15 September 1965), II: *AAS* 57 (1965), 776-777.

16. Address to the Council of the General Secretariat for the Special Assembly for Africa of the Synod of Bishops (23 June 1989), 1: *AAS* 82 (1990), 73; cf. Angelus (6 January 1989), 2: *Insegnamenti* XII/1 (1989), 40.

17. Address to the Council of the General Secretariat for the Special Assembly for Africa of the Synod of Bishops (23 June 1989), 5: *AAS* 82 (1990), 75.

18. Cf. Address to the Council of the General Secretariat for the Special Assembly for Africa of the Synod of Bishops, Yamoussoukro (10 September 1990), 3: *AAS* 83 (1991), 226.

19. Decree on the Bishops' Pastoral Office in the Church *Christus Dominus*, 6.

20. Cf. Apostolic Letter *Tertio Millennio Adveniente* (10 November 1994), 23: *AAS* 87 (1995), 19.

21. Synod of Bishops, Special Assembly for Africa, *Message of the Synod* (6 May 1994), 7: *L'Osservatore Romano* (English-language edition), 11 May 1994, 6.

22. Cf. Second Vatican Ecumenical Council, Decree on the Missionary Activity of the Church *Ad Gentes*, 38.

23. Second Vatican Ecumenical Council, Dogmatic Constitution on the Church *Lumen Gentium*. 13.

24. Cf. *Relatio ante disceptationem* (11 April 1994), 34: *L'Osservatore Romano*, 13 April 1994, 5.

25. Paul VI, Apostolic Exhortation *Evangelii Nuntiandi* (8 December 1975), 75: *AAS* 68 (1976), 66.

26. Cf. Synod of Bishops, Special Assembly for Africa, *Relatio ante disceptationem*, 34: *L'Osservatore Romano*, 13 April 1994, 5.

27. Apostolic Exhortation *Evangelii Nuntiandi* (8 December 1975), 76: *AAS* 68 (1976), 67.

28. Encyclical Letter *Centesimus Annus* (1 May 1991), 57: *AAS* 83 (1991), 862.

29. Cf. Message of the Eighth Plenary Assembly of SECAM (19 July 1987): *La Documentation catholique* 84 (1987), 1024-1026.

30. Address to the Council of the General Secretariat of the Special Assembly for Africa of the Synod of Bishops (23 June 1989), 6: *AAS* 82 (1990), 76.

31. Synod of Bishops, Special Assembly for Africa, *Report of the General Secretary* (11 April 1994), VI: *L'Osservatore Romano*, 11-12 April 1994, 10.

32. Cf. Synod of Bishops, Special Assembly for Africa, "The Church in Africa and her Evangelizing Mission Towards the Year 2000: 'You Shall Be my Witnesses' (Acts 1:8)": *Lineamenta*, Vatican City, 1990; *Instrumentum Laboris*, Vatican City, 1993.

33. Cf. *Instrumentum Laboris*. Of the thirty-four Episcopal Conferences in Africa and Madagascar, thirty-one sent in their observations, while the other three were unable to do so because of the difficult situations in which they found themselves.

34. *Relatio ante disceptationem* (11 April 1994), 1: *L'Osservatore Romano*, 13 April 1994, 4; cf. *Relatio post disceptationem* (22 April 1994), 1: *L'Osservatore Romano*, 24 April 1994, 8.

35. Second Vatican Ecumenical Council, Pastoral Constitution on the Church in the Modern World *Gaudium et Spes*, 22; cf. *Catechism of the Catholic Church*, No. 1260.

36. Address at the General Audience (21 August 1985), 3: *Insegnamenti* VIII/2 (1985), 512.

37. Message *Africae Terrarum* (29 October 1967), 3: *AAS* 59 (1967), 1074-1075.

38. *Ibid.*, 3-4: *loc. cit.*, 1075.

39. Homily at the Mass commemorating the Five Hundredth Anniversary of Evangelization in Angola, Luanda (7 June 1992), 2: *AAS* 85 (1993), 511-512.

40. Cf. "Situation of the Church in Africa and Madagascar: Some Factors and Observations," *L'Osservatore Romano*, 16 April 1994, 6-8; Office of Church Statistics, "The Church in Africa: Numbers and Statistics (1978-1992)," *L'Osservatore Romano*, 15 April 1994, 6.

41. Homily for the Canonization of Blessed Charles Lwanga, Matthias Molumba Kalemba and Twenty Companion Martyrs (18 October 1964): *AAS* 56 (1964), 905-906.

42. John Paul II, Homily for the closing celebration of the Special Assembly for Africa of the Synod of Bishops (8 May 1994), 6: *L'Osservatore Romano* (English-language edition), 11 May 1994, 2.

43. Address to the Symposium of Episcopal Conferences of Africa and Madagascar, Kampala (31 July 1969), 1: *AAS* 61 (1969), 575.

44. *Relatio ante disceptationem* (11 April 1994), 5: *L'Osservatore Romano*, 13 April 1994, 4.

45. Cf. No. 10: *L'Osservatore Romano* (English-language edition), 11 May 1994, 6.

46. Cf. *Relatio post disceptationem* (22 April 1994), 22-26: *L'Osservatore Romano*, 24 April 1994, 8.

47. Paul VI, Message *Africae Terrarum* (29 October 1967), 6: *AAS* 59 (1967), 1076.

48. *Relatio ante disceptationem* (11 April 1994), 2: *L'Osservatore Romano*, 13 April 1994, 4.

49. *Ibid.*, 4: *loc. cit.*

50. John Paul II, Homily at the Opening Liturgy of the Special Assembly for Africa of the Synod of Bishops (10 April 1994), 3: *AAS* 87 (1995), 180-181.

51. Cf. No. 36: *L'Osservatore Romano*, 11 May 1994, 8.

52. John Paul II, Encyclical Letter *Sollicitudo Rei Socialis* (30 December 1987), 42-43: *AAS* 80 (1988), 572-574.

53. *Message of the Synod* (6 May 1994), 39: *L'Osservatore Romano* (English-language edition), 11 May 1994, 8.

54. Cf. Synod of Bishops, Special Assembly for Africa, *Relatio ante disceptationem* (11 April 1994), 6: *L'Osservatore Romano*, 13 April 1994, 4.

55. Paul VI, Apostolic Exhortation *Evangelii Nuntiandi* (8 December 1975), 15: *AAS* 68 (1976), 14.

56. *Ibid.: loc. cit.*, 15.

57. *Ibid.*, 53: *loc. cit.*, 42.

58. *Relatio ante disceptationem*, (11 April 1994), 6: *L'Osservatore Romano*, 13 April 1994, 4.

59. Homily at the conclusion of the sixth Pastoral Visit in Africa, Lilongwe (6 May 1989), 6: *Insegnamenti* XII/1 (1989), 1183.

60. Cf. *Relatio ante disceptationem* (11 April 1994), 6: *L'Osservatore Romano*, 13 April 1994, 4.

61. Pontifical Commission "Iustitia et Pax," *The Church and Racism: Towards a More Fraternal Society* (3 November 1988), 12: Vatican City, 1988.

62. Cf. Synod of Bishops, Special Assembly for Africa, *Instrumentum Laboris*, 68; *Relatio ante disceptationem* (11 April 1994), 17: *L'Osservatore Romano*, 13 April 1994, 5; *Relatio post disceptationem* (22 April 1994), 6, 9, 21: *L'Osservatore Romano*, 24 April 1994, 8.

63. John Paul II, Apostolic Exhortation *Familiaris Consortio* (22 November 1981), 75: *AAS* 74 (1982), 173.

64. John Paul II, Angelus (20 March 1994), 1: *L'Osservatore Romano* (English-language edition), 23 March 1994, 1.

65. Cf. Synod of Bishops, Special Assembly for Africa, *Message of the Synod* (6 May 1994), 45-47: *L'Osservatore Romano* (English-language edition), 11 May 1994, 8.

66. John Paul II, Encyclical Letter *Sollicitudo Rei Socialis* (30 December 1987), 22: *AAS* 80 (1988), 539.

67. Synod of Bishops, Special Assembly for Africa, *Relatio ante disceptationem* (11 April 1994), 8: *L'Osservatore Romano*, 13 April 1994, 4.

68. Paul VI, Apostolic Exhortation *Evangelii Nuntiandi* (8 December 1975), 18: *AAS* 68 (1976), 17.

69. Paul VI, Apostolic Exhortation *Evangelii Nuntiandi* (8 December 1975), 14: *AAS* 68 (1976), 13.

70. *Ibid.*, 15: *loc. cit.*, 15.

71. *Ibid.*, 18: *loc. cit.*, 17.

72. Second Vatican Ecumenical Council, Decree on the Missionary Activity of the Church *Ad Gentes*, 17.

73. Paul VI, Homily at the Canonization of Blessed Charles Lwanga, Matthias Molumba Kalemba and Twenty Companion Martyrs (18 October 1964): *AAS* 56 (1964), 907-908.

74. Address to the Symposium of Episcopal Conferences of Africa and Madagascar, Kampala (31 July 1969), 1: *AAS* 61 (1969), 575; cf. *Propositio* 10.

75. Cf. *Propositio* 10.

76. *Propositio* 3.

77. Antiphon *O sacrum convivium*: Magnificat at Second Vespers for the Solemnity of the Body and Blood of Christ.

78. *Message of the Synod* (6 May 1994), 2: *L'Osservatore Romano* (English-language edition), 11 May 1994, 6.

79. *Propositio* 4.

80. Synod of Bishops, Special Assembly for Africa, *Message of the Synod* (6 May 1994), 9: *L'Osservatore Romano* (English-language edition), 11 May 1994, 6.

81. *Propositio* 4.

82. *Propositio* 3.

83. *Propositio* 4.

84. Cf. *Propositio* 6.

85. Cf. *ibid.* 6.

86. John Paul II, Apostolic Exhortation *Catechesi Tradendae* (16 October 1979), 53: *AAS* 71 (1979), 1319.

87. John Paul II, Encyclical Letter *Redemptoris Missio* (7 December 1990), 52: *AAS* 83 (1991), 229; cf. *Propositio* 28.

88. Cf. *Propositio* 29.

89. *Propositio* 30.

90. *Propositio* 32.

91. Cf. *Propositio* 33.

92. Nicene-Constantinopolitan Creed: *DS* 150.

93. Cf. John Paul II, Apostolic Exhortation *Catechesi Tradendae* (16 October 1979), 53: *AAS* 71 (1979), 1319.

94. Cf. John Paul II, Address at the University of Coimbra, Coimbra (15 May 1982), 5: *Insegamenti* V/2 (1982), 1695.

95. *Propositio* 28.

96. *Propositio* 31.

97. *Propositio* 32.

98. *Ibid.*

99. Cf. Second Vatican Ecumenical Council, Dogmatic Constitution on the Church *Lumen Gentium*, 6.

100. Cf. *Propositio* 8.

101. Cf. *ibid*.

102. *Ibid*.

103. Cf. *ibid*.

104. Second Vatican Ecumenical Council, Dogmatic Constitution on the Church *Lumen Gentium*, 1. See also Chapters I and II.

105. *Propositio* 34.

106. Cf. *Propositiones* 35-37.

107. *Propositio* 38.

108. *Propositio* 39.

109. *Propositio* 40.

110. Cf. *ibid*.

111. *Propositio* 41.

112. Cf. No. 23: *L'Osservatore Romano* (English-language edition), 11 May 1994, 7.

113. Cf. *Propositio* 41.

114. Cf. *ibid*.

115. *Propositio* 42.

116. Cf. *ibid*.

117. Paul VI, Apostolic Exhortation *Evangelii Nuntiandi* (8 December 1975), 31: *AAS* 68 (1976), 26.

118. Synod of Bishops, Special Assembly for Africa, *Lineamenta*, 79.

119. Paul VI, Apostolic Exhortation *Evangelii Nuntiandi* (8 December 1975), 31: *AAS* 68 (1976), 26.

120. *Ibid*., 33: *loc. cit.*, 27.

121. Pastoral Constitution on the Church in the Modern World *Gaudium et Spes*, 40.

122. John Paul II, Encyclical Letter *Redemptoris Missio* (7 December 1990), 15: *AAS* 83 (1991), 263.

123. John Paul II, Post-Synodal Apostolic Exhortation *Christifideles Laici* (30 December 1988), 36: *AAS* 81 (1989), 459.

124. Second Vatican Ecumenical Council, Pastoral Constitution on the Church in the Modern World *Gaudium et Spes*, 22.

125. *Sermo* XXI, 3: *SCh* 22a, 72.

126. Pastoral Constitution on the Church in the Modern World *Gaudium et Spes*, 41.

127. Cf. Encyclical Letter *Populorum Progressio* (26 March 1967), 48: *AAS* 59 (1967), 281.

128. *Ibid*., 87: *loc. cit.*, 299.

129. *Propositio* 45.

130. *Ibid*.

131. *Ibid*.

132. Cf. Paul VI, Encyclical Letter *Populorum Progressio* (26 March 1967), 48: *AAS* 59 (1967), 281.

133. John Paul II, Encyclical Letter *Sollicitudo Rei Socialis* (30 December 1987), 41: *AAS* 80 (1988), 572.

134. Synod of Bishops, Special Assembly for Africa, *Instrumentum Laboris*, 127.

135. Cf. *Message of the Synod* (6 May 1994), 45-46: *L'Osservatore Romano* (English-language edition), 11 May 1994, 8.

136. John Paul II, Encyclical Letter *Redemptoris Missio* (7 December 1990), 37: *AAS* 83 (1991), 285.

137. Angelus (6 January 1989), 2: *Insegnamenti* XII/1 (1989), 40.

138. John Paul II, Encyclical Letter *Redemptoris Missio* (7 December 1990), 46: *AAS* 83 (1991), 292.

139. *Ibid*., 47: *loc. cit.*, 293-294.

140. *Ibid.*, 7: *loc. cit.*, 255-256.

141. Synod of Bishops, Special Assembly for Africa, *Relatio ante disceptationem* (11 April 1994), 8: *L'Osservatore Romano*, 13 April 1994, 4.

142. John Paul II, Encyclical Letter *Redemptoris Missio* (7 December 1990), 83: *AAS* 83 (1991), 329.

143. Cf. Synod of Bishops, Special Assembly for Africa, *Message of the Synod* (6 May 1994), 33: *L'Osservatore Romano* (English-language edition), 11 May 1994, 8.

144. Second Vatican Ecumenical Council, Decree on the Apostolate of the Laity *Apostolicam Actuositatem*, 14.

145. Paul VI, Apostolic Exhortation *Evangelii Nuntiandi* (8 December 1975), 15: *AAS* 68 (1976), 14.

146. John Paul II, Address to the Episcopal Conference of Cameroon, Yaoundé (13 August 1985), 4: *Insegnamenti* VIII/2 (1985), 378.

147. Cf. *ibid.*, 5: *loc. cit.*, 378.

148. Paul VI, Apostolic Exhortation *Evangelii Nuntiandi* (8 December 1975), 75: *AAS* 68 (1976), 65.

149. *Ibid.*: *loc. cit.*, 65-66.

150. John Paul II, Encyclical Letter *Redemptoris Missio* (7 December 1990), 23: *AAS* 83 (1991), 269-270.

151. John Paul II, Address to the Italian National Congress of the Ecclesial Movement for Cultural Commitment (16 January 1982), 2: *Insegnamenti* V/1 (1982), 131.

152. Cf. Decree on the Missionary Activity of the Church *Ad Gentes*, 22.

153. Cf. *Propositio* 32; Second Vatican Ecumenical Council, Constitution on the Sacred Liturgy *Sacrosanctum Concilium*, 37-40.

154. *Propositio* 38.

155. John Paul II, Apostolic Exhortation *Familiaris Consortio* (22 November 1981) 75: *AAS* 74 (1982), 173.

156. *Ibid.*, 86: *loc. cit.*, 189-190.

157. Cf. *Propositio* 14.

158. Homily in the Basilica of the Annunciation, Nazareth (5 January 1964): *AAS* 56 (1964), 167.

159. John Paul II, Apostolic Letter *Mulieris Dignitatem,* (15 August 1988), 6: *AAS* 80 (1988), 1662-1664; cf. *Letter to Women* (29 June 1995), 7: *L'Osservatore Romano* (English language edition), 12 July 1995, 2.

160. John Paul II, Apostolic Exhortation *Familiaris Consortio* (22 November 1981), 22: *AAS* 74 (1982), 107.

161. *Propositio* 48.

162. John Paul II, Apostolic Exhortation *Familiaris Consortio* (22 November 1981), 13: *AAS* 74 (1982), 93-94.

163. *Ibid.*

164. Cf. Message to Mrs Nafis Sadik, Secretary General of the 1994 International Conference on Population and Development (18 March 1994): *AAS* 87 (1995), 190-196.

165. *Message of the Synod* (6 May 1994), 30: *L'Osservatore Romano* (English-language edition), 11 May 1994, 7.

166. John Paul II, Apostolic Exhortation *Familiaris Consortio* (22 November 1981), 42: *AAS* 74 (1982), 134.

167. *Propositio* 5.

168. Cf. *Propositio* 34.

169. Cf. *Propositio* 9.

170. Cf. John Paul II, Post-Synodal Apostolic Exhortation *Christifideles Laici* (30 December 1988), 45-56: *AAS* 81 (1989), 481-506.

171. Cf. John Paul II, Encyclical Letter *Redemptoris Missio* (7 December 1990), 71-74: *AAS* 83 (1991), 318-322.

172. Cf. *Propositio* 12.

173. *Propositio* 13.

174. *Propositio* 14.

175. Second Vatican Ecumenical Council, Dogmatic Constitution on the Church *Lumen Gentium*, 11.

176. Cf. John Paul II, Apostolic Exhortation *Familiaris Consortio* (22 November 1981), 52: *AAS* 74 (1982), 144-145.

177. Cf. *ibid.*, 55: *loc. cit.*, 147-148.

178. Cf. *ibid.*, 62: *loc. cit.*, 155.

179. *Catechism of the Catholic Church*, No. 1656, which quotes the Second Vatican Ecumenical Council, Dogmatic Constitution on the Church *Lumen Gentium*, 11.

180. *Catechism of the Catholic Church*, No. 1657, which quotes the Second Vatican Ecumenical Council, Dogmatic Constitution on the Church *Lumen Gentium*, 10; and the Pastoral Constitution on the Church in the Modern World *Gaudium et Spes*, 52.

181. Cf. *Propositio* 15.

182. Cf. *ibid.*

183. *Propositio* 16, which refers to the Second Vatican Ecumenical Council, Dogmatic Constitution on the Church *Lumen Gentium*, 43-47.

184. Cf. Second Vatican Ecumenical Council, Decree on the Missionary Activity of the Church *Ad Gentes*, 18; and Decree on the Appropriate Renewal of the Religious Life *Perfectae Caritatis*, 19.

185. *Propositio* 16.

186. Cf. *Propositio* 22.

187. Congregation for Religious and Secular Institutes and Congregation for Bishops, Directives for Mutual Relations between Bishops and Religious in the Church *Mutuae Relationes* (14 May 1978): *AAS* 70 (1978), 473-506.

188. Cf. *Propositio* 22.

189. *Propositio* 18.

190. *Ibid.*

191. *Ibid.*

192. *Propositio* 17.

193. *Propositio* 20.

194. Cf. John Paul II, Post-Synodal Apostolic Exhortation *Pastores Dabo Vobis* (25 March 1992), 70-77: *AAS* 84 (1992), 778-796; *Propositio* 20.

195. Second Vatican Ecumenical Council, Decree on the Ministry and Life of Priests *Presbyterorum Ordinis*, 16.

196. Cf. *ibid.*, 8.

197. Decree on the Bishops' Pastoral Office in the Church *Christus Dominus*, 11.

198. Cf. *Propositio* 21.

199. Cf. *Epistolarum Liber*, VIII, 33: *PL* 77, 935.

200. *Propositio* 23; cf. *Relatio ante disceptationem* (11 April 1994), 11: *L'Osservatore Romano*, 13 April 1994, 4.

201. *Propositio* 24.

202. *Ibid.*

203. *Ibid.*

204. *Propositio* 25.

205. *Propositio* 26.

206. Cf. Second Vatican Ecumenical Council, Decree on the Missionary Activity of the Church *Ad Gentes*, 15.

207. Cf. *Propositio* 27.

208. *Propositio* 45.

209. No. 43: *L'Osservatore Romano* (English-language edition), 11 May 1994, 8.

210. Cf. *Propositio* 46.

211. *Propositio* 47.

212. Synod of Bishops, Special Assembly for Africa, *Message of the Synod* (6 May 1994), 57: *L'Osservatore Romano* (English-language edition), 11 May 1994, 9.

213. Cf. John Paul II, Encyclical Letter *Ut Unum Sint* (25 May 1995), 40: *L'Osservatore Romano* (English-language edition), 31 May 1995, Supplement, VI.

214. Cf. John Paul II, Encyclical Letter *Sollicitudo Rei Socialis* (30 December 1987), 32: *AAS* 80 (1988), 556.

215. Cf. *Message of the Synod* (6 May 1994), 35: *L'Osservatore Romano* (English-language edition), 11 May 1994, 8.

216. Cf. *Propositio* 56.

217. *Message of the Synod* (6 May 1994), 34: *L'Osservatore Romano* (English-language edition), 11 May 1994, 8.

218. Cf. *Propositio* 54.

219. Cf. *ibid.*

220. Cf. Paul VI, Encyclical Letter *Populorum Progressio* (26 March 1967): *AAS* 59 (1967), 257-299; John Paul II, Encyclical Letter *Sollicitudo Rei Socialis* (30 December 1987): *AAS* 80 (1988), 513-586; Encyclical Letter *Centesimus Annus* (1 May 1991): *AAS* 83 (1991), 793-867; *Propositio* 52.

221. Cf. Synod of Bishops, Special Assembly for Africa, *Message of the Synod* (6 May 1994), 63: *L'Osservatore Romano* (English-language edition), 11 May 1994, 9.

222. Cf. *ibid.*

223. *Propositio* 51.

224. *Propositio* 45.

225. *Ibid.*

226. Paul VI, Address at Boys' Town for the Fifth World Day of Peace (1 January 1972): *AAS* 64 (1972), 44.

227. *Propositio* 49.

228. *Message of the Synod* (6 May 1994), 35: *L'Osservatore Romano* (English-language edition), 11 May 1994, 8.

229. *Ibid.*

230. Cf. *Propositio* 53.

231. Cf. Second Vatican Ecumenical Council, Pastoral Constitution on the Church in the Modern World *Gaudium et Spes*, 86; Paul VI, Encyclical Letter *Populorum Progressio* (26 March 1967), 54: *AAS* 59 (1967), 283-284; John Paul II, Encyclical Letter *Sollicitudo Rei Socialis* (30 December 1987), 19: *AAS* 80 (1988), 534-536; Encyclical letter *Centesimus Annus* (1 May 1991), 35: *AAS* 83 (1991), 836-838; Apostolic Letter *Tertio Millenneo Adveniente* (10 November 1994), 51: *AAS* 87 (1995), 36, which proposes as part of the preparation for the Great Jubilee of the Year 2000 "reducing substantially, if not cancelling outright, the international debt which seriously threatens the future of many nations"; Pontifical Commission "Iustitia et Pax," *At the Service of the Human Community: An Ethical Approach to the International Debt Question* (27 December 1986): Vatican City, 1986.

232. *Propositio* 49.

233. *Ibid.*

234. *Ibid.*

235. Cf. Apostolic Letter *Mulieris Dignitatem* (15 August 1988), 6-8: *AAS* 80 (1988), 1662-1670; *Letter to Women* (29 June 1995), 7: *L'Osservatore Romano* (English-language edition), 12 July 1995, 2.

236. *Propositio* 48.

237. Cf. *ibid.*

238. *Propositio* 57.

239. *Ibid.*

240. *Propositio* 61.

241. Cf. *Propositio* 58.

242. Cf. *Propositio* 60.

243. Address to the Bishops of Kenya, Nairobi (7 May 1980), 6: *AAS* 72 (1980), 497.

244. Cf. Paul VI, Apostolic Exhortation *Evangelii Nuntiandi* (8 December 1975), 50: *AAS* 68 (1976), 40.

245. No. 42.

246. *Relatio post disceptationem* (22 April 1994), 11: *L'Osservatore Romano*, 24 April 1994, 8.

247. Address to the Episcopal Conference of Senegal, Mauritania, Cape Verde and Guinea-Bissau, Poponguine (20 February 1992), 33: *AAS* 85 (1993), 150.

248. Encyclical Letter *Redemptoris Missio* (7 December 1990), 39: *AAS* 83 (1991), 287.

249. Decree on the Missionary Activity of the Church *Ad Gentes*, 20.

250. Angelus (6 January 1989), 2: *Insegnamenti* XII/1 (1989), 40.

251. John Paul II, Encyclical Letter *Redemptoris Missio* (7 December 1990), 63: *AAS* 83 (1991), 311.

252. Second Vatican Ecumenical Council, Decree on the Missionary Activity of the Church *Ad Gentes*, 29.

253. Decree on the Ministry and Life of Priests *Presbyterorum Ordinis*, 10.

254. Encyclical Letter *Redemptoris Missio* (7 December 1990), 67: *AAS* 83 (1991), 316.

255. *Ibid.*, 66: *loc. cit.*, 314.

256. Second Vatican Ecumenical Council, Decree on the Missionary Activity of the Church *Ad Gentes*, 38.

257. Encyclical Letter *Redemptoris Missio* (7 December 1990), 84: *AAS* 83 (1991), 331.

258. John Paul II, Address to a group of Bishops of Nigeria during their *ad Limina* Visit (21 January 1982), 4: *AAS* 74 (1982), 435-436.

259. Encyclical Letter *Redemptoris Missio* (7 December 1990), 90: *AAS* 83 (1991), 336-337.

260. *Ibid.*, 91: *loc. cit.*, 337-338.

261. Pontifical Commission "Iustitia et Pax," *The Church and Racism: Towards a More Fraternal Society* (3 November 1988), 22: Vatican City, 1988.

262. *Ibid.*, 20: *loc. cit.*

263. Second Vatican Ecumenical Council, Pastoral Constitution on the Church in the Modern World *Gaudium et Spes*, 22.

264. Nos. 77-79: *L'Osservatore Romano* (English-language edition), 31 May 1995, Special Supplement, XI.

265. John Paul II, Encyclical Letter *Sollicitudo Rei Socialis* (30 December 1987), 38: *AAS* 80 (1988), 565.

266. *Ibid.*, 40: *loc. cit.*, 568.

267. Second Vatican Ecumenical Council, Pastoral Constitution on the Church in the Modern World *Gaudium et Spes*, 39.

268. John Paul II, Encyclical Letter *Sollicitudo Rei Socialis* (30 December 1987), 48: *AAS* 80 (1988), 583.

269. Paul VI, Apostolic Exhortation *Gaudete in Domino* (9 May 1975), III: *AAS* 67 (1975), 297.

270. John Paul II, Homily at the Opening Mass of the Special Assembly for Africa of the Synod of Bishops (10 April 1994), 1: *AAS* 87 (1995), 179.

271. John Paul II, Apostolic Letter *Tertio Millennio Adveniente* (10 November 1994), 42: *AAS* 87 (1995), 32.

272. John Paul II, Homily at Mass, Khartoum (10 February 1993), 8: *AAS* 85 (1993), 964.

INDEX OF POST-SYNODAL APOSTOLIC EXHORTATION

CHAPTER III
EVANGELIZATION AND INCULTURATION

The Church's mission [55-56]
Proclamation [57-58]
Urgent need for inculturation [59]
Theological foundations [60-61]
Criteria and areas of inculturation [62]
The Church as God's family [63]
Areas of application [64]
Dialogue [65-67]
Integral human development [68-69]
Becoming the voice of the voiceless [70]
Means of social communication [71]

CHAPTER IV
IN THE LIGHT OF THE THIRD CHRISTIAN MILLENNIUM

I. Present-day Challenges [72]

Need for Baptism [73]
Urgency of evangelization [74]
Importance of formation [75]
Deepening the faith [76]
The power of witness [77]
Inculturating the faith [78]
A reconciled community [79]

II. The Family

Evangelizing the family [80]
The Holy Family as a model [81]
Dignity and role of man and woman [82]
Dignity and role of Marriage [83]
Saving the African family [84]
The family as open to society [85]

CHAPTER V
"YOU SHALL BE MY WITNESSES" IN AFRICA

Witness and holiness [86-87]

I. Agents of Evangelization [88]

Vital Christian communities [89]
Laity [90]
Catechists [91]
The family [92]
Young people [93]
Consecrated men and women [94]
Future priests [95]
Deacons [96]